Houghton Mifflin Company
Editorial Advisory Committee in Education

As the Twig Is Bent

Readings in Early Childhood Education

Edited by

Robert H. Anderson
Harvard University

Harold G. Shane
Indiana University

HOUGHTON MIFFLIN COMPANY · BOSTON
New York · Atlanta · Geneva, Ill. · Dallas · Palo Alto

Contents

Part Three
Education of the Young Child

Preface

Books of readings drawn from the current periodical literature have become a popular and effective device for updating and enriching discussion on dynamic topics. Access to the views of many authors on various aspects of a topic, especially one in which there is a wide spectrum of theory and practice, helps both the research worker and the practitioner acquire a solid background for the decisions they must make. Although it is true that each collection of readings reflects certain attitudes or biases on the part of the editor responsible, so that not every item will seem useful or justifiable, the editor nevertheless saves his readers a great deal of time and effort by sifting through the literature and selecting and organizing those pieces which seem particularly relevant and informative.

For several reasons this volume is somewhat unique within the readings literature. Most importantly, it grows out of a special issue of *Phi Delta Kappan*, with eleven articles from the issue comprising the backbone of the book. These articles appeared in March 1969 (volume L, number 7), and they are included with the gracious cooperation of the fourteen authors plus Phi Delta Kappa, acting through editor Stanley M. Elam. We, the two editors of this volume, were among the writers and we thank our colleagues for their significant contributions.

Eight of the Kappan articles appear here in their original form (articles 11, 15, 20, 25, 26, 31, 33, and 34), or with minor modifications. Authors Edward T. Hall (article 19), James B. Macdonald (article 23), and Harold G. Shane (article 1) chose to revise their pieces and so the reader will discover some new or amplified material.

Another unique feature of this volume is that, in association with articles or book chapters previously published, it includes three selections which were commissioned by the editors in order to meet a special need or provide a fresh perspective. The articles by Edith Dowley (#2), Frances Litman (#36), and Rochelle S. Mayer (#28) are therefore appearing in print for the first time. We are especially pleased to introduce these significant statements to their friends in early childhood education.

At the moment in 1970 that this volume was delivered to the publisher, several other collections of readings in the field of early childhood education were available on the market. We believe that the serious student will want to consult these as well as our own collection for a complete view of the options and opinions available. Our own book is, we think, a reasonably complete and solid entry, capable of standing alone; we have high regard, however, for the other volumes, and our own selections have been influenced by the fact that other useful materials are available. For instance, we admire the topical and useful emphasis on Montessori, Piaget, and cognitive development in the collection edited by Joe L. Frost.[1] Because the Frost volume has provided a rich background in those areas, we have been free to place these important topics within what we feel is now a better balanced view of the field of early childhood education. We are pleased to note that many of the highly regarded authors who contributed to the Frost volume are also represented in other selections in our own volume.

The second volume, edited by Auleta,[2] also includes some valuable selections. Noting, however, that the curriculum section dealt primarily with the school experiences of primary school children, we sought in our own volume to emphasize curriculum innovation at the pre-primary level.

As we planned this volume, we had certain priorities in mind. Almost half of the selections emphasize aspects related to the development of the preschool-age child. Early childhood educators in particular have taken seriously John Dewey's dictum of "education as development, and development as education." We hope the organization of our book is seen as a tribute to this approach. Thus, Part Two of the volume includes pieces on intellectual and motivational development, on language acquisition and communication, and on the many facets of personality development. Because our concern is to provide the reader with the most significant and meaningful insights available in the literature, rather than solely with the most current contributions, our selections include pieces which go back as far as 1950. Their contemporaneity, however, could hardly be disputed.

Another of our goals was to provide a volume of readings which would have relevance for all people concerned with the growth and education of young children. Lately, in keeping with the original aim of early education (see Lazerson's historical discussion), the disadvantaged child has become a major focus of interest. There is now accumulating a substantial literature specifically on the disadvantaged child. As we did not wish to duplicate these efforts — and therefore omitted important topics such as nutritional deprivation[3] which are available elsewhere—we did make a conscious effort to select pieces in Part Two where the author applied his insights to social class or ethnic differences.

We also felt, however, that we could make a special contribution by providing articles which allow us to question and examine some of the assumptions underlying compensatory preschool education—a topic not always included in works on the disadvantaged child. Thus, in Part One, which is intended to provide an historical perspective of early childhood education, we not only included general informative articles with an

[1] Joe L. Frost, *Early Childhood Education Rediscovered: Readings* (New York: Holt, Rinehart and Winston, 1968).
[2] Michael S. Auleta, *Foundations of Early Childhood Education: Readings* (New York: Random House, 1969).
[3] Rita Bakan, "Malnutrition and Learning," *Phi Delta Kappa,* LI (June 1970), pp. 527–530.

essentially positive orientation, but also two articles (3 and 4) which raise disturbing but important questions and are specifically concerned with compensatory education and the education of lower-class blacks.

Part Three is devoted to questions of educational practice. Here again our concern for providing material meaningful to people concerned with a variety of aspects of preprimary education is apparent. In addition to general articles providing an overview of the current state of the field, we included selections on day care, curriculum development and educational media, and administrative and program concerns.

The curriculum section not only addresses such questions as what to teach? and how? but provides a selection which analyzes various preschool education approaches, information sadly lacking in the current literature. In addition, the important areas of program research and evaluation are touched upon in the Glick article.

The selection on administrative and program concerns encompasses a wide range of important issues. In addition to examining some administrative decisions that are necessary or possible, it looks at the issue of parent participation, the role and training of paraprofessionals, and the needs of teachers for training.

In so dynamic a field, it is certain that other topics and problems will emerge during the next several years and there will be need for other volumes with newer material and different emphases. Already obvious, for example, is the need for a full-dress discussion of children's day care, the literature of which is only now reaching significant proportions. For those whose interest is in the general and educational welfare of the young child, the next decade promises to be a rich and fruitful one, indeed.

While it is scarcely possible for editors and readers to share a direct experience together, except as their paths may cross by chance, we nonetheless hope that those who use this volume will become as excited about the material as we did while working with it. We feel privileged to have our words alongside those that appear (or re-appear!) here, and we suspect that our readers will at the end conclude that early childhood education is a vibrant and robust enterprise.

ROBERT H. ANDERSON, *Cambridge, Mass.*
HAROLD G. SHANE, *Bloomington, Ind.*

ACKNOWLEDGMENT

Rochelle Selbert Mayer (Mrs. Eric S.), who wrote article 28, also served as our editorial assistant. It would be impossible to exaggerate the contribution that she made to the volume, or the pleasure that was ours in working with her.

R.H.A.
H.G.S.

Part One
Early Childhood Education in Perspective

I The Renaissance of Early Childhood Education

Harold G. Shane

The article which follows is an expansion of the editorial which opened the March 1969 issue of Phi Delta Kappan, *a special issue on early childhood education. To his original notes on twenty-first century education, Professor Shane, guest editor for that issue, has added his conjectures about the impact of early childhood education programs on elementary and secondary schooling.*

A major contemporary development in education—one which seems certain to influence public schools in the 1970s—is the widespread reawakening of interest in the very young child. It is important at this juncture for educational leadership to be aware of some of the factors and events which have led to this new concern for early childhood. In particular, thought needs to be given to the practices and policies which will be introduced, studied, and evaluated as a downward extension of the public schools occurs in the coming decade.

A Long History

For centuries great educators such as Comenius, Pestalozzi, Froebel, Basedow, and Montessori intuitively sensed the importance of children's experiences before the age of six. Also, during the past forty years, nursery and preschool specialists have made a strong case for the guidance of boys' and girls' early learning. Rose Alschuler, James Hymes, and Laura Zirbes are representative of the many contemporary figures who, beginning in the 1920s, made important contributions to preschool practice.

Sometimes this was accomplished through research, but more often through reasoned conjectures based upon empirical study and personal insight.

In years past, children were, of course, also made the object of quite careful medical and psychological research. For example, the writings of Arnold Gesell and Frances Ilg provided useful longitudinal child-growth data. Willard Olson and Robert Havighurst, respectively, made "organismic age" and "developmental tasks" standard pedagogical phrases, while Jean Piaget for a quarter century has been respected for his developmental-cognitive studies.

Phi Delta Kappan, Volume 50 (March 1969). This article (as revised) and ten other articles in this volume reprinted with permission of *Phi Delta Kappan.* Mr. Shane, of Indiana University, is co-editor of this volume.

But despite enthusiastic supporters and a substantial literature before 1960, no priority and frequently little heed was given by the public schools or the general community to the development of programs for children in the four-year span beginning at two and extending through age five. True, the Lanham Act expediently provided money for the care of children of working mothers during World War II, and some districts began to offer kindergarten programs for two or three hours a day. But for the most part, the importance of early childhood was honored more by words than by actions in the schools. Even today in many states considerable parental pressure (or tuition) is required before kindergarten programs are launched for four-year-olds. In wide areas there are no kindergartens at all.

Let us now look at the confluence of events and circumstances that have led to the present renaissance of interest, which holds promise for the long delayed provision for education of two- to five-year-olds.

Factors in Renaissance

The renaissance of interest in the very young has been stimulated by many things. An inventory of some of these elements and events follows.

Political decisions. To be both blunt and succinct, it seems rather obvious that policies and "politics" at the federal level have had a distinct bearing on the funding of educational programs begun prior to the kindergarten level. By the earlier sixties it was becoming clear that there was much social dynamite in the ghettos of the city and in Appalachia-type rural slums. One of a number of ways of postponing or precluding explosions was providing educational programs for the children of the poor.

Current social commentaries. Recent attention-capturing books that focus on the complex challenges and appalling conditions of ghetto education have helped to convince many citizens of the importance of an early, problem-preventive approach to educating our children of poverty. Although they vary appreciably in quality and insight, this genre of book includes such titles as *Education and Ecstacy, Our Children Are Dying, Death at an Early Age, How Children Fail,* and *The Way It 'Spozed To Be.*

The great national concern which has developed for the problems of rural areas and the inner city has quickened interest in the young child and lent support to providing for education of the culturally different. Educators have begun to point out that it is short-sighted and wasteful to have so-called compensatory education in elementary and secondary schools to repair damage done to boys and girls before they enter kindergarten or the primary school.

Head Start. Operation Head Start, as part of the war on poverty, is both a result of the new recognition for the importance of children's early experiences and a cause of the current awareness of these early years.[1]

Environmental mediation. One important influence in developing programs for very young children is the concept of environmental mediation —the idea that during the child's early life wholesome forms of intervention in his milieu can help him become more effective in his transactions and interactions with others. While a sentimental interest in improving the environment of children has existed for centuries, the concept of a deliberate, planned intervention is, for practical purposes, a phenomenon of the sixties.

Creating intelligence. Closely related to the point above is the accumulating evidence suggesting that the young child's intelligence is modifiable, that we can in effect "create" what we measure as an IQ. The old "ages and stages" concept simply does not correspond with new information about childhood, the ways in which children learn, and the ways in which they develop. Benjamin Bloom, Ira Gordon, and J. McVicker Hunt[2] are among writers who stress the significance of a facilitating environment for the optimal development of children and emphasize the importance of children's early years. Research done by David Krech[3] with infrahuman subjects strongly suggests that glia (memory) cells, brain size, and the blood supplied to the cerebral hemispheres actually can be increased by intervening in the milieu to create stimulating surroundings. His article on page 209 is especially provocative in that it implies that we may have been losing out on the best years of the learner's life by postponing his inschool education—until the ripe old age of six.

Psychoneurobiochemeducation. The rapidly developing field which Krech has called "psychoneurobiochemeducation" has implications for early contacts with children. Specialists in certain disciplines such as biochemistry have conducted experiments with both subhuman and human subjects that are beginning to demonstrate the use of drugs (such as pipradol, or magnesium pemoline) in influencing mind, mood, and memory. While pharmacies and surgical suites operated by boards of education seem unlikely to dominate our schools, there is reason to believe that very early school contacts for children having personality and learning problems may permit chemical therapy to reclaim these boys and girls who would otherwise become liabilities to society.

Experiments in early learning. Experiments in early learning, although not unique to the present decade, have fueled discussions and provided relevant—and sometimes disputed—data to the process of creating educational policies which will govern school practices in the 1970s. O.K. Moore's[4] inquiries into responsive environments, Dolores Durkin's[5] exploration of preschool reading instruction, and Bereiter and Engelmann's[6] controversial work on early academic learning through predominantly oral methods at the University of Illinois as they attempted early cognitive training are illustrative of contemporary projects.

Improved understanding of subcultures and group membership. Cultural anthropologists such as Edward T. Hall[7] have begun to point out the implications of membership in a given U.S. subculture. Accumulating evidence suggests that it is during the first four or five years of life that many personal behaviors—in language, attitude, values, even ways of learning—begin to take on the form they will retain for a lifetime. We now spend billions for remedial work, for penal and mental institutions, and for belated compensatory or supportive education necessitated, in a number of instances, because schools have not had early contacts with the children who will become their clientele.

The early influences of social class. Research by Jerome Kagan[8] has begun to suggest that social class membership—closely related to subculture group membership—begins permanently to influence personality, for better or worse, by the age of five or before.

Ethnicity as a mediating factor. Gerald Lesser[9] and his associates convincingly state, as a result of several replicated studies, that ethnicity (i.e., ethnic, subculture group membership) apparently causes children to learn in different ways.

Language development. For years now, Basil Bernstein's[10] work, which demonstrates that social class and one's linguistic characteristics are intimately related, has been widely accepted. The research cited, as well as analogous studies, which space precludes listing, are beginning to form a mosaic of data suggesting that these years of early childhood are more critical than any other stage of human development. In other words, if society, through its educational planning, does not vigorously begin to foster facilitating environments for every young children, it may be too late or immensely expensive to remove the psychological scar tissue that has long since formed on the personalities of certain young children before they enter school at the age of six.

Educational technology. A number of other elements have made educators more acutely interested in the initial years of childhood.[11] Improved technology has produced "talking" typewriters, "talking" books, and other teaching aids that can be used by boys and girls of three and four if they are in a school setting where they are available. Also, the progress made in developing Stage III computers promises to provide equipment that can be used in four- and five-year-old kindergartens.

Mass media: the phantom curriculum. The "phantom curriculum" to which mass media daily expose the child also has a bearing on early childhood education. By the time the child is enrolled in kindergarten or the primary school, he has an ill-assorted but important array of information.[12] There are those who not only contend that the massive sensory input of mass media is making children educable sooner, they also contend that the schools have a responsibility to help children at an early age acquire more coherent input. The problems here have been widely recognized, although much remains to be done in coping with them.

The rediscovery of Montessori, Piaget and Vygotsky. While it is difficult to determine whether it is a cause or a result of the renaissance in early childhood education, the rediscovery of the work of Montessori, Piaget, and Vygotsky certainly has helped to enliven the instructional scene. These distinguished persons focused their work on aspects of methods, cognition, human development, and language growth at age five or below.

A decline in the elementary school population. Finally, a small group of prescient educational leaders, persons who are of a pragmatic turn of mind, are casting a speculative eye on the two- to five-year-old group because of the widespread use of the "pill." In view of the drop in the U.S. birth rate in the last few years, there will be an inevitable decline in the gross elementary school population by 1975. One way of utilizing the staff and the space that are likely to become available will be to extend the school's responsibility downward.

"Shock Waves" from Early Childhood Education

It is more likely that "shock waves" generated by the impact of early childhood education programs will reverberate upward through the elementary school to the secondary school during the next decade. This phenomenon may well be the most important concomitant of the renaissance of interest in young children. Its importance resides in the likelihood that public school organization and policies will be triggered by programs for two- to five-year-olds which produce a "new client" for elementary teachers to serve.

Let us briefly examine some of the possible elements involved in the new educational "mix" which appears to be developing: possible changes in the children entering the primary years, potential innovations or changes in the primary and middle school, and developments that may occur at the secondary level.

A New Client for the Elementary School?

Although there is at present no satisfying longitudinal research which traces the influence of early childhood education experiences on a group of boys and girls in the two to five range, it seems inevitable that as experiences of this sort begin to be provided during the later 1970s, they will produce a different, improved client. What the six-year-old of 1980 will be like is a matter of conjecture, but some plausible hypotheses can be advanced.

Let us endeavor to suggest some of the possible benefits to or changes in the child who has come in contact with good school programs beginning no later than age three:

1. He should be more skilled in both receptive and expressive communication;
2. His major physical problems, if any, should have been identified and (hopefully) remedied insofar as possible;

3. He should be more secure and more skilled in his interactive control relationships with his environment;
4. Impediments imposed by certain types of social class membership should be reduced;
5. Behavioral differences due to membership in a given subculture should be less obvious;
6. The range of ability among his peers should be greater than was true during the previous decade;
7. Since early childhood education is unlikely to be a universal in the U.S. for some time to come, the group in which the child finds himself may vary more in chronological age than is the case in 1970 when some five-year-olds (and a rare four-year-old) are enrolled in the first year of primary school.

Whether the "new client" will be in groups that are easier or more difficult for teachers to cope with may depend on how successfully primary schools modify their present programs.

Possible Innovations in the Primary School

When speculating about possible changes in the primary school, four major innovations seem likely. First, prescribed experiences will be replaced by more flexible ones. Second, self-contained or one-teacher classrooms will more rapidly give way to cooperative teams or differentiated flexible partnerships of teachers. Third, the curriculum will become more of a seamless continuum and less a series of blocks or units. Fourth, the progress of the child during his primary and middle school years is likely to occur outside the graded structure now found in many elementary schools.

How will the downward extension of public education tend to bring about the four changes? In the first place, as even greater differences in ability and adjustment of children are recognized by the school, flexibility in planning the program of the individual learner becomes a professional responsibility. And the primary school of the late 1970s should have appreciably more data pertaining to boys and girls than is now the case. Indeed, one of the probable emerging purposes of the school's contacts with young children may prove to be that of obtaining or providing personal data for the planning of the child's instruction. Such data presumably would include dental, medical, social, and psychological information.

The idea that flexible teaching partnerships will further erode the policy of assigning one teacher to one classroom is supported by a growing trend to pool teachers' talents so that they may better serve the needs and purposes of children in the seamless curriculum. By the time a given group of children has been exposed for one or more years to an effective early childhood program, their composite profiles will be so varied and their needs—both academic and developmental—will be so wide-ranging that even a superior teacher, by himself in a self-contained classroom, could not expect to handle them all. A likely solution, then, is the differentiated, flexible teaching partnership: a cooperative form of staff employment in which teachers, paraprofessionals, and various educational specialists design the ways in which they can aid the development of a hundred or more children placed in their care for two or more consecutive years.

Potential Changes in the Middle School Years

Various modifications of the primary school inevitably will phase their way into the middle school. However, the most important changes are not merely those which extend flexible teaching partnerships or the seamless curriculum concept into the intermediate years. Rather the major changes will be those unique to the education of ten- to twelve-year-old preadolescents.

One of the major decisions to be made with respect to the middle school years is whether the emphasis shall be on the academic, on the cognitive, or on an enrichment approach as the faculty seeks to maximize human development. In view of the current emphasis on both more excellent and more humane (and humanizing) educational experiences, it seems both likely and desirable that the middle school will concentrate on developing excellence in social and economic literacy rather than on the improvement of academic work *per se*.

Again to illustrate, it seems reasonable that the middle school will emphasize even more strongly cognitive development but with respect to a broader concept of human and *humane* literacy and socially desirable attitudes rather than with respect to mastery of subject matter alone. Content presumably will be more of a means to developmental ends rather than an end in itself.

Conjectures as to Changes Rippling Upward to the Secondary Level

If a desirable developmental foundation is laid in early childhood and is strengthened in the primary and middle school years, the improvement in the learner in U.S. schools could be exponential during the late 1970s and 1980s.

That is, the most *visible* educational payoff for early childhood education might begin at the secondary level and increase thereafter throughout the post-secondary years.

Were this to happen, it probably would be foreshadowed by a distinct change in the role of the high school and in its present operation. Rather than preparing students for the world of work or for college, as it endeavors to do now, the secondary years might provide the equivalent to an advanced technical education or to a present-day university education prior to the student's entry into either the employment market or into the university. In the event of this not improbable development, the university may become primarily a graduate institution and would be able to focus more on research, on the development of programs offered in professional schools which lead to licensing (teachers, doctors, accountants, etc.), and on the vocational contributions of the arts and sciences to the professional schools.

One essential point must be added. The "secondary" school, as it begins to prepare its clients to the level of today's baccalaureate degree holders, almost certainly would need to include what are now labeled the junior college or community college years, and the "university" would need to encompass today's junior and senior college years and three or more years of graduate school. This is *not* intended to suggest that by 1980 or 1985 that there will be *separate* schools providing three years of early childhood education, six to eight years of elementary education, six to eight years of secondary, and five years at the university level. It *is* to suggest the probable emergence and great importance of an unbroken or seamless curriculum providing a flow of learning experiences and extending from early childhood through whatever secondary or university level education tomorrow's society deems desirable for its well-being.

Twenty-First Century Education

As we move toward the next century, a century that is closer to today than is the beginning of World War II, we may find that the renaissance of early childhood education is of greater importance to education as a whole than it is to childhood!

That is, its value may reside not only in the improvement of learning experience for the youngest but in the innovations and changes that the shock waves of its impact create throughout the structure of public education.

Changes of the sort hinted at here, of course, are broader and require greater creative thought and effort than the organizational changes and policies that must be designed to initiate and to sustain them. But most important of all will be the matter of the values that education will pursue as we conjecture about the preparation of children and youth who will spend most of their time in a new century.

As we study innovations we must often ask ourselves two questions: what kind of world are we preparing our children for, and what can we do through our policy decisions to shape society so that tomorrow will be better?

Let us begin our contemplation of programs for the youngest by first sweeping away some of the intellectual smog that continues to obscure many of our goals. The projects we initiate should be based not just on better knowledge of early childhood but on rationally examined values as well. These are values which should reflect a reasoned quest for a twenty-first century in which life has become more humane and secure, is marked by outreaching friendship for others, and is less confused and violent than the era through which we have been groping.

References

1. For a succinct assessment, see Keith Osborn, "Project Head Start," *Educational Leadership* (November 1965), pp. 98–102.

2. The following references are helpful: Benjamin S. Bloom, *Stability and Change in Human Characteristics* (New York: John Wiley and Sons, 1964); Ira J. Gordon, "New Conceptions of Children's Learning and Development," pp. 49–73, in *Learning and Mental Health in the School* (Washington, D.C.: Association for Supervision and Curriculum, 1966); J. McVicker Hunt, *Intelligence and Experience* (New York: Ronald Press, 1961).

3. David Krech, "The Chemistry of Learning," *Saturday Review* (January 20, 1968), pp. 48–50.

4. O.K. Moore, "Autoelectric Responsive Environments for Learning," pp. 184–219, in Ronald Gross and Judith Moore (eds.), *Revolution in the Schools* (New York: Harcourt, 1964).

5. Dolores Durkin, *Children Who Read Early* (New York: Teachers College, Columbia University, 1966).

6. Carl Bereiter and Seigfried Englemann, *Teaching Disadvantaged Children in the Preschool* (Englewood Cliffs, N.J.: Prentice-Hall, 1966).

7. See Edward T. Hall, *The Silent Language* (Garden City, N.Y.: Doubleday, 1965); idem, *The Hidden Dimension* (New York: Doubleday, 1966).

8. Jerome Kagan, "The Many Faces of Response," *Psychology Today* (January 1968), pp. 60–65.

9. Cf. the article by Fort, Watts, and Lesser in *Phi Delta Kappan*, L (March 1969), pp. 386–388. Cf. Susan S. Stodolsky and Gerald Lesser, "Learning Patterns in the Disadvantaged," *Harvard Educational Review* (Fall 1967), pp. 546–593.

10. Basil Bernstein, "Language and Social Class," *British Journal of Sociology* (November 1960), pp. 271–276.

11. Cf. the article by Meierhenry and Stepp in this volume.

12. John McCulkin, "A Schoolman's Guide to Marshall McLuhan," *Saturday Review* (March 18, 1967), pp. 51–53 ff.

2 Perspectives on Early Childhood Education

Edith M. Dowley

*"The history of early childhood education is a history of social change,"
says Edith Dowley. The following article delves into the foundations
of early childhood education, discussing some of the motivating theories,
people, and attempts in the field, and reviews some of the most recent
ideas about early childhood education.*

Early childhood education came into the seventies in a position
of unprecedented significance. Recognized as one of the foremost issues
of the day, it rates prime time, front page and cover story prominence in
the mass media, as well as scholarly treatment in some of the most distinguished journals of the arts and sciences. Books and publications relating
to the behavior, development and education of young children have been
marketed in such numbers in the past ten years that it is almost impossible to keep abreast of their growing influence on society. The toy and
educational-materials industries thrive on the current status of early cognitive stimulation. Nursery schools and kindergartens of every kind, from
public-supported to franchised-for-profit, are multiplying rapidly throughout the United States. There is legislation, on local, state, and national
levels, either passed or pending, which will affect the educational opportunities of a new generation of preschool children and regulate the
quality of preparation and performance of those who will teach them.
The importance of providing education for young children has captured
the imagination of the public today as never before.

Social and political unrest have characterized the climate of much of
the world in the past ten years. The public has grown more and more
impatient with war, poverty, racial discrimination, social injustice, and
a deteriorating environment. They demand immediate solutions to these
persistent problems. At the same time, new light on the human potential
has revealed that man has scarcely begun to develop his seemingly limitless capabilities. As his technology grows in complexity, it becomes apparent that there must be a radical redefinition of educational goals to
provide the tremendous knowledge and develop the skills which man
must have in order to control his machinery and manage his social
organization.

This paper was commissioned especially for this book of readings. Parts of it were
adapted from the author's article on "Early Childhood Education" in the *Encyclopedia
of Educational Research* (Macmillan, 1969). Edith M. Dowley is Director of Bing Nursery
School, and Associate Professor of Psychology and Education at Stanford University.

It is not surprising then that early learning has achieved priority rating at this time. One way, obviously, to speed up the learning process, is to begin education at a younger age. Therefore, when Hunt[1] suggested a psychological basis for preschool enrichment as an antidote for cultural deprivation, and Bloom et al.[2] advocated early compensatory education, they intrigued a whole new group of professionals to investigate the learning potential of young children. Social scientists "discovered" what educators of young children for half a century had taken for granted, that the preschool years are a crucial time not only for social and emotional but also for intellectual growth. Almost overnight, childhood became a precious commodity—a valuable national resource which had previously been underestimated.

Childhood is a comparative newcomer to art, literature, and to the social sciences.[3] Artists of the tenth century were unable to depict a child except as a man on a smaller scale, according to Ariès.[4] It is probable that there was no place in the medieval world for childhood as we know it. This was not because children were rejected or neglected, but because medieval society was not aware of the particular nature of childhood which makes the child different from the adult. As soon as the infant could live without his mother or his nanny he joined the society of adults.

Kesson[5] tells us that it was only yesterday in human history that the majority of children could be expected to live beyond their fifth year. In the two centuries of historical writings about children which he covered, he traced the profound changes which have occurred in western man's theory of the child. The child was the beneficiary of the physician's skill, the reformer's zeal and the object of speculation of philosophers and educators who found him an object of serious intellectual interest. Not until the turn of the century just past was science to claim the child in the research of biologists and psychologists. Sears et al.,[6] speculating about why science remained so long aloof from the study of child behavior, suggest that science was a male preoccupation and that even in the 1940s and 1950s those scientific and medical specialities which pertained to children attracted fewer than their share of men.

The history of early childhood education is a history of social change. As the political and economic conditions of human living are degraded by war, pestilence, and want, or encouraged by intervals of peace, public health, and productive plenty, the conditions of childhood are also affected. In the course of two centuries the young child has been the victim of every social ill or the beneficiary of social good depending on the times in which he lived and the position to which he was born. Educational leaders stand out in the history of childhood because they advocated better infant care, exposed the evils of child labor, pleaded for the prevention of cruelty to children, or contributed to the discovery of the almost limitless mind of the child.

Prototypes for almost every educational movement can be traced back to earlier periods of history. Comenius in the mid-seventeenth century expressed his appreciation of the teaching function of parents, which is a basic assumption of the modern nursery school movement. Although some of John Locke's judgmental and punitive attitudes toward children are unacceptably harsh in the light of modern attitudes toward mental health, in 1693 he articulated many principles and practices which are valued today.[7] He contended that curiosity should be encouraged in children as a valuable appetite for knowledge. He also viewed "spontaneous play" and the "delight in discovery" as assets to learning. In the eighteenth century, Rousseau, a radical thinker for his times, brought to childhood and to the very nature of the child a new dignity and respect. Pestalozzi and Froebel in the latter half of the eighteenth and beginning of the nineteenth centuries introduced learning through the use of "the senses" and the "freedom to investigate" into an educational system dominated by rote memory and harsh discipline. The concept of compensatory education which is currently emphasized as an antidote for cultural deprivation had its origins in the thinking of Pestalozzi and Froebel and was later expanded and implemented by Montessori and McMillan.

The current national interest in nursery education for deprived children about whom we have been concerned since 1959 can be traced back to Froebel. At the onset of the Industrial Revolution he conceived the "kindergarten" in Germany and gave it the name it carries to this day. His followers started kindergartens in the slums of Berlin and claimed success for them. Froebel advocated giving the child freedom of movement to explore the world and emphasized an ordered outer world which would in turn make for an ordered inner world. In addition, Braun[8] tells us, Froebel's use of language during the child's exploring was aimed at making the impressions of the child conscious and unified.

Early in this century Maria Montessori, agreeing with Froebel in allowing the child the freedom to explore and teach himself, worked with slum children of Rome in their preschool years. She replaced Froebel's materials with her own, which were larger and therefore more manageable and easier for the child to control. Her total environment was more in tune with the child's size. The child in her preschool was left to pursue his own interests and free to solve problems without interference. In this way she was able to develop and foster in him a sense of competence. Montessori is best known for the design for sensory training and the utilization of synthetic intellectual functions.

Margaret McMillan and her sister Rachel were originally concerned about children in the slum districts of London. They saw the nursery school as making up for poverty, apathy, and neglect. They included among their goals provisions for medical and dental care, for cognitive stimulation and work. (How familiar these ideas must sound to persons involved in Head Start programs for preschool children from low income families, organized nationally in 1965 as a part of the antipoverty programs of the Johnson administration!) The McMillans were influential in setting in motion the American nursery school, which, though it more typically served the middle-class child in this country, was patterned after the nursery schools they established in England.

Until the middle of the nineteenth century, the leaders in education were those who articulated a method or pleaded for educational reform. The history of early childhood was for the most part a history of the changing attitudes of society toward children and learning. Then Charles Darwin, with his concept of the hereditary determination of intelligence, sowed the seeds of the child study movement. G. Stanley Hall, impressed by Darwinian theory, and recognizing the importance of the empirical study of the child, became a leader of the new psychology in America. One of his students, Louis Terman, translated and adapted the intelligence test designed in France by Alfred Binet. In a short time the Stanford revision of the Binet-Simon Intelligence Scale became the most widely known test of intelligence in America. Terman and others communicated their faith in "fixed intelligence" to those who spread the testing movement in America.

In the first half of this century teaching was influenced tremendously by this theory and won such wide acceptance that it produced considerable controversy when in 1940 child psychologists at the Child Welfare Station of the University of Iowa[9] claimed positive effects on intellectual development from certain enriching experiences offered by the nursery school. They were so soundly criticized, however, by other leading psychologists[10] that their findings were put aside for almost two decades and only recently rediscovered by advocates of preschool enrichment for the educationally deprived.

The twenties and thirties saw an increase in experimental studies of children by psychologists. John B. Watson, the father of behaviorism, not only had an important influence on the child-rearing practices of the day, but on teacher-child relationships, as well. Widely distributed textbooks on preschool education by Foster and Mattson[11] and by Blatz et al.[12] reflect his dogmatism and his behaviorist theories about habit training, early socialization and absence of affect in the teaching of young children.

Arnold Gesell, who began his monumental study of growth and development early in this century, took exception to the behaviorists. He warned that their theories were fraught with undesirable consequences for the young child. In Gesell's thinking, the first six years of life exceeded all others in developmental importance. Early childhood education was to him a cultural instrument for strengthening the normal functions of a normal home.[13] His normative approach to development achieved tremendous popular acceptance and he became a revered authority figure for a whole generation of parents and teachers of young children.

During the depression years of the early thirties, nursery education was given national recognition in the United States for the first time. Federal legislation and support were instrumental in establishing nursery schools throughout the country under the Works Progress Administration. The

primary objective of the WPA nursery schools was to give work to unemployed teachers, nurses, and other helpers, and at the same time provide nutrition, protection, and a healthy and emotionally stable environment for 75,000 needy children from two to five years of age. Surplus
foods were made available to them in abundant supplies as a by-product
of economic support for farmers. The supervision and training programs
established for these nursery schools were carefully planned and organized under professional leadership.

World War II brought a second spurt in the growth of nursery schools.
Under the Lanham Act, funds were made available for the group care
of young children whose mothers worked in strategic war industries.
These child-care centers were mobilized on such a vast scale—because of
the urgent and immediate need for them—that they were not of uni-
formly high quality in their programs or in their teaching personnel.
They made at least two important contributions to education, however.
They introduced the concept of group care and guidance for young
children to a wider community; this in turn resulted in increasing awareness by the general public of the value of nursery education. Secondly,
because of the longer hours the children spent at school and the disturb-
ances in parent-child relationships which were a consequence of father-
absence[14] and mother-employment, teachers were forced to look for improved ways of working with children. Their search eventually led to a
revision of their objectives, their programs and the environment they
made for learning. It also gave them greater insight into the social and
emotional needs of young children.[15]

The idea that good nursery education is not only valuable, but for
some children essential, had not yet been accepted by the general public,
however. When the war ended, federal support for day-care centers was
withdrawn on the assumption that women, no longer needed in war-
related employment, would return to their former roles of full-time wives
and mothers. This was not always the case, however, and people tried
with varying and limited success to continue centers where the employment of mothers was determined to be necessary for the welfare of their
families.

The nursery school as a new, twentieth-century institution was not
bound by the same traditions of education which often determined the
direction of the kindergarten and elementary school. It had the freedom
and flexibility to work out its own philosophy and practice. Again the
education of young children took a new direction. During the war, parents of young children were made aware of the value of planned group
experiences for their preschool children. Some resourceful mothers banded
together to do something about securing the benefits of early childhood
education for their own children. The parent-cooperative nursery school
movement flourished in several parts of the country in the post-war years.
In California, where the growth of nursery schools was impressive, parent-

child observation classes have become parent-education classes with laboratory arrangements for mothers to observe their children one or more half days a week in supervised play and routine activities which sometimes even include a lunch and nap.

Following the war years, the influence of psychoanalytic theory began to be evident in preschool practice. Benjamin Spock[16] was changing the child-rearing practices of a large segment of the population by advocating greater permissiveness in the socialization of infants and in allowing the young child to learn in his own time and his own way. Frustration, aggression, and the ventilation of feelings were of concern to those who worked with young children. The attention of teachers was drawn to "the fundamental needs of the child,"[17] and the role of the teacher took on clinical as well as educational functions. Much attention was given to the phenomenon of anxiety in a child, especially "separation anxiety" and its harmful effects on groups of young children. In 1950 Erikson[18] at the White House Conference on Children and Youth introduced the concept of a healthy personality for every child in relation to his theory of the Eight Stages of Man (see article 10 of this volume).

The publication of research studies in child development and early learning, which had slowed down to a minimum in the war and post-war years, now gained new momentum in the early- to mid-fifties. The war had drawn attention to ethnic and cultural differences throughout the world in the care and rearing of children. Anthropologists and sociologists contributed insights into the effects of social position, skin color, economic and educational backgrounds on personality development and on the child's concept of himself. The concerns of the nursery school and kindergarten were with adjustment, freedom from prejudice, and learning to get along well with others.

Rediscovery of some of the earlier writings of Piaget in the late fifties inspired learning theorists to explore the cognitive aspects of development. An increase in experimental studies, which contributed to the knowledge of how children learn, followed. The effects of the high birth-rate which followed the war years resulted in larger elementary school classes and in an under-supply of well-prepared teachers to staff them. The American system of public education came in for some harsh criticism when a best seller by Rudolph Flesch in 1955 posed the question "Why Can't Johnny Read?" Then the launching of Sputnik I in 1957, by the USSR, resulted in a frantic search for reasons why American children were behind the Russians in academic achievement. The pressure for maximal utilization of our intellectual resources jolted the entire educational system and resulted in attempts to teach academic subjects to younger and younger children. Beginning instruction in reading as early as ten months of age was suggested, and new teaching aids such as teaching machines and talking typewriters were introduced. As Bronfenbrenner observed,[19] achievement began to replace adjustment as the highest goal of the American way of life. He predicted that the results might be children who are more aggressive, domineering, and cruel if education for academic excellence were pursued single-mindedly.

By the early sixties the direction of thought in early childhood education was toward rediscovering the mind of the child.[20] The influence of linguistics and the recognition at this time of the importance of language for educational growth stimulated great interest and research in language development.[21] The suspicion that too little was being done to foster intellectual development in young children began to creep into the literature.[22] Reviews of research related to teaching in the nursery school,[23] to the effects of early training on young children,[24] and to values in early childhood education,[25] revealed a considerable body of information and theory but also detected many gaps in knowledge and the absence of a clearly defined theory for nursery education.

The post-war years were a time of great technological expansion in the United States. Complex machinery was rapidly replacing manpower in performing many of the services and functions of human living. Highly skilled and professionally educated persons were in great demand to maintain and further the technology and human organization of the country. The gap between the affluent and the poor in the United States began to widen to an alarming degree.

A sense of overwhelming national guilt was felt when Hunt[26] and others exposed the effects of cultural and educational deprivation on a large segment of the population. Minority groups which had suffered the greatest disadvantage were understandably outraged. Experiments by Deutsch[27] indicated that preschool, kindergarten or day-care experience, or a combination of these, are associated with higher scores on intelligence tests than are achieved by children without such experiences. He also found that regardless of social class affiliation the advantage of preschool attendance is evident at first grade level and even more at fifth grade. The decision to utilize preschool enrichment as an antidote to poverty culminated in 1965 in federally funded preschool summer programs known as Project Head Start. As a part of the antipoverty program of the Johnson administration, over half a million children who had never before attended school were enrolled in programs which provided medical, dental, as well as educational services of a highly personal but professional nature.

In the years that followed, Head Start was established as a year-round program for young children. The success of the program has attracted the interest and concern of many scientists and citizens. Volumes have been written on the education of the disadvantaged in America as well as in other countries, particularly in Israel.[28]

The effects of enrichment in early childhood have not been limited to the disadvantaged; they have penetrated every social and cultural stratum of society. The business of educating young children is no longer the sole prerogative of parents and nursery school teachers. Government, scholars, business, all are involved and interested in shaping the future patterns for the education of young children.[29] Television, which for years held a powerfully influential though not always educationally sound or desirable position in the teaching of children, has now taken on the responsibility for selecting and imparting knowledge and for teaching skills and techniques to preschool children (Sesame Street, Mr. Rogers, Captain Kangaroo, etc.).

The mind of the young child of the seventies is truly a captive to his many and varied "discoverers."

In the first rush of excitement, in the mid-sixties some of the "discoverers of the mind of the child" discounted or ignored the substantial accumulation of more than four decades of knowledge and wisdom by nursery educators and criticized their principles and practices. The labels "traditional" and "establishment" were used to describe existing nursery schools, while "innovators" founded "Early Learning Centers" and "New Schools for Young Children." The concept of the nursery school, which from the beginning had been an adjunct to family living and an extension of the child's home outward, now tended to become a downward extension of the elementary school. Greater emphasis was given to cognitive learning, readiness for reading and the acquisition of language skills. Those who believed in the importance of play in early childhood now found themselves having to defend it.[30] As concerned parents and teachers pause to wonder if childhood is in danger of losing its identity, scientists continue to puzzle over the mystery of mental processes.

Early childhood education has come a long way in this century. The past five years of intensive research and experimentation have strengthened our old beliefs and given us new insights about what to value for children. Preschool programs have multiplied across the land. By 1967, 1,145,000 three- and four-year-olds were enrolled in preschool centers, and it is projected that by 1972 there will be 3,000,000.

Early childhood education has made a new place in the world of the seventies. So much importance has been attributed to the nursery years as a time for learning that some are beginning to wonder if childhood may be in danger of losing the gains made over the past century. Could childhood in the seventies return to the grim place it held in the middle ages when children were "miniature adults," exposed to all the serious artificialities of adult living rather than their involvement with the real world of children?

John Watson in the *Merrill-Palmer Newsletter* of March 1970 raises the question—is early learning good for a child? He wonders if a lot of learning tools that seem to make sense are really as beneficial as they appear. Elkind[31] tells us there is no evidence that preschool instruction has lasting effects on mental growth and development, and feels there is no justification for making the preschool bear the blame for failures in the elementary school. Too much education too early may result in "intellectually burned children," he warns. There is still much to be learned about optimal periods for acquiring knowledge and skill. It is wiser to avoid risking those which may discourage or handicap learning in later life.

The joy and delight of discovery in experimentation and exploration in an environment full of challenging, concrete, natural, childlike experiences have served childhood well for over half a century in nursery school. It seems wise to preserve and cherish them for children yet to come.

References

1. J. McVicker Hunt, "The Psychological Basis for Using Preschool Enrichment as an Antidote for Cultural Deprivation," *Merrill-Palmer Quarterly*, 10 (1964), pp. 209–248.

2. Benjamin S. Bloom *et al.*, *Compensatory Education for Cultural Deprivation* (New York: Holt, 1965).

3. Margaret Mead, "Theoretical Setting —1954," pp. 3–20, in Margaret Mead and Martha Wolfenstein (eds.), *Childhood in Contemporary Cultures* (Chicago: University of Chicago Press, 1963).

4. Philippe Ariès, *Centuries of Childhood: A Social History of Family Life* (trans. Robert Baldick) (New York: Knopf, 1962).

5. William Kesson, "Research in the Psychological Development of Infants," *Merrill-Palmer Quarterly*.

6. Robert R. Sears *et al.*, *Patterns of Child Rearing* (New York: Harper, 1957).

7. John Locke, *Some Thoughts Concerning Education* (Cambridge, England: Cambridge University Press, 1892).

8. Samuel J. Braun, "Nursery Education for Disadvantaged Children: An Historical Review," in *Montessori in Perspective* (National Association for the Education of Young Children, 1966).

9. Beth L. Wellman, "The Effects of Pre-School Attendance upon the I.Q." *Journal of Experimental Education*, 1 (1932), pp. 48–49; O. L. Crissey, "Mental Development as Related to Institutional Residence and Educational Achievement," *Iowa Study of Child Welfare*, 13 (1937).

10. Florence L. Goodenough, "New Evidence on Environmental Influence on Intelligence," *39th Yearbook, NSSE* (1940), pp. 407–365; Gwinn McNemar, "A Critical Examination of the University of Iowa Studies of Environmental Influences upon the I.Q.," *Psychological Bulletin* (1940), pp. 63–92.

11. Josephine C. Foster and Marion L. Mattson, *Nursery School Procedure* (New York: Appleton, 1929).

12. William E. Blatz *et al.*, *Nursery Education* (New York: Morrow, 1935).

13. Arnold Gesell, *The First Five Years: A Guide to the Study of the Preschool Child* (New York: Harper, 1940).

14. Lois M. Stolz *et al.*, *Father Relations of War-born Children* (Stanford, California: Stanford University Press, 1954).

15. Pauline S. Sears and Edith M. Dowley, "Research on Teaching in the Nursery School," in N. L. Gage (ed.), *Handbook on Research in Teaching* (Chicago: Rand McNally, 1963).

16. Benjamin Spock, *Common Sense Book of Baby and Child Care* (New York: Dell, 1946).

17. L. K. Frank, "Fundamental Needs of the Child," *Mental Hygiene*, 22 (1938), pp. 353–379.

18. Erik H. Erikson, *A Healthy Personality for Every Child*, Report of Midcentury White House Conference on Children and Youth (1951), pp. 6–25.

19. Urie Bronfenbrenner, "The Changing American Child: A Spectulative Analysis," *Merrill-Palmer Quarterly*, 7 (1961), pp. 73–84.

20. William E. Martin, "Rediscovering the Mind of the Child: A Significant Trend in Research in Child Development," *Merrill-Palmer Quarterly*, 6 (1960), p. 2.

21. Susan E. Ervin-Tripp, "Language Development," pp. 55–105, in Lois W. Hoffman and Martin L. Hoffman (eds.), *Review of Child Development Research*, vol. 2 (Beverly Hills, Calif.: Sage, 1966).

22. Kenneth D. Wann *et al.*, *Fostering Intellectual Development in Young Children* (New York: Teachers College, Columbia University, 1962); J. McVicker Hunt, *Intelligence and Experience* (New York: Ronald Press, 1961); William Fowler, "Cognitive Learning in Infancy and Early Childhood," *Psychol. Bulletin,* 59 (1962), pp. 116–152.

23. Kesson, "Research in Psychological Development."

24. Joan W. Swift, "Effects of Early Group Experience: The Nursery School and Day Nursery," pp. 249–281, in Martin L. Hoffman and Lois W. Hoffman (eds.), *Review of Child Development Research* (Beverly Hills, Calif.: Sage, 1964).

25. Evangeline Burgess, *Values in Early Childhood Education,* NEA, 1965.

26. J. McVicker Hunt, "The Psychological Basis for Using Preschool Enrichment."

27. Martin Deutsch, "The Disadvantaged Child and the Learning Process," pp. 163–181, in A. H. Passow (ed.), *Education in Depressed Areas* (New York: Teachers College, Columbia University, 1963).

28. Moshe Smilansky, "Fighting Deprivation in the Promised Land," *Saturday Review,* 49 (1966), pp. 82–86.

29. Barbara Biber, *Challenges Ahead for Early Childhood Education* (National Association for the Education of Young Children, 1969).

30. Milly Almy, "Spontaneous Play: An Avenue for Intellectual Development," *Young Children,* 22 (May 1967), pp. 268–277; L. K. Frank, "Play is Valid," *Childhood Education* (March 1968).

31. David Elkind, "Interpretive Essays on Jean Piaget," *Children and Adolescents* (Oxford University Press, 1970).

3 Social Reform and Early Childhood Education: Some Historical Perspectives

Marvin Lazerson

While many will argue that a good educational program for very young children can better society as a whole, this author contends that the "use of education as a surrogate for social reform" is a polite way of bypassing the real problems confronting society.*

To a historian, today's discussions of preschooling for urban children are particularly mortifying. The debates seem to make slight inroads into previously formulated conceptions. Admittedly, we have established an elaborate rationale for early childhood education. Psychologists and social scientists tell us that children can learn at an early age and warn us about the dire consequences of "cultural deprivation." Phrases like "social intervention" on behalf of the urban child, forging a bridge between home and school, and "learning to learn" seem to have become permanent parts of the regular incantations of American educators and their philanthropic and governmental colleagues. These gains may have led us to some educational breakthroughs. We seem to be committed to more and better schooling for the young, and the quality of our pedagogy may improve as a result. If nothing else, Head Start has made us critically aware of how children are brought up and what they do or do not accomplish in school. We are becoming sympathetic to the plight of children taught by those who doubt the youngsters' ability to learn, and hopefully this will enhance teacher training.

Despite all this, however, I am terribly pessimistic about the possibilities of substantive social change through preschooling. Too often discussions of educational reform appear to be a means of avoiding more complex and politically dangerous issues. As many of us have come to recognize, education is a lot cheaper than new housing and new jobs, and a lot less controversial than active enforcement of civil rights and antidiscrimination legislation. Preschool programs which tell us that

---

*Author's note: Much of the material in this article was compiled under a grant from the Bureau of Research, U.S. Office of Education, and a research fellowship from the Harvard-M.I.T. Joint Center for Urban Studies. I wish to thank David K. Cohen and Christopher Jencks for their criticisms of an earlier version of this essay.

"Social Reform and Early Childhod Education: Some Historical Perspectives," by Marvin Lazerson, is reprinted from *Urban Education* (April 1970), pp. 84–102, by permission of the publisher, Sage Publications, Inc.

their participants will succeed in school and life during the next two decades cannot really be tested at the present time, and in the meanwhile, we wait out the social problems which plague us. We are thus left with what has become a fairly typical example of educational reform: even greater calls for school responsibility while the social problems which have the greatest effect on schooling are largely ignored. The schools—in this case, preschooling—are asked to do too much, and are given too little support to accomplish what they are asked. A variety of interest groups, however, are satisfied: educators because they get status and funds, social reformers because they believe in education, and government officials because they pass positive legislation without upsetting traditional social patterns. In this light, the movement for early childhood education looks increasingly like a giant cop-out on the present, an elaborate ritual which focuses on the future as a way of avoiding meaningful action on today's pressing social needs.

All of this might seem unduly harsh. President Nixon, articulating proposals formulated during the Johnson administration, has called for "early intervention" to break the cycle of poverty. He has asked for a broadening of supportive services—preschooling before the ages of three and four now found in Head Start, more intensive year-round and follow-through programs, and expanded social services. Seeking expertise and efficiency, he has urged the transferral of Head Start from the experimental and frequently inefficient Office of Economic Opportunity to a newly proposed Office of Child Development in the Department of Health, Education and Welfare, the latter hardly a model of efficiency. Unfortunately, the President has simultaneously shown himself incapable of any real commitment to the problems of the urban areas. Adopting this attitude of "keep it cool," he shows little inclination to tell Americans that something is significantly wrong in our cities. His programs to counter poverty, discrimination, and unemployment are virtually nonexistent and where they appear, are often retrogressive. We are thus confronted with a situation in which the President emphatically calls for broad governmental involvement in education while withdrawing the government from active participation in social change.

In itself, this discrepancy between commitment and rhetoric would be depressing. But the problem of educational reform goes beyond the failings of the current administration and encompasses the widespread and historical use of education as a surrogate for social reform. Our assumptions about education and society, even more than our practices, lead me to pessimism about the fate of the early childhood education movement. In these terms, the particular policies offered by the Nixon administration are only part of an evolving tragedy. In the simplest terms, we confuse pedagogical reform with social change, and are satisfied with the former without realizing how little impact it has on the latter. While we discuss social issues, we so institutionalize our educational reforms that we narrow our practices, and in the process, divorce the schools from the communities they are supposed to serve. The results are tragic, for we continue to believe that an adequately functioning school is the basis for a society in which equality of opportunity is secured. That we risk such an occurrence becomes apparent when today's early childhood movement is compared to an earlier attempt at resolving ghetto problems through preschooling: the kindergarten of late nineteenth and early twentieth century America.

The Evolution of Kindergartens

Begun as an emancipatory institution for the cultured and affluent, designed to supplement the family, the home, and motherhood by recognizing the uniqueness of childhood, kindergartens were a major institutional adaptation to the needs of the young. Drawing upon new attitudes toward childhood—a sense of its special uniqueness and significance—early kindergartners tried to evolve a coherent view of the way in which a child grows. While very young, before the age of three, the child is self-centered, focusing on his body, his senses, and his powers of action. In the home and under his mother's tender care, the child can become selfish and egotistical. Refusing to postpone gratification, he learns to fulfill his needs, but fails to understand that a harmonious society depends upon shared and delayed satisfactions. To assure adequate socialization, Elizabeth Peabody, the patron saint of the kindergarten movement in America, wrote that an institution was needed which would allow the child "to take his place in the company of his equals, to learn his place in their companionship, and still later to learn wider social relations and their involved duties." Thus, brought together in a gathering of equals, each child's social instinct would be gratified and brought into equilibrium with his instinct of self-preservation. Unfortunately, society could not depend upon children to socialize perfectly; unless watched, children could indulge in evil, antisocial behavior. To the peer society was thus added a trained adult who kept order by uprooting evil tendencies. Like the gardener's cultivation of each plant until it reaches perfection, the trained kindergartner in her "garden" aided child development by carefully removing the weed-like obstacles to natural growth and by adding special nourishment to the soil. Just as the gardener had to understand plants, the kindergarten teacher had to know children. Thus, in this setting, the children's natural tendencies toward spontaneity and individuality would be channeled toward social adjustment and cooperation; in sum, order would evolve out of potential chaos.[1]

The mechanism for this development was, of course, play, that great discovery of late nineteenth-century America. Froebel's "gifts"—soft felt balls, blocks, sticks—activities such as paper cutting, cardboard construction, painting, even elementary sewing, as well as marching, dancing, singing, and a variety of outdoor activities were central to the kindergarten. Under the watchful eye of a trained teacher, play and work could be synthesized. Children could willingly and successfully work at play, and little else. It was thus mandatory that no school work in the form of books, writing, or reading exercises be introduced into the kindergarten. Childhood education was a unique phenomenon and had to be distinguished from the more traditional methods of teaching.

All of this was strikingly asocial—the kindergartners talked about the child, not classes of children. They could do this because at first they addressed only the wealthy and cultured. The early spokesmen and practitioners—Mrs. Horace Mann, Elizabeth Peabody, Kate Douglas Wiggin, and Mrs. Alma Kriege—were highly educated. When Miss Peabody opened her first kindergarten in Boston in the early 1860s, the tuition was fifty dollars a term, and she hired a French teacher to sing to the children. The kindergarten—with its small classes, play tools, French songs, and musical instruments—was expensive; it depended upon the considerable financial ability of its supporters.

But if the kindergarten began as a vehicle for the educational emancipation of the children of the well-to-do, it also became an institution for the poor. Stimulated by a rising tide of concern over immigrant life and urban poverty, settlement-house workers, philanthropists, and educators sought to make the kindergarten into a supplement for the children of poor, unstable families. This transition was dramatically portrayed by Kate Douglas Wiggin, author of *Rebecca of Sunnybrook Farm* and numerous other best-selling children's books. During the 1870s, Mrs. Wiggin ran a private kindergarten for the wealthy in Santa Barbara, California, when she suddenly had "a vision of how wonderful it would be to plant a child-garden in some dreary, poverty-stricken place in a large city, a place swarming with un-mothered, undefended, under-nourished child-life." Within a matter of months, she was in San Francisco's crowded ghettos in charge of a settlement kindergarten.[2]

The rationale for this commitment quickly became familiar. Parents who worked, were poor, spoke a foreign language, or seemed otherwise maladjusted to urban life should send their children to such classes because—as the editor of *Century Magazine* wrote—the kindergarten provides "our earliest opportunity to catch the little Russian, the little Italian, the little German, Pole, Syrian, and the rest and begin to make good American citizens of them."[3] And when the kindergarten attained general acceptance, and was transferred from the settlement houses to the public schools, it was still thought of as having special uniqueness for children of the poor. At the turn of the century, the superintendent of schools in Haverhill, Massachusetts, wrote:

> In my opinion the Kindergarten should be established not for the benefit of those children who come from homes of culture and refinement; but on the contrary, it should receive those children that have had little, if any,

good home training. If it were established in such a portion of our city, and were properly conducted, it would furnish a happy transition from the healthful schoolroom surroundings.[4]

The advocates of the urban kindergarten thus blended generalizations about all children with views about the particular needs of slum children. They emphasized the importance of getting the child early, while he was still susceptible to proper molding. They stressed the dangers of allowing the young to grow untutored. While they contended, for example, that children learned best through play, they rejected any notion that *unsupervised* play was properly educational—what the urban child learned on the street was harmful. City and family life outside the classroom appeared as hostile antagonists of the kindergarten, and to counteract their influence, children learned about birds and flowers, streams, and clean white houses. Kindergartners harped on the inadequacy of home and family for the urban poor, the threat of later social anarchy from youth and adults inadequately trained as children, and the difficulties of adult success for children not introduced to proper behavior patterns.

Kindergartners, then, were not concerned narrowly with children, but saw themselves as activists in broad social reform. "The real reform of poverty and ignorance," wrote the muckraker Jacob Riis, a strong supporter of kindergarten education, "must begin with children. . . . The little ones, with their new standards and new ambitions, become in a very real sense missionaries of the slums, whose work of regeneration begins with their parents."[5] Every teacher was asked to spend her afternoons visiting her pupils' homes, or inviting mothers into the classroom for special teas and talks on health and child care and discussions on the problems of their common existence. What happened in the classroom was supposed to be transferred to the home and neighborhood. Children who were clean and thrifty taught cleanliness and thrift to their parents. Through the child, the family could be reached, and through that, the society. In this way, kindergarten advocates saw preschooling as one of the great instruments of urban reform. If, in fact, the programs were based on hostility to the mothers and their way of life, if kindergartners visited the homes of the children to reinforce their essential antagonism to the way those homes were conducted, the conception did, at least, suggest that knowledge of the slums might become an integral feature of early childhood schooling.

Like the preschool programs of today, the kindergarten met resistance. It was expensive; to cut costs, as many as fifty or sixty children often would be herded into a single classroom—a continuing phenomenon in many parts of the country. It broke with traditional classroom ideas of decorum and order. Children could have "fun" on the playground or in the street, but the school was no place for such nonsense. Some also argued that the kindergarten gave preferential treatment to slum children, while others twisted the argument into the assertion that it was all right for such children, but irrelevant to the others who could depend upon their families for socialization. Even within the kindergarten movement, conflict over the nature of play and learning occurred. Froebel's gifts came under attack for not meeting all the needs of children, and for not taking into account the differing backgrounds and emotional stages of individuals. Liberal kindergartners rejected the notion that Froebel had provided all the answers, and called for modifications in technique to take account of nationality, class, age, environment, and social development. Similar questions and agitation occurred after the turn of the century when the Montessori methods made their appearance in America. But the most interesting conflicts were those between the newly emerging professional kindergartners and the teachers in the existing elementary schools. The former believed that the years three to six represented the key stages in a child's development, and felt that progress they achieved in the kindergarten was blunted or dissolved by the autocratic teaching techniques of the grade schools. By the turn of the century the kindergartners were in the middle of a raging war over the extension of kindergarten techniques into the primary grades. Unhappy children, they declared, could not learn; they would rebel, be chastized, and would finally suffer in alienated silence, waiting only until they could legally drop out of school. The kindergartners placed increasing stress upon the importance of a satisfactory elementary school experience as the key to continued participation in formal education. Ultimately, they wanted all teachers trained for teaching children, not subjects.

The primary school teachers' response to these criticisms was mixed. Some first grade teachers found that children with a kindergarten experience were more wide-awake, observing, and acquainted with the basic instruments of learning. Others agreed, but emphasized the child's ability to get along with his peers as the essential contribution of the kindergarten. Some held that kindergartens were particularly useful for the immigrant slum child because they introduced English into his life and provided the warm, tender, and motherly care such children were widely held to miss. A few primary school teachers even believed that kindergarten techniques should be introduced into their own classrooms, that the ideas of the kindergarten were valid for children over five and six. But to many of the primary school teachers, the kindergarten was unsettling. They thought kindergarten children intractable and unwilling to conform to the disciplined learning routine of the classroom. Since nonkindergarten children responded to lessons more readily, the teachers concluded that schools should remain schools and should not become play houses.

Conflicts within the kindergarten and between elementary school and kindergarten teachers profoundly affected the institutionalization of early childhood schooling. The early kindergarten had depended upon certain universalities: all children grew in a particular way, they needed similar training. Whether applied to the affluent or the slum, a uniform kindergarten program provided the most effective means of socializing the child. After 1900, however, growing doubts about the ability of slum children to learn, buttressed by a new emphasis on educational testing and upon the categorization of children, led to a differentiation of program. What was proper depended upon the ethnic, class, and social status groupings of the children; the deficiencies of slum life meant that slum children needed special educational techniques. Whereas the kindergartens of the upper classes focused on free play and the removal of restraint and inhibitions, providing an atmosphere of independence, occasional creativity, and a general expansion of home activities, most kindergartens, and especially those for the urban poor, committed themselves to the inculcation of discipline and orderly behavior patterns believed absent in the child's environment, and thought so necessary for success in the first grade. In the slum, where school discipline seemed to define the educational process itself, kindergartens became tiny military camps whose inhabitants marched, sang, and spoke in unison. Determined to combine order and activity, kindergarten teachers had their children march to the water fountain, to recess, and to their seats. In most school districts, kindergartens and elementary classes merged in practice, if not in theory, blurring the concept of early childhood education. Small classes, special consideration for teaching staff, and play equipment—regarded as essential to a properly functioning kindergarten—cost more than most urban school systems would accept, and under economic pressures, programs were cut back or eliminated. The nobility of childhood, once so proudly proclaimed by kindergarten advocates, became a barren phrase in the hands of American educators. While educators talked about the individual needs of each child, in practice they denied individuality by grouping children into a priori categories which had little to do with what children actually brought to the classroom. In effect, kindergarten educators drew their definitions from their perceptions of the social and economic conditions of their consumers. Independent play and creative learning became the domain of those who could afford private classes or affluent public school systems, those who came from homes that were considered motivated toward learning and which inculcated acceptable social values. For the urban poor, regimented play became the introduction to preschool learning. These children learned how to behave, a process they seemed incapable of learning outside the classroom and which would make elementary school easier for teacher and child.

Simultaneously, the professionalization of kindergarten education—its transfer from the social settlements and philanthropic-minded originators to elementary school educators concerned with establishing a secure identity and status—worked against the broader commitments to social change. Rather than seeking to reform life in the slum, kindergartens centered on the child's relationship to the school. Children were trained to enter the first grade; kindergarten teachers were responsible for that task, not for amelioration of slum problems. Reading readiness, not shared learning experiences between the generations, dominated kindergarten education. The early desire that kindergartners teach only one-half the day, spending the remainder with children in their homes or with parents in the classroom, dissolved as teachers now taught double sessions. While this change implicitly recognized that the teachers hostile to the life of the poor were not going to undertake substantive social reform, the withdrawal of the kindergarten from its social reformist orientation helped to isolate the urban school from the community it served. Educators, applauding the introduction of kindergartens, could ignore the social problems which shaped their work.[6]

The Preschool Compared and Contrasted

Historical analogies are at best tenuous and dangerous. Yet the issues in this case are important and the evidence compelling enough to allow us to draw parallels between the introduction of the kindergarten—the major innovation in early childhood education in the late nineteenth and early twentieth centuries—and the thrust of our present debates over preschool programs. In an earlier period, great urban tension revolving around the influx of non-English speaking immigrants and exposure to slum life produced a host of reform measures. Better housing, public health facilities and legislation, municipal reorganization, and the wave of social agitation forming the progressive era made reform and revision the dominant ethic of a generation. Much of that reform activity involved education: pedagogical change, social services in the school, licensing and professionalization of teachers, new curricula. This thrust toward social amelioration, when combined with a new enthusiasm for childhood and the child study movement, gave impetus to the kindergarten as a preschool innovation. Today's early childhood education movement derives from similar roots. The findings of cognitive psychologists like Martin Deutsch of the Institute for Developmental Studies, J. McVicker Hunt of the University of Illinois, and Benjamin Bloom of the University of Chicago have synthesized the importance of early childhood experience with the possibilities that children can learn more than we have given them credit for. When joined to the social reform thrust of the Kennedy-Johnson administration—the war on poverty and its adjuncts—preschooling seemed a logical approach to social problems, combining the possibilities for school achievement by the individual, and for community reform through the involvement of parents and paraprofessionals in the classroom. The middle class saw in Head Start a reiteration of the day nursery, the poor were anxious for day-care centers, and politicians could satisfy everyone by voting support for "our children." Both the earlier kindergarten and Head Start derive from a theory of cultural deprivation, the notion that parents of the poor—earlier, immigrants, today, blacks—cannot provide a foundation for success in the larger society. Then and now, educational reformers begin with a fundamental hostility to the home and life styles of the poor, and seek to overcome the gap between social classes by creating a bridge between school and home. In both time periods, the new preschool programs usually, but not always, represent pedagogical innovations and more individualized teaching; they recognize that children learn familiar, meaningful (to them) material which is sympathetically presented. In addition, innovation in preschooling has been a source of protracted conflict between the educational establishment and the new reformers. In the case of the kindergarten, the innovators made "childhood for the child" into a gospel with play as its testament, and sought to overturn ossified teaching methods. At the same time, social-settlement advocates wanted community-oriented education, as opposed to educators who wanted preschooling tied to the more traditional public school system. Today the advocates of play, having created the kindergarten, but finding themselves more comfortable in middle-class nursery schools, hold sway, while cognitive psychologists contend that the urban poor enter school intellectually malnourished and demand that preschool programs provide intellectual content as a basis for elementary school success. Similarly, the professional educators, centered in the Office of Education and state and local education systems, stand ready to protect the school from outsiders; they are determined to keep community activists out of the preschool program. At the present moment, they appear likely to succeed.

This is not to say that the kindergarten at the turn of the century and preschooling today are identical. We are considerably more sophisticated about education and psychological growth now than we were then. Federal involvement—financial and supervisory—has dramatically altered the arena of political debate and decision-making. Schools are more important now than ever before, if only because our use of them as certifying agencies has become more extreme. Decisions about them, therefore, are more crucial. The present preschool movement is explicitly aimed at the poor; kindergartens have always possessed a middle- and upper-class clientele, the nursery schools even more so. Head Start's strongest public justification is the argument that it will improve school achievement, while the kindergartens drew on other themes. Yet taking into account these differences, the parallels remain incredibly striking, and, I am afraid, present developments will too likely resemble those of the past. Innovation is being put to work in the interests of traditional goals. Like the incorporation of kindergarten techniques into the lower elementary grades and the loss of distinctiveness in kindergarten education, the findings of cognitive psychologists will probably find their way into preschool programs under conditions and assumptions which may well mystify their originators. Children will undoubtedly soon be "playing" at intellectual games. "Talking typewriters" founded on the assumption that each child should set his own pace and should generate his own curriculum as part of the learning process are now being purchased with the intention of providing preplanned curricula for the participating children. Having discovered that many of the innovations depend either upon expensive hardware or smaller ratios of pupils to teacher or both, most school systems, already severely pressed financially, will undertake cost savings that will quickly undercut what may have been distinctive about the original program, or may prevent the emergence of educational innovations.

All of this is rather depressing, but it hardly touches the most distressing facet of the analogy: the continuing belief among the educational policy makers and teachers that educational problems are going to be resolved in the schools. The kindergartners, at first, recognized the fallacy of this position. They recognized that learning problems were social problems and that they were not simply going to be resolved in the classroom no matter how innovative the programs were. Though they were naive in believing that home visits and mother's clubs would influence social behavior, they at least recommended that teachers get out of the classroom and into the community. For a variety of reasons —economic, hostility from public school authorities, the ideology of discipline, and a declining faith in the ability of the poor to succeed— the commitment to social reform, limited as it was, foundered, and kindergartners soon accepted the notion that the problems of learning could best and, in practice, only be solved in the classroom. They thus turned their programs into preparatory exercises for the first grade. That is, kindergartners began by raising the bold notion that educational questions were at the root of social questions, but ended by substituting pedagogical reforms for social reform. In effect, they had unwittingly participated in a process which made educational change synonymous with pedagogical change.

This seems to me the most striking feature of the contemporary preschool movement. Today's educators and laymen alike readily agree that the problems of the schools go beyond the classroom. Every policy statement on compensatory education begins by asserting that poverty, discrimination, and unemployment are the key determinants of school achievement, and that revised teaching methods, class size, physical facilities, and curriculum may provide satisfaction for the policy makers and teachers, and in some cases for the community involved, but they are not going to resolve the educational problems of the ghetto. The overwhelming impression gleaned from the studies like the United States Civil Rights Commission's *Racial Isolation in the Public Schools* is that our problems are, at heart, social problems. This, is crucial. We have got to see the broader issues involved in any educational reform. The schools cannot resolve our social problems, and conversely, if we want improved school achievement among the poor, we had better commit ourselves to substantial economic and community reform. School problems are thus not going to be resolved as long as the social conditions of the poor take second place to educational methodology, and American educators had better face up to that proposition.

But while this cautions against undue exaltation of school reforms, it is only a first step. This same argument has been used to justify poor achievement and inadequate teaching for some time, i.e., the schools cannot compensate for inadequate home life, or poor kids cannot learn. Nor does a recognition that educational and social reform are not the same thing mean that pedagogy is unimportant or irrelevant. The kindergartens of the turn of the century did represent improved childhood schooling, and in numerous ways the idea of happy children influenced our elementary schools to their benefit. Certainly better trained teachers, new approaches to learning, greater knowledge of children, and more realistic, relevant, and stimulating subject matter will improve the quality of our school systems. But educators are fooling themselves if they believe these are sufficient or even most important. They are deluding themselves if they think pedagogical adjustments are going to alter in any significant way the achievement patterns of the young, especially if they are carried out in isolation from the community involved.

It is here that I think our current preschool program is being misdirected. I am terribly afraid that two trends are emerging, with deleterious consequences to social reform. The first lies in the use of early childhood education as a panacea. Without a concomitant commitment to vast changes in our urban environment—a commitment we still lack—preschooling will not significantly improve school achievement. We will soon become frustrated by the discrepancy between expectations and fulfillment, and will withdraw from any further commitments to education. The second trend lies in the growing professionalization of early childhood education, and the related withdrawal from community activism. In its early stages, Head Start was closely connected to a host of local antipoverty projects. As part of the Office of Economic Opportunity, its participants saw themselves involved in community-wide reform. In Mississippi, for example, Head Start was intimately related to voter registration and civil rights. In a number of projects, mothers and neighborhood workers were brought into the classroom and participated in shared educational experiences with their children. Some of this continues, but increasingly professional educators are taking control of the preschooling movement. Those who have been hostile to the poor and have helped to give us static and deadening educational structures in the ghetto are now likely to turn early childhood education into a dull and barren learning experience. Demands are being made that parents be licensed if they are to aid in teaching, thereby once again setting up the dichotomy between the "good" education of the teacher and the "bad" education of the nonprofessional mother. What began in many areas as a community-based learning experience—and more important had the potential to become such a program—threatens instead to become another hostile intruder into the life of the poor. When attached to educators' unwillingness to fight for broad social reform, preschooling cannot be expected to be very meaningful to those it ostensibly serves.

I began this essay on a note of pessimism. Perhaps I am being unfair to the preschool movement, in many ways the most promising of the current activities on the educational scene since it continues to see itself in broad social terms and occasionally draws upon new insights in learning theory. Yet it is precisely for these reasons that I dread seeing all its energy, time, and money fall by the wayside, largely because the movement has failed to reflect upon what it is doing. Americans, as we are acutely aware, have tended to see their commitment to the schooling of the young as a reaffirmation of their faith in the future, an optimistic belief that in the child lies the well-being of society. Both the kindergarten movement at the turn of the century and the preschool programs of today assert that faith. There is, as I suggested, an alternative hypothesis. Early schooling for the child of poverty may represent an abdication of the present, an implicit statement that society is unwilling to grapple with the immediate issues of discrimination and poverty, but would rather postpone confrontation to a later date, naively expecting not to have to face the issues at all. Placing the child in school is an excellent means for achieving that postponement. In this sense, the preschoolers may once again settle for pedagogical rather than social reform, find that nothing has really changed, and give up hope in trying. Recognition of that possibility will, I hope, place our concern for early childhood schooling in a different light. Our policies in the past, however, provide little cause for optimism.

References

1. E. Peabody, *Lectures in the Training School for Kindergartners* (Boston: D. C. Heath, 1893).

2. K. D. Wiggin, *My Garden of Memory* (Boston: Houghton Mifflin, 1893), pp. 105–107 ff.

3. R. W. Gilder, "The Kindergarten: An Uplifting Social Influence in the Home and the District," *National Education Association Journal of Proceedings and Addresses* (1903), p. 390.

4. Haverhill, Massachusetts, School Committee, *Annual Report of the School Committee* (1897), p. 29.

5. J. Riis, "Children of the Poor," p. 92, in R. A. Woods *et al.* (eds.), *The Poor in Great Cities* (New York: Charles Scribner, 1895).

6. M. Lazerson, "Urban Reform and the Schools: Kindergartens in Massachusetts, 1870-1915." *History of Education Quarterly* (forthcoming).

4 Early Childhood Intervention: The Social Science Base of Institutional Racism

Stephen S. Baratz and Joan C. Baratz

Joan and Stephen Baratz examine the underlying assumptions of intervention programs that tacitly label Negro behavior as pathological. They suggest that the failure to recognize and utilize existing cultural forms of the lower-class Negro community to teach new skills not only dooms intervention programs such as Head Start to failure but also constitutes a form of institutional racism. An illustration of a pathological versus cultural interpretation of Negro behavior is presented when the Baratzes contrast the interventionists' statements that describe Negro children as verbally destitute and linguistically underdeveloped with current sociolinguistic data that indicate that Negro children speak a highly developed but different variety of English from that of the mainstream standard. The cultural difference model is presented as a viable alternative to the existing genetic inferiority and social pathology models, both of which share the view of the Negro as a "sick white man."

To understand the present political and academic furor over the efficacy—and therefore the future—of such early-intervention programs as Head Start, it is necessary first to examine the basic concepts and assumptions upon which these programs are founded and then to determine whether existing data can support such an approach to the problem of educating children from black ghettos.

This paper attempts (1) to present an overview of the interventionist literature with particular emphasis on the role of the social pathology model in interpreting the behavior of the ghetto mother, and (2) to illustrate how the predominant ethnocentric view of the Negro community by social science produces a distorted image of the life patterns of that community. The importance of this distortion is that, when converted into the rationale of social action programs, it is a subtle but pernicious example of institutional racism.

This paper is concerned with the goals of intervention programs that deal with altering the child's home environment, with improving his

Baratz, Stephen S. and Baratz, Joan C., "Early Childhood Intervention: The Social Science Base of Institutional Racism," *Harvard Educational Review*, 40, Winter 1970, pp. 29–50. Copyright © 1970 by President and Fellows of Harvard College. When this article appeared, Stephen Baratz was associated with the National Academy of Science, and Joan Baratz was connected with the Education Center.

language and cognitive skills, and most particularly with changing the patterns of child-rearing within the Negro home. These goals are, at best, unrealistic in terms of current linguistic and anthropological data and, at worst, ethnocentric and racist. We do not question the legitimacy of early childhood programs when they are described solely as nursery school situations and are not based on the need for remediation or intervention; nor do we question such programs when they increase chances for the employment of economically deprived Negroes. Finally, we do not question such programs when they are described as opportunities to screen youngsters for possible physical disorders, even though follow-up treatment of such diagnostic screening is often unavailable.

We wish to examine in more detail, however, the social pathology model of behavior and intelligence in Head Start* projects. We shall attempt to demonstrate that the theoretical base of the deficit model employed by Head Start programs denies obvious strengths within the Negro community and may inadvertently advocate the annihilation of a cultural system which is barely considered or understood by most social scientists. Some thirty years ago, Melville Herskovits made the following insightful observation when talking about culturally related behavioral differences:

> [We need to recognize the existence of] . . . the historical background of the . . . behavioral differences . . . being studied and those factors which make for . . . their existence, and perpetuation. When, for instance, one sees vast programs of Negro education undertaken without the slightest consideration given to the possibility of some retention of African habits of thought and speech that might influence the Negroes' reception of the instruction thus offered—one cannot but ask how we hope to reach the desired objectives. When we are confronted with psychological studies of race relations made in utter ignorance of characteristic African patterns of motivation and behavior or with sociological analyses of Negro family life which make not the slightest attempt to take into account even the chance that the phenomenon being studied might in some way have been influenced by the carry-over of certain African traditions, we can but wonder about the value of such work.[1]

It is one of the main contentions of this paper that most, if not all, of the research on the Negro has sorely missed the implications of Herskovits' statement. Rather, research on the Negro has been guided by an ethnocentric liberal ideology which denies cultural differences and thus acts against the best interests of the people it wishes to understand and eventually help.

---

*We recognize that no two Head Start projects are exactly alike. Head Start is used here as a generic term for intervention programs designed for under-privileged preschool children.

Socio-political Ideology and Studies of the Negro

Though it has seldom been recognized by investigators, it has been virtually impossible for social science to divorce itself from ideological considerations when discussing contemporary race relations. As Killian has pointed out with reference to the social science role after the 1954 Supreme Court Decision:

> Because of their professional judgment that the theories were valid and because of the egalitarian and humanitarian ethos of the social sciences, many sociologists, psychologists, and anthropologists played the dual role of scientist and ideologist with force and conviction. Without gainsaying the validity of the conclusions that segregation is psychologically harmful to its victims, it must be recognized that the typically skeptical, even querulous attitude of scientists toward each other's work was largely suspended in this case.[2]

Social science research with Negro groups has been postulated on an idealized norm of "American behavior" against which all behavior is measured. This norm is defined operationally in terms of the way white middle-class America is supposed to behave. The normative view coincides with current social ideology—the egalitarian principle—which asserts that all people are created equal under the law and must be treated as such from a moral and political point of view. The normative view, however, wrongly equates equality with sameness. The application of this misinterpreted egalitarian principle to social science data has often left the investigator with the unwelcome task of describing Negro behavior not as it is, but rather as it deviates from the normative system defined by the white middle class. The postulation of such a norm in place of legitimate Negro values of life has gained ascendance because of the pervasive assumptions (1) that to be different from whites is to be inferior and (2) that there is no such thing as Negro culture. Thus we find Glazer and Moynihan stating: "The Negro is only an American and nothing else. He has no values and culture to guard and protect."[3]

Billingsley has taken sharp objection to the Glazer and Moynihan statement, pointing out:

> The implications of the Glazer-Moynihan view of the Negro experience is far-reaching. To say that a people have no culture is to say that they have no common history which has shaped and taught them. And to deny the history of a people is to deny their humanity.[4]

However, the total denial of Negro culture is consonant with the melting-pot mythology and it stems from a very narrow conceptualization of culture by non-anthropologists.[5] Social science has refused to look beyond the surface similarities between Negro and white behavior and, therefore, has dismissed the idea of subtle yet enduring differences. In the absence of an ethno-historical perspective, when differences appear in behavior, intelligence, or cognition, they are explained as evidence of genetic defects or as evidence of the negative effects of slavery, poverty, and discrimination. Thus, the social scientist interprets differences in behavior as genetic pathology or as the alleged pathology of the environment; he therefore fails to understand the distortion of the Negro culture that his ethnocentric assumptions and measuring devices have created. The picture that emerges from such an interpretive schema may be seen as culturally biased and as a distortion of the Negro experience.

Liberals have eagerly seized upon the social pathology model as a replacement for the genetic inferiority model. But both the genetic model and the social pathology model postulate that something is wrong with the black American. For the traditional racists, that something is transmitted by the genetic code; for the ethnocentric social pathologists, that something is transmitted by the family. The major difference between the genetic model and the social pathology model lies in the attribution of causality, *not* in the analysis of the behaviors observed as sick, pathological, deviant, or underdeveloped. An example of the marked similarity between the genetic and the social pathology perspectives can be found in the literature concerning language abilities of Negroes.

Language Abilities of Negroes

Language proficiency is considered at length in both the social and the genetic pathology models. This concern is not accidental, but is the result of a basic assumption shared by both the social pathologists and the genetic racists that one's linguistic competence is a measure of one's intellectual capacity.

Thus we find Shaler, who believed in the genetic inferiority of the Negro, writing:

> His inherited habits of mind, framed on a very limited language—where the terms were well tied together and where the thought found in the words a bridge of easy passage—gave him much trouble when he came to employ our speech where the words are like widely separated stepping-stones which require nimble wits in those who use them.[6]

And later, Gonzales describes the language of the Carolina coastal Negroes called Gullahs in a similar manner:

> Slovenly and careless of speech, these Gullahs seized upon peasant English used by some of the early settlers and by the white servants of the wealthier colonists, wrapped their clumsy tongues about it as well as they could, and, enriched with certain expressive African words, it issued through their flat noses and thick lips as so workable a form of speech that it was gradually adopted by other slaves and became in time the accepted Negro speech of the lower districts of South Carolina and Georgia. With characteristic laziness, these Gullah Negroes took short cuts to the ears

of their auditors, using as few words as possible, sometimes making one
gender serve for three, one tense for several, and totally disregarding
singular and plural numbers.[7]

Hunt provides a similar description, but from the social pathology
perspective, when he writes of the parents of Negro children:

> These parents themselves have often failed to utilize prepositional relation-
> ships with precision, and their syntax is confused. Thus, they serve as
> poor linguistic models for their young children.[8]

And Deutsch, writing on the same subject, states:

> In observations of lower-class homes, it appears that speech sequences
> seem to be temporally very limited and poorly structured syntactically.
> It is thus not surprising to find that a major focus of deficit in the chil-
> dren's language development is syntactical organization and subject con-
> tinuity.[9]

Green gives us another example of the deficit orientation of social
pathology thinkers:

> The very inadequate speech that is used in the home is also used in the
> neighborhood, in the play group, and in the classroom. Since these poor
> English patterns are reconstructed constantly by the associations that these
> young people have, the school has to play a strong role in bringing about
> a change in order that these young people can communicate more ade-
> quately in our society.[10]

Finally, Hurst categorizes the speech of many Negro college freshmen
as:

> . . . [involving] such specific oral aberrations as phonemic and sub-pho-
> nemic replacements, segmental phonemes, phonetic distortions, defective
> syntax, misarticulations, mispronunciations, limited or poor vocabulary,
> and faulty phonology. These variables exist most commonly in unsyste-
> matic, multifarious combinations.[11]

Because of their ethnocentric bias, both the social pathologists and
the genetic racists have wrongly presumed that linguistic competence
is synonymous with the development of standard Englsh and, thus, they
incorrectly interpret the different, yet highly abstract and complex, non-
standard vernacular used by Negroes as evidence of linguistic incompetence
or underdevelopment.[12] Both share the view that to speak any linguistic
system other than standard English is to be deficient and inferior.

Since as early as 1859, when Müller[13] wrote the *History of Ancient
Sanskrit Literature,* the racist contention has been that languages (and
their cognitive components) could be hierarchically ordered. Müller
himself offered German as the "best" language for conceptualization,
but it will not surprise anyone to learn that at various times and
according to various writers, the "best" language has been the language
of the particular person doing the thinking about the matter. Thus,
the ethnocentrism of the social pathology model, which defines a dif-

ference as a deficit, forces the misguided egalitarian into testing a racist assumption that some languages are better than others.

The Logic of Intervention

It is important, then, to understand that the entire intervention model of Head Start rests on an assumption of linguistic and cognitive deficits which must be remedied if the child is to succeed in school. The current linguistic data, however, do not support the assumption of a linguistic deficit. The linguistic competence of black children has been well documented in a number of recent investigations.[14] Many lower-class Negro children speak a well ordered, highly structural, but different, dialect from that of standard English. These children have developed a language. Thus one of the basic rationales for intervention, that of developing language and cognitive skills in "defective" children, cannot be supported by the current linguistic data.

Nonetheless, the first intervention programs assumed that the causes of a Negro child's failure in school could be counteracted in those months prior to his entrance into school. Data soon became available concerning the effects of Head Start, indicating that three months was not enough time for intervention to be effective.[15] The social pathologists reasoned that the supposedly progressive deleterious effects of the early environment of the Negro child were so great they could not be overcome in a few months. This argument provided the basis for the extension of Head Start to a full year before school—and by extension into intervention programs which begin earlier and earlier in the child's life and which eventually call for interference with existent family and child-rearing activities.

This expanding web of concern is consistent with the deficit model. Postulation of one deficit which is unsuccessfully dealt with by intervention programs then leads to the discovery of more basic and fundamental deficits. Remediation or enrichment gradually broadens its scope of concern from the fostering of language competence to a broad-based restructuring of the entire cultural system. The end result of this line of argument occurs when investigators such as Deutsch and Deutsch[16] postulate that "some environments are better than others."

With the recognition of failures and limitations within Head Start and like programs with a social pathology base, proponents of intervention call for earlier and earlier intervention in the child's life. This follows from an interlocking set of assumptions which they frequently make:

1. that, upon entering school, the Negro disadvantaged child is unable to learn in the standard educational environment;
2. that this inability to learn is due to inadequate mothering;
3. that the ghetto environment does not provide adequate sensory stimulation for cognitive growth.

The first premise is buttressed by the continued reports of failure of black children in our schools. Indeed, they do not benefit from the standard educational environment. (That does not, however, say anything about whether they are capable of learning generally.) The second premise is an extension of the earlier work on mothering of institutionalized children as reported by Spitz,[17] Goldfarb,[18] Rheingold[19] and Skeels and Dye.[20] Much of this literature, however, is predicated on the total absence of a mother or mothering agent. Indeed, the Skeels follow-up study[21] indicates that a moronic mother is better than no mother at all. The difficulty in extending this logic to the ghetto child is that *he has a mother,* and his behavior derives precisely from her presence rather than her absence.

Then too, the sensory stimulation assumption was an over-extension of the earlier work of Krech *et al.*,[22] where animals were raised in cages with either considerable sensory stimulation or *none* at all. Again, the model was that of absence of stimulation rather than difference in type and presentation of stimulation.

The Inadequate Mother Hypothesis

It is important to understand that the inadequate mother hypothesis rests essentially on the grounds that the mother's behavior produces deficit children. It was created to account for a deficit that in actuality does not exist—that is, that ghetto mothers produce linguistically and cognitively impaired children who cannot learn. Black children are neither linguististically impoverished nor cognitively underdeveloped. Although their language system is different and, therefore, presents a handicap to the child attempting to negotiate with the standard English-speaking mainstream, it is nonetheless a fully developed, highly structured system that is more than adequate for aiding in abstract thinking. French children attempting to speak standard English are at a linguistic disadvantage; they are not linguistically deficient. Speaking standard English is a linguistic disadvantage for the black youth on the streets of Harlem. A disadvantage created by a difference is not the same thing as a deficit!

In addition, before reviewing some of the notions of the inadequate mother hypothesis, it is necessary to stress that the data presented in that literature fail to show anything more than correlations between child-rearing behaviors and school achievement. As has been discussed elsewhere,[23] these correlations cannot be utilized as if they are statements of cause and effect. Although available data do indeed indicate that these culturally different Negro children are not being educated by the public school system, the data fail to show (1) that such children have been unable to learn to think and (2) that, because of specific child-rearing practices and parental attitudes, these children are not able (and, presumably, will never be able) to read, write, and cipher—the prime teaching responsibilities of the public school system.

Nevertheless, the inadequate mother hypothesis has proliferated in the literature of educational psychology. Of chief concern in this literature is the mother-child interaction patterns of lower-class Negroes. Despite the insistence that these patterns are the chief cause of the child's deficits, the supporting data consist almost entirely of either (1) responses to sociological survey-type questionnaires or (2) interaction situations contrived in educational laboratories. There is almost no anthropologically oriented field work that offers a description of what actually does happen *in the home* wherein the deficit is alleged to arise.

One of the chief complaints leveled against the black mother is that she is not a teacher. Thus one finds programs such as Caldwell's[24] which call for the "professionalization of motherhood," or Gordon's[25] which attempts to teach the mother how to talk to her child and how to teach him to think.

The first assumption of such programs is that the ghetto mother does not provide her child with adequate social and sensory stimulation.[26] However, further research into the ghetto environment has revealed that it is far from a vacuum; in fact, there is so much sensory stimulation (at least in the eyes and ears of the middle-class researcher) that a contrary thesis was necessarily espoused which argues that the ghetto sensory stimulation is excessive and therefore causes the child to inwardly tune it all out, thus creating a vacuum for himself.[27]

More recently, studies of social interaction suggest that the amount of social stimulation may be quantitatively similar for lower-class and middle-class children. Thus, the quantitative deficit explanation now appears, of necessity, to be evolving into a qualitative explanation; that is, the child receives as much or even more stimulation as does the middle-class child, but the researchers feel this stimulation is not as "distinctive" for the lower-class child as it is for the middle-class child.[28] Of course, it is interesting to note here that, except for those environments where social and sensory deprivation are extremely severe or total, a condition which is certainly not characteristic of the ghetto environment, there is not evidence to suggest that the ghetto child is cognitively impaired by his mother's sensory social interactions with him.

It has further been suggested that the ghetto mother manages her home in such a manner that the child has difficulty developing a proper sense of time and space—i.e. the organization of the house is not ordered around regularly occurring mealtimes and is not ruled by the White Anglo-Saxon Protestant maxim "everything in its place, and a place for everything." To the middle-class observer, such a home appears to be disorganized and chaotic, while it is merely organized differently. Thus we have data which tell what the mother does not do, but we are missing the data which describe what she does do and explain how the household manages to stay intact. Again, there is no extant research that indicates that the development of a concept of time is either helped or hindered by a child's growing up in an environment where there are regularly occurring meals and bedtimes. There is, however, a considerable literature concerning cultural differences in the concept of time.[29]

Further, it is continually asserted that the ghetto mother does not talk or read to her child, thus supposedly hindering his intellectual growth and language development. Despite the fact that no study has ever indicated the minimal amount of stimulation necessary for the child to learn language, and despite the fact that *the child has in fact developed language,* the ghetto mother is still accused of causing language retardation in her infant.

The mother's involvement in reading activities is also presumed to be extremely important to the child's development and future school success. The conclusions of many studies of the black ghetto home stress the absence of books and the fact that ghetto mothers rarely read to their children. Although the presence of books in the home may be quite indicative of middle-class life styles, and stories when read may very well give pleasure to all children, there appears to be no evidence which demonstrates that reading to children is essential for their learning to read, or that such reading will enhance their real language development. Although Irwin's[30] landmark study indicates that children who are systematically read to babble more, it does not demonstrate that they are linguistically more proficient than those children who are not read to systematically.

A further factor is the mother's behavior which is continually blamed for deficits in the child is her lack of communication to him of the importance of school achievement. Although the literature presents a great many cases which illustrate that the lower-class mother verbalizes great achievement motivations concerning her children, these verbalizations are largely discredited in the eyes of some psychologists[31] who see little action—e.g., helping with homework, joining the PTA—underlying her statement of achievement motivation for her child. (Here, ironically, the supposedly nonverbal mother is now being penalized for her verbal behavior.) Indeed, her verbalizations tend to exhort the child to behave and achieve in class in relation to some assumed behavioral norm rather than to some educational reward; e.g., learn to read because the teacher says so, not because there are many things that one can learn from books.[32] Nonetheless, there do not appear to be any data which show that preschool children resist learning, avoid schooling, or generally do not wish to achieve in the classroom; nor are there data to suggest that intrinsic motivations (learn for learning's sake) are effective for teaching reading, or that extrinsic ones (do it because I tell you) are not. In fact, the behaviorist literature tends to indicate that different sub-groups (i.e., lower-class versus middle-class) respond differently to various reinforcements (for instance, food versus praise).

The recent work of Hess, Shipman, Brophy, and Bear[33] is sure to add considerable fuel to the inadequate mother hypothesis. Hess and his colleagues collected data on 163 black mothers and their four-year-old children. The mothers were divided into four groups: professional, skilled, unskilled-family intact, and unskilled-father absent. Social workers collected data in two extensive home interviews. Later, the mothers and children came to the university where IQ and other formal tests were administered. The mothers were also presented with theoretical situations and asked what they would do or say—e.g., what would you say to your child on his first day of school. In addition, the mothers were asked to teach their children a block-sorting task and to replicate a design on an etch-a-sketch box with their children. The Hess *et al.* data furnished a good deal of information concerning teaching styles of lower- and middle-class black women. These data, however, were undoubtedly influenced by the fact that the situations in which they were elicited (i.e., interviewing and a laboratory task) are much more typical of middle-class experiences. Nevertheless, many differences in maternal language and teaching styles appeared. It would be a mistake, however, to conclude that these differences in language and teaching style cause the child to be uneducable. What makes him appear "uneducable" is his failure in an educational system that is insensitive to the culturally different linguistic and cognitive styles that he brings to the classroom setting. The school, therefore, fails to use the child's distinct cultural patterns as the vehicle for teaching new skills and additional cultural styles.

One of the major difficulties with the work of Hess *et al.* lies in their concept of "educability." Superficially this refers to those skills which every child potentially possesses but which presumably are not developed if the mother's behavior is "restricted" and not similar to that of those middle-class mothers who produce children who succeed in school. Those skills which the child potentially possesses, however, are not defined by Hess *et al.* simply as language development, but rather more subtly as the use of standard English. Concept development is not seen as the development of language for thought (There are, of course, no languages that one cannot think in!) but rather, it is defined in terms of performance on standardized tasks or measures of verbal elaboration. Again, motivation is described not in terms of wanting to read, but rather in terms of books around the house and the use of the public library. "Educability" then, is really defined as specific middle-class mainstream behaviors rather than as the possession of universal processes through which specific behaviors can be channeled. The lower-class mother is a priori defined as inadequate because she is not middle-class.

In their discussions of the mothers' language behavior, Hess *et al.* rely heavily on the concepts of Basil Bernstein, who describes two different communicative styles generally used by lower- and middle-class English children. That the language and teaching behaviors of lower-class Negro mothers are different from those of middle-class mothers is beyond question. That the different behavior leads to cognitive defects has yet to be demonstrated. Carroll[34] has discussed the methodological issue of the relationship of language style to cognition. To say that a particular language has a deleterious effect on cognitive performance, speakers of that language must be tested for cognitive ability on a non-linguistic task —such a task has yet to be developed or tested.

The Hess data, while providing considerable information on maternal behavior differences in lower- and middle-class black women, do not indicate that the children from lower-class homes are any less ready to learn than are the middle-class children, nor do they demonstrate that these children will be less able—especially if they are placed in a school that takes advantage of their experiences, as the present school curriculum does in certain crucial regards for the middle-class child. The Hess data do show, however, that the behaviors of the middle-class Negro mothers are more typically mainstream and that what these mothers teach their children is more typically within mainstream expectations; therefore, such children tend to perform better in a testing situation—and subsequently in a school situation—which requires mainstream behaviors and heuristic styles than do lower-class children, who have learned something else.

There is much to be learned about maternal teaching styles and how they can be used to help the child function better in interactions with the mainstream culture. Research has indicated how unlike the middle-class mother the lower-class mother is, but there is very little description of who the lower-class mother is and what she does.

The Failure of Intervention

Intervention programs postulated on the inadequacy of the mother or the lack of environmental stimulation[35] fail after an initial spurt in IQ scores. This appears to be an artifact of the methodology, for the first contact with mainstream educational patterns (an agent intervening in the home, a Head Start Program, kindergarten or first grade in the public school) appears automatically to cause an increase in IQ for these children. This artifact is clearly evidenced in the "catch-up" phenomenon where non-Head Start children gain in IQ apparently as a result of exposure to a school environment. The additional observation, that increases in IQ of both Head Start *and* non-Head Start children decrease after second or third grade, is a further indication that early childhood intervention is not where the answer to the failure of children in public school lies.

Interventionists argue that what is needed are school-based programs

(Project Follow-Through) which maintain the "gains" of Head Start by changing the nature of the school environment. In effect, this argument is a specious one since it was the intervention program itself which was supposed to insure the child's success in the schools as they are presently constituted. For the early childhood interventionists then to turn around and say that the schools do not do their job in maintaining the increases which the school itself has generated in non-Head Start children (as well as the increases of Head Start children) is indeed to point to the crux of the matter: the failure lies in the schools, not the parents, to educate these children. This clearly indicates that critical intervention must be done, but on the procedures and materials used in the schools rather than on the children those schools service. Intervention which works to eliminate archaic and inappropriate procedures for teaching these children and which substitutes procedures and materials that are culturally relevant is critically needed. It is important to note here that such intervention procedures—e.g., the use of Negro dialect in the teaching of reading[36]—are not ends in themselves. The goal of such procedures is to have the children perform adequately on standardized achievement tests. It is the process, not the goals, of education that must be changed for these children. *The educational problems of lower-class culturally different Negro children, as of other groups of culturally different children, are not so much related to inappropriate educational goals as to inadequate means for meeting these goals.*

It is not, therefore, a particular program for early childhood intervention at a critical period which affects IQ scores. Rather it is the initial contact with mainstream middle-class behaviors that tends to raise temporarily the scores of young children. As the test items, however, begin to rely more and more heavily on the language style and usage of the middle-class, these culturally different dialect-speaking children tend to decrease in test performance. Unlike the behaviors which initially raise IQ scores and which the child learns simply from contact with the middle-class system, fluency in a new language style and usage must be taught formally and systematically for it to be mastered. Indeed, this failure to teach the mainstream language styles and usage by means of the child's already existing system may well explain why the initial test gains of these children are not maintained.

The early childhood programs, as well as public schools, fail in the long run because they define educability in terms of a child's ability to perform within an alien culture; yet they make no attempt to teach him systematically new cultural patterns so that the initial spurt in test scores can be maintained. Educability, for culturally different children, should be defined primarily as the ability to learn new cultural patterns within the experience base and the culture with which the child is already familiar. The initial test scores of culturally different children must not be misevaluated as evidence of "educability," but rather should be viewed as evidence of the degree to which the child is familiar with the mainstream system upon which the tests are based both in content and presentation.

Because of the misconception of educability and the misevaluation of the test data, interventionists and educators create programs that are designed (1) to destroy an already functionally adequate system of behavior because it is viewed as pathological and (2) to impose a system of behavior without recognizing the existence of a functionally adequate system of behavior already in place. (Thus it is comparable to attempting to pour water into an already wine-filled pitcher.) Education for culturally different children should not attempt to destroy functionally viable processes of the subculture, but rather should use these processes to teach additional cultural forms. The goal of such education should be to produce a bicultural child who is capable of functioning both in his subculture and in the mainstream.

However, since Head Start has disregarded or attempted unknowingly to destroy that which is a viable cultural system, we should not have been surprised by its failure in attempting to "correct" these behaviors. Head Start has failed because its goal is to correct a deficit that simply does not exist. The idea that the Negro child has a defective linguistic and conceptual system has been challenged by the findings of Stewart,[37] J. Baratz,[38] Labov,[39] and by Lesser and his colleagues,[40] who point to the structurally coherent but different linguistic and cognitive systems of these children. Indeed, the deficit model of Head Start forces the interventionist closer and closer to the moment of conception and to the possibility of genetic determination of the behavior now attributed to a negative environment. This position is plaintively described by Caldwell:

> Most of us in enrichment . . . efforts—no matter how much lip service we pay to the genetic potential of the child—are passionate believers in the plasticity of the human organism. We need desperately to believe that we are born equalizable. With any failure to demonstrate the effectiveness of compensatory experiences offered to children of any given age, one is entitled to conclude parsimoniously that perhaps the enrichment was not offered at the proper time.[41]

Elsewhere Caldwell refers to what she calls the Inevitable Hypothesis which we interpret as backing up further and further (intervene at four, at three, at one, at three months) until we are face to face with the possibility of genetic differences between Negroes and whites which forever preclude the possibility of remediation or enrichment. We are in Caldwell's debt for such a passionate statement of the real issue at hand. All educators concerned with intervention of any kind and unaware of the culture (and the alternative conceptual framework it offers) respond at a gut level to the implications which the failure of early childhood programs has for the overtly racist genetic model. The frustration due to the failure of intervention programs proposed by the social pathologists could lead to three possible lines of responses from those watching and participating in the unfolding of events. They are:

1. an increased preoccupation with very early intervention, at birth or shortly thereafter, to offset the allegedly "vicious" effects of the inadequate environment of the Negro child;
2. the complete rejection of the possibility of intervention effects unless the child is totally removed from his environment to be cared for and educated by specialists;
3. the total rejection of the environmentalist-egalitarian position in favor of a program of selective eugenics for those who seem to be totally unable to meet the demands of a technological environment—scientific facism.

Suffice it to say that recently we have seen an articulation of all three of these unfeasible positions.

The clearest line of thought currently evident comes from people such as Shaefer,[42] Gordon,[43] and Caldwell[44] advocating the introduction of specialists into the home who would not only provide the missing stimulation to the child, but also teach the mother how to raise her children properly. Thus, the new input is an intensive attempt to change totally the child's environment and the parent's child-rearing patterns.

But the fear is that even such a massive attempt will still fail to innoculate the child against failure in the schools. Recognizing this, Caldwell[45] provides the model for intervention programs which take the child completely out of the home for short periods of time for the purpose of providing him with the experiences unavailable to him during his first three years of life. It is only a short distance from this position to Bettelheim's statement[46] advocating total removal of Negro children to kibbutz-like controlled environments in order to overcome the effects of the allegedly negative values and practices of the ghetto—in short, the annihilation of distinctive Afro-American cultural styles.

Finally, the appearance of the scholarly article recently published by Arthur Jensen[47] in the *Harvard Educational Review* represents the attempt of a former social pathologist to deal with the failure of the intervention programs. He may find his position politically distasteful but, for a scientist who lacks a cross-cultural perspective and an historical frame of reference, it is the only way to maintain his scientific integrity. Like most scholars who come to advocate an unpopular thesis, Jensen has done his homework. His familiarity with the data indicates to him the futility of denying (1) that Negro children perform less well on intelligence tests than whites and (2) that Head Start has failed in its intent to produce permanent shifts in IQ which lead to success in the educational system. Since Jensen rejects the social pathology model but retains a concept that describes Negro behavior as defective, it is not at all surprising that he has no alternative other than a model of genetic inferiority.

However, like the social pathologists who had to create an explanation (i.e., inadequate mothering) for a nonexistent deficit, Jensen is also called upon to explain the reasons for a relative theory of genetic inferiority in the American Negro. His argument, similar to those of earlier genetic racists, states that the Negroes who were brought over as slaves "were selected for docility and strength and not mental ability, and that through selective mating the mental qualities present never had a chance to flourish."[48] Interestingly enough, this contention was decimated almost thirty years ago by Melville Herskovits in his book, *The Myth of the Negro Past*,[49] in which he presents historical and anthropological data to reject the notion of selective enslavement and breeding. It is precisely the absence of a sophisticated knowledge and perspective of cultural continuity and cultural change which has forced both the social pathologists and the genetic pathologists to feel that they have dealt with "culture" if they acknowledge that certain test items are "culture-bound." Such changes represent very surface knowledge of the concept of culture and, in particular, do not deal with subtle yet significant cultural differences. Many social scientists believe that they are dealing with the culture when they describe the physical and social environment of these children. One must not confuse a description of the environment in which a particular culture thrives for the culture itself.

Because historical and political factors have combined to deny the existence of a Negro culture,[50] social scientists have found themselves having to choose between either a genetic deficit model or a deficit model built on an inadequate environment (the "culture" of poverty). However, our view of the current status of research on the Negro in the United States indicates that we are on the brink of a major scientific revolution with respect to American studies of the Negro and the social action programs that derive from them. This revolution began with Herskovits and is being forwarded by the linguistic and anthropological studies of Stewart,[51] Szwed,[52] Abrahams,[53] Hannerz,[54] and others. The basic assumption of this research is that the behavior of Negroes is not pathological, but can be explained within a coherent, structured, distinct, American-Negro culture which represents a synthesis of African culture in contact with American European culture from the time of slavery to the present day.

Since the pathology model of the language and thought of Negroes as it is used in intervention programs has been created by the superimposition of a standard English template on a non-standard dialect system, producing a view of that non-standard system as defective and deviant, then the data gathered in support of that pathology view must be totally re-evaluated and old conclusions dismissed, not solely because they are non-productive, but also because they are ethnocentric and distorted and do not recognize the cultural perspective. The great impact of the misuse of the egalitarian model on social science studies of the Negro must be re-examined.

As long as the social pathology and genetic models of Negro behavior remain the sole alternatives for theory construction and social action, our science and our society are doomed to the kind of cyclical (environment to genes) thinking presently evident in race relations research. Fortunately, at this critical point in our history, we do have a third model available, capable of explaining both the genetic and social pathology views with greater economy and capable of offering viable research and societal alternatives.

The major support for the assertion of a revolution in scientific thinking about the Negro comes from the discovery that the urban Negro has a consistent, though different, linguistic system. This discovery is an anomaly in that it could not have been predicted from the social pathology paradigm. This finding, if we can judge from the incredulity expressed about it by our colleagues, violates many of the perceptions and expectations about Negro behavior which are built into the assumptive base of the social pathology model. This assumptive base, it is argued, has restricted our phenomenological field to deviations from normative behavior rather than to descriptions of different normative configurations. In the present case, it would appear that the defect and difference models of Negro behavior cannot exist side by side without a growing awareness of the need for change and radical reconstruction of our modes of theorizing and conceptualizing about Negro behavior.

However, there may be resistance to adopting the cultural difference model which stems not only from the inherent methodologies of the social pathology theory, but also from the much more vague, and often unexpressed sociopolitical view of the particular investigator seeking to support his view of our current racial situation—views which are unarticulated and therefore unexamined. Thus, the resistance we anticipate may be intensified by the fear that talking about differences in Negro behavior may automatically produce in the social pathologist the postulation of genetic differences. This fear, so often expressed, is related to the real fact that the genetic model itself relied on behavioral differences as the basis for its conclusions about genetic determination. Three points can be made here to deal with this concern: (1) it has not and should not be the role of rational scholarly discourse to dismiss data and knowledge simply because it does not fit a particular ideological position extant at a particular moment in history; (2) differences, which indicate that learning has taken place, are not deficits; and (3) the view of the current social pathology position is in many ways prone to the same criticisms leveled at the genetic pathology model. The current scientific crisis will resolve itself solely on the basis of scholarly research and not ideology or polemic. The basic assumptions of scholarly research must be examined and models tried out that offer more successful and economical explanations.

In summary, the social pathology model has led social science to establish programs to prevent deficits which are simply not there. The failure of intervention reflects the ethnocentrism of methodologies and theories which do not give credence to the cognitive and intellectual skills of the child. A research program on the same scale as that mounted to support the social pathology model must be launched in order to discover the different, but not pathological, forms of Negro behavior. Then and only then can programs be created that utilize the child's differences as a means of furthering his acculturation to the mainstream while maintaining his individual identity and cultural heritage.

References

1. M. Herskovits, "The Ancestry of the American Negro," *American Scholar,* 1938-39, reprinted in J. Herskovits (ed.), *The New World Negro* (Bloomington, Ind.: Indiana University Press, 1966), p. 127.

2. L. M. Killian, *The Impossible Revolution?* (New York: Random, 1968), p. 54.

3. N. Glazer and D. Moynihan, *Beyond the Melting Pot* (Cambridge, Mass.: MIT Press and the Harvard University Press, 1963).

4. A. Billingsley, *Black Families in White America* (Englewood Cliffs, N.J.: Prentice-Hall, 1968), p. 37.

5. S. and J. Baratz, *The Social Pathology Model: Historical Bases for Psychology's Denial of the Existence of Negro Culture,* APA Paper (Washington, D.C., 1969).

6. N. S. Shaler, "The Nature of the Negro," *Arena,* 3 (1890), pp. 23–25.

7. A. Gonzales, *The Black Border: Gullah Stories of the Carolina Coast* (South Carolina: The State Company, 1922), p. 10.

8. J. McV. Hunt, "Towards the Prevention of Incompetence," p. 31, in J. W. Carter (ed.), *Research Contributions from Psychology to Community Health* (New York: Behavioral Publications, 1968).

9. M. Deutsch, "The Disadvantaged Child and the Learning Process," p. 174, in A. H. Passow (ed.), *Education in Depressed Areas.* (New York: Columbia Teachers College, 1963).

10. R. Green, "Dialect Sampling and Language Values," p. 123, in R. Shuy (ed.), *Social Dialects and Language Learning* (Champaign, Ill.: NCTE, 1964).

11. C. G. Hurst, Jr., *Psychological Correlates in Dialectolalia* (Washington, D.C.: Howard University Communities Research Center, 1965).

12. See J. Baratz, "Language Development in the Economically Disadvantaged Child: A Perspective," *ASHA* (Marsh, 1968); idem, "Linguistic and Cultural Factors in Teaching English to Ghetto Children," *Elementary English,* 46 (1969), pp. 199–203; idem, "Language and Cognitive Assessment of Negro Children: Assumptions and Research Needs," *ASHA* (March 1969).

13. F. M. Müller, *History of Ancient Sanskirt Literature, so far as it illustrates the primitive religion of the Brahmans* (London: Williams and Norgate, 1859).

14. W. Stewart, "Continuity and Change in American Negro Dialects," *The Florida FL Reporter* (Spring 1968); W. Labov, and P. Cohen, "Systematic Relations of Standard Rules in Grammar of Negro Speakers," Project Literacy #7 (1967); W. Labov, "The Logic of Nonstandard Dialect," in J. Alatis (ed.), *School of Languages and Linguistics Monograph Series, No. 22.* (Washington, D.C.: Georgetown University, 1969), pp. 1–43; J. L. Dillard, *Black English in the United States* (New York: Random, 1969); J. Baratz, "Linguistic and Cultural Factors in Teaching English to Ghetto Children,"

Elementary English, 46 (1969), pp. 199–203; idem, "Language and Cognitive Assessment of Negro Children: Assumptions and Research Needs," *ASHA* (March 1969); W. Wolfram, *Sociolinguistic Description of Detroit Negro Speech* (Washington, D.C.: Center for Applied Linguistics, 1969).

15. M. Wolff, and A. Stein, "Head Start Six Months Later," *Phi Delta Kappan* (March 1967).

16. C. Deutsch, and M. Deutsch, "Theory of Early Childhood Environment Programs," in R. Hess and R. Bear (eds.), *Early Education: Current Theory, Research and Action.* (Chicago: Aldine, 1968).

17. R. Spitz, "Hospitalism: An Inquiry into the Genesis of Psychiatric Conditions in Early Childhood," *Psychoanalytic Study of the Child,* 1 (1945), pp. 53–74.

18. W. Goldfarb, "Emotional and Intellectual Consequences of Psychological Deprivation in Infancy: A Re-evaluation," in P. H. Hoch and J. Zobin (eds.), *Psychopathology of Childhood* (New York: Grune and Stratton, 1955).

19. H. Rheingold, "The Modification of Social Responsiveness in Institutional Babies," *Monograph of Society for Research and Child Development,* 21, Serial No. 63 (1956), p. 2.

20. H. Skeels and H. Dye, "A Study of the Effects of Differential Stimulation on Mentally Retarded Children," *Proceeding of the American Association for Mental Deficiency,* 44 (1939), pp. 114–136.

21. H. Skeels, "Adult Status of Children with Contrasting Early Life Experiences," *Monograph Society for Research in Child Development,* 31, 3 (1960), p. 1–65.

22. D. Krech, M. Rosenzweig, and E. L. Bennet, "Relations Between Brain Chemistry and Problem Solving Among Rats Raised in Enriched and Impoverished Environments," *Journal of Comparative and Physiological Psychology,* 55 (1962), pp. 801–807.

23. S. Baratz, "Social Science Research Strategies for the Afro-American," in J. Szwed (ed.), *Black America* (New York: Basic Books, in press).

24. B. Caldwell, "The Fourth Dimension in Early Childhood Education," in R. Hess and R. Bear (eds.), *Early Education: Current Theory, Research and Action* (Chicago: Aldine, 1968).

25. I. Gordon, "Research Report: Infant Performance." (Gainesville, Florida: Institute for Development of Human Resources, University of Florida, 1968).

26. J. McV. Hunt, *Intelligence and Experience* (New York: Ronald Press, 1961).

27. C. Deutsch and M. Deutsch, "Theory of Early Childhood Environment Programs," in R. Hess and R. Bear (eds.), *Early Education: Current Theory, Research and Action* (Chicago: Aldine, 1968); C. Deutsch, "Auditory Discrimination and Learning Social Factors," *Merrill-Palmer Quarterly,* 10 (1964), pp. 277–296.

28. J. Kagan, "His Struggle for Identity," *Saturday Review* (December 1968).

29. J. Henry, "White People's Time, Colored People's Time," *Transaction* (March-April 1965).

30. D. C. Irwin, "Infant Speech: Effect of Systematic Reading of Stories," *Journal of Speech and Hearing Research,* 3 (1960), pp. 187–190.

31. I. Katz, "Research Issue on Evaluation of Educational Opportunity: Academic Motivation," *Harvard Educational Review,* 38 (1968), pp. 57–65.

32. R. Hess, V. Shipman, J. Brophy, and R. Bear, *The Cognitive Environments of Urban Preschool Children* (The Graduate School of Education, University of Chicago, 1968).

33. *Ibid.*

34. J. Carroll, *Language and Thought* (Englewood Cliffs, N.J.: Prentice-Hall, 1964).

35. E. Shaefer, "Home Tutoring, Maternal Behavior and Infant Intellectual Development," *APA* Paper (Washington, D.C., 1969); I. Gordon, "Research Report: Infant performance" (Gainesville, Florida: Institute for Development of Human Resources, University of Florida, 1968); R. A. Klaus, and S. W. Gray, 'The Early Training Project for Disadvantaged Children: A Report after Five Years," *Monograph SRCD,* 33 (1968).

36. S. and J. Baratz, "Negro Ghetto Children and Urban Education: A Cultural Solution," *Bulletin of the Minnesota Council for the Social Studies* (Fall 1968), Reprinted in *Social Education,* 33, 4 (1969), pp. 401–404; J. Baratz and R. Shuy (eds.), *Teaching Black Children To Read* (Washington, D.C.: Center for Applied Linguistics, 1969).

37. W. Stewart, "Urban Negro Speech: Sociolinguistic Factors Affecting English Teaching," in R. Shuy (ed.), *Social Dialects and Language Learning,* NCTE (Champaign, Ill., 1964); idem, "Sociolinguistic Factors in the History of American Negro Dialects," *The Florida FL Reporter,* 5 (Spring 1967); idem, "Continuity and Change in American Negro Dialects," *The Florida FL Reporter* (Spring 1968); idem, "Sociopolitical Issues in the Linguistic Treatment of Negro Dialect," *School of Languages and Linguistics Monograph Series No. 22* (Washington, D.C.: Georgetown University, 1969), pp. 215–223; idem, "Historical and Structural Bases for the Recognition of Negro Dialect," *School of Languages and Linguistics Monograph Series, No. 22* (Washington, D.C.: Georgetown University, 1969), pp. 239–247.

38. J. Baratz, "Language and Cognitive Assessment of Negro Children: Assumptions and Research Needs, *ASHA* (March 1969).

39. W. Labov, "The Logic of Nonstandard Dialect," pp. 1–43, in J. Alatis (ed.), *School of Languages and Linguistics Monograph Series, No. 22* (Washington, D.C.: Georgetown University, 1969).

40. G. Lesser, G. Fifer, and D. H. Clark, Mental Abilities of Children from Different Social Class and Culture Groups," *Monograph of Society for Research in Child Development,* 30 (1965), p. 647; S. Stodolsky, and G. Lesser, "Learning Patterns in the Disadvantaged," *Harvard Educational Review,* 37 (1967), pp. 546–593.

41. B. Caldwell, "The Fourth Dimension in Early Childhood Education."

42. E. Shaefer, "Tutoring the 'Disadvantaged,'" *The Washington Post* (February 9, 1969); idem, "Home Tutoring, Maternal Behavior and Infant Intellectual Development," APA Paper (Washington, D.C., 1969).

43. Gordon, "Infant Performance."

44. B. Caldwell, "What is the Optimal Learning Environment for the Young Child?" *American Journal of Orthopsychiatry,* 37 (1967), pp. 9–21.

45. *Ibid.*

46. B. Bettelheim, "Psychologist Questions Value of Head Start Program," *New York Times* (March 17, 1969).

47. A. Jensen, "How Much Can We Boost IQ and Scholastic Achievement?" *Harvard Educational Review,* 39 (1969), pp. 1–123.

48. I. Edson, "jensenism, n. The Theory that I.Q. is Largely Determined by the Genes," *New York Times* (August 31, 1969), p. 10 ff.

49. M. Herskovits, *The Myth of the Negro Past* (New York: Harper and Brothers, 1941).

50. S. and J. Baratz, *Social Pathology Model.*

51. W. Stewart, "Urban Negro Speech: Sociolinguistic factors affecting English teaching," in R. Shuy (ed.), *Social Dialects and Language Learning,* NCTE (Champaign, Ill., 1964); W. Stewart, "Social dialects," in E. Gordon (ed.), *Research Planning Conference on Language Development in Disadvantaged Children* (Yeshiva University, 1966); W. Stewart, "Sociolinguistic factors in the history of American Negro dialects," *The Florida FL Reporter,* 5, 2 (Spring, 1967); W. Stewart, "Sociopolitical issues in the linguistic treatment of Negro dialect," *School of Languages and Linguistics Monograph Series No. 22* (Georgetown University, 1969), pp. 215–223; W. Stewart, "Historical and structural bases for the recognition of Negro dialect," *School of Languages and Linguistics Monograph Series, No. 22* (Georgetown University, 1969), pp. 239–247; W. Stewart, "Continuity and change in American Negro dialects," *The Florida FL Reporter,* 3 (Spring 1968); W. Stewart, "On the use of Negro dialect in the teaching of reading," in J. Baratz and R. Shuy (eds.), *Teaching Black Children To Read.* (Washington, D.C.: Center for Applied Linguistics, 1969); W. Stewart, "Teaching black language: A forum lecture for Voice of America," Washington, D.C., (May 1969).

52. J Szwed, "Ethnohistory of the Afro-American in the United States," APA Paper (Washington, D.C., 1969); J. Szwed, *Black America* (New York: Basic Books, in press).

53. R. Abrahams, *Deep Down in the Jungle,* revised edition (Hatboro, Pa. Folklore Associates, 1967).

54. U. Hannerz, *Soulside Inquiries in Ghetto Children and Community.* (Stockholm, Sweden: Almquist & Wiksele, 1969).

Part Two
Growth and Development of the Young Child

SECTION A

Intellectual and Motivational Development

5 The Epigenesis of Intrinsic Motivation and Early Cognitive Learning

J. McV. Hunt

As an introduction to this unit, Professor Hunt emphasizes the influence of external stimuli on the child's interests and abilities. He abandons the ideas "that intelligence is fixed and that development is predetermined," and provides strong arguments for those who advocate increased activity in the field of early childhood education.

Even as late as fifteen years ago, a symposium on the stimulation of early cognitive learning would have been almost impossible. It would have been taken by most people as a sign that both participants and members of the audience were too soft-headed to be considered seriously. Even as late as fifteen years ago, there was simply no point in talking about such a matter, for no possibility of altering cognitive capacity, or intelligence, was conceived to exist. To be sure, there was, before World War II, some evidence that suggested, even strongly, that cognitive capacities might be modified by early experience; but such evidence as existed was "too loose" to convince anyone who embraced the assumptions that intelligence is fixed and that development is predetermined.[1] These two assumptions—and I believed and taught them just as did most of us—were considered to be among the marks of a "sound" and "hard-headed" psychologist. Had we psychologists absorbed the implications of Johannsen's[2] distinction between the genotype and the phenotype and his notion that the phenotype is always a product of continuous, ongoing, organism-environment interaction, we should

"The Epigenesis of Intrinsic Motivation," by J. McVicker Hunt, reprinted with permission from editor and publisher of Ralph N. Haber (ed.), *Contemporary Theory and Research in Visual Perception* (New York: Holt, Rinehart, and Winston, 1968).
J. McVicker Hunt is Professor of Psychology at the University of Illinois.

never have held these two assumptions with such certainty; but of the two fathers of the science of genetics we knew only Mendel. Since World War II, however, the various investigations of the effects of infantile experience have piled up sufficient evidence to nearly destroy the credibility of these two dominant assumptions of our post–Darwinian tradition.

The change in conceptions started with the work of Sigmund Freud, but it has recently taken some abrupt new turns. Freud's[3] theory of psychosexual development attributed great importance to the effects of early infantile experience and especially to the preverbal fates of instinctive modes of pleasure-getting. The earliest studies of the effects of infantile experience assumed these effects to be on the emotional rather than on the intellectual aspects of personality.[4] Yet the studies of the effects of the richness of environmental variations encountered during infancy on adult maze-learning ability in rats[5] and in dogs[6] have proved to be most regularly reproducible. These studies stemmed from the neuropsychological theorizing of Donald Hebb[7] and his distinction between "early learning," in which "cell-assemblies" are developed, and "later learning," in which these assemblies are connected in various kinds of "phase sequences." The studies showed that those rats encountering the larger number of environmental variations during infancy received higher scores on the Hebb-Williams[8] maze-test of animal intelligence than did those encountering fewer variations.[9]

In Hebb's[10] original study of this kind, the number of variations in environment ranged from the many supplied by pet-reared rats in a human home to the few supplied by cage-rearing in the laboratory. A similar approach was employed by Thompson and Heron,[11] and dogs pet-reared from weaning until eight months of age proved to be markedly superior in performance on the Hebb-Williams test at eighteen months of age (after ten months with their cage-reared litter-mates in a dog pasture) to those litter-mates individually cage-reared from weaning to eight months. In fact, the pet-reared dogs appeared to differ more from their cage-reared litter-mates than did the pet-reared rats from their litter-mates. From this I am inclined to infer that the degree of the adult effect of such infantile experience increases as one goes up the vertebrate scale. I tend to attribute this apparent increase in the effect of infantile experience to the increasing proportion of the brain that is without direct connections with receptor input and/or motor output.[12] I refer here, of course, to the notion of the A/S ratio first put forth by Hebb.[13]

This notion, that the degree of effect of the richness of variations in environment encountered during infancy on adult cognitive capacities increases with the size of the A/S ratio, suggests that the results of these animal studies should probably generalize to the human species. Incontrovertible evidence concerning this suggestion is hard to come by. Nevertheless, a combination of observations strongly supports the suggestion that such early experience has marked effects on the rate of human development and perhaps also has effects on the level of adult intellectual ability.

First, the evidence concerning effects of early experience upon the rate of human intellectual development is fairly compelling. It has long been noted that children being reared in orphanages show retardation in both their functional development and their motivational apathy. These observations were long discounted because of the notion that only those genotypically inferior remain in orphanages, but the well-known studies of René Spitz[14] helped to rule out this attribution of the retardation to a selection of genotypes. Unfortunately, Spitz's observations could be discounted on other grounds.[15] More recently, however, Wayne Dennis,[16] whose prejudices would appear from his previous writings to favor the traditional assumptions of "fixed intelligence" and "predetermined development," has found two orphanages in Teheran where retardation is even more extreme than that reported by Spitz. Of those infants in their second year, 60 percent were still unable to sit up alone; of those in their fourth year, 85 percent were still unable to walk alone. Moreover, while children typically creep on all fours rather than scoot, as did the children in a third orphanage in Teheran (one for demonstration purposes), those in these two typically chose scooting. By way of explanation, Spitz emphasized the emotional factors associated with lack of mothering (a one-to-one interpersonal relationship) as the basis for the greater retardation observed at "foundling home" than at "nursery." Dennis, on the other hand, has attributed the extreme retardation in sitting and walking to lack of learning opportunities, or more specifically, to the "paucity of handling, including failure of attendants to place children in the sitting position and the prone position."[17] These may well be important factors, but I suspect that yet another factor is of sufficient importance to deserve specific investigative attention—namely, a paucity of variation in auditory and visual inputs, or, perhaps I should say a paucity of meaningful variation in these inputs. On the visual side, these Teheran infants (i.e., those in the orphanages in which 90 percent of the children are recorded as having been under one month of age at the time of admission) had plenty of light, but they continually faced homogeneous off-whiteness interrupted only by passing attendants who seldom stopped to be perceived. On the auditory side, while the noise level of the surrounding city was high and cries of other children were numerous, seldom did clear variations in sound come with such redundancy as to become recognizable and very seldom did such sound variations herald any specific changes in visual input. Thus, opportunities for the development of specific variations in either type of input and opportunities for auditory-visual coordinations were lacking. Moreover, since no toys were provided, the children had little opportunity to develop intentional behavior calculated to make interesting spectacles last. Dennis has reported the most extreme case of mass retardation of which I know. Although signs of malnutrition were present, Dennis was inclined not to consider it a major factor because of the vigor he observed in such automatisms as head shaking and rocking back and forth, and because he could see no way in which malnutrition could call forth scooting rather than creeping. Moreover, the role of heredity was minimized by the facts that the children in the demonstration orphanage, where retardation was much less marked, came from the one admitting neonates, and that they were probably chosen from those most retarded at the time of transfer.

Second, the evidence concerning the permanence of such effects is highly suggestive if less compelling than that concerning rate of development. Whether or not such retardation as that observed in Teheran inevitably leaves a permanent deficit cannot be stated with certainty. You will recall that Dennis observed that once these children in the orphanage learned to walk, they appeared to walk and run as well as other children do. But do not most intellectual and social functions demand a much more broadly integrated and more finely differentiated set of autonomous central processes than do such motor functions as walking and running? Certainly this is suggested by the fact that the dogs pet-reared by Thompson and Heron[18] are much superior to those cage-reared in solving various problems in the Hebb-Williams mazes even after a period of ten months of running free in the dog pasture. Moreover, permanence of the effects of infantile experience is also strongly suggested by the results of Goldfarb's studies,[19] in which adolescents, orphanage-reared for approximately their first three years, showed lower IQs, less rich fantasies, less tendency to take and hold onto a task, and more social problems than did adolescents (matched with those orphanage-reared for educational and socioeducational status of their mothers) who were reared in foster homes for those first three years. And again, permanence of intellectual deficit is also suggested by the finding in Israel that children of Jewish immigrants from the Orient persist in their scholastic inferiority to children of Jewish immigrants from Western countries, and by the observations that children from the slums in America persist in scholastic inferiority to children from middle-class parents even though the slum children may be advanced at least in motor development at ages from one to two years. In spite of these strong suggestions, it would be exceedingly interesting to have direct evidence from test performances at adolescence of these orphanage-reared Iranians for comparison with the test performances of family-reared Iranians or of adolescents reared in the demonstration orphanage. It is also important to determine whether the intellectual deficit from defective early experience is irreversible, or persists because of the way in which human children are usually treated once they achieve certain ages. If the latter alternative is the case, it should be possible to devise corrective experiences to overcome the deficit. This would be re-studying the issues that concerned Itard and Seguin. Getting the evidence necessary to decide such issues is exceedingly difficult.

Early Cognitive Learning and the Development of Intrinsic Motivation

Combining such bits of evidence as I have indicated with the geneticist's conception of genotype-environment interaction and with the biologist's notion of organism-environment interaction now makes it quite sensible to attempt to stimulate early cognitive learning. This evidence, however, hardly indicates how to go about it. Perhaps the most fruitful source of suggestions about how to proceed comes from an examination of the relationship between the development of intrinsic motivation and early cognitive learning.

Changes in Traditional Assumptions of Motivation

One of the leading traditional assumptions about motivation, namely, that painful stimulation during infancy leads inevitably (through something like Pavlovian conditioning) to increased proclivity to anxiousness and to reduced capacity for adaptation or learning, has been called into serious question by evidence from studies of the effects of painful infantile experience. Various investigators have found that rats submitted to painful electric shock, like those handled and petted, defecate and urinate less in an unfamiliar situation than do those left unmolested in the maternal nest.[20] If proneness to defecate or urinate in an unfamiliar situation is an index to anxiousness, these findings appear to deny the notion that anxiousness is an inevitable consequence of painful stimulation and to suggest that painful stimulation may be a special case of the principle that variation in inputs helps to immunize an animal to fear of the strange. Moreover, investigators have found that encounters with electric shock before weaning may increase the adult ability of rats to learn, at least when this ability is indexed by means of the number of trials required to establish an avoidance response to painful stimulation.[21] Encounters with painful electric shock in infancy appear to share with petting and handling the same kind of effects upon avoidance conditioning just as they share similar effects upon later defecation and urination in an unfamiliar situation. At least, this appears to be true for rats, but it may not be true for mice.[22]

Perhaps this surprising similarity in the effects of painful stimulation and in the effects of petting and handling is an artifact of comparing the effects of each of these kinds of encounters with the effects of leaving the infant rat unmolested in the maternal nest. In such comparisons, painful shock, petting, and handling all constitute variations in receptor inputs or in environmental encounters. It has been argued that these various kinds of input are equivalent in their effects on still unweaned rat pups and that it is only stimulation per se that counts in early infancy.[23] This, however, can hardly be so, for Salama and Hunt[24] have found that rats shocked daily during their second ten days of life show substantially less "fixation" effect of shock at the choice-point in a T-maze than do their litter-mates that were petted or handled. The petted and handled rats in this experiment showed "fixation" effects that did not differ significantly from those of litter-mates left unmolested in the maternal nest. The findings of this experiment show that some of the effects of shock in early infancy differ markedly from those of petting and handling, but the fact that shock in infancy reduces rather than increases the "fixation" effects of shock at the choice-point in the maze is again highly dissonant with the assumption that painful stimulation must inevitably increase proclivity to anxiousness. Long ago, the Spartans based their child-rearing on the principle that infants should be exposed to pain and cold to toughen them against future encounters with such exigencies. The evidence may indicate that they were not entirely wrong. On the other hand, the status of this issue is hardly such as to warrant any abrupt change in our tradition of protective tenderness toward our young.

Another change in our conception of motivation derives from recognition that there is a motivating system inherent in an organism's informational interaction with the environment. Although it is quite clear that painful stimulation, homeostatic needs, and sex all constitute genuine motivating systems, a very large share of an organism's interaction with the environment is informational in character. It occurs through the distance receptors, the eyes and the ears, and, to a much lesser degree, through touch. Elsewhere I have documented the basis for the notion that a motivating system inheres within this informational interaction.[25] For instance, the Russian investigators have found both an emotional aspect and an attentional aspect to even an infant mammal's response to change in visual or auditory input. This is what they call the "orienting response." The emotional aspect of this "orienting response" can be registered by such expressive indicators as vascular changes (plethysmograph), changes in blood pressure (sphygmomanometer), changes in heart rate (cardiotachometer), changes in palmar sweating (electrical conductance of the skin), changes in muscular tension (electromyograph), and changes in brain potentials (electroencephalogram). For these changes, see Razran.[26] The attentional aspect can be seen in the cessation of ongoing activities and the efforts to turn to the source of input. The fact that this "orienting response" is present at birth, or as soon as the ears are cleared and the eyes are open, indicates that it is a fundamental, ready-made mechanism. The fact that this response has both emotional and attentional aspects indicates, at least to me, that it is motivational, and the fact that the "orienting response" occurs to changes of ongoing inputs through the eyes and ears indicates that its motivational power is intrinsic within the organism's informational interaction with the environment.

Stage One in the Epigenesis of Intrinsic Motivation: the "Orienting Response"

Indications of the motivational importance of this "orienting response" and of encounters with variations in inputs derive from the marked retardation observed in children whose auditory and visual inputs have been severely restricted. Here the extreme retardation observed by Dennis in the Teheran orphanages has the dramatic import, if I am correct, that the major factor in its causation lies in homogeneity of reception input. Furthermore, in light of our traditional behavioristic belief that the observable motor response is all-important in development, it is worth noting that the marked retardation that I am attributing to homogeneity of input does not occur with inhibition of motor function during the first year. Again, this latter observation is by Dennis, or by Dennis and Dennis.[27] You will recall that the distribution of ages for the onset of walking in Hopi children cradled for their first year did not differ from the distribution of ages for onset of walking in Hopi children reared in an unrestrained fashion. While the motions of the legs and arms of the cradled infants were restrained during most of their waking hours, the fact that these cradled infants were often carried about, once they were forty days old, means that they probably encountered an enriched variety of redundant changes in auditory and visual input. Such a comparison suggests that it may be changes in perceptual input rather than opportunity for motor response that is most important in the motivation of psychological development during the earliest months.[28]

First suggestion for stimulating early cognitive learning. This brings me to my first concrete suggestion for stimulating cognitive development during the earliest months, and the process can begin at the child's birth. I suggest that the circumstances be so arranged that the infant will encounter a high variety of redundant changes of auditory, visual, and tactual inputs.

But this suggestion needs elaboration. While changes in ongoing stimulation are probably of basic motivational importance, it may not be mere change in itself that is sufficient to foster cognitive development; redundance of the input changes and of intermodal sequences of input changes are probably necessary. Piaget's[29] observations of his own infants suggest that, during approximately the first half-year, one of the major accomplishments of interaction with the environment consists in the coordination of what are at birth largely independent sensorimotor systems. According to Piaget, these systems include sucking, listening, looking, grasping, vocalizing, and wriggling. Without use, any one of these systems will wane. As is well known to any farm boy who has pail-fed a calf, the sucking wanes after ten days or two weeks of pail-feeding and the calf can be trusted completely among fresh cows with full udders. Moreover, the work of Alexander Wolf[30] and of Gauron and Becker[31] on the effects of depriving infant rats of audition and vision on the readiness of these systems to respond in adulthood, coupled with the work of Brattgard[32] and of Riesen[33] showing that the visual system fails to develop properly when rabbits and chimpanzees are reared in darkness, indicates that this principle holds for listening and looking as well as sucking. Parenthetically, I should add that the role of organism-environment interaction in early development appears also to be tied biochemically with later capacity to synthesize RNA, as the work of Brattgard,[34] Hydén,[35] and others (see Riesen)[36] appears to indicate. Perhaps the earliest of such interactions serve chiefly to sustain and to strengthen and develop the individual ready-made sensorimotor organizations or, as Piaget terms them, the "reflexive schemata." Very shortly, under typical circumstances, however, the sounds that evoke listening come to evoke looking, and the things seen come to evoke grasping and reaching, and the things grasped come to evoke sucking, etc. Such changes indicate progress in the coordination of the originally separate systems. During this phase, which is the second stage in Piaget's[37] system, the progressive organization of schemata consists chiefly in such coordination, and it appears to consist in sequential organization, of which Pavlov's *conditioning* and Guthrie's *contiguity learning* are special cases.

If one tries to imagine how one can introduce redundant changes in visual and auditory inputs in order to provide for the sequential coordination of listening with looking, of looking with reaching, etc., one finds it no easy matter without actually having on hand human beings whose approaches and withdrawals supply the auditory-input changes that are regularly followed by visual-input changes. I have found myself wondering if the emphasis on mothering may not have a somewhat justified explanation in that it is the human infant's informational interaction with this coming and going of the mother that provides the perceptual basis for this coordination of relatively independent schemata.

Stage Two in the Epigenesis of Intrinsic Motivation

But the nature of this intrinsic motivational process changes with experience. Any attempt to stimulate early cognitive learning must, I believe, take this change in form, or epigenesis, into account if it is to be at all successful. Moreover, if this epigenesis is taken into account, the circumstances encountered by the infant should not only motivate a rapid rate of cognitive development but should contribute substantially to the satisfaction the infant gets from life. As observers of infant development have long noted, the human infant appears to learn spontaneously, that is, in the absence of the traditional extrinsic motivators, and to get a superb enjoyment from the process.[38] This is a new notion to most of us, but it is also old. For instance, it was implicit in the "self-activity" of Froebel[39] and in the "intrinsic interest" of Dewey.[40] Moreover, Maria Montessori,[41] to whose work I shall return shortly, built her system of education for young children on the notion that children have a spontaneous interest in learning.

In what appears to be the first major transition in the structure of intrinsic motivation, the infant, while continuing to respond to changes in ongoing stimulation, comes to react toward the cessation of inputs which have been encountered repeatedly in a fashion designed to continue them or to bring them back into perceptual ken. Piaget[42] called this a "reversal tranformation." He considered it to be the beginnings of intention. Each of you who has ever dandled an infant on your knee is familiar with at least one example: when you stop your motion, the infant starts a motion of his own that resembles yours, and when you start again, the infant stops. The prevalence of infants' actions that are instigated by an absence of repeatedly encountered changes in input suggests, at least to me, that the repeated encounters with a given pattern of change in receptor input lead to recognition that provides one basis, and I believe it an important one, for cathexis, emotional attachment, and positive reinforcements.[43] My colleague Morton Weir prefers to refer to what attracts the infant as "predictability." Perhaps this is the better term. I have, however, preferred "recognition" because I suspect that what is happening is that the repeated encounters with a pattern of change in ongoing input serve to build into the storage of the posterior intrinsic system of the cerebrum a coded schema that can be matched to an input from the repeatedly encountered pattern of change. As the pattern is becoming recognizable, or when it is newly recognized, I suspect it provides a joyful basis of cathexis and positive reinforcement. I believe, at least tentatively, that it is this recognition that is one of the most consistent evokers of the infant's smile. Such an interpretation gains some support from the fact that maternal separation and encounters with unfamiliar persons bring little emotional disturbance, anxiety, or grief until the second half of the first year of life.[44] In fact, these observations of emotional disturbance are important indicators that the cathexis or maternal attachment has been formed. It is this emotional disturbance that supports the observation that an infant acts to retain or to obtain a pattern of familiar input that attests his cathexis of that pattern. Moreover, it should be noted that emotional distress accompanies maternal deprivation only after the age at which objects have begun to acquire permanence for the child. Presumably this permanence of objects is based on the development, in the course of repeated encounters with a pattern of change in input, of a set of semiautonomous central processes that can represent the pattern deriving from an encounter with an object.

Parenthetically, may I suggest also that the following-response within what is called "imprinting" may well be a special case of this more general principle that emotional attachment grows out of the recognition coming from repeatedly encountering an object, place, or person; the fact that the following-response occurs after a shorter period of perceptual contact with an object in a species such as the grey-leg goose, or in the sheep or deer, than is required in species such as the chimpanzee or man suggests that the number of encounters, or duration of perceptual contact required may well be a matter of the portion of the brain without direct connections with receptors or motor units, or what Hebb[45] has termed the A/S ratio.

Out of such observations comes the empirical principle, which I have imbibed from Piaget,[46] that "the more an infant has seen and heard, the more he wants to see and hear." The avidity of an infant's interest in the world may be seen to be in large part a function of the variety of situations he has encountered repeatedly. Moreover, it would appear to be precisely the absence of such avid interest that constitutes the regularly observed apathy of orphanage-reared children who have encountered only a very limited variety of situations. It may well be that this seeking of inputs that have been made familiar by repeated encounters is what motivates the behavior Dennis and Dennis[47] have termed "autogenous." Outstanding examples of such behavior are the hand-watching and the repetitive vocalizations called "babbling." It is, apparently, seeking to see the hands that motivates the motions to keep them within view, thereby providing the beginnings of eye-hand coordination. It is, apparently, seeking to hear voice sounds that motivates spontaneous vocalizing and keeps it going, thereby providing the infant with a beginning of ear-vocal coordination.

Second Suggestion for the Stimulation of Early Cognitive Learning. This brings me to my second suggestion for fostering early cognitive learning. It comes in connection with the development of intrinsically motivated intentions or plans, as the terms *intention* and *plan* are utilized by Miller, Galanter, and Pribram.[48] In fact, it is in connection with this development of intrinsically motivated intentions or plans that one basis for this change in the conception of motivation may be seen. Psychologists and psychoanalysts have conceived of actions, habits, defenses, and even of every thought system, as an attempt to reduce or eliminate stimulation or excitation within the nervous system arising out of painful stimulation, homeostatic need, or sex. To anyone who has observed and pondered the struggle of a young infant to reach and grasp some object he sees, it is extremely difficult to find such an extrinsic motivational basis for his reaching and grasping. What is suggested by Piaget's observations is that in the course of repeated encounters with an object, there comes a point at which seeing that object becomes an occasion for grasping it. In this coordination between looking and grasping, it would appear that grasping the object becomes a goal even though it is quite unrelated to pain, to homeostatic need, or to sex. Once an infant has the grasping goal of an object he has seen repeatedly, his various other motor schemata of striking, pushing, and even locomotion become also means to achieve this goal. Anyone who ponders this phenomenon in the light of the traditional theory of extrinsic motives will ask, "but why grasp the object?" And, "why grasp one object rather than another?" My tentative answer to these questions is that the object has become attractive with the new-found recognition that comes with repeated visual or auditory encounters. While reading

Piaget's[49] observations, one gets the impression that a smile very frequently precedes the effort to grasp, as if the infant were saying, "I know what you are, I'll take hold of you." Of course, nothing is so explicit; he has no language; he is merely manifesting a kind of primordial plan or intention. It is my hypothesis that this primordial intention is instigated by recognitive perception. If this hypothesis is true, then once an infant is ready to grasp things and to manipulate them, it is important that he have perceptual access to things he can grasp. It is important that there be a variety of such things that he has encountered earlier. The more varied the objects that are available, the more interest the infant will have in his world and the more sources of attractive novelty he will have later on.

As already indicated, it is probably also important that the infant have an opportunity to interact with human beings as well as with inanimate objects. Perhaps one of the chief functions of early interaction with human beings is to make the vocalized phones of the parental language and the gestures of communication familiar, for one of the most common forms of action designed to hold onto newly recognized inputs is imitation.* Such imitation is important for socialization and for intellectual development because the roots of human culture reside in the sounds of language and the various gestures of communication. An infant imitates first those phones and gestures that are highly familiar to him. In fact, one of the most feasible ways to start an interactive relationship with a young infant is to make one of the sounds that he is making regularly or to perform one of his characteristic gestures. The very fact that the sounds or gestures are the infant's helps to insure his recognition of them. Seeing them in another person commonly brings delighted interest and, not infrequently, imitative effort to recover them when the adult has stopped. The infant's jouncing in the dandling relationship is a special case of such imitative effort. Again we have a kind of encounter hard to arrange without involving human beings. This paucity of encounters that can be arranged without human beings supports the idea that the stories of feral men, including Romulus and Remus, are probably myths.

Stage Three in the Epigenesis of Intrinsic Motivation

The second major transformation in intrinsic motivation appears to occur when repeatedly encountered objects, places, and events become "old stuff." The infant then becomes interested in novelty. The breakdown of the meaning of a given input with repeated perceptual encounters and the monotony that comes with repeated participation in given events are phenomena that psychologists have long observed.[51] Hebb,[52] moreover, has observed that a major source of pleasure resides in

---

*This conception of imitation differs radically from that given by Miller and Dollard,[50] but it does not deny that their conception may be true under certain circumstances.

encountering something new within the framework of the familiar. The sequence—of "orienting response" to stimulus change, recognition with repeated encounters, and interest in the variations within the familiar— may well be one in the interaction of an organism with each completely new class of environmental phenomena. What look like stages in the development of the first year may possibly be derived from the fact that an infant tends to be repeatedly encountering a fairly extended variety of situations at a fairly consistent rate. In any event, in his observations of his own children, Piaget[53] noted that this interest in novelty appears toward the end of the first year.

There are those who dislike the very motion of such an epigenesis in the structure of motivation. There are those who seek single explanatory principles. Some have tried to explain this series of transformations in terms either of a process in which the new is continually becoming familiar or of a process whereby the earlier interest in the familiar exists because recognizability itself is novel at this phase. We may someday get a biochemical understanding of this phenomenon, but such attempts to find a unitary psychological principle of explanation are probably doomed to failure. Numerous studies indicate very clearly that organisms first respond to change in ongoing inputs. It is less certain that they next prefer the familiar, but the evidence is abundant that they later prefer objects and situations that are relatively less familiar than others available.[54] There is one instance in which a study shows that the lowly rat will endure even the pain of electric shock to get from his familiar nest-cage to an unfamiliar situation where there are novel objects to manipulate.[55] Studies also exist, moreover, in which organisms withdrew in fear from "familiar objects in an unfamiliar guise." These were objects that could never have been associated with painful stimulation in their previous experience because the animals had been reared under known conditions at the Yerkes Primate Laboratory. Festinger[56] has, also, found people withdrawing from information dissonant with their strong held beliefs, plans, or commitments.

It is no easy matter to characterize properly what is essential in that glibly called "novelty." I believe, however, that we can say that novelty resides within the organism's informational interaction with its environment. I have termed this essence "incongruity";[57] Berlyne[58] has written of the "collative variables" underlying "arousal potential"; Festinger[59] has talked of "dissonance"; Hebb[60] has written of the stage of development in cortical organization; and Munsinger and Kesson[61] are using the term "uncertainty." Whatever this essence is called, too much of it gives rise to withdrawal and gestures commonly connoting fear. Too little appears to be associated with boredom. That novelty that is attractive appears to be an optimum of discrepancy in this relationship between the informational input of the moment and the information already stored in the cerebrum from previous encounters with similar situations.

Once interest in novelty appears, it is an important source of motivation. Perhaps it is the chief source of motivation for cognitive learning. Interest in novelty appears to motivate the improvement of locomotor skills, for the novel objects "needing" examination or manipulation are typically out of reach. It appears to motivate imitation of unfamiliar verbal phones and unfamiliar gestures and even of fairly complex actions. Imitated vocalizing of unfamiliar phones and vocal patterns appears to be exceedingly important in the acquisition of language. The notion that all infants vocalize all the phones of all languages[62] has long been hard to believe. The social side of language acquisition appears to be more than the mere reinforcing with approval or notice of those vocal patterns characteristic of the parents' language. If the interest in novelty provides an intrinsic motivational basis for (imitatively) vocalizing phones that have never been a part of the infant's vocal repertoire, then we have a believable explanation for the fact that most of the first pseudo-words are approximations of adult vocalizations that have occurred repeatedly in connection with novel and exciting events. Repetition of encounters with a given class of events may be presumed gradually to establish central processes representative of that class of events, that is, *images,* if you will. Imitation of the novel phones verbalized by adults in association with the class of events may provide the infant with a vocalization that can serve him as a sign of his image. Later, reinforcement, partially based on approval-disapproval and partially based on growing cognitive differentiation, may lead gradually to images and phonemic combinations that are sufficiently like those of the people taking care of an infant to permit communication.

Once language is acquired, the human child comes into basically the same existential situation in which all of us find ourselves. He then has two major sources of informational input: first, the original one of perceiving objects and events, and second, the new one of learning about them through the language of others. One of his major intellectual tasks is to make what he learns about the "real world" through the communications of others jibe with what he learns about it directly through his own receptors. This is a creative task of no mean proportion, and it is not unlike the task with which mature men of science are continuously concerned. This is one of George Kelly's[63] major points.

The considerations already outlined in connection with my suggestions concerning repeated encounters with a given class of stimulus change and "recognition" show again the basis for the principle that "the more a child has seen and heard, the more he wants to see and hear" and do. If an infant has encountered a wide variety of changes in circumstances during his earliest days, and if he has encountered them repeatedly enough to become attached to them through recognition, and if he has had ample opportunity to act upon them and to manipulate them, he will become, I believe, ready to be intrigued by novel variations in an ample range of objects, situations, and personal models.

The fact that too much novelty or incongruity can be frightening and too little can be boring, however, creates a problem for those who would stimulate cognitive development. They must provide for encounters with materials, objects, and models that have the proper degree of that incongruity.[64] This is one aspect of what I have termed the "problem of the match."[65]

Third Suggestion for the Stimulation of Early Cognitive Learning. Consideration of the problem of the match brings me to my third concrete suggestion for stimulating cognitive learning in the very young. I must confess that I have borrowed this suggestion from Montessori.[66] The first portion of this suggestion is that careful observation be made of what it is in the way of objects, situations, and models for imitation that interests the infant. Once it is clear what objects and models are of interest, then I suggest providing each infant with an ample variety of them and with an opportunity to choose spontaneously the ones that intrigue him at a given time. This latter suggestion assumes, of course, that the infant is already comfortable, that he feels safe, and that he is satisfied so far as homeostatic needs are concerned. I really feel that we do not have to worry too much about gratifying the sex appetite of a child under three years of age.

When I wrote *Intelligence and Experience,*[67] this problem of providing a proper match between the materials with which a child is confronted by teachers and what he already has in his storage loomed large because of our tremendous ignorance of the intricacies involved. This ignorance is a major challenge for investigation; in the meantime, however, as Jan Smedslund pointed out to me in a conversation in Boulder last summer, Montessori long ago provided a practical solution. She based her system of education on intrinsic motivation, but she called it "spontaneous learning." She provided young children with a wide variety of materials, graded in difficulty and roughly calculated to be the range of materials that would provide a proper match for children of ages three to six if they were given opportunity for choice. She also gave each of the children in her school an opportunity to occupy himself or herself with those materials of his or her own individual choice. To do this, she broke the lock-step in the educational process. A Montessori school was socially so constructed that the children were obviously expected to occupy themselves with the materials provided. Moreover, by having together within a single room children ranging in age from three to six years, she provided a graded series of models for the younger children and an opportunity for some of the older children to learn by teaching the younger ones how to do various things. You will be interested to know that a substantial proportion of the slum children in Montessori's school began reading and writing before they were five years old. In the Casa di Bambini, which Montessori founded in 1907 in the basement of a slum apartment-house in Rome, the teacher was the apartment-house superintendent's sixteen-year-old daughter who had been trained by Montessori. You will also be interested to know that the old nursery school bugaboo that children have very brief spans of attention did not hold. Dorothy Canfield Fisher[68]—the novelist who spent the winter of 1910–1911 at the original Casa di Bambini—has written that it was common to see a three-year-old continuously occupied with such a mundane task as buttoning and unbuttoning for two or more hours at a stretch.

Montessori's contributions to the education of the very young were discussed with excitement in America until the time of World War I. Thereafter the discussion ended almost completely. I suspect that this occurred because Montessori's theoretical views were so dissonant with what became about then the dominant views of American psychologists and American educators. Her theory that cognitive capacity could be modified by proper education was dissonant with the dominant and widely-prevailing notions of "fixed intelligence" and "predetermined development." These notions were implicit in the doctrine of a constant IQ. Her notion of spontaneous learning was sharply dissonant with the doctrine that all behavior is extrinsically motivated by painful stimulation, or homeostatic need, or sex. Moreover, the importance she attributed to sensory training was dissonant with what became the prevailing presumption that it is the observable motor response that counts. We need to reexamine her contributions in the light of the theoretical picture that has been emerging since World War II. I am grateful to Jan Smedslund for calling her contributions to my attention.

My discourse has skipped roughly half of the second year and all of the third year of life, because interest in novelty typically makes its earliest appearance toward the end of the first year or early in the second. (Montessori's schools took children only at three years of age or older.) I suspect that the basic principle involved in stimulating cognitive learning is fairly constant once the interest in novelty appears. On the other hand, I would not be surprised if it were precisely during this period between eighteen months and three years of age that lower-class families typically most hamper the kind of cognitive learning that is later required for successful performance in school and in our increasingly technological culture. Let me explain briefly.

During the first year, the life of an infant in a family crowded together in one room—as Oscar Lewis[69] has described such living in his *Children of Sanchez* and as I have observed it in the slums of New York—probably provides a fairly rich variety of input. On the other hand, once an infant begins to use his new-found locomotor and linguistic skills, his circumstances in a lower-class setting probably become anything but conducive to appropriate cognitive learning. Using his new locomotor skills gets him in the way of problem-beset adults and, all too likely, may bring punishment which can be avoided only by staying out of their way. This in turn deprives the infant of the opportunity to hear and imitate the verbal phones that provide the basis for spoken language. If a slum child should be lucky enough to acquire the "learning set" that things have names and to begin his repetitive questioning about "what's that?", he is not only unlikely to get answers but also likely to get his ears cuffed for asking such silly questions. Moreover, in the slum setting of lower-class family life, the models that an infant has to imitate are all too often likely to result in the acquisition of sensorimotor organizations and attitudes that interfere with rather that facilitate the kinds of cognitive learning that enable a child to succeed in school and in a technological culture such as ours. How long such interference with development can last without resulting in a permanent reduction in cognitive potential remains an unsolved problem. It is likely, however, that day-care centers and nursery schools prepared to face such children with situations, materials, and models that are not too incongruous with the schemata and attitudes that they have already acquired, can counteract much of the detrimental effect of lower-class life. Such preschool experience during the second and third, and possibly even during the fourth, years of life can perhaps serve well as an antidote to this kind of cultural deprivation.[70]

Summary

I have limited my discussion to the implications, for the stimulation of early cognitive learning, of the epigenesis of intrinsic motivation that I believe I can see taking place during preverbal development. I have identified three stages of intrinsic motivation that are separated by two major "reversal transformations." In the first of these, repeated encounters with patterns of change in perceptual input lead to recognition that I now believe to be a source of pleasure and a basis for cathexis or for affectional attachment. The second consists in a transition from an interest in the familiar to an interest in the novel. During the first few months, when the child is responsive chiefly to changes in the character and intensity of ongoing stimulation, I suspect it is most important to provide for repeated encounters with as wide a variety as possible of changes in receptor input. It may also be important to provide for sequential arrangements of these inputs that will provide a basis for a coordination of all combinations of the ready-made reflexive sensorimotor systems. As the infant becomes attached to objects, people, and situations by way of the hypothetical joys of new-found recognition, it is probably most important to provide opportunities for him to utilize his own repertoire of intentional activities to retain or elicit or manipulate the objects, people, and situations, again in as wide a variety as is feasible. Once interest in novelty appears, I suspect it is most important to give the child access to a variety of graded materials for manipulation and coping and to a variety of graded models for imitation. With what little we now know of what I call the "problem of the match," I suspect it is important to follow Montessori's principle of trusting to a considerable degree in the spontaneous interest of the individual infant instead of attempting to regiment his learning process in any lock-step method of preschool education.

References

1. J. McV. Hunt, *Intelligence and Experience* (New York: Ronald Press, 1961).

2. W. Johannsen, *Über Erblichkeit in populationen und in reinen Linien* (Jena: Gustav Fisher, 1903).

3. S. Freud, "Three Contributions to the Theory of Sex" (1905), in A. A. Brill (tr. and ed.), *The Basic Writings of Sigmund Freud* (New York: Modern Library, 1938).

4. J. McV. Hunt, "The Effects of Infant Feeding Frustration Upon Adult Hoarding in the Albine Rat," *Journal of Abnormal Social Psychology*, 36 (1946), pp. 338–360.

5. D.O. Hebb, "The Effects of Early Experience on Problem-Solving at Maturity," *American Psychology*, 2 (1947), pp. 306–307.

6. W. R. Thompson and W. Heron, "The Effects of Restraining Early Experience on the Problem-Solving Capacity of Dogs," *Canadian Journal of Psychology*, 8 (1964), pp. 17–31.

7. D.O. Hebb, *Organization of Behavior* (New York: Wiley, 1964).

8. D.O. Hebb and K. Williams, "A Method of Rating Animal Intelligence," *Journal of Genetic Psychology*, 34 (1946), pp. 59–65.

9. D. G. Forgays, and Janet W. Forgays, "The Nature of the Effect of Free Environmental Experience in the Rat," *Journal of Comparative and Physiological Psychology*, 45 (1952), pp. 32–328; R. H. Furgus, "The Effect of Early Perceptual Learning on the Behavioral Organization of Adult Rats," *Journal of Comparative and Physiological Psychology*, 47 (1954), pp. 331–336; B. Hymovitch, "The Effects of Experimental Variations on Problem-Solvings in the Rat," *Journal of Comparative and Physiological Psychology*, 45 (1952), pp. 313–321.

10. Hebb, "Effects of Early Experience."

11. Thompson and Heron, "Effects of Restraining Early Experience."

12. K. H. Pribram, "A Review of Theory in Physiological Psychology," *Annual Review of Psychology*, 11 (1960), pp. 1–40.

13. Hebb, *Organization of Behavior*.

14. R. A. Spitz, "Hospitalism: An Inquiry into the Genesis of Psychiatric Conditions in Early Childhood," *Psychoanalytic Study of the Child*, 1 (1945), pp. 54–74; idem, "Hospitalism: A Follow-up Report," *Psychoanalytic Study of the Child*, 2 (1946), pp. 113–117.

15. S.R. Pinneau, "The Infantile Disorders of Hospitalism and Anaclitic Depression," *Psychological Bulletin*, 52 (1955), pp. 429–459.

16. W. Dennis, "Causes of Retardation Among Institutional Children: Iran," *Journal of Genetic Psychology*, 96 (1960), pp. 47–59.

17. *Ibid.*, p. 58.

18. Thompson and Heron, "Effects of Restraining Early Experience."

19. W. Goldfarb, "Emotional and Intellectual Consequences of Psychologic Deprivation in Infancy: A Re-evaluation," pp.105–119, in P. Hoch and J. Zubin (eds.), *Psychopathology of Childhood* (New York: Grune and Stratton, 1955).

20. V. H. Denenberg, "The Interactive Effects of Infantile and Adult Shock Levels Upon Learning," *Psychological Reports*, 5 (1959), pp. 357–364; idem, "The Effects of Early Experience," Ch. 6, in E. S. E. Hafez (ed.), *The Behavior of Domestic Animals* (London: Balliere, Tindall, and Cox, 1962); Denenberg and G. G. Karas, "Interactive Effects of Age and Duration of Infantile Experience on Adult Learning," *Psychological Reports*, 7 (1960), pp. 313–322; Denenberg, J. R. C. Morton, N. S. Kline, and L. J. Grota, "Effects of Duration of Infantile Stimulation Upon Emotionality," *Canadian Journal of Psychology*, 16 (1962), pp. 72–76; S. Levine, "A Further Study of Infantile Handling and Adult Avoidance Learning," *Journal of Personality*, 27 (1956), pp. 70–80; idem, "Infantile Experience and Consummatory Behavior in Adulthood," *Journal of Comparative and Physiological Psy-*

chology, 50 (1957), pp. 609–612; idem, "Effects of Early Deprivation and Delayed Weaning on Avoidance Learning in the Albino Rat," *Archives of Neurology and Psychiatry*, 79 (1958), pp. 211–213; idem, "The Effects of Differential Infantile Stimulation on Emotionality at Weaning," *Canadian Journal of Psychology*, 13 (1959), pp. 243–247.

21. K. H. Brookshire, R. A. Littman, and C. N. Stewart, "Residua of Shocktrauma in the White Rat: A Three-Factor Theory," *Psychological Monographs*, 75 (1961), p. 514; K. H. Brookshire, "An Experimental Analysis of the Effects of Infantile Shock-trauma," *Dissertation Abstracts*, 19 (1958), p. 180; V. H. Denenberg, "The Interactive Effects of Infantile and Adult Shock Levels upon Learning," *Psychological Reports*, 5 (1959), pp. 357–364; Denenberg and R. W. Bell, "Critical Periods for the Effects of Infantile Experience on Adult Learning," *Science*, 131 (1960), pp. 227–228; Denenberg and Karas, "Interactive Effects," S. Levine, "Infantile Handling"; idem, "Effects of Early Deprivation"; S. Levine, J. A. Chevalier, and S. J. Korchin, "The Effects of Early Shock and Handling on Later Avoidance Learning," *Journal of Personality* 24 (1956), pp. 475–493.

22. G. Lindzey, D. T. Lykken, and H. D. Winston, "Infantile Trauma, Genetic Factors, and Adult Temperament," *Journal of Abnormal Social Psychology*, 61 (1960), pp. 7–14.

23. S. Levine, "Effects of Differential Infantile Stimulation."

24. A. A. Salama and J. McV. Hunt, "'Fixation' in the Rat as a Function of Infantile Shocking, Handling, and Gentling," *Journal of Genetic Psychology*, 105 (1964) pp. 131–162.

25. J. McV. Hunt, "Motivation Inherent in Information Processing and Action," in O. J. Harvey (ed.), *Motivation and Social Organization: The Cognitive Factors* (New York: Ronald Press, 1963).

26. G. Razran, "The Observable Unconscious and the Inferable Conscious in Current Society Psychophysiology; Interoceptive Conditioning, Semantic Conditioning, and the Orienting Reflex," *Psychological Review*, 68 (1961), pp. 81–147.

27. W. Dennis, "Causes of Retardation Among Institutional Children: Iran," *Journal of Genetic Psychology*, 96 (1970), pp. 47–59; W. Dennis and Marsena G. Dennis, "The Effect of Cradling Practice Upon the Onset of Walking in Hopi Children," *Journal of Genetic Psychology*, 56 (1940), pp. 77–86.

28. Cf. D. W. Fiske and S. R. Maddi, *Functions of Varied Experience* (Homewood, Ill.: Dorsey Press, 1961).

29. J. Piaget, *The Origins of Intelligence in Children*, 1936 (trans. Margaret Cook) (New York: International Universities Press, 1952).

30. A. Wolf, "The Dynamics of the Selective Inhibition of Specific Functions in Neurosis: A Preliminary Report," *Psychosomatic Medicine*, 5 (1943), pp. 27–38. Reprinted in S. S. Tomkins (ed.), *Contemporary Psychopathology*, Ch. 31 (Cambridge: Harvard University Press, 1943).

31. E. F. Gauron and W. C. Becker, "The Effects of Early Sensory Deprivation on Adult Rat Behavior Under Competition Stress: An Attempt at Replication of a Study by Alexander Wolf," *Journal of Comparative and Physiological Psychology*, 52 (1959), pp. 689–693.

32. S. O. Brattgard, "The Importance of Adequate Stimulation for the Chemical Composition of Retinal Ganglion Cells During Post-natal Development," *Acta Radiologica* (Stockholm, 1952).

33. A. H. Riesen, "The Development of Visual Perception in Man and Chimpanzee," *Science*, 106 (1947), pp. 107–108; A. H. Riesen, "Plasticity of Behavior: Psychological Aspects," pp. 425–450, in H. F. Harlow and C. N. Woolsey (eds.), *Biological and Biochemical Bases of Behavior* (Madison: University of Wisconsin Press, 1958); idem, "Stimulation as a Requirement for Growth and Function in Behavioral Development," in D. W. Fiske and S. R. Maddi (eds.), *Functions of Varied Experience* (Homewood, Ill.: Dorsey Press, 1961).

34. Brattgard, "Importance of Adequate Stimulation."

35. H. Hydén, "Biochemical Changes in Glial Cells and Nerve Cells at Varying Activity," pp. 64–89, in F. Brucke (ed.), *Proceedings of the 4th International Congress of Biochemistry, III, Bio-*

chemistry of the Central Nervous System (London: Pergamon Press, 1959).

36. Riesen, "Development of Visual Perception."

37. Piaget, *Origins of Intelligence.*

38. J. M. Baldwin, *Mental Development in the Child and in the Race* (New York: Macmillan, 1895); K. Buhler, *Die Giestige Entwicklung des Kindes* (Jena: Fischer, 1918); idem, "Displeasure and Pleasure in Relation to Activity," Ch. 14, in M. L. Reymert (ed.), *Feelings and Emotions: the Wittenberg Symposium* (Worcester, Mass.: Clark University Press, 1928); I. Hendrick, "The Discussion on the 'Instinct to Master,'" *Psychoanalytic Quarterly,* 12 (1943), pp. 561–565; B. Mittelman,: Motility in Infants, Children, and Adults," *Psychoanalytic Study of the Child,* 9 (1954), pp. 142–177.

39. F. Froebel, *The Education of Man* (trans., W. T. Harris) (New York: Appleton, 1887).

40. J. Dewey, *The School and Society* (Chicago: University of Chicago Press, Phoenix Books, P3, 1960).

41. Maria Montessori, *The Montessori Method* (New York: Frederick A. Stokes, 1912).

42. Piaget, *Origins of Intelligence.*

43. J. McV. Hunt, "Piaget's Observations as a Source of Hypotheses Concerning Motivation," *Merrill-Palmer Quarterly,* 9 (1963), pp. 253–275.

44. Anna Freud and Dorothy Burlingham, *Infants Without Families* (New York: International Universities Press, 1944).

45. Hebb, *Organization of Behavior.*

46. Piaget, *Origins of Intelligence.*

47. W. Dennis, and Marsena G. Dennis, "Infant Development Under Conditions of Restricted Practice and Minimum Social Stimulation," *Genetic Psychology Monographs,* 23 (1941), pp. 149–155; also as: "Development Under Controlled Environmental Conditions," III-one, in W. Dennis (ed.), *Readings in Child Psychology* (New York: Prentice-Hall, 1951).

48. G. A. Miller, E. H. Galanter, and K. H. Pribram, *Plans and the Structure of Behavior* (New York: Holt, 1960).

49. Piaget, *Origins of Intelligence;* Piaget, *The Construction of Reality in the Child,* 1937 (trans. Margaret Cook) (New York: Basic Books, 1954).

50. N. E. Miller and J. Dollard, *Social Learning and Imitation* (New Haven, Conn.: Yale University Press, 1941).

51. See E. B. Titchener, *A Text-book of Psychology* (New York: Macmillan, 1926), p. 425.

52. Hebb, *Organization of Behavior,* p. 224.

53. Piaget, *Origins of Intelligence.*

54. W. N. Dember, R. W. Earl, and N. Paradise, "Response by Rats to Differential Stimulus Complexity," *Journal of Comparative and Physiological Psychology,* 50 (1957), pp. 514–518; D. O. Hebb, and Helen Mahut, "Motivation et Recherche du Changement Perceptif Chez le Rat et Chez l'Homme," *Journal de Psychologie Normale et Pathologique,* 48 (1955), pp. 209–220; K. Montgomery, "A Test of Two Explanations of Spontaneous Alternation," *Journal of Comparative and Physiological Psychology,* 45 (1952), pp. 287–293; idem, "Exploratory Behavior as a Function of 'Similarity' of Stimulus Situations," *Journal of Comparative and Physiological Psychology,* 46 (1953), pp. 129–133.

55. H. W. Nissen, "A Study of Exploratory Behavior in the White Rat by Means of the Obstruction Method," *Journal of Genetic Psychology,* 37 (1930), pp. 361–376.

56. L. Festinger, *A Theory of Cognitive Dissonance* (Evanston, Ill.: Row, Peterson, 1957).

57. Hunt, "Motivation Inherent in Information Processing."

58. D. E. Berlyne, *Conflict, Arousal, and Curiosity* (New York: McGraw-Hill, 1960).

59. Festinger, "Theory of Cognitive Dissonance."

60. Hebb, *Organization of Behavior.*

61. H. Munsinger and W. Kessen, "Uncertainty, Structure and Preference," *Psychological Monographs,* 78 (1964), p. 586.

62. F. H. Allport, *Social Psychology* (Boston: Houghton Mifflin, 1924).

63. G. A. Kelly, *A Psychology of Personal Constructs* (New York: Norton, 1955).

64. Hunt, "Motivation Inherent in Information Processing."

65. J. McV. Hunt, *Intelligence and Experience,* p. 267 ff.

66. Montessori, *Montessori Method;* Dorothy Canfield Fisher, *A Montessori Mother* (New York: Holt, 1912).

67. Hunt, *Intelligence and Experience.*

68. Fisher, *Montessori Mother.*

69. O. Lewis, *The Children of Sanchez* (New York: Random House, 1961).

70. J. McV. Hunt, "The Psychological Basis for Using Pre-School Enrichment as an Antidote for Cultural Deprivation," *Merrill-Palmer Quarterly,* 10 (1964), pp. 209–248.

6 Wishful Thinking About Children's Thinking

Millie Almy

One of the first significant commentaries on the relevance and mean-
ing of Piaget's theories for early childhood education, this article is
a landmark in the literature. This 1961 statement by a top person in
the field exemplifies the willingness on the part of early childhood edu-
cators to integrate, evaluate, and apply new insights even when it means
revising long-held assumptions and convictions.

"So little for the mind," say the critics. Some react against school
programs where "doing" seems to supersede learning; others against
situations where memorization and repetition seem ascendant over
problem solving and critical or creative thinking. So educators, ever
mindful of the pressure of public opinion and not insensitive to the
criticism from within their own ranks, turn their attention more and
more to the mind and to the processes of thinking.

Support for their interest comes from the psychologists, who, following
some years of preoccupation with more directly observable aspects of
human behavior, are now increasingly interested in the ways man
acquires knowledge of himself and of his environment. As their research
in the cognitive processes grows, some of them extend their concerns
beyond the laboratory and into the classroom. This territory was once
off limits to all but the educational psychologist, and even he was seldom
completely at home there.

But the psychologist does not share his interest in thinking with the
educator alone. The scientist, the mathematician, and the linguist have
also begun to inquire into the nature of children's thinking, looking for
evidence that children can think effectively. They are concerned that
the school equip its graduates to deal more adequately with the com-
plexities of a changing world.

Different Views

Representing different disciplines and different professions, each of
these individuals has a characteristic way of looking at thinking. The
educator, perhaps, is most aware of what the teacher does or says in
attempting to influence thinking; the psychologist centers his attention
on the responses of the individual children, whereas the other specialists

Reprinted with permission from *Teachers College Record*, February 1961. Dr. Almy is
Professor of Psychology and Education in Teachers College, Columbia University.

are concerned with the logical structure of their particular subjects. Eventually, if the children are to be taught to think effectively and to the satisfaction of all concerned, these differing viewpoints need to be reconciled.

Perhaps, when specialists with differing outlooks view the intellectual life of the classroom simultaneously, they can avoid the inclination to think wishfully, rather than realistically, about the ways that children think. Many adults reveal this wishful tendency when they assume that the thinking of the five- or ten-year-old basically resembles their own, and again when they take whatever he says to mean what they would mean if they were saying the same things.

The process of education would be considerably simplified if children, once having acquired speaking vocabularies resembling those of adults, also shared with them similar ways of explaining and viewing the world. If youngsters of seven and seventeen did indeed think alike, the second grade teacher and the high school teacher could use similar methods, and the presentation of subject matter could be determined by its own particular logic.

Childhood Limitations

Much of the literature related to the curriculum is replete with statements implying that the processes of concept formation differ little, if at all, from the kindergarten or even the nursery-school years to adulthood. Similarly, many of the principles cited in educational methods courses rest on the assumption that children and adults arrive at and understand new concepts in basically similar ways. Such principles, unfortunately, gloss over what appear to be important limitations in the thinking abilities of children as compared to adults.

These limitations are not such as to necessitate a curriculum of intellectual pabulum in the elementary school. The problem is not that children are unable to cope with ideas, but rather that they apprehend them in ways that are characteristic of their level of development. To postpone opportunities to deal in their own fashion with certain aspects of science, mathematics, art, or literature until they have reached the age of high school or even college may be to offer them only the bare bones of abstraction stripped of real significance. The danger in current attempts to erase the idea that the "public schools are easy schools," generating mediocrity in thinking, appears to lie less in the attempt to inject more content into the curriculum than in failure to recognize that each level of development contributes its own special understandings of that content.

Like many other educators interested in the kindergarten and primary grades, the writer long believed that the only important difference between the reasoning abilities of younger and older children lay in the greater experience of the older youngsters. Qualitatively, the thinking of five-year-olds and six-year-olds should be similar to that of older children. If this were the case, the kinds of experience provided in the early childhood curriculum should importantly influence children's thinking, both immediately and later. To test this notion, a study of children's thinking about natural phenomena was undertaken. For many years the curriculum for young children in kindergarten and in elementary school has included attention to this area. But the kinds of understanding that may be possible at this level of development have not been much investigated.

The exploratory phases of the study[1] were designed to examine the efficacy of the demonstration-interview as a technique for revealing children's conceptions about such presumably familiar aspects of their world as air, water, objects that float and those that sink, living and non-living things. Two groups of kindergarten children were interviewed at mid-year and end of kindergarten and again at the end of first grade. Eighty interviews with children ranging in age from three-and-a-half to seven years were conducted by students in developmental psychology. The results suggested explanations for some of the many discepancies to be found among studies of children's thinking using the interview as a method and between those studies and others based on observations of children at work and play. But the most significant result of the exploratory study lay in its assault on the writer's own wishful belief that the child's words had the same meaning to him as they did to her and that his logic was basically no different from her own.

Adult Difficulties

Some consolation for finding herself in this position has come from the realization that other educators and psychologists, as well as scholars from various other disciplines, are also prone to indulge in wishful thinking about children's thinking. When one reads the literature on concept formation, begins to examine the thought processes lying behind the verbal façade children present in the classroom, and then listens to what educators say the children are thinking and what scholars assert the children should be thinking, the difficulties of maintaining a realistic view of children's thinking are obvious.

Mistaken assumptions about the nature of a young person's thinking are perhaps most likely to occur in relation to early childhood. Most of the illustrative material for this article is drawn from this stage of development. But there is little reason to believe that those who are concerned with learning in the high school as well as in the middle and upper elementary school years (and perhaps even in college and graduate school) are not also sometimes inclined to be influenced by their desires.

Wishful thinking on the part of teachers is readily demonstrable. They are easily misled by a glib response, an expected answer, or even an eager look, forgetting that a facile memory and a sensitivity to adult expectation may mask meanings and understandings that are quite different from those the teacher expects. But those who build the curriculum, who are concerned with either the earliest or the most strategic moments for teaching particular concepts, are also not immune to wishfulness. They reveal it when they imply that first and second graders can readily become miniature physicists and mathematicians. They and others reveal their own predilections when they assign priorities to either concrete or abstract thinking. That children do indeed learn by doing is surely not debatable, but that activity must *dominate* the curriculum from kindergarten to college is open to question.

It also appears that some scholars, perhaps a few psychologists, and at least an occasional educator would like to center all attention on a kind of pure thought, analytic thinking undefiled by emotion or fantasy. Granted that logical thinking is essential, the important contribution of intuition, insight, and imagination to effective thought ought not be overlooked.

Similarly, recent attempts to plan the curriculum of the school around the logical structure underlying the various disciplines are promising in many respects. But here again, one must question whether some scholars are not prone to assume that whatever approach leads to effective thinking in their own discipline will probably apply to others as well. Undoubtedly, the underlying logical structure has been made considerably more explicit in certain disciplines than in others. This is perhaps reflected in the fact that the most comprehensive research in the nature of children's thinking has been in the area of physical science and mathematics. The bulk of it has been contributed by Piaget and is best represented in English by his work with Inhelder, *The Growth of Logical Thinking from Childhood to Adolescence*.[2]

In studying thinking processes, Piaget has played the dual role of logician and psychologist. This approach has alienated him from many of his American colleagues. Yet, what appears to be his basic idea has considerable potential appeal for those who plan the content of children's schooling. Essentially, he uses symbolic logic as an instrument for describing the thinking processes necessary to the understanding of the structure of a given discipline. Confronting children of successive ages with representative problems, he has been able to demonstrate the sequence of appearance of increasingly complex reasoning abilities.

Nevertheless, the author's study of kindergarten children's thinking about natural phenomena was based partially on a conviction that Piaget's assertion of limited reasoning abilities in young children failed to take into sufficient account the possibility that experience of a kind that could be provided in a classroom could readily modify their thinking. She was unprepared to have the children, almost as though they had read and comprehended Piaget, demonstrate so many of the limitations in reasoning that he describes as characteristic of early levels of development. On the other hand, the children also revealed that they were accumulating, classifying, and organizing a great deal of information about their world. These findings raised many provocative questions and led to what now appears to be a more intelligent grappling with ideas about cognitive development, of which Piaget's remains most fruitful.

Piaget's Views

Piaget's unique contribution lies in his use of "operations." Operations are actions or ways of getting information from the world of reality into the world of thought. During infancy, the child is capable only of direct action on his world. Later, he internalizes his actions and is able to carry them out symbolically. But it is not until he is also able to cancel or "reverse" them mentally (i.e., to be aware of a previous thought) that he can comprehend the world in the way the adult does. Not until this point can the adult hope to teach him the most elementary concepts of physics or mathematics. Similarly, it is not until he can mentally handle potentiality or possibility as effectively as reality that he can comprehend mathematics or physics in abstract terms. At this point, he is no longer limited to considering what "is" but can deal with "might be." He can theorize that under certain conditions, certain variables may behave in a variety of ways. He does not need to create the conditions or actually to manipulate the variables in order to predict the outcome.

During the period ordinarily encompassed by the elementary and high school years, the child, according to Piaget, moves from the stage of *intuitive thought,* in which his experience is predominantly perceptual, into a stage of *concrete operations.* At this level, he can reason similarly to an adult, but not until he reaches the stage of *formal operations* does genuine abstract thinking become possible. The shift from intuitive thinking to concrete operations appears to take place by age seven, while progress from concrete toward formal operations begins around eleven. Age is used here, of course, only as an indication of general maturity level. Piaget's studies are not normative, and considerable variability among children can be assumed.

Thinking remains on the intuitive level so long as the child confronting the world is dominated by his immediate perception. It appears, for example, when he believes that a given amount of liquid placed in a tall slender vessel is not the same when it is spread out in a shallow wide vessel. This notion persists even when he seems to understand that the point at issue is not the appearance of the liquid but the amount "to drink." Or he may think that a friend has more clay than he has when, after having received an identical amount, the friend breaks his into small bits, distributing them over a large area.

In this stage, the child cannot hold on mentally to the before and after aspects of a particular phenomenon. He cannot coordinate relationships. His comments, for example, may indicate that he deals first with the height of the tall vessel and then with the width of the shallow one. He is not yet able to think of the height of the one as related to the width of the other. Nor will it occur to him, as it will later, to test the relationships by pouring the liquid from one vessel to another.

At this intuitive level, the child does not yet understand "conservation," the fact that the substance or material of an object remains constant even while it undergoes changes in appearance or that a given number of objects remains the same regardless of how they may be arranged. He also lacks what Piaget terms "reversibility," the ability to cancel mentally a transformation that he has seen occur. It is though, for example, having thought about the size of an object, he can not go back to a previous thought about its weight. Once these ideas are attained, the child can begin to handle logical relationships, although he does so through direct actions rather than abstractly. He has reached a stage of *concrete operations.*

With these operations, the child can in an orderly fashion handle the equivalences among a group of objects—say, a collection of toy soldiers—and also deal systematically with their differences. Thus, he recognizes that the "soldiers" include both all the plastic soldiers and all the metal soldiers, and that there are more "soldiers" than either plastic or metal soldiers. But he can also sort them into classes of "privates" and "sergeants" and include in those classes both those that are metal and those that are plastic. He can also create a series, arranging them in order of size or, perhaps, even according to their authority (who gives orders to whom).

The ability to form classes and series considerably enhances the child's ability to manipulate and to understand number, space, and time. Various aspects of his physical world take on additional meaning.

Up to this point, however, the child cannot deal with sheer possibilities except experimentally, by actual trial and error. Not until he moves into the stage of *formal operations* can he examine the consequences of various combinations of factors in a systematic and orderly fashion. His thinking is then no longer bound to the immediate task. Rather, he is able to devise theories, state them verbally, and then test them in actual experience. He can reason in the same way as the logician, even though he has not been taught logic.

Supporting Views

The sequence of intellectual development described by Piaget corresponds with the findings in other studies of concept formation, although it is doubtful whether any other single investigator has covered so many concepts over so wide an age range.

Studies like those by Welch,[3] for example, have indicated that conceptualization proceeds from simple levels (men and women are all people) to more complex levels (such as the understanding that potatoes are vegetables, apples are fruit, and that both vegetables and fruit are food). Piaget notes, however, that a child may learn these ideas without being able to manipulate them effectively. By the age of eight, according to Welch, children can conceptualize on these levels but cannot deal with more remotely abstract classifications. Such inclusive classes as "living substance" or, still more abstractly, "substance" are too difficult.

Reichard, Schneider, and Rapaport,[4] using sorting tests, found three levels of development. At the concretistic level up to five or six years, children classified objects on the basis of nonessential incidental features. A functional level, where classification was made on the basis of use, extended to the age of eight, and the abstract level was not much used before the age of ten.

Studies summarized by Heinz Werner[5] similarly indicate a sequence in concept formation from a "naming" or describing level to later concrete and abstract levels. Werner, however, holds to a theory of mental development that suggests a spiral evolution rather than a series of stages. He appears to agree with Piaget when he indicates that a task can be achieved by genetically different analogous processes, but he also notes that at any stage of development, the level of performance depends on the relative novelty of the task.

The challenge put to the educator by such studies of the development of thinking processes is that of ascertaining, on the one hand, the level at which children can think and, on the other, the level of thinking the material presented demands if it is to be understood. Can adults, who have put away (or believe that they have put away) their own childish ways of thinking, readily recapture them to understand what is going on in the minds of children? Some of the resistance to the observations made by Piaget, and also evidence from other studies of concept formation, suggests that such a return is difficult. Yet Piaget seems to say that unless the adult can enter into the thinking of the child, he can have very little influence over it.

The problem the adult faces is perhaps most acute when the children he wishes to teach are still at an intuitive level of thought, still too caught up in the perceptions of the moment to be able to deal logically with the relationships between various aspects of their experience. To what extent are children in kindergarten, first, and, perhaps, even second grade thinking in these ways, and how is their ability to learn affected?

Thinking in the Classroom

The unexpected results of the exploratory study prompted a further examination of assumptions about young children's thinking in both the practice of early childhood education and the literature related to it.

Instances of wishful thinking about what might be going on in the minds of children were easy to find. But, there were also some realistic efforts to get behind the verbal façade. On the whole, it seems that neither the limitations the child has in his thinking, nor the special contribution this level of development may make to eventual adult thinking, are fully appreciated. One suspects that an inquiry related to the period of transition between "concrete" and "formal" thinking would yield similar results.

Few would deny that many five-year-olds come to kindergarten with a background of experience broader than that brought by their fathers and mothers twenty years ago. Undoubtedly, they have traveled more miles, whether by car or plane. They have had the stimulation of television and probably of children's records and books. It is likely that their vocabularies are larger. Certainly, the information they have available concerns a somewhat different variety of things from those their parents knew about. Does this mean that the beginning school child of the 1960s has reached a level where he is able to think more logically, to deal with more complex relationships than his parents were? Can he cope more readily with the abstract symbols involved in reading? Will he move more directly to computation in arithmetic? Are space rockets and dinosaurs more appropriate for his science curriculum than the geography of his neighborhood and the care of rabbits and turtles? Must his social studies center around the "community helpers," or can he begin to understand the structures of laws, taxation, and administration that supports the fireman and the policeman?

One has only to eavesdrop for awhile on the spontaneous conversations of any group of five- or six-year-olds to recognize that many if not all of them are keenly alert to pictures and their captions, whether in books, magazines, or TV commercials. They recognize a variety of signs. They handle nickels and dimes and quarters as they buy lollipops and Good Humors. They talk about planets and satellites, and they refer to historic and even prehistoric events. They know something about income taxes and sales taxes. Their teachers say that they are forming concepts. But what kinds of concepts? What kinds of understandings lie behind their glibness? Are their "concepts" stable enough so that they can be related to one another, classified, compared? Or are the responses the teacher labels "concepts" still pretty much names or labels for personal experience?

Recently, several kindergarten teachers, who had been introduced to Piaget's theory that children of five or six are likely to be in a transitional state between intuitive and operational thought, attempted to gather evidence about the kinds of thinking their children revealed. Coming from privileged homes, these youngsters were verbally facile, competent in managing most of their own affairs, and generally alert to their environment.

At the beginning of the kindergarten year, all in one group of eighteen children were able to count, some of them to one thousand. Yet, the teacher discovered none of them had any stable notion of numbers beyond three. Asked to select four pebbles to match those held by the teacher, they scooped up as many as twelve. Only one child was ingenious enough to count off the number the teacher had with her own four fingers, and then apply the same four fingers to her pile of pebbles.

In the same group, a highly verbal youngster demonstrated how extensively his thinking was dominated by his perception when he attempted an explanation of the reason certain objects stayed on the flannel board when others did not. He volunteered the notion that the material on the board was rough and that the material on the back of the pictured objects was also rough. Not misled by his apparent logic, the teacher picked up a piece of paper and inquired as to whether he thought it would stick to the board. The child replied that it would not because it was "round," whereas the other objects were not.

In another group, almost at the end of the year, the children were confronted with the problem of building a larger enclosure for some chickens they had received at Easter. Using blocks, they constructed a building almost as tall as they were. Gradually, the realization that they could not get the chickens out of the enclosure dawned on them. But for some time none of them were able to fathom the relationship between their height and the depth of the enclosure. They summoned their teacher, and when she could not reach into it either, advised her to get a stool to stand on. She did so, but, of course, to no avail. Still unsatisfied, they asked her to get a step ladder and remained baffled by the results.

Concepts as Conceptions

Clearly, all of these children were still thinking largely on a perceptual level. Although their teachers might say that they were developing concepts of number, of causality, and of height, none of them had really gone (at least in these examples) beyond a stage of naming certain aspects of their own experience. They had labels for experiences such as "four," "rough," "round," "deep," "tall," "high"; but they were unable to relate or compare the properties they could describe.

One reason for confusion here lies in the fact that the term "concept" is used in quite different ways by the teacher, the psychologist, and the person representing a particular discipline such as mathematics or physics. The teacher thinks of a concept as something that she wants children to learn. The psychologist often regards a concept as a system of related meanings held by an individual. In contrast, the mathematician or the physicist views concepts as integral parts of the logical structure of a particular discipline. He is not concerned about *personal* meanings; his attention is concentrated on those common or agreed-upon meanings which make possible scientific communication.

Failure to distinguish adequately between *concepts* as "abstractable, public, essential forms" and *conceptions* as "individual mental images and symbols"[6] leads to inevitable confusion. In recent years, psychologists and others have tried to show teachers how importantly the array of meanings a child brings to a particular problem influences his solutions of it. Accordingly, curriculum has emphasized the provision of "meaningful experience." Sometimes, however, educators lose sight of the fact that for the solution of certain problems, the application of meanings other than those that are public and abstract is a hindrance to efficient solution. There comes a time when the concrete is no longer enriching. In mathematics, for example, the child cannot indefinitely perform calculations with counters, beads, and so on. Numbers and their relationships must eventually be dealt with abstractly. In physics, the notions that some objects float and others sink, followed by the awareness that objects of equivalent size may have different weights, must eventually be replaced with the abstract idea of specific gravity as a quantifiable relationship.

If teachers at all levels of education could understand the kinds of thinking demanded by the material they present to their students and recognize whether or not the students are coping with it as anticipated, much time and effort might be saved. The kindergarten teacher, for example, would not be satisfied that the children had arrived at any particular generalizations about transportation merely because they had all looked and talked about pictures of trains and airplanes. The elementary school teacher would rely more on the children's demonstration of their understandings than on their comments. Teachers of algebra and geometry would check for evidence of ability to deal with abstraction before proceeding to teach further abstractions.

Teaching Concepts

Inhelder has suggested that,

> . . . it might . . . be interesting to devote the first two years of school to a series of exercises in manipulating, classifying, and ordering objects in ways that highlight basic operations of logical addition, multiplication, inclusion, serial ordering, and the like. For surely these logical operations are the basis of more specific operations and concepts of all mathematics and science. It may indeed be the case that such an early science and mathematics "pre-curriculum" might go a long way toward building up in the child the kind of intuitive and more inductive understanding that could be given embodiment later in formal courses in mathematics and science. The effect of such an approach would be, we think, to put more continuity into science and mathematics and also to give the child a much better and firmer comprehension of the concepts which, unless he has this early foundation, he will mouth later without being able to use them in any effective way.[7]

The crucial question, perhaps, is whether it is possible to provide experiences for young children that involve more than memorization, or the automatic repetition of the correct response. Inhelder's use of the term "exercise" does not do justice to the active inquiry the child has to bring to problems like those represented in Piaget's demonstrations, nor does it adequately represent the opportunities available to the child for learning from his own mistakes.

Inhelder's proposal also implies a formality of approach that seems incompatible with active, energetic American first and second graders. However, the experience she envisions could be made an inherent part of any program concerned with the adequacy of children's thinking. Isaacs[8] has suggested, for example, that the planning, constructing, and building, and the opportunities for learning by error that typify the modern infant school offer numerous possibilities for the intuitive child to develop toward an operational mode of thinking.

In the long run, the important contributions of the kindergarten and possibly even the first grade to later intellectual development may lie as much in the nurture of the normal child's curiosity and zest for learning as in the early exercise of incipient logical thinking. The encouragement of keen observation, furtherance of the awareness of the properties and the actions of the objects that make up his world, and the development of a vocabulary adequate to describing them, all appear to be appropriate educational goals. Indeed, if the children in the exploratory study, particularly those coming from lower socio-economic backgrounds, provide a good example, such goals may sometimes take priority over the early promotion of "concrete operations."

Thinking and Emotion

Surely the present, possibly belated, swing of the educational pendulum towards a re-emphasis on the school's responsibility for intellectual development carries with it all that is currently known about children. But some individuals who are concerned with schools are prone to overlook much that is known. They think that strict concentration on the intellectual or the academic aspects of education will obviate most if not all, of the problems that have beset the schools in recent years. They are either unconcerned with or ignore the emotional aspects of children's thinking. In contrast, another group of individuals are alarmed at the present emphasis on the intellectual. They assume that such emphasis *necessarily* implies a rejection of the emotional. Both groups seem to be thinking more wishfully than realistically.

It is of course possible to look at the outcomes of cognitive processes, the materials mastered, or the problems solved, as something apart from the motives involved in the individual's thinking. Piaget takes note of this when he says that cognitive "structures" are unaffected by affect; but he notes at the same time that there is no cognitive mech-anism without its emotional element and, conversely, no state of pure emotion without its cognitive element.[9] Feelings of success or failure may influence a child's solution of a mathematical problem, but his addition can still be viewed as either right or wrong.

Despite Piaget's insistence on the constant interaction between emo-tions and intellect, his studies, with the possible exception of his in-vestigations of the thinking of the very young child, do not seem to have exploited the relationship very fruitfully. He indicates, for example, that under conditions of stress a child regresses to an earlier level of thinking. But he gives little attention to the implications of optimal motivation either for a given level of development or for the facilita-tion of transition from one level to another.

Work with children with learning difficulties indicates how emotion can distort thinking. Underachieving ten- and eleven-year-olds, who, according to Piaget's theory, should be able to function logically, are often unable to understand the problems, much less cope with them in the way that other youngsters of their age do. Like preschool children, they are too bound to their immediate perceptions to deal effectively with any complex relationships. Their perceptions, in turn, seem dominated by fears and anxieties, preventing their attainment of a more mature level of cognitive development.

If unresolved emotional conflict at one level of development may permeate thinking at a later level, what are the more usual contribu-tions of one level to the next? Piaget's theory accounts for the emergence, stage by stage, of the ability to use logical abstractions. But this repre-sents only one area of cognitive functioning. It does not account, for instance, for critical and creative thinking. Drawing on imagination and intuition, these may be as firmly rooted in the early childhood period as the ability to think operationally seems to be in the years from seven or eight onward.

It is perhaps more than coincidence that the developmental stage labeled "intuitive" by Piaget is seen as a period of developing initiative and "power testing" by psychoanalytic ego psychologists. Not yet under-standing which aspects of his environment are likely to remain constant and which will change momentarily, the young child lives, at least for the time, in a world of many possibilities. Thus, he is often much more inclined to experiment and try than is the older youngster, who knows, for example, that water does not stay in a sieve or that a cake of sand inevitably falls apart. However limited they may be in handling complex relationships, children in the "intuitive" stage are probably as apt in perceiving analogies as they will ever be. If such ability could be nur-tured, it should contribute importantly to later insight and cognitive inventiveness.

Similarly, Piaget's period of concrete operational thought is paralleled in psychoanalytic theory by a period of achievement and mastery.

Provided the preceding period has been resolved in such a way that the child is emotionally free to tackle new learnings with zest, he relishes acquiring new skills and knowledge. His thinking at this stage may be less ebullient than at the earlier level, but he is acquiring better ability to direct it and to check its outcomes. Thus, he is building an important resource for adolescence, a period that will confront him with new kinds of problems, both emotional and intellectual.

Thought and Personhood

When thinking, whether logical or intuitive, is thus viewed as an aspect of the developing personality, motivated in the same ways as other kinds of behavior, the fallacy of a belief that concentration on the outcomes of thinking can free the school from concern with personality development seems clear. The mind has its entity in the person. To comprehend a child's mind adequately is to know him and those who are like him. It is to know how he views the world and what is meaningful to him; and good teaching requires that he then be offered the means and the challenge to build further meanings. As more is known about the nature of thinking and the processes of cognitive development, it is clear that the teacher can aid and abet the student's thinking more effectively. But it is still possible to overestimate, perhaps wishfully, the extent of his influence.

The Prophet may yet be sustained. Speaking of children he says, "They have their own thoughts." When the teacher is indeed wise he does not bid his students enter the house of his wisdom but, rather, leads them to the "threshold of their own minds."[10]

References

1. Millie Almy, *Young Children's Thinking About Natural Phenomena.* Interim Report to Horace Mann Lincoln Institute of School Experimentation (New York: Teachers College, Columbia University, 1960).

2. J. Piaget and Barbel Inhelder, *The Growth of Logical Thinking from Childhood to Adolescence* (New York: Basic Books, 1958).

3. L. Welch, "A Behavorist Explanation of Concept Formation," *Journal of Genetic Psychology*, 41 (1947), pp. 201–202.

4. Suzanne Reichard, M. Schneider, and D. Rapaport, "The Development of Concept Formation in Children," *American Journal of Orthopsychiatry*, 14 (1944), pp. 152–162.

5. H. Werner, *Comparative Psychology of Mental Development* (Chicago: Follet, 1948).

6. Susanne K. Langer, *An Introduction to Symbolic Logic* (New York: Dover Publications, 1953).

7. B. Inhelder, J. S. Bruner, *The Process of Education* (Cambridge, Mass.: Harvard University Press, 1960), p. 46.

8. N. Isaacs, *Piaget's Work and Progressive Education* (Bulletin, National Froebel Foundation, 1955).

9. J. Piaget, *Les Relations entre l'Affectivité et l'Intelligence dans le Developpement Mental de l'Enfant* (Paris: Centre de Documentation Universitaire, 1954).

10. K. Gibran, *The Prophet* (New York: Alfred A. Knopf, 1958).

7 Children's Conception of Reality: Some Implications for Education

Charles D. Smock

The following is a more recent (1968) discussion of the insights that Piaget's work holds for early childhood education. Smock examines three of the basic assumptions that derive from current research, and moves to an elaboration of some of Piaget's central ideas on intellectual development. He concludes with an interesting set of new principles which he dubs the three T's.

I would not go so far as many experts in the area, but I do realize the tremendous role that education must play in the challenges that confront our society and the world today. Not only are we confronted with the challenge and magnificance of a knowledge explosion in many areas, but there is currently an increased awareness of the role that education *must* play in creating truly equal educational opportunities for all people, at home and abroad. The transformation our society is undergoing, we hope, will be directed on such a course that our traditional values and beliefs concerning the nature of human existence will be maintained.

These challenges make educational theory and practice the most exciting of all time. Certainly some of the most significant advances have been in the technological sector; e.g., the teaching machine. However, in my opinion, we have recently devoted relatively too much time to teaching machines and too little to the characteristics of our "learning machines"; that is, to the children who are the targets for educational innovation.

Fortunately, recent theoretical and research emphasis, particularly that of the Swiss psychologist Piaget, has begun to draw appropriate attention to the child once more.

During the past decade, psychologists have discovered or rediscovered three important aspects of the early phases of child development that are of central importance for education:

1. The tremendous plasticity of the human organism: These discoveries range from the fact that infants are capable of form discrimination within the first few days of life,[1] to that of the tremendous effects of the structure of the environmental factors impinging on the infant,

Reprinted with permission from *Journal of Speech and Development in Education*, Vol. 1, No. 3, Spring 1968, Athens, Georgia. Charles Smock is affiliated with the University of Georgia.

to intellectual growth, and to the realization that relatively young children can learn to read.

2. The effects of early stimulation and early environmental systems on infant and early child development are tremendously complex. Some of these early experiences appear highly persistant, but many are not. The Head Start program is an excellent example. We now know a short period of intervention, whether it be for three months or for a full year, is not likely to have lasting effects on the child's ultimate intellectual level. In fact, the "follow-through" and "upward bound" programs are insufficient as well. We also need programs of adult education that might be entitled "stay on top" and "operation retread."

Further, the possible delayed effects of many early experiences have been curiously ignored. The most dramatic example of this is derived from the work of Harlow[2] on the development of affective systems in mammals. The initial experiments indicated no undesirable consequences of substituting a piece of velvet for a biological mother during infancy. Follow-up studies, however, indicated behavior consistant with what clinicians might call a severe form of psychopathology. As adolescents and adults, the chimpanzees did not establish social emotional relations with other members of their species. While such procedures, at the human level, might help solve the population explosion, I'm quite sure that other desirable goals of society would be lost. In any case, it is important to approach all of these problems of early stimulation with the understanding that hardly anything is known about the *long term effects* of such experiential innovations.

3. The third major discovery (or more correctly I should say rediscovery) of recent years is that children have a mode of reasoning that characterizes their understanding of reality that is different from that of adults. To understand the child's conception of reality is the necessary ingredient for truly innovational education strategy. Until we do understand the principles underlying child thought, our innovations will not persist, will be neglected and misinterpreted and probably misused if used at all. Such has been the fate of most important educational innovations in the past.

The most dramatic of yesterday's discoveries about the child's world was the Freudian one that the child has an emotional life of fantasy more or less secret and inaccessible. Perhaps of equal or even more importance, however, was the discovery of people like John Dewey and G. Stanley Hall that a child has an intellectual life of his own. The idea was not entirely new. At the turn of the century, for example, Darwin had been concerned with early intellectual development, but previous educational thought had defined the child largely as a small replica of the adult. That is, the child differed from the adult mainly in terms of his lack of what he is not rather than what he is in terms of ignorance, incompetence and probably original sin.

Progressive education arose in opposition to these notions of the child as an unformed adult. In its initial stages, and certainly as it was formulated, it proposed that the objective of education was the cultivation and stimulation of the child's world so that the child would grow into an adult with an adult's understanding of his world in reality. Unfortunately the careful thought and research which would give substance to this vision has been very slow in coming. And, I might add, progressive education in its original form was never really tried in the public schools despite the fact it has become the whipping boy for all that is wrong in our society today. It did gain some foothold in preschool education but there it became transformed into an educational strategy that can be summed up by "be patient, be nice, don't push, let the child play."

Emerging from a number of social forces (e.g. Sputnik) and new theoretical and research knowledge, we have recently been confronted with a contrasting point of view. A number of psychologists and educators are proposing that a child can be taught anything if only the right gimmicks, the right teaching techniques, and the "right" theory of learning are used.[4] Such a position is embarrassing to me as a child psychologist and acceptance of it should be embarrassing to any educator. While some outstanding success and significant discoveries have been achieved by this approach, I anticipate little lasting good to come from uncritical acceptance of such a position. To anticipate my conclusion, I believe that no matter how clever our programs are for the teaching of specific skills such as reading at the sensory motor level (i.e., during the first three years), they are secondary to the educational goals of general cognitive stimulation related to the natural world view and thought of the young child. Educational approaches designed to be consistent with this latter view will neither make the absurd mistake of separating the emotional-social development from the child's intellectual development nor ignore the importance of constructing an educational environment that instills a continuing desire to learn and particularly one that lasts beyond the second or third grade.

To return to my main theme. To give substance to the notion that a child has his own view of reality after so many years, we rely heavily on the forty years of child study by Jean Piaget. In innumerable books and research reports he and his colleagues have presented results of interviews, observations and experiments on young children dealing with the stages in the child's development of concepts of reality including space, time, number, logic, causality, and so on.

On the basis of these data Piaget concluded that a radical change occurs in the child's modes of reasoning about at age three and again about age five or six. According to his theory the thinking or reasoning of the preschool child has a logic of his own, a logic that is quite different from the adult rather than being simply a weaker form of an adult logic or a reflection of ignorance of adult concepts.

Although American psychologists rejected Piaget's observations and conclusions for a number of years because of methodological inexactitude, today psychologists and educators are taking a new and very close look at his ideas, methods, and findings. In fact, it is not too strong to say he is the dominant force in child psychology and education today. Regardless of the outcome of attempts to verify his findings and the conformation or disconformation of his theory, the strategy he has proposed in the study of cognitive development will at least, if followed, finally give substance to the idea that the child's world is different from that of the adult. Most specifically he emphasizes, and it cannot be overemphasized, that the child helps to build his own concepts of reality, the child participates in the construction of reality and will not accept the ready-made adult-imposed reality as his own.

Two aspects of children's reality concepts that are central to Piaget's thinking, albeit a limited aspect of his general theory, are: first, that children fail to make distinction between "subjective" and "objective" aspects of the world; and secondly, that in acquiring an "objective" view, or adult mode of reasoning, children move through an invariant sequence of cognitive structures that determine their learning characteristics. Both of these general ideas or working hypotheses are significant for educators and should be subjected to continual thought and analysis in terms of the various subject matter areas and goals of education.

The child's failure to differentiate subjective experiences from objective reality components of his experience pervades his behavior and thinking. A wide range of illustrative examples are available from current and past researches. Let's take first what may appear to be an irrelevant example. We all realize that children find it difficult, at times, to separate day-dreams or night-dreams from real happenings. Piaget insists we should not dismiss the child's interpretation of his dream experience as due to the inadequacy of the child's mind but rather as a product of the inherent logic of the child's thought processes and its consequent "realism" characteristic.[6] One aspect of realism is confusion of thoughts with things and things with that for which symbols stand. Children between ages two and three often seem to react to dreams, to pictures and toys of animals, and objects as though they were really the animals they represented. Perhaps you have had the experience of a young son or daughter who broke into tears as you cut the bunny off the Easter cake or who became quite upset that you were unwilling to accept his dream experience as real. These everyday examples of children's reactions to dreams are, then, quite relevant to what happens in other areas of their early learnings. The failure to differentiate subjective and objective realm components is characteristic of a child's adaptations to his environment including the educational environment and the concepts we attempt to teach him.

One of the major results of the differentiation of subjective and objective is the construction of a world of permanent and unchanging objects and events systems. The infant under eight to ten months does not have a conception of the permanent object when he is reaching toward a bright toy, and if [it is] covered with a handkerchief, he stops reaching. The toy no longer exists for him. By one-and-one-half he knows objects permanently exist but he cannot see them; however, it is not until the age of six or seven that he begins to view physical dimensions and identity as unchangeable things that only appear to vary under different conditions.

For example, we could take a five-year-old from a kindergarten and seat her in front of the table with two brightly colored necklaces laying side by side. The necklaces are of equal length and their ends are neatly aligned. The child is told to pretend the *blue* one is "hers" and the *red* one is "mine" and our problem is to decide which necklace is longer. The little girl will probably be a little puzzled by the question since she replies with conviction that both necklaces are the "same length." I pick up one necklace and make a circle of it and ask her to tell me which necklace is "longer" or is mine still as "long as yours." The little girl stretches her arms to illustrate length and beams, "Mine is the longest. You made yours into a ring and mine is all this long."

Or a young child might be presented with two boards about two feet square, covered with green cloth. On each board there are several barns and a cow. The child is asked to pretend this is a countryside and to indicate which cow has the more grass to eat. Interestingly enough, but consistent with our earlier statements, when the barns on both fields are solidly packed in one corner the child answers "the cows have the same amount to eat in each field." However, if we spread the barns on one field into various locations and leave the barns on the other field grouped together, she then indicates the cow on the field with the barns in various locations has less to eat than on that field where the barns are closely grouped.[7]

Examination of these kinds of ideas, including the child's conception of length, substance, and space, led Piaget to discover the child's thought during this so-called prelogical stage is not due to the child being illogical in the adult sense but to the fact he places too much trust in appearances: i.e., the child tends to respond to the perceptual and subjective elements of the situation. By the time the child is six or seven, however, she will know the length of a string of beads is conserved: that is the length will not change even if its "longness" disappears when it's ends are joined in a circle. The basic question is how does she gain the concept of length as a dimension so that the perceptual cues presented by the changes in shape are ignored. Today most psychologists, along with Piaget, see that the child's mind is internally consistent and yet externally illogical, a kind of Alice in Wonderland where lengths, widths, weights, distances have as much consistency and constancy as Silly Putty.[8]

This new picture has aroused widespread debates among psychologists and educators. It raises a host of questions about the understanding of mental processes in general and the education of young children in particular. For example, is intellectual development pre-set, as in the child's physical growth, or can it be speeded up by experience through teaching? Does the child develop through a series of specific stages on his way to adult reasoning? What are the long range consequences of attempts to speed up the child's acquisition of adult forms of reasoning? Piaget's theory and research, and research of many American psychologists, has begun to give us some tentative answers. By six or seven, children have developed the idea of logical necessity in the adult sense within a restricted range of their experience. This acquisition is manifested through the "conservation" of length and area, as mentioned above, as well as a number of other concepts pertaining to the physical world. For example, at about age six or seven the number of elements in a collection remains unchanged regardless of how the elements are displaced or arranged. Conservation of substance and length occurs at about age seven or eight and weight and volume at ten to fourteen years of age. (These ages for the various acquisitions of the conservation concepts are, of course, only gross averages but do not in any way detract from Piaget's major conclusion that the attainment of conservation points to the formation of a new stage in the child's mental development.) Thus, most psychologists have been convinced these phenomenon represent qualitative changes in the child's mode of reasoning and that the phenomena Piaget describes are stable and accurate descriptions of cognitive development processes.

A second aspect of Piaget's position has not been accepted so readily, however. He maintains that changes in thought processes are largely spontaneous and occur independently of teaching or specifically directed experiences. The controversy centers on two basic questions. (1) Can the child's logic, as indicated by the conservation acquisitions, be explained as resulting from qualitatively different modes of reasoning characteristic of the preoperational stage *or* is it merely the result of a naive trust in, and strong tendency to respond to, perceptual aspects of the situation? (2) Does the transformation from prelogical to logical modes of reasoning represent an *invariant order or sequence of development?* The answer to the first question now is fairly clear, in my opinion: the child's performance on the conservation task is not due to merely a naive trust in perceptual cues nor to inadequate development of language facility.

The answer to the second question must be more tentative but the evidence to date indicates that some sort of ordering or developmental sequencing is most probable. Cultural and environmental factors, or innate capabilities, may make one child or group of children reach a given stage of development earlier than another, but all children appear to go through the same order of modes of reasoning regardless of environmental structure or amount of direct teaching. It would appear the differentiation of the subjective from the objective world is a major developmental transformation (or task, if you wish) requiring considerable experience, time, and active participation of the child. Further, children appear to move through a series of qualitatively different modes of reasoning from birth through adolescence before there is adequate achievement of this distinction in a large number of areas.

We should mention one other factor. Besides the issues we've discussed so far, there is one major problem which must be faced before we can say a young child has a cognitively different experience of reality than the adult. The child's acceptance of the subjective as real may *not* be simply verbal or cultural ignorance but could be due to the child being more swayed by his wishes and fears than are adults. This is the explanation favored by psycholoanalytic-oriented psychologists. The Freudian view sees the young child as dominated by the pleasure principle. Without denying that desires, wishes and fears are reflected in many problem-solving tasks, the explanation is inadequate. We find children's reality attitudes are highly consistent whether situations involve fears or wishes concerning quite neutral topics. The consistency across many levels of "emotional" involvement cannot be explained by the child's acceptance of "unreality" if it were only a product of wishes and fears.

The general conclusion to be drawn from recent research is largely confirmatory of Piaget's view that young children's mode of thinking and experience of reality are different than the adults and that these differences are not due to the children's ignorance, or to lack of teaching, or to lack of control over wishes and fears. If the young child's sense of reality is different than the adults, should we exploit this difference by stimulating the child's exploration of the world he will later consider unreal or should we stimulate his development of a more mature sense of reality? Often the young child's openness to the world of magic and [the] unreal is considered a unique capacity for imagination in creativity. Preschool could be considered as fundamentally the best time for such exploration through play. At the other extreme is the view the child should be taught objective skills (the three R's) and knowledge as soon as possible.

Neither of the above views takes into account that the preschool orientation to reality is a developmental stage which needs to be intergrated with later stages of development. To put off reality until elementary school is only to divorce the child's preschool world of the subjective from the elementary school child's world of the more objective.[9]

To focus during early cognitive development on training for specific skills is to teach the child a body of information whose meaning to the child is full of subjective distortions. The child may invest these early verbal and number skills with magical meanings which interfere with later learning and, more important, may create the aversion to self-motivated learning we note so much of in adults and older children.

The controversy surrounding these issues has proved a healthy stimulant for educational innovation. Too often, however, the proponents of each position have taken an "all or none" stance and thus attracted non-thinking disciples to their particular fold. Education is devoted to multiple goals and I would like to see educators and psychologists continue to explore the multiple possibilities of generating optimal educational strategies for educating young children. Neither Piaget, nor other modern theorists, offers specifics; but there are many significant and far ranging issues and problems to be solved that are not apparent in the polemics of the dogmatic "innovators." More innovations, more experimental approaches, more ideas—these we need from all educators whether teachers, curriculum advisors, or administrators.

The dogma of the three R's needs to be replaced with a new set of principles (probably to become dogma in its own good time) which we might call the three T's: Titillation, Time and Tools. These terms describe an orientation and educational strategy that are independent of particular subject matter area. But they are, in my mind, three indispensible aspects of learning at any stage of development and are of particular importance in early childhood education. Taken together they can provide the kind of environmental-educational situation that promotes not only intellectual growth but the total organismic development of the child.

Titillation refers to a set of environmental conditions in which the teacher and curriculum materials together represent an educational strategy capitalizing on the particular prior experience and current cognitive development of children. The experiments in English schools have clearly demonstrated that if children are provided a sufficiently informal setting and broad range of educational activities, they will select the appropriate activities in much the same way that free selection of food results in children meeting appropriate nutrient requirements. Certainly we can force children to learn many kinds of things and have done so often. The consequences of such forcing techniques however have been generally undesirable, resulting in lethargy, lack of curiosity, and a continual need to force children to learn things by offering external and extrinsic rewards such as grades, money, and/or honors. Once again it is time that educators at all levels begin to recognize a dualism with respect to motivation: that is the difference between intrinsic and extrinsic motivation.[10] Children are always motivated to learn where the problems with which they are confronted represent areas designed to capitalize upon the adaptive requirements and capacities of the child at that particular stage of development. We too often confound the problem of motivating children by either failing to match the task with his current cognitive capacities or fail to recognize that many skills and much knowledge can be taught through many different media. We too often segregate subject matter into neat little compartments that fit our conception of reality, or that of our teachers, and fail to recognize that children can learn much about measuring or quantitative concepts while engaging in what we might term "art." Further, we are so fascinated by our own conversation and voice that we over-emphasize the value of verbal learning when much of the same material could be learned much more readily, easily and with more permanent effects where we allow the child to participate in a concrete way and with concrete materials in solving problems requiring the same skills.

Time refers to two aspects of the educational problem: first, the timing of educational experiences; and secondly, the necessity for recognizing variation in amount of time children require to acquire certain skills or knowledge. The timing of educational experiences must be geared to the characteristics of the child (of which I have emphasized so much in this paper); and secondly, it may involve a value decision. I know neither evidence nor reasons, from the point of view of our current knowledge of learning capacities of children, why children cannot be taught to read during preschool, for example. Whether or not such early skill learning might have later undesirable side effects is yet to be determined. Nor do we know for sure that it has all the positive side effects that have been so emphasized. But certainly the time spent in such training should not deprive the child of opportunities for other kinds of acquisitions equally important for later learning whether they be in terms of a specific knowledge and skills or related to the personal-social characteristics that are desirable from the point of view of society. (Or the extent or persistence of motivation to learn.)

Time is also important with respect to variation in children's ability to solve particular problems. There is probably no ideal variation of optimum spacing of a particular task with respect to the amount of time necessary to all children to learn. The over-emphasis on clock hours and definite temporal end-points for "education" is as detrimental to the preschool child's cognitive growth as it is to that of the graduate student.

Finally, *tools* refer to the basic skills that are anticipatory of the child's adaptive requirements during later years. In later childhood and adulthood the child is confronted with complicated technical and cognitive problems as well as social, moral and political ones. Each child needs a certain set of specific *tools* such as reading and mathematics to be a constructive citizen and to live a good life. People may vary as to what these basic skills or *tools* might be, but I am sure we would all agree that reading, mathematics, logic and understanding of social interaction dynamics are among the most important ones. Each of these, however, can be taught with an infinite variety of subject matter content. It is very difficult to separate economics from history or history from art or art from many other contents. The important thing is to provide a variety of possible contents which will tap the variety of interests, experiential backgrounds and cognitive level of the child. But in any case the world of the child and the natural processes of his development to adulthood are such that an educational strategy is demanded which places appropriate emphasis upon *titillation, time,* and *tools.*

A final comment is, perhaps, in order. The new discoveries referred to earlier (relatively high-level capacity of young infants, plasticity of the human organism during early development, and the different modes of reasoning during early childhood) indicate the potentiality for accelerating cognitive development of children in diverse ways. Moving all or some of the three R's, and other subjects, to the preschool level need not distress us, nor is it inconsistent with the broad generalizations to be drawn from the current theory and research on cognitive development. Such decisions, however, need to be viewed in the proper perspective of the multiple *goals of education* and more essentially, the *nature of the thought process* during the early stages of development.

References

1. R. L. Frantz, "Pattern Vision in New-born Infants," *Science,* 140 (1963), pp. 296–297.

2. H. Harlow and R. R. Zimmerman, "Affection in the Infant Monkey," *Science,* 130 (1959), pp. 421–423.

3. J. Piaget, *Construction of Reality in the Child* (New York: Basic Books, 1954).

4. J. S. Bruner, *Toward a Theory of Intuition* (Cambridge: Harvard University Press, 1966); J. S. Bruner *et al., Studies in Cognitive Growth* (New York: Wiley & Sons, Inc., 1966).

5. B. Inhelder, C. D. Smock, and M. and H. Sinclair, "Cognitive Development: Comments on Bruner's Piagetism

Theory," *American Psychologist,* 21 (1966), pp. 160–164.

6. Piaget, *Construction of Reality.*

7. J. Piaget, *Psychology of Intelligence* (London: Routledge and Kegen Paul, 1947).

8. See Joachim F. Wohlwill, "The Mystery of the Prelogical Child," *Psychology Today.*

9. Lawrence Kohlberg, "Cognitive Stages in Preschool Education," *Human Development* (1966), pp. 5–17.

10. C. D. Smock and B. G. Holt, "Children's Reactions to Novelty: An Experimental Study of 'Curiosity Motivation,'" *Child Development,* 33 (1962), pp. 631–642.

8 The Role of Play

Barbara Biber

The articles which follow were published separately but are here pre-
sented together in a specially adapted version. Section I, popular in
tone, grew out of a talk to a parent audience almost twenty years ago.
It reveals and develops a viewpoint which is also present in Section II,
the latter describing play within the broader context of developmental
theory.

Reader please note: our bias concerning the importance of play to the
growth process inspires us to include this material not only in Part II
on Growth and Development, but specifically within the section on
Intellectual and Motivational Development.

I. Play as a Growth Process

What do we have in mind when we think of play? What do
children do when they play? Children's play has the quality of intense,
absorbing experience, a bit of life lived richly and fully. There is zest
and wonder and drama and a special kind of immediacy that is without
thought for the passing of time. There is nothing to be accomplished, no
sense of what is right or wrong to check the flow of spontaneity, no
direction to follow. Whatever is at hand can become the suitable materials for play. The essence of the play experience is subjective, something within the child that may not necessarily become obvious to the
one who observes the course or the form of his activity.

Play as an activity may take any one of numberless forms. It may be
just physical activity, an overflow of energy, of exuberance. Besides
running, skipping, hopping, children like to slide, seesaw and swing.
Although these play experiences require a degree of patterning in coordination, they belong among the natural playful uses which a child
makes of his body. If his play is as free as his energy is boundless, he is
likely to embroider the basic patterns: he soon finds it more fun to
hop on one foot, to slide down on his belly instead of his bottom, to
swing standing up.

Playing may be something quite different from the lively expression

Play as Growth Process, by Barbara Biber, Ph.D., reprinted with permission from *Vassar*
Alumnae Magazine XXXVII, 2, 1951. Reissued 1959, 1963, 1965.
The section on *Synthesis* is excerpted sections of a chapter from a paper by Barbara
Biber entitled "A Learning-Teaching Paradigm Integrating Intellectual and Affective
Processes." Reprinted from Eli M. Bower and William G. Hollister (eds.), *Behavioral*
Science Frontiers in Education. (New York: Wiley, 1967) by permission from the
publisher.
Barbara Biber is a Distinguished Research Scholar at the Bank Street College in New
York City.

of physical energies. It may take quite delicate forms such as playing with sounds and words. The chanting of younger children, the nonsense rhyming of the older ones are play forms.

The child is playing when, with his hands, he impresses himself on things around him. He pounds the clay and smears the paint. He creates with blocks even when he is only stacking them high or lining them up low. He makes the mud take shape. He fits things together and takes them apart. There is pleasure and satisfaction in what one's hands can make of the physical world and the child, in his playful remaking of the world around him, lays the cornerstone of his feeling about himself in relation to that world.

Now we come to the world of play that is most challenging and enticing: dramatic play. Here the child can take flight. He needs no longer be a child. He can make himself over and be a wolf or an engineer or a mother or a baby who is crying. He can re-create the world not only as he really experiences it but even in the strange aspects that symbolize some of his deepest wishes and fears. It is this kind of play— or rather the values that it has for growth—that I would like to talk about most today.

What do play experiences do for child growth? If a child can have a really full wholesome experience with play, he will be having the most wholesome kind of fun that a child can have. For a child to have fun is basic to his future happiness. His early childhood play may become the basic substance out of which he lays down one of his life patterns, namely, not only that one can *have* fun but that one can *create* fun. Most of us as adults enjoy only a watered-down manufactured kind of fun—going to the movies, shopping, listening to a concert, or seeing a baseball game and do not feel secure that some of the deepest resources for happiness lie within ourselves, free of a price of admission. This is one of these securities that compose a positive attitude toward life, in general.

In dramatic play, children also find a sense of confidence in their own impulses. There are no directions to follow, no rules to stick to. Whatever they do will be good and right. Wherever their impulses lead them, that is the way to follow. This is the freedom children should have in their play, an absence of boundaries and prescriptions that we cannot grant them outside of their play lives.

Another important by-product of play is the feeling of strength it yields to the child, a relief from the feelings of powerlessness and helplessness that many children feel keenly as junior members of our well-ordered adult world. In play we give them an opportunity to counteract this powerlessness to a degree. It is the child's chance to lay the plans, to judge what is best, to create the sequence of events. Dramatic play is one of the basic ways in which children can try out their talents for structuring life. The fact that they deal with symbols rather than realities does not detract from the sense of mastery.

As you watch children playing, you see the ingredients of the child world spread out before you, differing in complexity and elaboration according to the level of maturity. When a two- or three-year-old plays train, he does so simply. The train goes. It makes sounds. Just a block and a child saying "choo" may be Johnnie's idea of a train but very soon he meets up with Mary who has been very much impressed with the odd way that people sit in trains, looking at each other's backs. To another child in the group a train is not a train unless it whistles. Soon, a composite train emerges: it goes, it says "Choo," it whistles intermittently, people sit in it one behind the other. Children, at all levels, pool their ideas in free dramatic play, expose each other to new impressions, stimulate each other to new wondering and questioning. Can we fail to recognize this process as learning? Can we neglect to notice that here is learning going on in a social atmosphere full of pleasure and delight? In re-living and freely dramatizing his experience the child is thinking at his own pace with other children. He is learning in the best possible way.

More than that, the ways of the world are becoming delicious to him. He is tasting and re-tasting life in his own terms and finding it full of delight and interest. He projects his own pattern of the world into the play and in so doing, brings the real world closer to himself. He is building the feeling that the world is his, to understand, to interpret, to puzzle about, to make over. For the future, we need citizens in whom these attitudes are deeply ingrained.

We would be seriously in error, however, were we to assume that all play of young children is clear and logical. Horses are more likely to eat lamb stew than hay and what starts out to be a boat often ends as a kitchen stove without any obviously clear transitions. Often when play violates the line of adult logic we can see that it has a special kind of coherence all its own—perhaps the coherence of an action rather than a thinking pattern. Playing dentist may take the form of sitting on a keg and whirling one's feet around because the wonderful dentist's chair is the outstanding recall for the child. Teeth and drills may be altogether omitted while the child accentuates through his play what impressed him most. It makes sense in child terms even though it may not to the adult who is told that the children are playing dentist when what meets the eye looks like a crowd of whirling Dervishes. To understand children's play we must loose our imaginations from the restrictions of adultness and the limitations of logic that is tied in within literalness and objective reality.

If free play is to yield these values in terms of children's growth needs, it requires a skilled guiding hand, especially where children are collected in groups as they are in nursery schools. There is a way of setting the stage and creating an atmosphere for spontaneous play. Most important in this atmosphere is the teacher's sensitive understanding of her own role. Sometimes the teacher needs to be ready to guide the play, especially among the fives, sixes and sevens, into channels that are beyond the needs of the nursery years. But she must guide only in terms of the children's growth needs. Her guidance may be in terms of her choice of stories, materials, trips, experiences. It may function through discussions. Without skillful guidance, a free play program for successive years can become stultified and disturbing to children.

One of the main problems with respect to play which we are working through as teachers is—How much shall the teacher get involved in the children's play? Shall she correct, suggest, contribute, participate? I don't have the answer, but I hope teachers will continue to think about and talk about this problem. We have left behind the stage of education in which the teacher was relegated to the background. We have still to discover what are the optimal points at which the teacher can step in, offering new material, or ideas to enrich the play. In our teacher training institutes we encourage teachers to have imagination and use it but if you teach this too well, the teachers themselves (and this goes for parents, too) will be expressing themselves in the play, and before you know it they will have taken away the play from the child. This, naturally, is closely related to teacher personality. Some people intuitively know when it is best to withdraw and take a passive role, when a new idea will not be an intrusion and when stimulation had best be indirect. It behooves us all as teachers to think: are we stimulating and developing the children by our active teaching or are we becoming so active that the children are overwhelmed and restricted by the flood of our bright ideas?

Day in, day out, we affect children's play by the things we provide for them to play with. We choose equipment and materials with care and thought and have accepted the premise that a good share of play materials should be of the "raw" variety—things like clay, blocks, paper, mud which the child can freely shape to his own purposes and upon which he can impress his own pattern. These are in contrast to the finished dolls and trains, trucks and doll dishes which come in finished form and are adapted, as established symbols, into the flow of the child's free play. One of the interesting questions in education today has to do with what balance shall be kept between raw and finished materials, recognizing that each kind serves a different function with respect to play and may meet varying needs of different individual children. This is an area for study and experimentation in which we have made only a fair beginning.

To return briefly to the point that children's play cannot always be understood from the vantage point of logic and realistic accuracy. The inner coherence of play is as often based on emotion as it is on logic or action. If it seems incomprehensible, rambling or slightly insane it is because we cannot read the deep emotional life of children, because we do not understand adequately how feeling can transform thought, at all ages.

We know that children are full of feeling—deep and good, hard and strong feeling. They get mad and glad with intensity. Their feelings are as quick, as volatile as they are deep. This vital aspect of their life experience needs outlet through play quite as much as their developing curiosities and their effervescent energies. Many of us who can accept play as a child's way of interpreting life intellectually, often stop short at allowing children full freedom in expressing the feeling aspects of their lives. Or else we make the error of thinking of emotional expression of this kind in terms of negative feeling, of avoiding repression of hostility and such. This, to be sure, is an important aspect of wholesome growth. The chance to express negative feeling through play can save the child considerable anguish. The dolls he is allowed to hit leave him more able to face his real life problems successfully.

But there is the positive aspect of a child's emotional life which should not be overlooked. Covering the doll lovingly with layers of blankets is as deep and important an experience as the smacking and the spanking. What we must remember through all of this is that the child does not necessarily play out what his actual experience has been. He may instead be playing out the residue of feeling which his experience has left with him —quite another dimension, psychologically. It has been possible only to indicate this latter point briefly.

Summing up, we can say that play serves two different growth needs in the early years—learning about the world by playing about it (realizing reality) and finding an outlet for complex and often conflicting emotions (wherein reality and logic are secondary). We, the adults, need to understand this process more deeply than we do and to continue to improve our techniques for providing experiences through play by means of which the child can freely express feeling and creatively master reality.

II. Synthesis

Goal

Anxiety about the deficiencies of education is not limited to those who have taken the initiative in revising method and subject matter in the interest of advancing the intellectual level of children. Psychologists and educators who have a special interest in creativity, both as a deepening personal process and as a requisite for a healthy society, have been working with equal energy and commitment on needed reorientation in educational practice and thinking.

In 1959, Guilford wrote "the preservation of our way of life and our future security depend upon our most important natural resources: our intellectual abilities and, more particularly, our creative abilities."[1] Torrance begins to close in on the image of the creative person:

> "It takes very little imagination to recognize that the future of our civilization—our very survival—depends upon the quality of the creative imag-

ination of our next generation. . . . Democracies collapse only when they fail to use intelligent, imaginative methods for solving problems. The kind of citizen here called for is a far cry from the model of a quiz-program champion of a few years ago, and he is also more than a 'well-rounded individual' . . ."[2]

Out of the prodigious amount of work and complex findings on creativity in recent years, certain themes appear concerning the relation between creativity and intellectual, motivational, and personality factors. Intellectual functioning is known to be infinitely complicated, multifaceted, having at least "three faces." Certain intellectual factors are considered to contribute directly to creative power, others less directly. The kind of thinking in which variety of response is produced, for example, and in which the thinker allows himself to go off in different directions, sometimes called "divergent thinking," appears to be important to creativity; this is also true for the kind of intellectual activity represented in "transformation," that is, changes of arrangement, organization, or meaning.[3] A long list of other intellectual manifestations—the tendency to toy with ideas, to see patterns in data, the capacity to be puzzled, to sense ambiguities, or to discriminate—have been associated with creative functioning through studies of "creative" individuals. On two points there seems to be general agreement. First, it is these aspects of intellectual functioning that have traditionally been neglected in education and, second, conventional measures, especially the IQ, are inadequate and incomplete measures of intelligence when its full complexity is taken into account. These studies have frequently led to suggestions for changes in education that would foster creativity. Actually, these suggested changes overlap greatly with the recommendations made by those concerned with raising the level of cognitive mastery. Their recommendations are to value self-initiated learning, to revise readiness concepts, to develop self-concept, to remove the constraints against questioning and exploration, and to shift away from an assumed dichotomy of work and play.

Still the question of creativity appears more complex than can be seen when its relation to intellectual functioning is mainly considered. From his studies of creativity in mature professional life, MacKinnon concludes ". . . we may have overestimated in our educational system the role of intelligence in creative achievement."[4] He advocates closer attention to nonintellectual factors "ultimately associated with creative talent," such as "openness to experience and especially to experience of one's inner life," "disposition to admit complexity and even disorder into their perceptions without being made anxious by the resulting chaos," and thus a preference for the "richness of the disordered to the stark barrenness of the simple."[5] Barron places his experimental work in a framework of psychoanalytic theory. Like MacKinnon, he sees the creative person as having a stronger impulse to render experience intelligible, to find order where none may be apparent. By his more dynamic view, he sees this disposition of the creative person to integrate diverse stimuli as supported in part by concomitant respect and contact with irrational elements in the person himself; he sees a general intimacy with nonrational processes leading up to a commitment and ability to effect complex personal synthesis.[6]

At this point concepts of creativity and ego-strength seem to share common ground. The idea that optimal psychological functioning is synonymous with a synthesis of processes—personal and impersonal, subjective and objective, rational and nonrational—has gained in general importance, especially in recent years, as criteria of positive mental health, of maturity, of ego-strength have been conceptualized as processes rather than as traits or behavior patterns. The application of this postulate to education and the learning process has had, however, very few articulate spokesmen; and unfortunately, this view of learning, in its full complexity, seems largely absent from the most prominent revisions of curriculum and teaching method. Gardner Murphy has argued against the contemporary trend to extrapolate thought processes from the impulsive and motivational life of the child, making specific reference to the role of the teacher:

> ". . . the nurture of rationality may perhaps lie in other efforts than the sheer encouragement of rational thought . . . the learner must not be deprived of the riches of his impulse life, and the teacher must be a quickener of that impulse life through which thought can grow, indeed a shaper and molder of impulse into the rationality which comes from a healthy craving for contact with reality . . . there is, moreover, within us a world of inner stimulation and challenge, an inner world of physiological response, of memories, of images, and of fantasies . . . the teacher who responds to this inner world can convey it just as she or he can respond to the outer world . . . these two forms of motivation—the impulse to know and the impulse to gratify the inner needs—are two aspects of one reality. The cognitive need is as commanding and constraining, and at the same time as fulfilling, as any realization of the more primitive organic needs."[7]

It is the concept of synthesis of inner and outer worlds, of rational and nonrational processes, elaborated in studies of creative functioning, that is closely related to the goal of *supporting the synthesis of learning experience through opportunity for symbolic expression.* This goal is really part of a general view that learning as experience is incomplete unless it is carried through to a synthesizing phase in which new material is absorbed by being processed through the child's individual, prior store of ideas, images, feelings, and strivings. Piaget's analysis of assimilation and accommodation provides us with a theoretical foundation of the processes whereby known and unknown, in the cognitive realm, are joined.[8] A solution to a problem or a new concept uniting previously disparate facts represents one kind of synthesis. The use of newly learned arithmetic manipulations in some practical operation of measurement is a more functional example of synthesis. But synthesis of another kind, cutting across the cognitive and affective domains, occurs when the outcome of the learning experience takes symbolic form and results in a transformation of some part of the child's encounter with the outer world that reflects and utilizes the forces—the cumulated meanings, feelings, wishes, conflicts—of his inner life of impulse and affect.

There is an assumption behind the interest [in] and emphasis on providing materials, techniques, and a climate of values that support symbolic re-expression as a basic part of learning. The assumption is that the admission of nonrational processes into the learning life of children adds an additional dimension of power to potential mastery of objective material. This appears to be borne out by Torrance,[9] who found that a group of "high creative" children matched the academic performance of a comparative group of "low creative" children who had a significantly higher IQ rating; the "high creative" group attained this with less obvious strain or pressure. Torrance attributes this difference to the incidental learning that can take place when learning is enjoyed in the relaxed spirit of "playing around."[10] Might it not be that the success of the creative group was also related to the qualities of "openness to experience of one's inner life" and the freedom from rigidity associated with access to and utilization of the nonrational processes identified with creativity? The goal, stated in more general terms elsewhere,"[11] is "to develop people whose deep feelings remain generative in connection with their intellectual functioning and channel and qualify the nature of their performance."

Method and Rationale

In terms of curriculum, the presence of a variety of materials—paint, clay, blocks, or musical forms—and the opportunity to choose and use them freely without the constraints of models or established evaluative criteria, is one way of fulfilling this goal. In such settings the children engage in the process of "play." The mechanism of free dramatic play, the "pretending" and "make believe" that young children use to make their lives more encompassable and endurable, has been developed as a major teaching technique. Growing mastery of reality is expressed in play through the increasing detail and differentiation of the activities reproduced, through the widening scope of experience selected for representation in the play world, and through the progress from short, simple, almost momentary play schemes, to involved, prolonged, connected series of imagined events. Transactions in play contain the same interweaving of thought and emotion that characterizes molar life experience. Whether the figures of the play are people, animals, or anthropomorphized objects, their interactions, as agents or subjects, carry the charge of love, hate, destruction, rescue, loss, recovery, wish, defeat, pain, conquest—emotion that is relieved and externalized from the inner personal life history, sometimes directly, more often indirectly, through symbolic forms, displacements, or distortive mechanisms that grant the safety of distance from that part of the subjective life that is inevitably conflict-laden.

The younger the child, the less does the product of his dramatic play have to adhere to the logic of reality; for older children, who no longer permit themselves open distortion of reality to meet their inner needs or wishes, the projective channels are narrowed; but free-form dramatizing* still affords an opportunity to re-express idea content, in a matrix derived less from identification and more from empathy of what it feels like to be this or that person in this or that situation.

Thus dramatic play is a special kind of tool for learning, suited to the idiom of childhood, which fuses the wondering, problem-solving, and conceptualizing of the groping child mind with the symbolic expression of the wishes and fears, longings for strength, pleasures, and pains of the forming inner self. The fact that this fusion takes place actively in dramatic play is further reason to recognize it as a form of learning contributing to mastery and ego-strength. Thus, Erikson: ". . . to hallucinate ego-mastery is the purpose of play . . ." and ". . . the child's play is the infantile form of the human ability to deal with experience by creating model situations and to master reality by experiment and planning . . .,"[12] and in Omwake ". . . play of this nature provides a proving ground for the development and gradual refinement of the full range of emerging ego functions. These include language, motor skills, memory, concept formation, reality testing, control of impulse, and secondary process thinking . . ."[13]

Furthermore, if the importance placed by investigators in the field of creativity, MacKinnon and Barron particularly, upon "openness to one's feeling life" and "valuing nonrational components of experience" is valid, then the use of dramatic play and free-form dramatizing represents a kind of teaching method that should encourage creativity, originality, and invention because of the externalization and active fusion of subjective and objective meanings which these forms of play facilitate.

References

1. J. P. Guilford, "Three Faces of Intellect," *American Psychologist*, 14, 8 (1959), pp. 469–480.

2. E. P. Torrance, "Education and Creativity," p. 55, in C. W. Taylor (ed.), *Creativity: Progress and Potential* (New York: McGraw-Hill, 1964).

3. Guilford, "Three Faces of Intellect."

4. D. W. MacKinnon, "The Nature and Nurture of Creative Talent," *American Psychologist*, 17, 7 (1962), pp. 484–495.

5. *Ibid.*

---

*This term refers to play making in the upper elementary years when children dramatize freely around a given theme, using factual information that they have gathered. The properties and dramatic business of their production is original.

6. F. Barron, "The Needs for Order and for Disorder as Motives in Creative Activity," pp. 119–128, in C. W. Taylor (ed.), *The Second (1957) Conference on the Identification of Creative Scientific Talent* (Salt Lake City: University of Utah Press, 1958).

7. G. Murphy, "Non-rational Processes in Learning," pp. 158, 162, 163, in R. Gross and Judith Murphy (eds.), *The Revolution in the Schools* (New York: Harcourt, Brace and World, 1964).

8. J. Piaget, *The Origins of Intelligence in Children* (1936) (New York: International Universities Press, 1952).

9. Torrance, "Education and Creativity."

10. *Ibid.*

11. Barbara Biber and Patricia Minuchin, "The Role of the School in the Socialization of Competence," working paper for Conference on Socialization for Competence, Social Science Research Council (Puerto Rico, April 1965), Bank Street College of Education. Also (abbreviated version) in B. Rosen *et al.* (eds.), *Achievement in American Society* (Cambridge, Mass.: Schenkman Publishing Co., 1967).

12. E. H. Erikson, *Childhood and Society* (New York: W. W. Norton, 1950).

13. Eveline B. Omwake, "The Child's Estate," in A. J. Solnit and Sally A. Provence (eds.), *Modern Prospectives in Child Development* (New York: International Universities Press, 1963).

Personality Development

9   Defense and Growth

Abraham Maslow

No discussion of human growth would be complete without reference to the seminal thinking of the late Abraham Maslow. Here, in a particularly central chapter in his book on being and becoming, Maslow elaborates the conditions under which children either flourish or fail to actualize their potential.

This chapter is an effort to be a little more systematic in the area of growth theory. For once we accept the notion of growth, many questions of detail arise. Just how does growth take place? Why do children grow or not grow? How do they know in which direction to grow? How do they get off in the direction of pathology?

After all, the concepts of self-actualization, growth and self are all high-level abstractions. We need to get closer to actual processes, to raw data, to concrete, living happenings.

These are far goals. Healthily growing infants and children don't live for the sake of far goals or for the distant future; they are too busy enjoying themselves and spontaneously living for the moment. They are *living,* not *preparing* to live. How can they manage, just being, spontaneously, not *trying* to grow, seeking only to enjoy the present activity, nevertheless to move forward step by step? i.e., to grow in a healthy way? to discover their real selves? How can we reconcile the facts of Being with the facts of Becoming? Growth is not in the pure case a goal out ahead, nor is self-actualization, nor is the discovery of Self. In the child, it is not specifically purposed; rather it just happens. He doesn't so much search as find. The laws of deficiency-motivation and of purposeful coping do not hold for growth, for spontaneity, for creativeness.

The danger with a pure Being-psychology is that it may tend to be static, not accounting for the facts of movement, direction, and growth. We tend to describe states of Being, of self-actualization as if they were

Nirvana states of perfection. Once you're there, you're there, and it seems as if all you could do is to rest content in perfection.

The answer I find satisfactory is a simple one, namely, that growth takes place when the next step forward is subjectively more delightful, more joyous, more intrinsically satisfying than the previous gratification with which we have become familiar and even bored; that the only way we can ever know what is right for us is that it feels better subjectively than any alternative. The new experience validates *itself* rather than by any outside criterion. It is self-justifying, self-validating.

We don't do it because it is good for us, or because psychologists approve, or because somebody told us to, or because it will make us live longer, or because it is good for the species, or because it will bring external rewards, or because it is logical. We do it for the same reason that we choose one dessert over another. I have already described this as a basic mechanism for falling in love, or for choosing a friend, i.e., kissing one person gives more delight than kissing the other, being friends with *a* is more satisfying subjectively than being friends with *b*.

In this way, we learn that we are good at, what we really like or dislike, what our tastes and judgments and capacities are. In a word, this is the way in which we discover the Self and answer the ultimate questions Who am I? What am I?

The steps and the choices are taken out of pure spontaneity, from within outward. The healthy infant or child, just Being, as *part* of his Being, is randomly, and spontaneously curious, exploratory, wondering, interested. Even when he is non-purposeful, non-coping, expressive, spontaneous, not motivated by any deficiency of the ordinary sort, he tends to try out his powers, to reach out, to be absorbed, fascinated, interested, to play, to wonder, to manipulate the world. *Exploring, manipulating, experiencing,* being interested, choosing, delighting, *enjoying* can all be seen as attributes of pure Being, and yet lead to Becoming, though in a serendipitous way, fortuitously, unplanned, unanticipated. Spontaneous, creative experience can and does happen without expectations, plans, foresight, purpose, or goal.

> But paradoxically, the art experience cannot be effectively *used* for this purpose or any other. It must be a purposeless activity, as far as we understand "purpose." It can only be an experience in *being*—being a human organism doing what it must and what it is privileged to do—experiencing life keenly and wholly, expending energy and creating beauty in its own style—and the increased sensitivity, integrity, efficiency, and feeling of well-being are by-products.[1]

It is only when the child sates himself, becomes bored, that he is ready to turn to other, perhaps "higher" delights.

Then arise the inevitable questions. What holds him back? What prevents growth? Wherein lies the conflict? What is the alternative to growth forward? Why is it so hard and painful for some to grow forward? Here we must become more fully aware of the fixative and regressive power of ungratified deficiency-needs, of the attractions of safety and security, of the functions of defense and protection against pain, fear, loss, and threat, of the need for courage in order to grow ahead.

Every human being has *both* sets of forces within him. One set clings to safety and defensiveness out of fear, tending to regress backward, hanging on to the past, *afraid* to grow away from the primitive communication with the mother's uterus and breast, *afraid* to take chances, afraid to jeopardize what he already has, *afraid* of independence, freedom and separateness. The other set of forces impels him forward toward wholeness of Self and uniqueness of Self, toward full functioning of all his capacities, toward confidence in the face of the external world at the same time that he can accept his deepest, real, unconscious Self.

I can put all this together in a schema, which though very simple, is also very powerful, both heuristically and theoretically. This basic dilemma or conflict between the defensive forces and the growth trends I conceive to be existential, imbedded in the deepest nature of the human being, now and forever into the future. If it is diagrammed like this:

$$Safety \longleftarrow\!\!\blacktriangleleft PERSON \blacktriangleright\!\!\longrightarrow Growth$$

then we can very easily classify the various mechanisms of growth in an uncomplicated way as:
   a. Enhancing the growthward vectors, e.g., making growth more attractive and delight producing;
   b. Minimizing the fears of growth;
   c. Minimizing the safetyward vectors, i.e., making it less attractive;
   d. Maximizing the fears of safety, defensiveness, pathology and regression.

We can then add to our basic schema these four sets of valences:

$$Enhance\ the\ dangers \text{————————} Enhance\ the\ attractions$$

$$Safety \longleftarrow\!\!\blacktriangleleft PERSON \blacktriangleright\!\!\longrightarrow Growth$$

$$Minimize\ the\ attractions \text{————————} Minimize\ the\ dangers$$

Therefore we can consider the process of healthy growth to be a never ending series of free choice situations, confronting each individual at every point throughout his life, in which he must choose between the delights of safety and growth, dependence and independence, regression and progression, immaturity and maturity. Safety has both anxieties and delights; growth has both anxieties and delights. We grow forward when the delights of growth and anxieties of safety are greater than the anxieties of growth and the delights of safety.

So far it sounds like a truism. But it isn't to psychologists who are mostly trying to be objective, public, behavioristic. And it has taken many experiments with animals and much theorizing to convince the students of animal motivation that they must invoke what P. T. Young[2] called a hedonic factor, over and above need-reduction, in order to explain the results so far obtained in free-choice experimentation. For example, saccharin is not need-reducing in any way and yet white rats will choose it over plain water. Its (useless) taste *must* have something to do with it.

Furthermore, observe that subjective delight in the experience is something that we can attribute to *any* organism, e.g., it applies to the infant as well as the adult, to the animal as well as to the human.

The possibility that then opens for us is very enticing for the theorist. Perhaps all these high-level concepts of Self, Growth, Self-realization, and Psychological Health can fall into the same system of explanation with appetite experiments in animals, free choice observations in infant feeding and in occupational choice, and the rich studies of homeostasis.[3]

Of course this formulation of growth-through-delight also commits us to the necessary postulation that what tastes good is also, in the growth sense, "better" for us. We rest here on the faith that if free choice is *really* free and if the chooser is not too sick or frightened to choose, he will choose wisely, in a healthy and growthward direction, more often than not.

For this postulation there is already much experimental support, but it is mostly at the animal level, and much more detailed research is necessary with free choice in humans. We must know much more than we do about the reasons for bad and unwise choices, at the constitutional level and at the level of psychodynamics.

There is another reason why my systematizing side likes this notion of growth-through-delight. It is that then I find it possible to tie it in nicely with dynamic theory, with *all* the dynamic theories of Freud, Adler, Jung, Schachtel, Horney, Fromm, Burrow, Reich, and Rank, as well as the theories of Rogers, Buhler, Combs, Angyal, Allport, Goldstein, Murray, Moustakas, Perls, Bugental, Assagioli, Frankl, Jourard, May, White, and others.

I criticize the classical Freudians for tending (in the extreme instance) to pathologize everything and for not seeing clearly enough the healthward possibilities in the human being, for seeing everything through brown-colored glasses. But the growth school (in the extreme instance) is equally vulnerable, for they tend to see through rose-colored glasses and generally slide over the problems of pathology, of weakness, of *failure* to grow. One is like a theology of evil and sin exclusively; the other is like a theology without any evil at all, and is therefore equally incorrect and unrealistic.

One additional relationship between safety and growth must be specially mentioned. Apparently growth forward customarily takes place in little steps, and each step forward is made possible by the feeling of being safe, of operating out into the unknown from a safe home port, of daring because retreat is possible. We may use as a paradigm the toddler venturing away from his mother's knee into strange surroundings. Characteristically, he first clings to his mother as he explores the room with his eyes. Then he dares a little excursion, continually reassuring himself that the mother-security is intact. These excursions get more and more extensive. In this way, the child can explore a dangerous and unknown world. If suddenly the mother were to disappear, he would be thrown into anxiety, would cease to be interested in exploring the world, would wish only the return of safety, and might even lose his abilities, e.g., instead of daring to walk, he might creep.

I think we may safely generalize this example. Assured safety permits higher needs and impulses to emerge and to grow towards mastery. To endanger safety means regression backward to the more basic foundation. What this means is that in the choice between giving up safety or giving up growth, safety will ordinarily win out. Safety needs are prepotent over growth needs. This means an expansion of our basic formula. In general, only a child who feels safe dares to grow forward healthily. His safety needs must be gratified. He can't be *pushed* ahead, because the ungratified safety needs will remain forever underground, always calling for satisfaction. The more safety needs are gratified, the less valence they have for the child, the less they will beckon, and lower his courage.

Now, how can we know when the child feels safe enough to dare to choose the new step ahead? Ultimately, the only way in which we can know is by *his* choices, which is to say only *he* can ever really know the right moment when the beckoning forces ahead overbalance the beckoning forces behind, and courage outweighs fear.

Ultimately the person, even the child, must choose for himself. Nobody can choose for him too often, for this itself enfeebles him, cutting his self-trust, and confusing his *ability* to perceive his own internal delight in the experience, his *own* impulses, judgments, and feelings, and to differentiate them from the interiorized standards of others.

> From the moment the package is in his hands, he feels free to do what he wants with it. He opens it, speculates on what it is, recognizes what it is, expresses happiness or disappointment, notices the arrangement of the contents, finds a book of directions, feels the touch of the steel, the different weights of the parts, and their number, and so on. He does all this before he has attempted to do a thing with the set. Then comes the thrill of doing something with it. It may be only matching one single part with another. Thereby alone he gets a feeling of having done something, that he can do something, and that he is not helpless with that particular article. Whatever pattern is subsequently followed, whether his interest extends to the full utilization of the set and therefore toward further gaining a feeling of greater and greater accomplishment, or

whether he completely discards it, his initial contact with the erector set has been meaningful.

The results of active experiencing can be summarized approximately in the following way. There is physical, emotional, and intellectual self-involvement; there is a recognition and further exploration of one's abilities; there is initiation of activity or creativeness; there is finding out one's own pace and rhythm and the assumption of enough of a task for one's abilities at that particular time, which would include the avoidance of taking on too much; there is gain in skill which one can apply to other enterprises, and there is an opportunity each time that one has an active part in something, no matter how small, to find out more and more what one is interested in.

The above situation may be contrasted with another in which the person who brings home the erector set says to the child, 'Here is an erector set, let me open it for you.' He does so, and then points out all the things in the box, the book of directions, the various parts, etc., and, to top it off, he sets about building one of the complicated models, let us say, a crane. The child may be much interested in what he has seen being done, but let us focus on one aspect of what has really been happening. The child has had no opportunity to get himself involved with the erector set, with his body, his intelligence, or his feelings, he has had no opportunity to match himself up with something that is new for him, to find out what he is capable of or to gain further direction for his interests. The building of the crane for him may have brought in another factor. It may have left the child with an implied demand that he do likewise without his having had an opportunity to prepare himself for any such complicated task. The end becomes the object instead of the experience involved in the process of attaining the objective. Also, whatever he may subsequently do by himself will look small and mean compared to what had been made for him by someone else. He has not added to his total experience for coming up against something new for the next time. In other words, he has not grown from within but has had something superimposed from the outside. . . . Each bit of active experiencing is an opportunity toward finding out what he likes or dislikes, and more and more what he wants to make out of himself. It is an essential part of his progress toward the stage of maturity and self-direction.[4]

If this is all so, if the child himself must finally make the choice by which he grows forward, since only he can know his subjective delight experience, then how can we reconcile this ultimate necessity for trust in the inner individual with the necessity for help from the environment? For he does need help. Without help he will be too frightened to dare. How can we help him to grow? Equally important, how can we endanger his growth?

The opposite of the subjective experience of delight (trusting himself), so far as the child is concerned, is the opinion of other people (love, respect, approval, admiration, reward from others, trusting others rather than himself). Since others are so important and vital for the helpless baby and child, fear of losing them (as providers of safety, food, love, respect, etc.) is a primal, terrifying danger. Therefore, the child, faced with a difficult choice between his own delight experiences and the experience of approval from others, must generally choose approval from others, and then handle his delight by repression or letting it die, or not noticing it or controlling it by willpower. In general, along with this will develop a disapproval of the delight experience, or shame and embarrassment and secretiveness about it, with finally, the inability even to experience it.

> How is it possible to lose a self? The treachery, unknown and unthinkable, begins with our secret psychic death in childhood—if and when we are not loved and are cut off from our spontaneous wishes. (Think: what is left?) But wait—victim might even "outgrow" it—but it is a perfect double crime in which he him-it is not just this simple murder of a psyche. That might be written off, the tiny self also gradually and unwittingly takes part. He has not been accepted for himself, *as he is.* "Oh, they 'love' him, but they want him or force him or expect him to be different! Therefore he *must be unacceptable.* He himself learns to believe it and at last even takes it for granted. He has truly given himself up. No matter now whether he obeys them, whether he clings, rebels or withdraws—his behavior, his performance is all that matters. His center of gravity is in 'them,' not in himself—yet if he so much as noticed it he'd think it natural enough. And the whole thing is entirely plausible; all invisible, automatic, and anonymous!
>
> This is the perfect paradox. Everything looks normal; no crime was intended; there is no corpse, no guilt. All we can see is the sun rising and setting as usual. But what has happened? He has been rejected, not only by them, but by himself. (He is actually without a self.) What has he lost? Just the one true and vital part of himself: his own yes-feeling, which is his very capacity for growth, his root system. But alas, he is not dead. 'Life' goes on, and so must he. From the moment he gives himself up, and to the extent that he does so, all unknowingly he sets about to create and maintain a pseudo-self. But this is an expediency—a 'self' without wishes. This one shall be loved (or feared) where he is despised, strong where he is weak; it shall go through the motions (oh, but they are caricatures!) not for fun or joy but for survival; not simply because it wants to move but because it has to obey. This necessity is not life—not his life—it is a defense mechanism against death. It is also the machine of death. From now on he will be torn apart by compulsive (unconscious) *needs* or ground by (unconscious) conflicts into paralysis, every motion and every instant canceling out his being, his integrity; and all the while he is disguised as a normal person and expected to behave like one!
>
> In a word, I saw that we *become* neurotic seeking or defending a pseudo-self, a self-system; and we *are* neurotic to the extent that we are self-less.[5]

The primal choice, the fork in the road, then, is between others' and one's own self. If the only way to maintain the self is to lose others, then the ordinary child will give up the self. This is true for the reason already mentioned, that safety is a most basic and preponent need for children, more primarily necessary by far than independence and self-actualization. If adults force this choice upon him, of choosing between the loss of one (lower and stronger) vital necessity or another (higher and weaker) vital necessity, the child must choose safety even at the cost of giving up self and growth.

In principle there is no need for forcing the child to make such a choice. People just *do* it often, out of their own sicknesses and out of ignorance. We know that it is not necessary because we have examples enough of children who are offered all these goods simultaneously, at no vital cost, who can have safety and love *and* respect too.

Here we can learn important lessons from the therapy situation, the creative educative situation, creative art education and I believe also creative dance education. Here where the situation is set up variously as permissive, admiring, praising, accepting, safe, gratifying, reassuring, supporting, unthreatening, non-valuing, non-comparing, that is, where the person can feel completely safe and unthreatened, then it becomes possible for him to work out and express all sorts of lesser delights, e.g., hostility, neurotic dependency. Once these are sufficiently catharted, he then tends spontaneously to go to other delights which outsiders perceive to be "higher" or growthward, e.g., love, creativeness, and which he himself will prefer to the previous delights, once he has experienced them both. It often makes little difference what kind of explicit theory is held by the therapist, teacher, helper, etc. The really good therapist who may espouse a pessimistic Freudian theory, *acts* as if growth were possible. The really good teacher who espouses verbally a completely rosy and optimistic picture of human nature, will *imply* in actual teaching, a complete understanding and respect for regressive and defensive forces. It is also possible to have a wonderfully realistic and comprehensive philosophy and belie it in practice, in therapy, or teaching or parenthood. Only the one who respects fear and defense can teach; only the one who respects health can do therapy.

Part of the paradox in this situation is that in a very real way even the "bad" choice is "good for" the neurotic chooser, or at least understable and even necessary in terms of his own dynamics. We know that tearing away a functional neurotic symptom by force, or by too direct a confrontation or interpretation, or by a stress situation which cracks the person's defenses against too painful an insight, can shatter the person altogether. This involves us in the question of *pace* of growth. And again the good parent, or therapist or educator *practices* as if he understood that gentleness, sweetness, respect for fear, understanding of the naturalness of defensive and regressive forces, are necessary if growth is not to look like an overwhelming danger instead of a delightful prospect. He implies that he understands that growth can emerge only from safety. He *feels* that if a person's defenses are very rigid this is for a good reason and he is willing to be patient and understanding even though knowing the path in which the child "should" go.

Seen from the dynamic point of view, ultimately *all* choices are in fact wise, if only we grant two kinds of wisdom, defensive-wisdom and growth-wisdom. Defensiveness can be as wise as daring; it depends on the particular person, his particular status and the particular situation in which hc has to choose. The choice of safety is wise when it avoids pain that may be more than the person can bear at the moment. If we wish to help him grow (because we know that consistent safety-choices will bring him to catastrophe in the long run, and will cut him off from possibilities that he himself would enjoy if only he could savor them), then all we can do is help him if he asks for help out of suffering, or else simultaneously allow him to feel safe and beckon him onward to *try* the new experience like the mother whose open arms invite the baby to try to walk. We can't *force* him to grow, we can only *coax* him to, make it more possible for him, in the trust that simply experiencing the new experience will make him prefer it. *Only* he can prefer it; no one can prefer it for him. If it is to become part of him, *he* must like it. If he doesn't, we must gracefully concede that it is not for him at this moment.

This means that the sick child must be respected as much as the healthy one, so far as the growth process is concerned. Only when his fears are accepted respectfully, can he dare to be bold. We must understand that the dark forces are as "normal" as the growth forces.

This is a ticklish task, for it implies simultaneously that we know what is best for him (since we *do* beckon him on in a direction we choose), and also that only he knows what is best for himself in the long run. This means that we must *offer* only, and rarely force. We must be quite ready, not only to beckon forward, but to respect retreat to lick wounds, to recover strength, to look over the situation from a safe vantage point, or even to regress to a previous mastery or a "lower" delight, so that courage for growth can be regained.

And this again is where the helper comes in. He is needed, not only for making possible growth forward in the healthy child (by being "available" as the child desires) and getting out of his way at other times, but much more urgently, by the person who is "stuck" in fixation, in rigid defenses, in safety measures which cut off the possibilities of growth. Neurosis is self-perpetuating; so is character structure. We can either wait for life to prove to such a person that his system doesn't work, i.e., by letting him eventually collapse into neurotic suffering, or else by understanding him and helping him to grow by respecting and understanding both his deficiency needs and his growth needs.

This amounts to a revision of Taoistic "let-be," which often hasn't worked because the growing child needs help. It can be formulated as "helpful let-be." It is a *loving* and *respecting* Taoism. It recognizes not only growth and the specific mechanism which makes it move in the right direction, but it also recognizes and respects the fear of growth, the slow pace of growth, the blocks, the pathology, the reasons for not growing. It recognizes the place, the necessity and the helpfulness of the outer environment without yet giving it control. It implements inner growth by knowing its mechanisms and by being willing to help *it* instead of merely being hopeful or passively optimistic about it.

All the foregoing may now be related to the general motivation theory, set forth in my *Motivation and Personality*, particularly the theory of need gratification, which seems to me to be the most important single principle underlying all heathy human development. The single holistic principle that binds together the multiplicity of human motives is the tendency for a new and higher need to emerge as the lower need fulfills itself by being sufficiently gratified. The child who is fortunate enough to grow normally and well gets satiated and *bored* with the delights that he has savored sufficiently, and *eagerly* (without pushing) goes on to higher, more complex, delights as they become available to him without danger or threat.

This principle can be seen exemplified not only in the deeper motivational dynamics of the child but also in microcosm in the development of any of his more modest activities, e.g., in learning to read, or skate, or paint, or dance. The child who masters simple words enjoys them intensely but doesn't stay there. In the proper atmosphere he spontaneously shows eagerness to go on to more and more new words, longer words, more complex sentences, etc. If he is forced to stay at the simple level he gets bored and restless with what formerly delighted him. He *wants* to go on, to move, to grow. Only if frustration, failure, disapproval, ridicule come at the next step does he fixate or regress, and we are then faced with the intricacies of pathological dynamics and of neurotic compromises, in which the impulses remain alive but unfulfilled, or even of loss of impulse and of capacity.

I think it is possible to apply this general principle to Freudian theory of the progression of libidinal stages. The infant in the oral stage, gets most of his delights through the mouth. And one in particular which has been neglected is that of mastery. We should remember that the *only* thing an infant can do well and efficiently is to suckle. In all else he is inefficient, incapable and if, as I think, this is the earliest precursor of self esteem (feeling of mastery), then this is the *only* way in which the infant can experience the delight of mastery (efficiency, control, self expression, volition.)

But soon he develops other capacities for mastery and control. I mean here not only anal control which though correct, has, in my opinion, been overplayed. Motility and sensory capacities also develop enough during the so-called "anal" stage to give feelings of delight and mastery. But what is important for us here is that the oral infant tends to play out his oral mastery and to become bored with it, just as he becomes bored with milk alone. In a free choice situation, he tends to give up the breast and milk in favor of the more complex activities and tastes, or anyway, to add to the breast these other "higher" developments. Given sufficient gratification, free choice and lack of threat, he "grows" out of the oral stage and renounces it himself. He doesn't have to be "kicked upstairs" or forced on to maturity as is so often implied. He *chooses* to grow on to higher delights, to become bored with older ones. Only under the impact of danger, threat, failure, frustration, or stress does he tend to regress or fixate; only then does he prefer safety to gowth. Certainly renunciation, delay in gratification and the ability to withstand frustration are also necessary for strength, and we know that unbridled gratification is dangerous. And yet it remains true that these qualifications are *subsidiary* to the principle that sufficient gratification of basic needs is *sine qua non*.

What we wind up with then is a subjective device to add to the principle of the hierarchical arrangement of our various needs, a device which guides and directs the individual in the direction of "healthy" growth. The principle holds true at any age. Recovering the ability to perceive one's own delights is the best way of rediscovering the sacrified self even in adulthood. The process of therapy helps the adult to discover that the childish (repressed) necessity for the approval of others no longer need exist in the childish form and degree, and that the terror of losing these others with the accompanying fear of being weak, helpless and abandoned is no longer realistic and justified as it was for the child. For the adult, others can be and should be less important than for the child.

Our final formula then has the following elements:

1. The healthily spontaneous child, in his spontaneity, from within out, in response to his own inner Being, reaches out to the environment in wonder and interest, and expresses whatever skills he has,

2. To the extent that he is not crippled by fear, to the extent that he feels safe enough to dare.

3. In this process, that which gives him the delight-experience is fortuitously encountered, or is offered to him by helpers.

4. He must be safe and self-accepting enough to be able to choose and prefer these delights, instead of being frightened by them.

5. If he *can* choose these experiences which are validated by the experience of delight, then he can return to the experience, repeat it, savor it to the point of repletion, satiation or boredom.

6. At this point, he shows the tendency to go on to more complex, richer experiences and accomplishments in the same sector (again, if he feels safe enough to dare.)

7. Such experiences not only mean moving on, but have a feedback effect on the Self, in the feeling of certainty ("This I like; that I don't for *sure*"); of capability, mastery, self-trust, self-esteem.

8. In this never ending series of choices of which life consists, the choice may generally be schematized as between safety (or, more broadly, defensiveness) and growth, and since only that child doesn't need safety who already has it, we may expect the growth choice to be made by the safety-need gratified child. Only he can afford to be bold.

9. In order to be able to choose in accord with his own nature and to develop it, the child must be permitted to retain the subjective experiences of delight and boredom, as *the* criteria of the correct choice for him. The alternative criterion is making the choice in terms of the wish of another person. The Self is lost when this happens. Also this constitutes restricting the choice to safety alone, since the child will give up trust in his own delight-criterion out of fear (of losing protection, love, etc.)

10. If the choice is really a free one, and if the child is not crippled, then we may expect him ordinarily to choose progression forward.*

11. The evidence indicates that what delights the healthy child, what tastes good for him, is also, more frequently than not, "best" for him in terms of far goals as perceivable by the spectator.

12. In this process the environment (parents, therapists, teachers) is important in various ways, even though the ultimate choice must be made by the child:

a. it can gratify his basic needs for safety, belonging, love and respect, so that he can feel unthreatened, autonomous, interested and spontaneous and thus dare to choose the unknown;

b. it can help by making the growth choice positively attractive and less dangerous, and by making the regressive choice less attractive and more costly.

13. In this way the psychology of Being and the psychology of Becoming can be reconciled, and the child, simply being himself, can yet move forward and grow.

References

1. F. Wilson, "Human Nature and Esthetic Growth," p. 213, in C. Moustakas (ed.), *The Self* (New York: Harper, 1956).

2. P. T. Young, *Motivation and Emotion* (New York: Wiley, 1961).

3. W. B. Cannon, *Wisdom of the Body* (New York: Norton, 1932).

4. B. Zuger, "Growth of the Individual's Concept of Self," *AMA American Journal on Diseased Children*, 83 (1952), p. 179.

5. Anonymous, "Finding the Real Self," a letter with a foreword by Karen Horney, *American Journal of Psychoanalysis*, 9 (1949), p. 7.

---

*A kind of pseudo-growth takes place very commonly when the person tries (by repression, denial, reaction-formation, etc.) to convince himself that an ungratified basic need has really been gratified, or doesn't exist. He then permits himself to grow on to higher-need-levels, which of course, forever after, rest on a very shaky foundation. I call this "pseudo-growth by bypassing the ungratified need." Such a need perseverates forever as an unconscious force (repetition compulsion).

10 A Healthy Personality for Every Child

Once every so often a statement appears which is so informative and useful that it continues to have value for the field over several decades. The significant White House Conference Paper by Erik H. Erikson, towering figure in the fields of psychology and psychoanalysis, is here presented in digest form. His conceptualization of eight stages in the life cycle of man helps the educator see growth as a continuous process. The first four stages are particularly relevent to early childhood educators.

Many attempts have been made to describe the attributes of healthy personality. They have been put succinctly as the ability to love and the ability to work. A recent review of the literature suggests that the individual with a healthy personality is one who actively masters his environment, shows a unity of personality, and is able to perceive the world and himself correctly. Clearly, none of these criteria applies to a child. It seems to us best, then, to present . . . an outline that has the merit of indicating at one and the same time the main course of personality development and the attributes of a healthy personality.

This developmental outline was worked out by Erik H. Erikson, a psychologist and practicing psychoanalyst who has made anthropological field studies and has had much experience with children. It is an analysis that derives from psychological theory, to which is added knowledge from the fields of child development and cultural anthropology. The whole is infused with the author's insight and personal philosophy.

In each stage of child development, the author says, there is a central problem that has to be solved, temporarily at least, if the child is to proceed with vigor and confidence to the next stage. These problems, these conflicts of feeling and desire, are never solved in entirety. Each shift in experience and environment presents them in a new form. It is held, however, that each type of conflict appears in its purest, most unequivocal form at a particular stage of child development, and that if the problem is well solved at that time the basis for progress to the next stage is well laid.

In a sense personality development follows biological principles. Biologists have found that everything that grows has a groundplan that is laid out at its start. Out of this groundplan the parts arise, each part having its time of special ascendancy. Together these parts form a functioning whole. If a part does not arise at its appointed time, it

A Healthy Personality for Every Child: A Digest of the Fact Finding Report to the Midcentury White House Conference on Children and Youth, 1951, pp. 6-25.

will never be able to form fully since the moment for the rapid out-growth of some other part will have arrived. Moreover, a part that misses its time of ascendancy or is severely damaged during its formative period is apt to doom, in turn, the whole hierarchy of organs. Proper rate and normal sequence is necessary if functional harmony is to be secured.

Personality represents the most complicated functioning of the human organism and does not consist of parts in the organic sense. Instead of the development of organs, there is the development of locomotor, sensory, and social capacities and the development of individual modes of dealing with experience. Nevertheless, proper rate and proper sequence are as important here as in physical growth, and functional harmony is achieved only if development proceeds according to the groundplan.

In all this it is encouraging for parents and others who have children in charge to realize that in the sequence of his most personal experiences, just as in the sequence of organ formation, the child can be trusted to follow inner laws of development, and needs from adults chiefly love, encouragement, and guidance.

The operation of biological laws is seen, also, in the fact that there is constant interplay between organism and environment and that problems of personality functioning are never solved once and for all. Each of the components of the healthy personality to be described below is present in some form from the beginning, and the struggle to maintain it continues throughout life.

For example, a baby may show something like "autonomy" or a will of his own in the way he angrily tries to free his head when he is tightly held. Nevertheless, it is not until the second year of life that he begins to experience the whole conflict between being an autonomous creature and a dependent one. It is not until then that he is ready for a decisive encounter with the people around him, and it is not until then that they feel called upon to train him or otherwise curb his free-questing spirit. The struggle goes on for months and finally, under favorable circumstances, some compromise between dependence and independence is reached that gives the child a sense of well-being.

The sense of autonomy thus achieved is not a permanent possession, however. There will be other challenges to that sense and other solutions more in keeping with later stages of development. Nevertheless, once established at two or three years of age, this early sense of autonomy will be a bulwark against later frustrations and will permit the emergence of the next developmental problem at a time that is most favorable for its solution.

So it is with all the personality components to be described. They appear in miniature early in life. The struggle to secure them against tendencies to act otherwise comes to a climax at a time determined by emergence of the necessary physical and mental abilities. There are, throughout life, other challenges and other responses but they are seldom so serious and seldom so decisive as those of the critical years.

In all this, it must be noted in addition, there is not the strict dichotomy that the analysis given below suggests. With each of the personality components to be described, it is not all or nothing: trust *or* mistrust, autonomy *or* doubt, and so on. Instead, each individual has some of each. His health of personality is determined by the preponderance of the favorable over the unfavorable, as well as by what manner of compensations he develops to cope with his disabilities.

The Sense of Trust

The component of the healthy personality that is the first to develop is the sense of trust. The crucial time for its emergence is the first year of life. As with the other personality components to be described, the sense of trust is not something that develops independent of other manifestations of growth. It is not that the infant learns how to use his body for purposeful movement, learns to recognize people and objects around him, and also develops a sense of trust. Rather, the concept "sense of trust" is a short-cut expression intended to convey the characteristic flavor of all the child's satisfying experiences at this early age. Or, to say it another way, this psychological formulation serves to condense, summarize, and synthesize the most important underlying changes that give meaning to the infant's concrete and diversified experience.

Trust can exist only in relation to something. Consequently a sense of trust cannot develop until the infant is old enough to be aware of objects and persons and to have some feeling that he is a separate individual. At about three months of age a baby is likely to smile if somebody comes close and talks to him. This shows that he is aware of the approach of the other person, that pleasurable sensations are aroused. If, however, the person moves too quickly or speaks too sharply the baby may look apprehensive or cry. We will not "trust" the unusual situation but will have a feeling of uneasiness, of mistrust, instead.

Experiences connected with feeding are a prime source for the development of trust. At around four months of age a hungry baby will grow quiet and show signs of pleasure at the sound of an approaching footstep, anticipating (trusting) that he will be held and fed. This repeated experience of being hungry, seeing food, receiving food, and feeling relieved and comforted assures the baby that the world is a dependable place.

Later experiences, starting at around five months of age, add another dimension to the sense of trust. Through endless repetitions of attempts to grasp for and hold objects, the baby is finally successful in controlling and adapting his movements in such a way as to reach his goal. Through these and other feats of muscular coordination the baby is gradually able to trust his own body to do his bidding.

The baby's trust-mistrust problem is symbolized in the game of peek-a-boo. In this game, which babies begin to like at about four months of age, an object disappears and then reappears. There is a slightly tense expression on the baby's face when the object goes away; its reappearance is greeted by wriggles and smiles. Only gradually does a baby learn that things continue to exist even though he does not see them, that there is order and stability in his universe. Peek-a-boo proves the point by playful repetition.

Studies of mentally ill individuals and observations of infants who have been grossly deprived of affection suggest that trust is an early-formed and important element in the healthy personality. Psychiatrists find again and again that the most serious illnesses occur in patients who have been sorely neglected or abused or otherwise deprived of love in infancy. Similarly, it is a common finding of psychological and social investigators that individuals diagnosed as a "psychopathic personality" were so unloved in infancy that they have no reason to trust the human race and, therefore, no sense of responsibility toward their fellow men.

Observations of infants brought up in emotionally unfavorable institutions or removed to hospitals with inadequate facilities for psychological care support these findings. A recent report says: "Infants under six months of age who have been in an institution for some time present a well-defined picture. The outstanding features are listlessness, emaciation and pallor, relative immobility, quietness, unresponsiveness to stimuli like a smile or a coo, indifferent appetite, failure to gain weight properly despite ingestion of diets which are entirely adequate, frequent stools, poor sleep, an appearance of unhappiness, proneness to febrile episodes, absence of sucking habits."[1]

Another investigation of children separated from their mothers at six to twelve months and not provided with an adequate substitute comes to much the same conclusion: "The emotional tone is one of apprehension and sadness, there is withdrawal from the environment amounting to rejection of it, there is no attempt to contact a stranger and no brightening if a stranger contacts him. Activities are retarded and the child often sits or lies inert in a dazed stupor. Insomnia is common and lack of appetite universal. Weight is lost, and the child becomes prone to current infections."[2]

Most significant for our present point, these reactions are most likely to occur in children who up to the time of separation at six to nine months of age had a happy relation with their mothers, while those whose relations were unhappy are relatively unaffected. It is at about this age that the struggle between trusting and mistrusting the world comes to a climax, for it is then that the child first perceives clearly that he and his environment are things apart. That at this time formerly happy infants should react so badly to separation suggests, indeed, that they had a faith which now was shattered. Happily, there is usually spectacular change for the better when the maternal presence and love are restored.

It is probably unnecessary to describe the numerous ways in which stimuli from without and from within may cause an infant distress. Birth is believed by some experts to be a painful experience for the baby. Until fairly recently doctors were likely to advise that babies be fed on schedule and that little attention be paid to their cries of hunger at other times. Many infants spent many of the waking hours of the first four months doubled up with colic. All of them had to be bathed and dressed at stated times, whether they liked it or not. Add to these usual discomforts the fact that some infants are handled rather roughly by their parents, that others hear angry words and loud voices, and that a few are really mistreated, and it will not be difficult to understand why some infants may feel the world is a place that cannot be trusted.

In most primitive societies and in some sections of our own society the attention accorded infants is more in line with natural processes. In such societies separation from the mother is less abrupt, in that for some time after birth the baby is kept close to the warmth and comfort of its mother's body and at its least cry the breast is produced. Throughout infancy the baby is surrounded by people who are ready to feed it, fondle it, otherwise comfort it at a moment's notice. Moreover, these ministrations are given spontaneously, wholeheartedly, and without that element of nervous concern that may characterize the efforts of your mothers made self-conscious and insecure by our scientific age.

We must not exaggerate, however. Most infants in our society, too, find smiles and the comfort of mother's soft, warm body accompanying their intake of food, whether from breast or bottle. Coldness, wetness, pain, and boredom—for each misfortune there is prompt and comforting relief. As their own bodies come to be more dependable, there is added to the pleasures of increasing sensory response and motor control the pleasure of the mother's encouragement.

Moreover, babies are rather hardy creatures and are not to be discouraged by inexperienced mothers' mistakes. Even a mother cat has to learn, and the kittens endure gracefully her first clumsy efforts to carry them away from danger. Then, too, psychologists tell us that mothers create a sense of trust in their children not by the particular techniques they employ but by the sensitiveness with which they respond to the children's needs and by their over-all attitude.

For most infants, then, a sense of trust is not difficult to come by. It is the most important element in the personality. It emerges at the most vulnerable period of a child's life. Yet it is the least likely to suffer harm, perhaps because both nature and culture work toward making mothers most maternal at that time.

The Sense of Autonomy

The sense of trust once firmly established, the struggle for the next component of the healthy personality begins. The child is now twelve to fifteen months old. Much of his energy for the next two years will center around asserting that he is a human being with a mind and will of his own. A list of some of the items discussed by Spock under the heading, "The One Year Old," will serve to remind us of the characteristics of that age and the problems they create for parents. "Feeling his oats." "The passion to explore." "He gets more dependent and more independent at the same time." "Arranging the house for the wandering baby." "Avoiding accidents." "How do you make him leave certain things alone?" "Dropping and throwing things." "Biting humans." "The small child who won't stay in bed at night."

What is at stake throughout the struggle of these years is the child's sense of autonomy, the sense that he is an independent human being and yet one who is able to use the help and guidance of others in important matters. This stage of development becomes decisive for the ratio between love and hate, between cooperation and wilfulness, for freedom of self-expression and its renunciation in the make-up of the individual. The favorable outcome is self-control without loss of self-esteem. The unfavorable outcome is doubt and shame.

Before the sense of autonomy can develop, the sense of trust must be reasonably well-established and must continue to pervade the child's feeling about himself and his world. Only so dare he respond with confidence to his new-felt desire to assert himself boldly, to appropriate demandingly, and to hurl away without let or hindrance.

As with the previous stage, there is a physiological basis for this characteristic behavior. This is the period of muscle-system maturation and the consequent ability (and doubly felt inability) to coordinate a number of highly conflicting action patterns, such as those of holding on and letting go, walking, talking, and manipulating objects in ever more complicated ways. With these abilities come pressing needs to use them: to handle, to explore, to seize and to drop, to withhold and to expel. And, with all, there is the dominant will, the insistent "Me do" that defies help and yet is so easily frustrated by the inabilities of the hands and feet.

For a child to develop this sense of self-reliance and adequacy that Erikson calls autonomy, it is necessary that he experience over and over again that he is a person who is permitted to make choices. He has to have the right to choose, for example, whether to sit or whether to stand, whether to approach a visitor or to lean against his mother's knee, whether to accept offered food or whether to reject it, whether to use the toilet or to wet his pants. At the same time he must learn some of the boundaries of self-determination. He inevitably finds that there are walls he cannot climb, that there are objects out of reach, that, above all, there are innumerable commands enforced by powerful adults. His experience is much too small to enable him to know what he can and cannot do with respect to the physical environment, and it will take him years to discover the boundaries that mark off what is approved, what is tolerated, and what is forbidden by his elders whom he finds so hard to understand.

As problems of this period, some psychologists have concentrated particularly on bladder and bowel control. Emphasis is put upon the need for care in both timing and mode of training children in the performance of these functions. If parental control is too rigid or if training is started too early, the child is robbed of his opportunity to develop, by his own free choice, gradual control of the contradictory impulses of retention and elimination.

To others who study child development, this matter of toilet training is but a prototype of all the problems of this age range. The sphincters are only part of the whole muscle system, with its general ambiguity of rigidity and relaxation, of flexion and extension. To hold and to relinquish refer to much more than the bowels. As the child acquires the ability to stand on his two feet and move around, he delineates his world as me and you. He can be astonishingly pliable once he has decided that he wants to do what he is supposed to do, but there is no reliable formula for assuring that he will relinquish when he wants to hold on.

The matter of mutual regulation between parent and child (for fathers have now entered the picture to an extent that was rare in the earlier stage) now faces its severest task. The task is indeed one to challenge the most resourceful and the most calm adult. Firmness is necessary, for the child must be protected against the potential anarchy of his as yet untrained sense of discrimination. Yet the adult must back him up in his wish to "stand on his own feet," lest he be overcome by shame that he has exposed himself foolishly and by doubt in his self-worth. Perhaps the most constructive rule a parent can follow is to forbid only what "really matters" and, in such forbidding, to be clear and consistent.

Shame and doubt are emotions that many primitive peoples and some of the less sophisticated individuals in our own society utilize in training children. Shaming exploits the child's sense of being small. Used to excess it misses its objective and may result in open shamelessness, or, at least, in the child's secret determination to do as he pleases when not observed. Such defiance is a normal, even healthy response to demands that a child consider himself, his body, his needs, or his wishes evil and dirty and that he regard those who pass judgment as infallible. Young delinquents may be produced by this means, and others who are oblivious to the opinion of society.

Those who would guide the growing child wisely, then, will avoid shaming him and avoid causing him to doubt that he is a person of worth. They will be firm and tolerant with him so that he can rejoice in being a person of independence and can grant independence to others. As to detailed procedures, it is impossible to prescribe, not only because we do not know and because every situation is different but also because the kind and degree of autonomy that parents are able to grant their small children depends on feelings about themselves that they derive from society. Just as the child's sense of trust is a reflection of the mother's sturdy and realistic faith, so the child's sense of autonomy is a reflection of the parents' personal dignity. Such appears to be the teaching of the comparative study of cultures.

Personal autonomy, independence of the individual, is an especially outstanding feature of the American way of life. American parents, accordingly, are in a particularly favorable position to transmit the sense of autonomy to their children. They themselves resent being bossed, being pushed around; they maintain that everybody has the right to express his opinion and to be in control of his affairs. More easily than people who live according to an authoritarian pattern, they can appreciate a little child's vigorous desire to assert his independence and they can give him the leeway he needs in order to grow up into the upstanding, look-you-in-the-eye kind of individual that Americans admire.

It is not only in early childhood, however, that this attitude toward growing children must be maintained. As was said at the outset, these components of the healthy personality cannot be established once and for all. The period of life in which they first come into being is the most crucial, it is true. But threats to their maintenance occur throughout life. Not only parents, then, but everybody who has significant contact with children and young people must respect their desire for self-assertion, help them hold it within bounds, and avoid treating them in ways that arouse shame or doubt.

This attitude toward children, toward all people, must be maintained in institutional arrangements as well. Great differences in educational and economic opportunity and in access to the law, discrimination of all kinds are threats to this ingredient of mental health. So, too, may be the over-mechanization of our society, the depersonalization of human relations that is likely to accompany large-scale endeavor of all kinds.

Parents, as well as children, are affected by these mattters. In fact, parents' ability to grant children the kind of autonomy Americans think desirable depends in part on the way they are treated as employees and citizens. Throughout, the relation must be such as affirms personal dignity. Much of the shame and doubt aroused in children result from the indignity and uncertainty that are an expression of parents' frustrations in love and work. Special attention must be paid to all these matters, then, if we are to avoid destroying the autonomy that Americans have always set store by.

The Sense of Initiative

Having become sure, for the time being, that he is a person in his own right and having enjoyed that feeling for a year or so, the child of four or five wants to find out what kind of person he can be. To be any particular kind of person, he sees clearly, involves being able to do particular kinds of things. So he observes with keen attention what all manner of interesting adults do (his parents, the milkman, the truck driver, and so on), tries to imitate their behavior, and yearns for a share in their activities.

This is the period of enterprise and imagination, an ebullient, creative period when phantasy substitutes for literal execution of desires and the meagerest equipment provides material for high imaginings. It is a period of intrusive, vigorous learning, learning that leads away from the child's own limitations into future possibilities. There is intrusion into other people's bodies by physical attack, into other people's ears and minds by loud and aggressive talking. There is intrusion into space by vigorous locomotion and intrusion into the unknown by consuming curiosity.

By this age, too, conscience has developed. The child is no longer guided only by outsiders; there is installed within him a voice that comments on his deeds, and warns and threatens. Close attention to the remarks of any child of this age will confirm this statement. Less obvious, however, are experts' observations that children now begin to feel guilty for mere thoughts, for deeds that have been imagined but never executed. This, they say, is the explanation for the characteristic nightmares of this age period and for the over-reaction to slight punishment.

The problem to be worked out in this stage of development, accordingly, is how to will without too great a sense of guilt. The fortunate outcome of the struggle is a sense of initiative. Failure to win through to that outcome leaves the personality overburdened, and possibly over-restricted by guilt.

It is easy to see how the child's developing sense of initiative may be discouraged. So many of the projects dreamed up at this age are of a kind which cannot be permitted that the child may come to feel he is faced by a universal "No." In addition he finds that many of the projects are impossible of execution and others, even if not forbidden, fail to win the approval of the adults whom he has come to love. Moreover, since he does not always distinguish clearly between actuality and phantasy, his over-zealous conscience may disapprove of even imaginary deeds.

It is very important, therefore, for healthy personality development that much leeway and encouragement be given to the child's show of enterprise and imagination and that punishment be kept at a minimum. Boys and girls at this stage are extraordinarily appreciative of any convincing promise that someday they will be able to do things as well, or maybe better, than father and mother. They enjoy competition (especially if they can win) and insistence on goal; they get great pleasure from conquest. They need numerous examples of the kinds of roles adults assume, and they need a chance to try them out in play.

The ability that is in the making is that of selecting social goals and persevering in the attempt to reach them.

If enterprise and imagination are too greatly curbed, if severe rebukes accompany the frequently necessary denial of permission to carry out desires, a personality may result that is over-constricted. Such a personality cannot live up to its inner capacities for imagination, feeling, or performance, though it may over-compensate by immense activity and find relaxation impossible.

Constriction of personality is a self-imposed constriction, an act of the child's over-zealous conscience. "If I may not do this, I will not even think it," says conscience, "for even thinking it is dangerous." Resentment and bitterness and a vindictive atitude toward the world that forces the restriction may accompany this decision, however, and become unconscious but functioning parts of the personality. Such, at least, is the warning of psychiatrists who have learned to know the inmost feelings of emotionally handicapped children and adults.

This developmental stage has great assets as well as great dangers. At no time in life is the individual more ready to learn avidly and quickly, to become big in the sense of sharing obligation and performance. If during this preschool period the child can get some sense of the various roles and functions that he can perform as an adult, he will be ready to progress joyfully to the next stage, in which he will find pleasurable accomplishment in activities less fraught with phantasy and fear.

There is a lesson in this for later periods of personality development as well. As has been said before, these conflicts that come to a head at particular periods of a child's life are not settled once and for all. The sense of initiative, then, is one that must be continually fostered, and great care must be taken that youngsters and young people do not have to feel guilty for having dared to dream.

Just as we Americans prize autonomy, so too do we prize initiative; in fact, we regard it as the cornerstone of our economic system. There is much in the present industrial and political mode of life that may discourage initiative, that may make a young person think he had best pull in his horns. What these tendencies are and what they may do to youngsters and to their parents, who too must feel free if they are to cultivate the sense of initiative in their children, is a subject that warrants much serious discussion.

The Sense of Accomplishment

The three stages so far described probably are the most important for personality development. With a sense of trust, a sense of autonomy, and a sense of initiative achieved, progress through the later stages is pretty well assured. Whether this is because children who have a good environment in their early years are likely to continue to be so favored, or whether it is because they have attained such strength of personality that they can successfully handle later difficulties, research has not yet made clear. We do know that nearly all children who get a good start continue to develop very well, and we know that some of those who start off poorly continue to be handicapped. Observations of this sort seem to support psychological theory in the conclusion that personality is pretty well set by about six years of age. Since, however, some children develop into psychologically healthy adults in spite of a bad start, and since some who start well run into difficulties later, it is clear that much research is needed before this conclusion can be accepted as wholly correct.

To return to the developmental analysis, the fourth stage, which begins somewhere around six years of age and extends over five or six years, has as its achievement what Erikson calls the sense of industry. Perhaps "sense of accomplishment" would make the meaning clearer. At any rate, this is the period in which preoccupation with phantasy subsides, and the child wants to be engaged in real tasks that he can carry through to completion. As with the other developmental stages, there are foreshadowings of this kind of interest long before six years of age. Moreover, in some societies and in some parts of our own society children are trained very early to perform socially useful tasks. The exact age is not the point at issue. What is to be pointed out is that children, after a period characterized by exuberant imagination, want to settle down to learning exactly how to do things and how to do them well.

In contrast to the preceding stages and to the succeeding ones, this stage does not consist of a swing from a violent inner upheaval to a new mastery. Under reasonably favorable circumstances this is a period of calm, steady growth, especially if the problems of the previous stages have been well worked through. Despite its unspectacular character, this is a very important period, for in it is laid a firm basis for responsible citizenship. It is during this period that children acquire not only knowledge and skills that make for good workmanship but also the ability to cooperate and play fair and otherwise follow the rules of the larger social game.

The chief danger of this period is the presence of conditions that may lead to the development of a sense of inadequacy and inferiority. This may be the outcome if the child has not yet achieved a sense of initiative, or if his experiences at home have not prepared him for entering school happily, or if he finds school a place where his previous accomplishments are disregarded or his latent abilities are not challenged. Even with a good start the child may later lapse into discouragement and lack of interest if at home or school his individual needs are overlooked—if too much is expected of him, or if he is made to feel that achievement is beyond his ability.

It is most important for health of personality, therefore, that schools be conducted well, that methods and courses of instruction be such as

will give every child the feeling of successful accomplishment. Auto-
biographies of juvenile delinquents show time and again a boy who
hated school—hated the fact that he was marked out as stupid or awkward, as one who was not as good as the rest. Some such boys find in
jobs the sense of accomplishment they miss at school and consequently
give up their delinquent ways. Others, however, are handicapped in job
finding and keeping by the very fact that in school they did not develop
the sense of industry; hence they have work failure added to their other
insecurities. Nor is delinquency the only or the most likely outcome of
lack of success in school. Many children respond in a quieter way,
by passive acceptance of their inferiority. Psychologically they are perhaps even more harmed.

Our Puritan tradition maintains that children will not work except
under the spur of competition, so we tend to fear the suggestion that
all should succeed. To help children develop a sense of accomplishment does not mean, however, merely giving all of them good marks
and passing them on to the next grade. Children need and want real
achievement. How to help them secure it, despite differences in native
capacity and differences in emotional development, is one of the school's
most serious challenges.

School, of course, is not the only place in which children at this stage
of development can secure the sense of industry. In work at home
there are many opportunities for a child to get a feeling of mastery
and worthwhile endeavor. Rural youth groups and their urban counterparts cater to this need, and many recreation programs put as much
emphasis on work as on play. School, however, is the legally constituted
arrangement for giving instruction to the young, so it is upon teachers
that the professional responsibility for helping all children achieve
a sense of industry and accomplishment rests.

In addition to aiding personality development in this way, teachers
have many opportunities for reconfirming their pupils' sense of trust,
autonomy, and initiative or for encouraging its growth in children who
have been somewhat hampered by previous life experiences. Teachers
cannot work alone, of course, either in aiding a child in the development of new capacities or in strenthening old ones. Jointly with
parents and others they can do much, not only for children of already
healthy personality but also for many whose development has been
handicapped.

The Sense of Identity

With the onset of adolescence another period of personality development begins. As is well known, adolescence is a period of storm and
stress for many young people, a period in which previous certainties
are questioned and previous continuities no longer relied upon. Physiological changes and rapid physical growth provide the somatic base

for the turmoil and indecision. It may be that cultural factors also play a part, for it has been observed that adolescence is less upsetting in some societies than in others.

The central problem of the period is the establishment of a sense of identity. The identity the adolescent seeks to clarify is who he is, what his role in society is to be. Is he a child or is he an adult? Does he have it in him to be someday a husband and father? What is he to be as a worker and an earner of money? Can he feel self-confident in spite of the fact that his race or religion or national background makes him a person some people look down upon? Over all, will he be a success or a failure? By reason of these questions adolescents are sometimes morbidly preoccupied with how they appear in the eyes of others as compared with their own conception of themselves, and with how they can make the roles and skills learned earlier jibe with what is currently in style.

In primitive societies adolescents are perhaps spared these doubts and indecisions. Through initiation rites, often seemingly cruel in character, young people are tested out (and test themselves out) and are then welcomed into a socially recognized age category in which rights and duties and modes of living are clearly defined. In our society there are few rituals or ceremonies that mark the change in status from childhood to youth. For those who have religious affiliations, confirmation, joining the church, may serve this purpose in part, since the young people are thereby admitted, in this one segment of their lives at least, to the company of adults. Such ceremonies serve, in addition, to reaffirm to youth that the universe is trustworthy and stable and that a way of life is clearly laid out.

Graduation ceremonies might play a part in making a new status were it not that, in present-day America, status is so ill defined. What rules of law and custom exist are too diverse to be of much help. For example, legal regulations governing age of "consent," age at which marriage is permitted, age for leaving school, for driving a car, for joining (or being required to join) the Army or Navy mark no logical progressions in rights and duties. As to custom, there is so much variation in what even families who live next door to each other expect or permit that adolescents, eager to be on their way, are practically forced into standardizing themselves in their search for status. In this they are ably abetted by advertisers and entertainers who seek their patronage, as well as by well-meaning magazine writers who describe in great detail the means by which uniformity can be achieved.

In this urge to find comfort through similarity, adolescents are likely to become stereotyped in behavior and ideals. They tend to form cliques for self-protection and fasten on petty similarities of dress and gesture to assure themselves that they are really somebody. In these cliques they may be intolerant and even cruel toward those they label as different. Unfortunate as such behavior is and not to be condoned, intolerance serves the important purpose of giving the group members at least the negative assurance that there is something they are not.

The danger of this developmental period is self-diffusion. As Biff puts it in *The Death of a Salesman,* "I just can't take hold, Mom. I can't take hold of some kind of a life." A boy or girl can scarcely help feeling somewhat diffuse when the body changes in size and shape so rapidly, when genital maturity floods body and imagination with forbidden desires, when adult life lies ahead with such a diversity of conflicting possibilites and choices.

Whether this feeling of self-diffusion is fairly easily mastered or whether, in extreme, it leads to delinquency, neurosis or outright psychosis, depends to a considerable extent on what has gone before. If the course of personality development has been a healthy one, a feeling of self-esteem has accrued from the numerous experiences of succeeding in a task and sensing its cultural meaning. Along with this, the child has come to the conviction that he is moving toward an understandable future in which he will have a definite role to play. Adolescence may upset this assurance for a time or to a degree but fairly soon a new integration is achieved, and the boy or girl sees again (and with clearer vision) that he belongs and that he is on his way.

The course is not so easy for adolescents who have not had so fortunate a part or for those whose earlier security is broken by a sudden awareness that as members of minority groups their way of life sets them apart. The former, already unsure of themselves, find their earlier doubt and mistrust reactivated by the physiological and social changes that adolescence brings. The latter, once secure, may feel that they must disavow their past and try to develop an "American" personality.

Much has been learned and written about the adolescent problems of the boys and girls whose early personality development has been impaired. How they can be helped, if their disorders are not too severe, is also fairly well known. The full implications of these findings for parents, teachers, and others who would guide youth are still to be worked out but, even so, there is considerable information.

Less well understood are the difficulties and the ways of helping adolescents who grew up in cultures that are not of the usual run. These boys and girls may have been privileged in having had a childhood in which there was little inhibition of sensual pleasures, and in which development proceeded by easy, unselfconscious stages. For them, difficulties arise if their parents lose trust in themselves or if their teachers apply sudden correctives, or if they themselves reject their past and try to act like the others. The new role of middle-class adolescent is often too hard to play. Delinquency or bizarre behavior marks the failure.

How to reach these boys and girls, how to help them attain their desire, is a matter not well understood. It is clear, however, that they should not be typed by pat diagnoses and social judgments, for they are ever ready to become the "bums" that they are called. Those who would guide them must understand both the psychology of adolescence and the cultural realities of the day. There is trust to be restored and doubt and guilt and feelings of inferiority to be overcome. The science of how to do this is still pretty much lacking, though here and there teachers, clergymen, probation officers and the like are highly success-ful in the task.

Hard though it be to achieve, the sense of identity is the individual's only safeguard against the lawlessness of his biological drives and the authority of an over-weening conscience. Loss of identity, loss of the sense that there is some continuity, sameness, and meaning to life, exposes the individual to his childhood conflicts and leads to emotional upsets. This outcome was observed time and again among men hard pressed by the dangers of war. It is clear, then, that if health of per-sonality is to be preserved much attention must be given to assuring that America makes good on its promises to youth.

The Sense of Intimacy

After the sense of identity, to a greater or less extent, is achieved it becomes possible for the next component of the healthy personality to develop. This is the sense of intimacy, intimacy with persons of the same sex or of the opposite sex or with one's self. The youth who is not fairly sure of his identity shies away from interpersonal relations and is afraid of close communion with himself. The surer he becomes of himself, the more he seeks intimacy, in the form of friendship, love and inspiration.

In view of the early age at which boy and girl attachments are encouraged today, it may seem strange to put the critical period for the development of the sense of intimacy late in adolescence. The explana-tion is that, on the one hand, sexual intimacy is only one part of what is involved, and, on the other, boy-girl attachments of earlier age periods are likely to be of a somewhat different order. Regarding the latter point, it has been observed by those who know young people well that high-school age boys and girls often use each other's company for an endless verbal examination of what the other thinks, feels, and wants to do. In other words, these attachments are one means of defining one's identity.

In contrast to this use of friendship and companionship, boys and girls late in adolescence usually have need for a kind of fusion with the essence of other people and for a communion with their own inner resources. If, by reason of inadequacies in previous personality develop-ment, this sense of intimacy cannot be achieved, the youth may retire into psychological isolation and keep his relations with people on a formal, stereotyped level that is lacking in spontaneity and warmth or he may keep trying again and again to get close to others, only to meet with repeated failure. Under this compulsion he may even marry, but the role of mate is one he can rarely sustain, for the condition of true two-ness is that each individual must first become himself.

In this area of personality development as in the others, cultural factors play a part in sustaining or in discouraging the individual in his development. American culture is unusually successful in encouraging the development of the feelings of independence, initiative, industry, and identity. It is somewhat less successful in the area of intimacy, for the culture's ideal is the subordination of sexuality and sensuality to a life of work, duty, and worship.

Consequently, American adolescents are likely to be unsupported by their parents and to find little confirmation in story or song for their desire to sense intimately the full flavor of the personality of others. In many of them, then, the sense of intimacy does not develop highly and they have difficulty in finding in close personal relations the outlet for tension that they need.

There is some evidence that a change in conventions and customs in this respect is in the making, however. Too abrupt change in any such cultural matter is not to be urged, but it is to be hoped that gradual, frank discussion can bring about gradual alteration in attitude and overcome the dangers inherent in the traditional rigidity.

The Parental Sense

"Parental sense" designates somewhat the same capacity as that implied in the words, creativity or productivity. The individual has normally come to adulthood before this sense can develop fully.

The parental sense is indicated most clearly by interest in producing and caring for children of one's own. It may also be exhibited in relation to other people's children or by a parental kind of responsibility toward the products of creative activity of other sorts. The mere desire for or possession of children does not indicate that this component of the healthy personality has developed. In fact, many parents who bring their children to child guidance clinics are found not to have reached this stage of personality development.

The essential element is the desire to nourish and nurture what has been produced. It is the ability to regard one's children as a trust of the community, rather than as extensions of one's own personality or merely as beings that one happens to live with.

Failure to develop this component of the healthy personality often results in a condition which has not been adequately categorized clinically. Although a true sense of intimacy has not developed, the individual may obsessively seek companionship. There is something of egotism in this as in his other activities, a kind of self-absorption. The individual is inclined to treat himself as a child and to be rivalrous with his children, if he has any. He indulges himself, expects to be indulged, and in general behaves in an infantile or immature manner.

There are both individual and social explanations of the failure to develop an adequate parental sense. Individually, the explanation may be found in the inadequate development of the personality components previously described. In some people this failure goes far back. Because of unfortunate experiences in childhood they did not arrive at a firm sense of trust, autonomy, and the rest. In others it is only inadequacies in later stages, especially in the development of the sense of intimacy, that are at fault.

Socially, as has been suggested throughout this analysis, healthy personality development depends upon the culture's ideals and upon the economic arrangements of the society. In order that most people may develop fully the sense of being a parent, the role of parent, both mother and father, must be a respected one in the society. Giving must rank higher than getting, and loving than being loved. The economy must be such that the future can be depended upon and each person can feel assured that he has a meaningful and respected part to play. Only so can most individuals afford to renounce selfish aims and derive much of their satisfaction from rearing children.

The Sense of Integrity

The final component of the healthy personality is the sense of integrity. In every culture the dominant ideals—honor, courage, faith, purity, grace, fairness, self-discipline—become at this stage the core of the healthy personality's integration. The individual, in Erikson's words, "becomes able to accept his individual life cycle and the people who have become significant to it as meaningful within the segment of history in which he lives."

To continue Erikson's description, "Integrity thus means a new and different love of one's parents, free of the wish that they should have been different, and an acceptance of the fact that one's life is one's own responsibility. It is a sense of comradeship with men and women of distant times and of different pursuits, who have created orders and objects and sayings conveying human dignity and love. Although aware of the relativity of all the various life styles that have given meaning to human striving, the possessor of integrity is ready to defend the dignity of his own life style against all physical and economic threats. For he knows that, for him, all human dignity stands or falls with the one style of integrity of which he partakes."

The adult who lacks integrity in this sense may wish that he could live life again. He feels that if at one time he had made a different decision he could have been a different person and his ventures would have been successful. He fears death and cannot accept his one and only life cycle as the ultimate of life. In the extreme, he experiences disgust and despair. Despair expresses the feeling that time is too short to try out new roads to integrity. Disgust is a means of hiding the despair, a chronic, contemptuous displeasure with the way life is run. As with the dangers and the solutions of previous periods, doubt and despair are not difficulties that are overcome once and for all, nor is integrity so achieved. Most people fluctuate between the two extremes. Most, also, at no point, either attain to the heights of unalloyed integrity or fall to the depths of complete disgust and despair.

Even in adulthood a reasonably healthy personality is sometimes secured in spite of previous misfortunes in the developmental sequence. New sources of trust may be found. Fortunate events and circumstances may aid the individual in his struggle to feel autonomous. Imagination and initiative may be spurred by new responsibilities, and feelings of inferiority be overcome by successful achievement. Even late in life an individual may arrive at a true sense of who he is and what he has to do and may be able to win through to a feeling of intimacy with others and to joy in producing and giving.

Evidence of such changes is found in the case records of psychiatrists and social workers. Common sense observation attests that similar changes in health of personality are sometimes accomplished without benefit of any form of psychotherapy. Much remains to be learned about this, however, especially about how life itself may serve as therapeusis.

For the healthy personality development of children and youth it is necessary that a large proportion of adults attain a sense of integrity to a considerable degree. Not only parents but all who deal with children have need of this quality if they are to help children maintain the feeling that the universe is dependable and trustworthy. Integrity is relatively easily attained and sustained when the culture itself gives support, when a meaning to life is clearly spelled out in tradition and ceremony, and roles are clearly defined. Our culture, with its rapidly changing technology and its diversity of value standards, leaves much for the individual to work out for himself. In the American dream, however, and the Judaeo-Christian tradition on which it is based there are values and ideals aplenty. In the interest of the welfare of children and youth, in order that a generation of happy individuals and responsible citizens be reared, it is highly important that these values and ideals be brought into prominence and that the promise of American life be kept.

References

1. Harry Bakwin, "Emotional Deprivation in Infants," *Journal of Pediatrics,* 35 (October 1949), pp. 512–529.

2. John Bowlby, M.D., Summary of Dr. René Spitz's observations, unpublished manuscript.

11   The Beginnings of the Self: The Problem of the Nurturing Environment

Ira J. Gordon

*In the preceding selection the significance of the early stages in the child's
further development was noted. Gordon expands upon this, and draws
from recent research to develop a more complete understanding of the
growth of the self and the self concept.*

The concept of the self is an old one in religion and philosophy
and has been discussed endlessly as a part of man's search for identity,
as he sought to answer the question, "Who am I?" For Descartes the answer was, *"Cogito ergo sum"*—I think, therefore I am. This statement
marked a sharp break with medieval thought, and contributed to the
age of reason. For Descartes, cognition or reason was superior to emotion. Knowing was the self's primary function. The self was active,
aware, free; the senses and emotions were passive, or confused influences
upon the mind. From the early seventeenth until the late nineteenth
century, this view reigned.

Freud broke with this tradition by centering upon the emotions,
by denying free will, and by focusing upon the influence of the child's
experiences in the earliest years. Since Freud, the Descartian answer
is insufficient. We now seek to define ourselves in ways which include
our feelings as well as our thoughts, and look for the origins of our
personality in the first dim moments of life long before cognition
seemed possible. Because of Freud, our notion of self-definition has
required that its origins be in early childhood and that it be developed
from the experiences we have had in that most intimate of circles—our
family. For modern man, this is a truism; but it also leaves unanswered
a myriad of questions concerning how we got that way.

The first step in self-awareness is both affective and cognitive: the
discovery of one's own body as distinct and pleasurable. When the
infant puts thumb in mouth, he experiences sensation in both his thumb
and his mouth and learns that the thumb is part of him. When the
numerous other objects that the infant places in his mouth do not yield
the double sensation, he separates self from other. This process, labeled
"self-sentience" by Sullivan,[1] provides the infant with his first anchorage point, his first awareness of separateness. To paraphrase Descartes,

Phi Delta Kappan, March 1969. Reprinted by permission.
Mr. Gordon is Professor of Education and Director of the Institute for Development of
Human Resources, College of Education, University of Florida, Gainesville.

if the infant could speak, he might say, "I experience me, therefore I am."

The second marking point is the awareness of "other." The separation of "I" or "me" from "not me" requires the introduction of people and objects from outside the child. The child needs enough of them, with enough frequency and consistency, that they can be differentiated. The infant at three months engages in social smiles,[2] but much has gone on before this time to enable the child to reach this major social event. It is not purely the "maturation" of an inadequate organism toward social behavior. William James, at the turn of the century, defined the world of the infant as a blooming, buzzing confusion, but current research in learning indicates that infants are able to make much more elaborate differentiations of their physical environment in terms of sight and sound and sense than James would have thought possible.

For example, Lipsett's research at Brown[3] indicates the ways in which both operant and classical conditioning can occur in infancy. Although its approach is not psychoanalytic, current research in infant learning substantiates the psychoanalyst's view of the infant's ability to learn and thus supports the notion of the importance of this early period. But what is it the child learns, in addition to such behaviors as feeding or cooing responses, smiles, and cries? The period of infancy has been seen as the time the child learns basic trust.[4] The nature of the inputs— that is, the way he is handled and fondled, dealt with and responded to, and how his body reacts to these events—teaches the child whether or not the world is a safe or terrifying place, and whether he can trust it or not.

Since the separation of self and world is incomplete, the self-concept, the "I," is part of the world. It is both cognitive and affective, active and passive. "I" is not only in the brain but also in the viscera. It is both Cartesian and Freudian.

Specifically, what are some of the inputs in the very early years which influence the initial picture of the self? Robert Sears and his colleagues,[5, 6] in a series of studies which applied learning theory rigor to psychoanalytic concepts, indicated that parental attitudes and behavior (disciplinary techniques, permissiveness, severity, temperamental qualities, and aspirations) exhibited in the areas of hunger, elimination, dependency, sex, and aggression were important factors in development and in sex-role identification, a major dimension of the self-concept. But these external inputs emphasize the affective side of life. They do not adequately consider either the cognitive dimension or the role of the child himself.

Current thought emphasizes the competence of the infant and brings together both the cognitive and affective elements of the child into one system. It emphasizes the importance of not only the characteristic child-rearing patterns described by Sears, and the family drama so dear to the psychoanalyst, but also the role of the infant himself as an active, striving, curious, learning organism, who makes his impact on his family. This is no *tabula rasa* child. And the child's view of himself is not simply a mirror image of the external events which surround him early in life. From the very beginning it includes his own organism as it senses, feels, learns, and assigns meaning to these external stimuli. The child learns who he is from what happens to him, from the language that surrounds him, from the people who are dear to him, from the opportunities to deal with the objects and events in his immediate world, and from his own responses to the welter of stimuli. His self-esteem represents his unique organization of his own biological makeup, the evaluations made of him by significant adults, and his own learning from trial and manipulation and feedback from his world. Cognitive development is inseparable from personality development.

The child obviously cannot define "self" as distinct from "other" before he has a permanent frame of reference. One measure of this frame is Piaget's "object permanence," manifested by the individual's recognition that an object continues to exist even though it is no longer visible to him. He arrives at this point somewhere in the second year of life. It is a growth marker because now he can relate affectively to other individuals in some consistent fashion, and cognitively he has achieved a level where he can actively engage in searching his environment. Gaining this ability is a giant step forward and gives the child a sense of competence in relating to his world.

We can make an intuitive leap from object permanence to Erikson's basic trust. Both mean that the child has now organized at least a portion of his world so that it is orderly and predictable—and therefore manageable. With this he can structure a positive self-concept. Without a sense of object permanence, he is powerless. Psychological inputs are important here, because only on the basis of broad experience can the child discover that both people and things have external reality. With the establishment of "other," the child's own behavior can now include role-taking and role-playing.[7] This process enables him to shift from Piaget's "egocentric" stage toward "decentration." That is, he develops from seeing others as just like him toward a recognition of the fact that what one sees and believes depends upon where he stands and what he already knows. Parents not only influence opportunities for such role-playing, but also provide the basic models for imitation. Through the ways in which they teach or deny opportunities for dramatic play, they influence both the cognitive and affective dimensions of the self-concept. Smilansky[8] has described the way parents affect this phase of learning.

Piaget's theoretical exposition of cognitive development returns us to the epistemological position of Descartes, but with added knowledge from Freud and the behavioral scientists. Decarie,[9] for example, was able to investigate both Piagetian and psychoanalytic views about the process, timing, and meaning of arrival at object permanence. Generally, she found empirical support for both, and concluded that parents are the most effective agents in presenting both cognitive and affective experience to the young child. Piaget wrote in 1954:

> The other person is of course an emotional object to the highest degree but at the same time is the most interesting cognitive object, the most alive, the most unexpected. . . . The other person is an object which implies a multitude of exchanges in which cognitive as well as effective factors play a role, and if this object is of paramount importance in one of these respects, it is, I think, equally important in the other.[10]

How important are these early years? Gardner Murphy has indicated that the self-picture is fairly well integrated by the third year of life. Once it has developed, it becomes the evaluator, selector, judger, and organizer of future experience, and the child's behavior may be seen as organized to enhance and maintain his view. Such a picture sounds harsh and deterministic if we did not understand that possibilities for change are always present. Life is not over at age three, but the general view toward the world and toward one's self is already present.

The longitudinal data which support the importance of early childhood are fairly consistent. Bloom indicated on the basis of reviews of longitudinal research[11] that half of what accounts for the variance in adults in aggressiveness in males and dependence in females seems to be present by age four. Not only Bloom's summary but also the classical longitudinal studies conducted in California[12] and the longitudinal studies of the Fels Institute at Yellow Springs, Ohio,[13] demonstrated the effects of parental behavior in the child's first six years of his behavior and attitudes in subsequent years.

One of Bayley's findings is that the mother's affectional behavior toward her son in the first three years of his life was related to his friendship, cooperation, and attentiveness when he became a school child and an adolescent. These behaviors may be inferred to be reflections of feelings of security, a fundamental dimension of self-concept.

One of Freud's contributions is the concept of identification, and, more specifically, sex-role identification. We noted earlier that Sears adopted this concept and applied general behavior methodology to its investigation. It is central also to Kagan and Moss. For them, the notion of sex-role identification is a core concept in influencing stability of behavior from childhood through adulthood. Events early in life lead not only to the child's sex-role identification but also determine his general social expectancy for all behavior. Boys are expected to behave more aggressively, more competently, and in more task-oriented fashions; girls are to be more nurturant, more person-oriented. Parent behavior in the first six years of life influences the child's identity and the standards he will set for typical sex-related behavior. Kagan and Moss conclude that the individual's own desire to make his behavior agree with the culture's definition of sex is a major factor determining the stability of his behavior over time.

Longitudinal studies indicate how very important it is to analyze data about children by sex as well as by age. They indicate the differential effects of parental behavior on boys and girls. This should not surprise us, but it often gets overlooked. In both the cognitive and affective aspects of the self, boys and girls view themselves differently, tend to use different learning styles, tend to evaluate different aspects of self and world as important. The origins lie both in biology and in differential treatment.

Unfortunately, most of the children studied in longitudinal research have been middle-class, from somewhat stable families, where conditions might generally foster the mix of intellectual and emotional inputs that lead to positive views of the self. They fit Lois Murphy's observation that "Each experience of mastery and triumph sets the stage for better efforts in the next experience. Confidence, hope, and a sense of self-worth are increased along with the increase in cognitive and motor skills, which can contribute to better use of the resources."[14] Their world provides them with both intellectual challenge and emotional support. Both the cognitive and affective "matches"—the connection between the child's motives and cognitive level on the one hand and the experiences being offered to him on the other[15, 16]—are in phase. His positive self-image receives verification from his competence in dealing with the world.

Unfortunately, not all children have the sense of triumph described by Lois Murphy, nor do their selves match the world's demands. Yarrow's studies[17] of maternal deprivation indicate the difficulties encountered by children who lack a mother figure to provide them with some stable anchorage points. In the social domain, Clark,[18] Deutsch,[19] Smilansky,[20] Marans,[21] and Wortis,[22] among others, point out the devastating effects of social deprivation on building positive self-esteem. Although the child's view of himself does not mirror and is not an exact replica of his world's picture of him, for many youngsters it comes quite close. If the larger society conceives of the child as not worthwhile and demonstrates consistently to him that it so judges him, it is difficult for the child to value himself. Children in the ghetto, children classified as slow learners, children who for a variety of reasons are told even in these early years that they are not quite good enough or smart enough or handsome enough tend to devalue themselves and thus to set the stage for continuously poorer levels of performance than might otherwise be their lot. These images are already set before entry into school.[23] Children growing up in psychologically disorganized homes suffer similar fates, as Pavenstedt[24] has indicated about South Boston children.

"As the twig is bent . . ." has long been part of Western folklore. Scientific data now support this view. The origins of the self lie in the early years. How the child will see himself is influenced by the way he is treated, the opportunities provided for him, how he is evaluated as he copes with these opportunities, and how he perceives these evaluations.

If these early years are crucial in determining school performance through the mechanism of the self-concept, then society cannot shrug off its responsibility. For very young children, negative self-views may be as damaging as physical illness or actual physical handicap. We are rapidly making provision for medical help. We need to create nurturing environments early in life so that children's concepts of themselves may possibly emerge as positive. Whether the school systems as now constructed are the appropriate agencies to reach down to the younger years is open to debate. The example of Head Start programs and the present Parent and Child Center movement indicate that new social agencies consisting of and requiring the participation of those for whom the service is intended may provide effective vehicles for change. What is needed is education so designed that parents can provide children not only with an *affective* climate which tells them they are loved and worthy but also with a *cognitive* climate that allows the child to be competent as well as feel loved. Adequate self-esteem requires this combination.

A characteristic of the American society is its own self-concept that it is capable of solving the problems which afflict it, once the problems are pointed out. The issue is clear. What is required now are social engineering skills. Intervention is essential. We have some ideas of what it should be and who should render it. Now we need to develop the types of programs which provide for all children the psychological inputs which lead to positive self-esteem.

References

1. H. S. Sullivan, *The Interpersonal Theory of Psychiatry* (New York: W. W. Norton, 1953).

2. René Spitz, *The First Year of Life* (New York: International Universities Press, 1965).

3. L. Lipsitt, "Learning in the Human Infant," pp. 225–228, in H. W. Stevenson, E. H. Hess, and H. L. Rheingold (eds.), *Early Behavior: Comparative and Developmental Approaches* (New York: Wiley, 1967).

4. E. Erikson, *Childhood and Society* (New York: Norton, 1951).

5. R. Sears, E. Maccoby, and H. Levin, *Patterns of Child Rearing* (Evanston, Ill.: Row Peterson, 1957).

6. R. Sears *et al.*, *Identification and Child Rearing* (Stanford, Calif.: Stanford University Press, 1965).

7. G. H. Mead, *Mind, Self and Society* (Chicago: University of Chicago, 1940).

8. S. Smilansky, *The Effects of Sociodramatic Play on Disadvantaged Preschool Children* (New York: Wiley, 1968).

9. T. Decarie, *Intelligence and Affectivity in Early Childhood* (New York: International Universities Press, 1965).

10. J. Piaget, *Les Relations Entre l'Affectivité et l'Intelligence Dans la Developpement Mental de l'Enfant* (Paris: Centre de Documentation Universitaire, 1954).

11. B. Bloom, *Stability and Change in Human Characteristics* (New York: Wiley, 1964).

12. N. Bayley, "Consistency of Maternal and Child Behaviors in the Berkeley Growth Study," *Vita Humana* (1964), pp. 73–95.

13. J. Kagan and H. Moss, *Birth to Maturity* (New York: Wiley, 1962).

14. L. Murphy and associates, *The Widening World of Childhood* (New York: Basic, 1962).

15. J. McV. Hunt, *Intelligence and Experience* (New York: The Ronald Press, 1961).

16. Ira J. Gordon, *Studying the Child in School* (New York: Wiley, 1962).

17. L. Yarros, "Separation from Parents During Early Childhood," pp. 89–136, in Martin L. Hoffman and Lois W. Hoffman (eds.), *Review of Child Development Research,* vol. 1 (New York: Russell Sage, 1964).

18. K. Clark, *Dark Ghetto* (New York: Harper, 1965).

19. M. Deutsch and associates, *The Disadvantaged Child* (New York: Basic, 1967).

20. Smilansky, 1968.

21. A. Marans, D. Meers, and D. Huntington, "The Children's Hospital in Washington, D.C.," pp. 287–301, in Laura L. Dittman (ed.), *Early Child Care, the New Perspective* (New York: Atherton, 1968).

22. H. Wortis et al., "Child-Rearing Practices in a Low Socioeconomic Group," *Pediatrics,* 32 (1963), pp. 298–307.

23. B. Long and E. Henderson, "Social Schemata of School Beginners: Some Demographic Correlates," in *Proceedings, 75th Annual Convention,* American Psychological Association (1967), pp. 329–330.

24. E. Pavenstedt (ed.), *The Drifters* (Boston: Little, Brown, 1967).

12   His Struggle for Identity

Jerome Kagan

Why do boys usually have more difficulty in adapting to school than do girls? What are some of the contributory factors in the success of many middle-class children and the failure of many lower-class children in a school environment? In the following article Jerome Kagan cites some of the current research and hypotheses about how different attitudes and environments are significant in the education of the child.

The newborn child is a remarkably capable organism from the moment he begins to breathe. He can see, hear, and smell, and is sensitive to pain, touch, and change in position. The only one of the five senses that may not be functioning immediately at birth is taste.

The newborn's behavioral equipment is also remarkably well developed. When only two hours old, he will follow a rapidly moving light with his eyes; his pupils will dilate in darkness and constrict in light; he will suck a finger or nipple inserted into his mouth; he will turn in the direction in which his cheek or the corner of his mouth is touched. He can cry, cough, turn away, vomit, lift his chin from a prone position, and grasp an object placed in his palm. His body will react to a loud sound. He can flex and extend his limbs, smack his lips, and chew his fingers.

It is fortunate that the infant is so competent at birth because his new environment outside his mother's body subjects him suddenly to such unfamiliar stresses as hunger, heat, cold, and pain. During the first weeks of life, most of his behavior is in direct response to the unexpected interferences with his equilibrium. If he is hungry, he cries. If he is excited, he babbles. If he is in pain, he cries to the accompaniment of thrashing arms and legs.

These innate reactions alter his environment significantly by bringing another person to tend him. When this happens, the child—who instructed his mother more than she instructed him during his period in the womb—enters the active influence of the society to which he belongs. Thenceforth, according to the talents of those who serve him, certain of the infant's behaviors will be selectively strengthened and certain others will be selectively weakened.

The relation between infant and mother is a ballet, in which each partner responds to the steps of the other. If, when the infant cries, the mother bestows care and affection, the infant will be likely to cry on the next occasion when he is distressed. Thus the mother's actions are molding the infant's behavior. But the frequency and regularity with which the mother acts toward the child are also being affected by the infant. The mother is more likely to leave the living room and go to the infant's room if the infant cries than if the infant is quiet. As a result, irritable babies, who are more often boys than girls, typically share their mother's company more often than do placid, quiet babies. If a mother's attempts to soothe her infant are successful, she is more likely to come to the infant when he calls. The infant who smiles will elicit more smiling from the mother than a non-smiling baby. The infant girl who babbles provokes more imitative babbling from the mother than the infant who is quiet. In this sense, the infant is clearly shaping the mother's behavior as much as the mother influences the infant.

Another major determinant of the mother's actions, in addition to the child's moment-to-moment behavior, is her set of goals for the child. Most American middle-class mothers want their boys to be independent and self-reliant because contemporary American society rewards independence and competitiveness. Most Japanese middle-class mothers, by contrast, want their sons to be interdependent with the family and less self-reliant. The mothers' actions flow from these idealized models. Each mother loves her child equally and thinks she is doing the best for him.

Each set of parents has the difficult task of deciding what kind of child they wish to create. The decision can become excruciatingly difficult in times of great flux, like those through which we are now passing. The increasing population density in our cities, coupled with growing alienation of citizens from a sense of community, is causing many Americans to question whether individualism, carried to present-day extremes, is healthy. How does a particular set of parents react to this question? Depending on the strength of their commitment to traditions of competitive individualism versus their eagerness to participate in evolution of new cultural designs, their values may conflict with the values of their neighborhood. And if the characteristics of the child do not adapt him to whatever values are accepted by the parents, there is conflict within conflict.

The child whose personality traits do not match the values of his society is not likely to be well adjusted. Such a child might be much happier in a society governed by a quite different set of values. The parental decision regarding the child is an overwhelmingly moral one, not to be decided on scientific evidence alone. Parents should appreciate that there is no ideal set of personality characteristics for a child nor any ideal set of parental practices. Each is relative to its own time and cultural context.

The child's perception of whether he is loved or rejected is also relative. If the child knows that the parents are poor, and it is a sacrifice for them to buy him a toy worth five dollars for Christmas, he will interpret receipt of that toy as an act of love and affection; for he recognizes that the parents have given him something that required a personal sacrifice. The child of an affluent family who receives the same toy is not likely to view it as reflecting any special affection. For this boy, perhaps, a long walk in the forest, which is a sacrifice for a busy executive father, is the gift that is symbolic of love. Love or rejection is not contained in any specific set of behaviors by a mother or a father. Love or rejection is relative to the child's perceptions; for love, like beauty, is in the mind of the beholder.

The same reasoning holds for punishments. There is no specific effect of a verbal chastisement, a spanking, or a banishment from the company of parents or siblings. The effect of each of these punishments on the child is always dependent on the child's interpretation of that punishment. Each parent will be better able to socialize his child if he has access to the "tote board" of values the child holds. It is not an easy accomplishment, but its attainment is worth great effort.

The first year of life is marked by rapid development of perceptual structures in the child. Although we now know that the newborn child is far from being an amorphous bundle of insensitive flesh and bone, our contemporary understanding of cognitive growth resembles the state of chemical theory in the seventeenth century, when a scientist could relate either natural or purposive causes to obvious changes in the color, weight, smell, or texture of substances but could not explain what happened to bring the changes about.

Long before anything at all was known about the human brain, pre-scientific philosophies taught that the heart was the seat of human personality. Therefore, it is interesting that modern scientific research with children should demonstrate—as it has—that the heart-beat is a dependable signal of the child's attention. Experiments in our own and other laboratories during the last decade have tracked the processes of the infant mind by noting the occasions when the child's heartbeat suddenly slows. The resting heart rate of infants ranges from 120 to 180 beats per minute, with an average of about 145 beats. Experience has confirmed that decelerations greater than six or seven beats are most often associated with an attentive posture, and facial or motor responses indicating surprise. By measuring the child's heartrate and the duration of his gaze at various events, one can easily see that the earliest determinant of the infant's attention is high rate of change in the physical parameters of a stimulus. Lights that blink on and off are more likely to capture his attention than is a steady light source. Intermittent tones of sound are more attention getting than continuous ones. Visual events with high black-white contour contrast possess more power to recruit sustained attention than stimuli with minimal contour contrast. These conditions produce distinctiveness naturally. They elicit attention without prior learning. These factors dominate the attention during the first twelve weeks.

After that time, the infant's reactions show increasing signs of being controlled by experience. In other words, the child is beginning to think about what he sees. Attention is focused more and more in relation to the degree to which the elements of an event are a distortion or discrepancy from an established schema.

A schema is a representation of an external event. Like a caricature, it is defined by a set of distinctive elements. If the distinctive elements change, the schema changes. The four-month-old child's schema of a human face probably consists of an oval outline and two symmetrically placed eyes. When an infant of that age is shown a sketch of a face with asymmetric eyes or a face with no eyes, the child smiles markedly less than he smiles at a face with symmetrically placed eyes, with or without the presence of nose and mouth. The smile seems to be his "Aha" reaction—his way of saying the stimulus is familiar to him.

A child pays maximal attention to an event that is a slight deviation from the distinctive elements of his schema. The four-month-old baby will look longer at a photograph of a face—regular or moderately disfigured—than he would at a randomly generated nonsense figure with a high degree of black-white contrast. Furthermore, his cardiac deceleration will be greater to it than to the black-white nonsense figures. Since each child develops his own schema at his own rate, it follows that information intended to command his attention must be tailored to fit his schema.

Let us consider some economic class differences in cognitive functioning in light of the above. Our Harvard laboratory has studied more than 160 first-born Caucasian infants from lower-middle-class, middle-class, and upper-middle-class families. Lower-class infants come from families where one or both parents did not complete high school and where the fathers were in unskilled occupations. Upper-middle-class infants came from families where both parents were college graduates.

Each infant was exposed to two visual episodes in the laboratory at four months of age. In the first episode, each child was shown each of four different achromatic depictions of human faces. The four stimuli were a photograph of a male face, a schematic outline of a regular male face, a collage of the photograph of the face, and a collage of the schematic regular face. After a short recess, each child was shown a series of three-dimensional sculptured faces painted flesh color, and four presentations each of four different faces: a regular male face; a collage of that face with eyes, nose, and mouth rearranged; a regular face with no eyes; and a completely blank face with neither eyes, nose, nor mouth.

The children from the lowest economic level displayed the smallest cardiac decelerations to all the stimuli. How are we to interpret this?

The lower-middle-class infants look as long at the faces as the upper-class babies do, but do not decelerate their heartbeats because the faces are not close enough to their schema for the faces of their parents. The favorite explanation for this difference in response is that the mother's face is a more distinctive stimulus for the upper-middle-class child than for the less privileged child. We believe that well educated mothers are more likely to engage in frequent, distinctive, face-to-face contact with their children, more likely to create conditions that will make the parent's countenance distinctive.

The most dramatic differences between lower- and middle-class children of preschool or school age involve language skills. Documentation for this conclusion is everywhere. A fast and often glib interpretation of it rests on the belief that lower-class parents talk less often to their children. This may be too simple an interpretation. We certainly do not wish to reject the idea totally but we prefer to balance it with the possibility that lower-class children are not so much deprived of parental vocalization as they are deprived of distinctive vocalization. The lower-class child does not receive distinctive verbal stimulation from adults and, as a result, is less likely to attend to human speech.

Some of the lower- and middle-class children mentioned above were observed with their mothers in their homes for a day when the infants were four months old. A selected set of mother and child variables was recorded every five seconds. The observer wore in her ear a small, inconspicuous battery-powered device which produced a brief auditory signal every five seconds, and the observer recorded, in five-second units, variables that belonged to a prearranged code. Some of the variables included: mother vocalize to infant, mother touch infant, mother vigorously manipulate infant, mother pick up infant, child vocalize, child extend limbs, and child thrash.

Computation of the percentage of time the mother vocalized to the infant, regardless of what else she was doing, or where she was in the home, disclosed only a slight and nonsignificant tendency for the upper-middle-class mothers to vocalize more often than lower- or middle-class mothers to their daughters. There were even less striking differences for sons. However, when we examined the distinctiveness of the mothers' vocalization—vocalization that occurred when mother was face-to-face with her infant and doing nothing else but talking to her—more dramatic differences appeared.

Let us describe a hypothetical experience of an upper-middle-class girl and a lower-class girl.

The middle-class child is lying in her crib in her bedroom on the second floor of a suburban home. She wakes, the room is quiet, her mother is downstairs baking. The infant studies the crib and her fingers. Suddenly the quiet is broken as the mother enters, looks down at her baby, and speaks. This auditory intrusion is maximally distinctive and likely to orient the infant to her mother and to the vocalization. If the child responds vocally, the mother is apt to continue the dialogue.

An infant girl in a ghetto is lying on a couch in a two-room apartment with the television going and siblings peering into her face. The child lies in a sea of sound; like the sea, the sound is homogeneous. The mother approaches the child and says something. This communication is minimally distinctive from background noise and, as such, is not likely to recruit the infant's attention. Many of the infant's vocalizations during the day are not likely to be responded to by anyone nor are they likely to elicit a special response.

This research generates implications for preschool enrichment programs for lower-class children. There is a zealous attempt to bombard the lower-class child with pictures, crayons, books, speech, and typewriters, as if an intellectual deficit was akin to hunger and the proper therapy required filling of his cerebral gulleys with stuff.

I would like to argue for a more paced strategy, a self-conscious attempt to intervene when the intrusion is likely to be maximally distinctive. For example, teaching reading or vocabulary should be individual or in very small groups, and background context should be simple so that the material to be learned has maximal distinctiveness. Instructional speech should be paced so that each communication holds the attentional stage solo and does not share the child's limited attentional capacities with other attractions. We must initiate explicit attempts to diagnose the content and articulateness of the child's existing schema and to plan interventions that are moderate discrepancies from his schema.

Distinctiveness of events recruits the child's attention and can maintain it for five, ten, or even twenty seconds. But sustained attention for minutes requires more than discrepancy; it requires the possession of structures or chains of cognitive units that are specifically activated by the event. When one sees a three-year-old devote a half hour to exploration of an old telephone, there is a temptation to smile and mumble something about the child's natural curiosity. However, long periods of sustained involvement are neither inherent in the event nor part of the child's natural equipment. It can be taken for granted that this particular child has either watched a telephone being used, or spoken into a telephone mouthpiece himself, or heard his parents explain what a telephone is for. Sustained involvement of any child is dependent on that child's previous acquisition of a set of hypotheses and reactions appropriate to the object. Without such prior learning, a potential thirty-minute exploration can be reduced to less than thirty seconds.

I recall a teacher who brought to class a dozen packs of Cape Cod seaweed stuffed with attractive samples of shells of diverse species. She gave each pair of six-year-old children one of these attractive toys and withdrew, expecting the pupils to display natural curiosity. Each child devoted less than ten seconds to the material before returning to his previous game. The teacher had failed to explain to the children that the shells were once inhabited by different kinds of animals, and that by looking carefully at a shell one could tell not only what kind of animal had lived there but how old the animal was when it left the shell.

A second anecdote is equally forceful. One of our graduate students raised an infant rhesus monkey from birth. The animal became an interesting sight around William James Hall on the Harvard campus. My daughter, twelve years old, begged to see the monkey. We arranged to have the student and monkey come to dinner. My daughter excitedly informed the neighborhood of the event. A few minutes after the student and monkey were seated in our living room, six children, from seven to eleven years of age, rang the doorbell. They ran to the monkey, looked and poked for about two minutes, and then casually walked off one by one to more interesting activities. We hadn't prepared the children to ask themselves logical questions about the monkey—what makes him afraid, what makes him run, what makes him smack his lips?

In short, curiosity may be only a romantic name for that phenomenon that occurs when a child tries out a set of acquired hypotheses on some new object that captures the child's attention.

In addition to the distinctive elements of new material, the child's motivation is another factor that controls the intensity of attention the child will devote to a task. The child's desire to be proud of his parents and similar to them in word and deed is one strong motivational force.

Lower-class parents may exhort their children to work hard for good grades in school, but the children do not perceive their parents as persons who publicly engage in or express a value in intellectual mastery themselves. As a result, the children cannot view mastery of intellectual skills as a way of being similar to their parents, or of gaining the adult resources of power and competence that the child perceives his parents to possess.

The peer group is not unimportant in the development of standards and motives surrounding intellectual mastery. The child selects models from among his classmates once he begins school. As with the lower-class family, the lower-class peer group is biased against school achievement in favor of those behaviors that the boys and girls themselves define as masculine or feminine. This situation has serious consequences for school performance. The child of six years wants to maximize his similarity to whatever standards his schoolmates set for his sex. The child has learned that he or she is called a boy or a girl and rushes to elaborate this operational definition.

How does the child decide what events, objects, or actions are masculine or feminine? He works by a reliable formula. He implicitly computes the ratio of males to females associated with an event or action. If the ratio is lopsided in one direction, that activity is assigned the sex role of the majority party. Fishing is masculine, sewing is feminine. Any five-year-old will tell you this. School is usually classified as feminine by six-year-olds because in over 90 percent of the primary grades in this nation, the activity of the classroom is monitored by a woman.

One implication of these data argues for the wisdom of segregating the sexes, especially in the primary grades of school. In a sex-segregated class, each child might learn to maximize in the school experience the sex role appropriate to himself. The presence of a man in the classroom would obviously have the strongest impact on a boy. But even changing the content of the reading curriculum should have some benefit.

Aside from the importance of modeling, the peers mediate other mechanisms that engage the motive to master academic tasks. Most children, especially boys, have a strong motive for power, a desire to play the dominant role in an interpersonal dyad. The uncorrupted sign of power for all children is strength. Strength is the only legitimate currency of power which cannot be corrupted, and children recognize this principle. The culture, in its wisdom, preaches substitute signs for power. Prowess at athletics, skill at adult activities, signs of intelligence can function as badges of potency if the group accepts that currency. The middle-class child is likely to find himself in a peer group where the right to dominate is given to the child with good grades, to the child with a quick answer, to the child with a catalogue of facts. Lower-class peer cultures rarely adopt this translation of power. Thus the lower-class child, already unable to find models for intellectual striving in his parents, is further deprived of a primary motive to master intellectual skills.

The two themes in this brief essay stress the dramatic psychological growth that occurs in the opening years and the importance of the parent-child relationship for that growth. It is believed that a large share of the child's desire to adopt the values and skills of society, including the wish to master the tasks of the school, derive from a close parent-child relationship in the first few years of life. The child comes to value the parent and is, therefore, receptive to adopting the parent's motivations for him. There is growing interest in establishing day-care centers for economically underprivileged mothers who wish to work and need a place where they can leave their infant for most of the day. We believe this plan has potential dangers for the child's growth, for it could produce a child who has a seriously diluted tie to his parents. It will also weaken the emotional involvement of the mother with her own child. It would perhaps be wise to consider paying the mothers to stay with the children and beginning strong educational programs for parents, to educate them into the nature of the child and the nature of his psychological growth.

However, implementation of this suggestion will not by itself ameliorate the awesome educational deficiencies of many economically deprived children. The poor progress of these children in school is probably the result of many factors, including low income, residence in a slum neighborhood, an unstable family organization, absence of a father, a peer group that does not value school success, and, in some cases, inadequate nutrition of the individual child. It is not possible to state with confidence which of these factors produces the child's problems in school. Cures are most effective when diagnoses are accurate. We must therefore be cautious about simple plans or devices that promise to solve "the problem" when we are still unclear about the fundamental nature of the problem.

13 Why Some Three-Year-Olds Get A's — and Some Get C's

Maya Pines

How do you determine what constitutes "excellence" and "competence" in three-year-olds? And once you have decided that, what factors have contributed to one child's capabilities exceeding those of another child? Here the author tells of some "natural environment" research of children and their interactions with their mothers. The resulting classifications of mothers—Super-Mother, Smothering-Mother, Almost-Mother, Overwhelmed Mother, and Zoo-Keeper Mother—are amusing, but reveal a lot about the influence of the home environment on the development of the child.

The all-American, exceptionally competent three-year-old—the model for future generations, if a group of Harvard researchers has its way—is a frighteningly mature and verbal creature who scores high in seventeen abilities which seem to hold the key to his success.

He can, for example, "dual focus." (While two children argued and one screamed, "I'll murder you!" Sally barely looked up from her block-building, muttered, "Not *me*, though!" and continued what she was doing.)

He can sense dissonance or discrepancy. (When another boy held up a streaked drawing and announced, "It's the moon," Jimmy replied at once, "A moon doesn't have hair!")

He can anticipate consequences. (Seeing his friend carelessly pick up a basket filled with toys, George shouted, "Carry it, carry it, *use both hands!*")

Relying on thousands of simple, detailed observations like these, rather than on IQ tests, the Harvard School of Education's Pre-School Project believes it can now pick out the abilities which distinguish the most able three-year-olds from the most inept. Nine of these abilities, including the three above, involve intellect (or "intellectual skills," if you like). The eight others involve social factors; for illustration, the Harvard researchers note that when something gets in the way of the inept child (they tag him "C"), he may be reduced to tears, or throw a tantrum, while the competent child ("A") will be quietly persistent (he might even "con" someone into giving him what he wants—

The New York Times Magazine, July 6, 1969, © 1969 by The New York Times Company. Reprinted by permission.

Maya Pines is the author of *Revolution in Learning: The Years From Birth to Six* (Harper & Row, 1967), a study of the education of preschoolers.

in a socially acceptable way). Also the "C" child may be locked into either sheeplike docility or rebellion, while the "A" child knows both how to lead and how to follow. And as early as two years of age, the most competent group will be able to understand complex, unexpected instructions, such as, "Put the spoon under your foot," or the reverse, "Put your foot under the spoon," while the "C" group cannot.*
(The average, or "B," child was not covered in the study.)†

The goal of the Harvard project is to find out how the two groups of children got that way—what it was in their earliest environment that produced the startling differences between them. But why concentrate on youngsters of age three and under especially? "There has been a striking shift of interest, unprecedented in history, toward the first three years of life," declares Prof. Burton L. White, the Pre-School Project's director. A no-nonsense, pipe-smoking man whom everyone in his group calls "Bud," he notes that the original conception behind the Government's Project Head Start was that "something's wrong with these children at age six. There was no appreciation of how early that something comes about."

"Head Start began," he says, "with a few weeks in the summer before the child entered kindergarten or first grade—the Head Start summer program. Then they decided to take the child for a whole year before he is six. Next they decided to take him two years before he is six. And now, at last, they've begun to run parent-and-child centers for children from birth on. It's always seemed clear to a number of us that the place to begin is with the first days of life."

Throughout the nation, large numbers of psychologists, computer experts, educators, sociologists, linguists and others are coming to the same conclusion. Working backward to a younger and younger age, they are creating a new field, encompassing what Harvard's Jerome Bruner has dubbed "the growth sciences." This new composite discipline concentrates on the period other researchers had chronically neglected because the child seemed so inaccessible—the time between his fifth day of life, when the newborn usually leaves the hospital, and his entry into nursery school at three. Abandoning their rats, pigeons and other

---

*Other intellectual abilities include: dealing with abstractions, making interesting associations, planning and carrying out a sequence of activites, makng effective use of resources. Other social abilities: showing pride in accomplishment, making-believe being adult, expressing both affection and hostility to peers and adults.

† The researchers concentrate on the A and C children because they provide the greatest contrasts in abilities. These contrasts become focus points for the researchers, who otherwise would lose their way in the mass of material involved in so broad an undertaking as a study of over-all competence in children. The exclusion of B children —whose middle-level abilities do not provide such visible contrasts for investigation— cuts down the workload of researchers enormously. This does not mean, however, that B children are not studied at all. "Our errors allow us to study the B's," says one Harvard psychologist—that is, many children classified as A's and C's are, upon later assessment, reclassified as B's.

experimental subjects, including older children, hundreds of scientists are now focusing on the young child's mind—encouraged by the influx of Government funds for programs to stop the epidemic of school failure among the children of the poor, and by some new developments in psychology itself.

Just five years ago Benjamin S. Bloom of the University of Chicago shook up his colleagues with "Stability and Change in Human Characteristics," a thin book filled with statistics based on a thousand different studies of growth. Each of these studies followed up certain children and measured them at various points in their development. Although made by different people over the last half-century, these studies showed such close agreement that Bloom began to see specific laws of development emerging, rather than mere trends. For each human characteristic, Bloom found, there is a growth curve. Half of a child's future height, for instance, is reached by the age of two-and-one-half. By [the] age of four, his IQ becomes so stable that it is fairly accurate indicator of his IQ at seventeen. To a large extent, therefore, the die may be cast before a child ever begins his formal education.

Bloom emphasized that the child's environment has a maximum impact on a developing characteristic—during that characteristic's period of most rapid growth. Thus, since human intelligence grows most rapidly before the age of four this is the time when the environment can influence it most easily. As time goes on, Bloom declared, more and more powerful forces are required to produce a given amount of change in a child's intelligence, if it can be produced at all—and the emotional cost of this change is increasingly severe.

Meanwhile, other researchers were focusing on the differences between the children of the poor and the affluent. By kindergarten age, these differences are painfully obvious, with poor children's IQs running five to fifteen points below those of middle-class youngsters, and their verbal ability trailing even further behind. The Head Start programs were showing it was not easy to bridge the gap at that stage. So, when President Nixon announced that "Head Start must begin earlier in life, and last longer, to achieve lasting benefits," people in the growth sciences took new hope—especially those increasingly vocal, who want to concentrate on reaching children even before the age of three.

If their research confirms that the first three years of life largely determine a human being's future competence, these years can no longer be left to chance, they believe. Thus, armies of tutors could conceivably be sent into the homes of disadvantaged infants, and thousands of expectant parents enrolled in crash programs to teach them modern child-rearing. We may be witnessing the end of society's traditional laissez-faire about the earliest years of a human being's life.

Harvard has clearly taken the lead in the growth sciences at this point, with at least three nuclei of research on the child's early development. Each one, in its own way, has had to start practically from scratch, devising new tools to measure young children's progress and new techniques to rate their environment. "Assume that you are studying the great-chested Jabberwocky," Bruner advised his students.

The Pre-School Project, for one, had not originally intended to focus on children so young, but began by studying six-year-olds. And, initially, it did not even try to measure competence, but looked for "educability" —how ready a child was for formal education by the age of six. This turned out to be a knotty problem, however, all tied up with certain virtues which the school system rewards—passivity, obedience, being "a nice, organization child," as one of the researchers put it—but which the project did not much like. "Is the child who's geared up to the Boston educational system the kind of child we want to set as a model?" the Project's Dr. E. Robert LaCrosse recalls asking himself. And the answer was, "My God, NO!" Therefore, they decided to look for competence—all-around excellence in coping with problems in the yard as well as in the schoolroom.

"What specifically is competence at six?" Dr. White wanted to find out. "If you don't know the answer to that question, you can't have any idea of what you're trying to achieve." With disadvantaged children, at least you know clearly that you want to wipe out their deficits in language and whatever else goes into poor IQ development, he says, and there are programs for four- and five-year-olds that do this with some efficiency. "But that's not the same as asking, how are you going to rear your child so he will be *optimally* developed? We're not just responding to an emergency; we're looking for answers that will help *all* children."

Three years ago, then, White and a dozen other researchers armed with clipboards and tape recorders set out like naturalists to look for examples of excellent as well as poor development in children. In weekly visits to various local nursery schools, kindergartens and Head Start centers, they selected one group of outstanding three- to six-year-olds, their "A" group, and a parallel group of children who were not sick, but couldn't quite cope, their "C" group. They followed 440 "A" and "C" children closely for a year, noting the differences between them and checking their ratings of the children against the teachers' ratings of the children, and then they realized that they had come too late: "With our 'A' kids, the three-year-old children had basically the same cluster of abilities, in perhaps less polished form, as the six-year-old children," says LaCrosse, "and, in fact, they were more advanced than the six-year-old 'C's' in terms of both social and non-social skills."

This came as a shock to the project. "We were surprised, really, and kind of excited," says LaCrosse, one of the strongly committed young psychologists who have been flocking to the growth sciences. "Big Daddy Freud had said everything was over at five, with the resolution of the oedipal conflict, but we tended to disbelieve this. Then suddenly, we found that if you're talking about competence, the action comes before the age of three."

As a result, the Pre-School Project did an about-face and began studying children between the ages of one and three—in their natural habitat, of course. Off went LaCrosse and four associates into the homes of thirty toddlers to take regular running records of what actually goes on in a small child's life. Their assignment was to construct a new maternal behavior scale, later to become "a *human* behavior scale, that we can plug any human being into," LaCrosse explained. They followed the mothers and children from kitchen to bedroom to bahtroom, furiously recording in the manner of a sports announcer what happened to the child and what the mother was trying to do.

At first these intrusions into the privacy of the home seemed strange. "We had to fight the 'girdle-on' phenomenon," recalls La-Crosse. "You know—the first day we arrive, there's the mother with false eyelashes and hair freshly done, and the house perfect, at nine o'clock in the morning! Then one day, perhaps three visits later, we'll arrive and find the mother in a housecoat and the kitchen in chaos, the beds unmade—at that point, the girdle is off and we have achieved a certain rapport." The families were all known to the project from its earlier work with older children, and they were paid five dollars a half day for their services.

While LaCrosse and his group concentrated on the mothers, other project teams visited 170 different homes to record how the children spent their time and to study the development of specific characteristics. It took a year and a half to boil down their material on child activities to thirty-six categories of things that these youngsters do. It is taking even longer to work out useful scales covering the development of the selected characteristics.

Now the information from all these probes is just beginning to produce promising patterns, as the children's activities are related to their development and to their mothers' behavior. "We think we have spotted five prototype mothers," says LaCrosse. "There is, first of all, the Super-Mother. She wants to provide educational opportunities for her child; she slips in from time to time to teach the kid something, but she's not frantic about it. She enjoys the child as he is. She tends to do a great deal of labeling with him—'This is a ball'—and to elaborate on his sentences, adding new bits, such as 'This is a *red* ball,' or related ideas. There is a good balance between activities that she initiates and those initiated by the child.

"Then there is the Smothering Mother. All the kid does all day is respond to her commands. She seems discontented with where the child is right now. She's very busy preparing him for Harvard.

"The Almost Mother enjoys and accepts her child, but she is confused and frequently unable to meet his needs. She may lack a capacity for intellectual input—she usually waits for the child to initiate activities, then often can't understand what he wants. If she reads to her child, her spontaneous comments may be, "See the ball!" or "See the hill!" while the Super-Mother may ask, "What's he going to meet at the bottom of that hill?"

"The Overwhelmed Mother finds just living from day to day so overwhelming that she has almost no time for her child. The children may be raised by older siblings, or by themselves, in a chaotic home. Usually the mother has eight kids and a thirty-dollar-a-week food budget, but there are middle-class mothers of this type, too.

"Finally there is the Zoo-Keeper Mother, who tends to be middle- to upper-middle-class. She has a highly organized household routine, and the child will be materially well cared for, but will spend most of his time alone—perhaps in a crib filled with educational toys. She doesn't monitor her child's behavior, doesn't interact—in fact, there's a striking lack of contact between this mother and her child. This produces a child with highly repetitive, stereotyped behavior, despite the variety of toys."

These five mothers represent extreme types—since the mothers of "B" children were not included in this study. The Super-Mother naturally raises an all-around "A" child. The Smothering Mother's offspring rates "A" in cognitive* capacity, but not in emotional maturity—he tends to be shy or incredibly infantile. The Overwhelmed Mother produces a "C" child. The Almost Mother does a very good job until the child is fourteen to sixteen months old, when the mind-stretching aspects of care become more important, and then she fails. While the Super-Mother's child continues to grow rapidly, the child of the Almost Mother reaches a plateau which eventually turns him into a "B" child.

These differences cut across class lines. The project knows of at least one woman from a very poor neighborhood, a black activist, who is a Super-Mother, as well as numerous middle-class women who raise "C" children. However, the central tendency favors the middle-class child, both black and white, and one of the project's main contributions, so far, is that it documents for the first time just how the daily experiences of poor and middle-class children differ in the second and third year of life.

Take the matter of purposeless behavior—sitting and doing nothing, without looking at anything in particular, or else moving about in apparently aimless fashion. According to preliminary data, the child of an Overwhelmed Mother, who is usually very poor, spends forty-one times as much of his waking hours in such vapid behavior as the child of a Super-Mother, who tends to be middle-class. Since the Overwhelmed

---

*The word cognition is used in psychology to mean the study of how knowledge is acquired, retained and used. The child rated "A" above has a good learning capacity.

Mother often attempts to cope with her children by giving them food or candy, he also spends much more of his time eating.

The child of a Super-Mother, on the other hand, spends nearly one fifth of his day at an activity almost unknown to the offspring of an Overwhelmed Mother: make-believe, pretending to be someone or something else, a characteristic of children who are doing well around the age of two. Throughout this study, middle-class youngsters were found role-playing five times more frequently than lower-class children of the same age.

Since poor children are often accused of lacking a drive for achievement in school, it is very revealing that the middle-class children in this study spent fifty percent more of their time constructing things or practicing skills which give a sense of mastery. They also benefited from far more tutorial experiences. And they devoted more of their day to the one predominant occupation of nearly all children between the ages of one and three: staring at a person or thing with intensity, as if to study its features.

The extraordinary amount of time spent staring in this way—an average of twenty-two percent of the children's day—is "a revelation," says White. "It has authenticity and is not disputable." He warns that the relationship between the types of mothers and the children's activities remains to be verified, however.

These differences occur mostly after the baby is one-year-old, White believes, because until then most parents do things that are essentially the same. There are, of course, instances of extreme deprivation which can seriously retard or damage a child. But, in general, parents don't yet know how to enrich their babies' environment in a meaningful way, and even researchers such as White have only limited information on the subject. A few years ago, White showed that when infants in a bland hospital nursery were given a chance to look at and touch colorful stabiles, they learned to reach for objects above them—a landmark in development—in less than half the time it took other infants in the same nursery. He has raised his own three-year-old on the same principle, offering him plenty of interesting things to interact with at each stage in his development. Yet a lot more research needs to be done before parents can be given firm recommendations about the first year of life, he believes.

Meanwhile, White is convinced that the behavior of parents really begins to diverge during the child's second year, when the growing baby —now walking around and talking—forces himself on the attention of adults. The toddler's insatiable curiosity at that age, his zest for learning, and his obvious grasp of language, all lead the effective mother to produce a rich flow of talk and try in various ways to satisfy his drives. To other types of mothers, however, this growth means only two things: danger to the child, and much more work for them. In an extremely poor family where the mother is barely able to get through the day and has many other children to take care of, "you can predict what that will mean," says White. "She'll concentrate on keeping him out of the way; she cannot nurture his curiosity, and she won't do much talking."

In a two-year follow-up of the original "A" and "C" children, now five to eight years old, the project has found amazing continuity in their levels of ability. The "A" group is still doing extremely well in kindergarten through second grade and also testing high on the seventeen critical abilities. The "C" group is still inept—some sad and teary, some just oblivious, some every bit as likable as the more competent children —a diverse group that has one thing in common: Whatever its members are given to do, they don't do it well, either through lack of persistence or through lack of skill.

As soon as White has collected enough solid information about what causes these early differences, he plans to start teaching the Almost Mothers and the average mothers to use the best methods. Within thirty to fifty years, he predicts, the kind of child who is rated outstanding today will be considered merely normal, as a result of more skillful child-rearing.

The Pre-School Project's offices in Cambridge are cluttered and busy. Across Harvard Square, on the eleventh floor of the imposing concrete structure known as the William James Hall for the Behavioral Sciences, one encounters a more rarified atmosphere. Here is the Center for Cognitive Studies, headed by psychologist Bruner, a man of electric energy who paces up and down his spacious study, speaking volubly, with gestures. Until recently he studied how children between the ages of three and twelve process information—how they acquire it, retain it, transform it, and communicate it. But now, to find the *sources* of intelligent action, he concentrates on infancy. Under his guidance the entire center, with its staff of psychologists, linguists and researchers, has turned to an examination of the first two years of life—though no one here follows individual children, studies homes, or tries to intervene in the domestic situation in any way.

These researchers seem filled with a sense of wonder at how the human infant—so helpless and limited at birth—learns to control his environment and himself. At first, they find, the baby appears stupider than chimpanzees of the same age. But by the age of two or three the normal child has achieved one of the most difficult intellectual feats he may ever perform: he has reinvented the rules of grammar, all by himself, and he has learned to speak. He begins with what the linguists call holophrases—single words such as "Mummy" or "see," or very short phrases that are used as one word ("gimme"). Then, suddenly, around eighteen months of age, he takes one holophrase and combines it with many other words ("see doggie," "see light").

"At this particular point," notes Bruner, "as far as I am concerned, he enters the human race as a speaker, because I think you can find examples of holophrastic utterances in higher primates, but you will never find combinatorial grammar."

Besides learning language, the normal two-year-old constructs a fairly complex mental model of the world. (This allows him to manipulate various aspects of the world in his thoughts and fantasies.) He has also learned to control his own behavior so accurately that he can mobilize various skill patterns whenever he needs them. This is a formidable set of achievements, and the Center for Cognitive Studies is only beginning to unravel how the baby attains them.

Behind a partly closed room at the center, overlooking all of Harvard, a mother nurses her three-month-old infant. He has just been to a specially constructed baby "theater" where, reclining on a tiny chair resembling a car seat (safely strapped to it, in fact, by belly-and-breech cloth), he watched a swinging red ball, with exciting black and white bull's-eye stripes and a central row of shiny pearls, as it moved gently before his eyes. It was an experiment in depth perception, to discover whether infants of that age have any idea of what is graspable: Would the baby move his arms more when the shiny ball was up close than when it was far away? Did he have any sort of mental map of where he was? Finding, on both questions: Yes. Three-month-old infants have much more depth perception than was thought possible only a few years ago, the center finds. On the day of their birth, it has been determined, infants can track a triangle with their eyes. By one month of age, they notice when objects have been changed. In fact, infants are in every way much more aware of their surroundings than scientists had surmised—which helps explain the speed with which they build their model of the world.

To trace the development of this world-model, Bruner and two associates recently put three groups of babies of different ages through an experiment in which a jingly toy was placed behind a small transparent screen, open on one end. The youngest babies, only seven months old, simply reached for the toy with the nearest hand and bumped into the screen. After banging on and clawing at the screen for a while, they lost interest and gave up. The next group, the one-year-olds, began in the same fashion, but then let their hands follow the edge of the screen and reached behind it in a sort of backhand grasp until they got the toy. Only the eighteen-month-olds knew right away how to reach the toy efficiently, and did so. Over sixteen trials each, none of the babies ever changed his initial strategy: this was the best he was capable of at that stage.

The babies who take part in these experiments are usually the offspring of graduate students, brought there in response to ads in the Harvard Crimson. Asked how much time he actually spends with these babies, Bruner gestured helplessly. "Depends on what's going on in the Yard!" he exclaimed. "Which babies do you have in mind?" During the student strike, the faculty meetings took up most of his time. Now that the troubles seem to be over, he can go back to his main interest —studying how babies discover how to use their hands intelligently.

In babies' hands, Bruner believes, lie clues to much of their later development, and he particularly wants to find out how babies learn the value of two-handedness. Nobody teaches infants this skill, just as nobody teaches them to talk. Yet around the age of one, a baby will master the "two-handed obstacle box," a simple puzzle devised by the center to study this process. Seated on his mother's lap, he will suddenly use one hand to push and hold a transparent cover, while the other hand reaches inside the box for a toy.

To Bruner this is extraordinary, for it shows that the baby has learned to distinguish between two kinds of grip—the power or "holding" grip, which stabilizes an object, and the precision or "operating" grip, which does the work. Monkeys and apes have developed a precision grip, Bruner says, but "it is not until one comes to man with his asymmetry that the power grip migrates to one hand (usually the left) and the precision to the other." From then on, he emphasizes, many routines can be devised for holding an object with one hand while working it with the other, leading to the distinctly human use of tools and tool-making.

The experiments at the center are essentially very simple, but their interpretations are not. Some of these interpretations parallel Noam Chomsky's "transformational" approach to linguistics, which reduces language to basic kernel sentences, each one made up of a noun phrase and a verb phrase. Early in childhood every human being learns the logical rules which allow him to transform these kernels into any possible sentence. Bruner speculates that when a baby learns to differentiate between the two kinds of manual grip, this foreshadows "the development of topic and comment in human language"—the basic sentence form of subject/predicate, which may be found in all languages, with no exception whatsoever, and which a baby expresses when he combines a holophrase with another word. Thus, man may be uniquely predisposed, at birth, to reinvent the rules of grammar, to process information, and to develop "clever hands." He is born with a highly complex programing system, the result of millions of years of evolution.

What about disadvantaged children, then—why should they be different, if they are born with the same programing system? "Mind you, you can *ruin* a child's inheritance, too," warned Bruner, "with an environment where he acquires helplessness. You can also be trained to be stupid."

Before man's marvelous programing system can be activated for language, for instance, a baby must learn a series of primitive codes— and these require interaction with an adult. "What seems to get established very quickly between infant and parent is some sort of code of mutual expectancy," Bruner said, "when the adult responds to an initiative on the part of the child, thus converting some feature of the child's spontaneous behavior into a signal." Right from the start, parent and infant are busy communicating through eye-to-eye contact, smiles and sounds. As early as at four months of age, an infant will smile more to a face that smiles back than to one that does not respond; and if the adult face then stops smiling back, the infant will look away. In some cases, he may even struggle bodily to look away. A child's other attempts at learning can similarly be brought to a halt when his expectancy is thwarted, and things stop making sense.

Much of the center's work is based on the findings of the famous Swiss psychologist, Jean Piaget, who first described the stages through which young children construct their mental model of the world. How well and rapidly this model is built depends largely on the children's environment: the more new things a child has seen and heard, Piaget noted, the more he wants to see and hear. The greater variety of things a child has coped with, the greater his capacity for coping, and the more new methods he is able to invent by combining or re-combining what he has learned before. Both Piaget and Bruner disclaim an interest in early childhood *education,* however. What they are studying is early childhood itself. The mind of the human infant is still so deep a mystery, said Bruner, that he himself intends to stay with it for the rest of his life—"or until we give up, in final despair."

While Bruner concentrates on the process of learning, and White attempts to find the keys to individual children's competence, Professor Jerome Kagan of Harvard's Department of Social Relations focuses on differences in the development of young children from different social classes. These are sometimes so acute, he has found, that poor homes can be considered actually crippling—at least for life in our society. This is not a racial matter: Kagan's study of 180 youngsters deals entirely with white families. For nearly three years he saw and tested these 180 children at regular intervals in his laboratory, begining when they were four months old.

"Class differences emerge clearly by twelve months of age, and show up even earlier for girls—in some cases as early as at eight months," Kagan declares. They appear in every one of the basic skills which the child learns during his first three years. Middle-class children are at an advantage, for instance, in learning specific "schema" for the events around them. By one year of age, they are way ahead of poorer children in discriminating between similar stimuli. As Kagan explains it, the reason for this superiority is the middle-class youngsters' greater experience with *distinctive* stimulation—slight transformations or discrepancies from what is ordinary.

"Middle-class mothers seem unconsciously to try to surprise their infants," he says, "and that's very good! They play peek-a-boo, or make unexpected sounds. In slum areas the mothers don't do this—they don't think of it, or may have no time—yet it's important." Infants who live in crowded homes where they are surrounded by noise all the time, from television and from many voices, learn to "tune it out" right from the beginning. "You don't learn anything in a Tower of Babel," says Kagan. "The main question is, is the mother distinctive?"

Kagan was among the first to use electronic equipment to record babies' heartbeats during tests of attention. This is a useful way to determine whether an infant is actually looking at something, or just staring blankly: when a baby's heartbeats slow down, he is alerted and paying attention. With this equipment lightly and painlessly hooked up to the child's chest, Kagan could display various kinds of normal-looking or distorted masks and know exactly which ones surprised the infants. He learned that by the age of one, middle-class children are more attentive to unusual events—they look longer at strange faces and forms. Kagan interprets this to mean that middle-class children have a bigger stock of schemata with which to try and explain unexpected things in their environment, which makes them less likely to turn away until they understand the event.

He also found that middle-class babies form closer attachments to their mothers, and therefore, he says, are more likely to accept the mother's values and goals. This closer attachment, which can be observed by the greater amount of crying among middle-class infants between the age of six and ten months when their mother leaves the room, has nothing to do with the quality of the mother's love, he points out. "The fact is that the human caretaker is a target for the baby's clinging, scanning, vocalizing and smiling," explains Kagan. "The mother is a toy—just like the terry-cloth 'mothers' with which [psychologist Harry] Harlow's monkeys were raised in an experiment, and which they preferred [for reasons still unknown] to the wire 'mothers,' even when the latter provided them with milk. The more you play with this object, the more you get attached to it." And, according to a recent study by one of Kagan's graduate students, middle-class mothers do indeed spend a lot more time "entertaining their babies—talking, smiling, playing face-to-face—than do poorer women.

"We don't imply that the lower-class mother doesn't love her child," Kagan warns. "There is no difference in kissing, nor in the total amount of talking, as opposed to face-to-face talking. However, the lower-class mother is more apt to talk from another room, or issue orders, and not take time for long periods of reciprocal play with her child."

This leads to obvious differences in the quality of language among the poor and the affluent. The poor child, then, is at a disadvantage in all these things—learning schemata, forming the kind of attachments which lead him to accept the mother's values, and speaking. He is also less persistent at difficult tasks, Kagan has noted; worse at nonverbal problems, such as perceptual puzzles; and, in addition, has learned a sort of impotence.

"When a mother tends to a child in distress as soon as he cries, this leads the child to believe there is something he can do," says Kagan. "He learns he can have an effect upon the world—make things go, or stop. If he is not tended, he will learn helplessness." He describes a recent study with newborn dogs and cats which were placed in a situation where there was nothing they could do to ward off mild electric shocks. When these animals were later given the opportunity to act on their environment, they could not learn to do so.

Since all these differences occur so early, "we should think of changing the behavior of the mothers of poor children during the first two years of the child's life," Kagan suggests. He believes this will require a major national commitment.

Each in its own way, then, the three Harvard groups conclude that some fundamental learning patterns are set very early in life—well before the age of three and that during this period the child is particularly open to environmental influences, for good or for bad.

Does this mean that, once past the age of three, a child who has not learned the right patterns is doomed and cannot be changed? "No," replies Kagan. The child remains quite malleable during his first seven years, but the longer you wait, the more radically you need to change his environment—and the *probability* of change becomes a little less with each successive year.

Is it true that "compensatory education . . . apparently has failed," as psychologist Arthur Jensen wrote in a recent issue of the Harvard Education Review? No, answer the growth scientists, compensatory education has not failed, because it has never really been tried—at least never properly, or on a large scale. They tend to dismiss the only massive effort, Head Start, as too little, too late, and too unfocused in its present form. "Just eight weeks [of training], a couple of hours a day? That's not very much!" says Kagan. "That's not a radical change in a child's environment." The growth scientists also object that Head Start children are comparatively old (two-thirds of them are five or six, and only five percent of the total are under the age of four). More powerful programs, they believe, are needed for children between the ages of three and six lasting the full year, and focused so as to teach cognitive skills.

What the people in the growth sciences really want, however, is not emergency treatment for disadvantaged children, but *prevention* of handicaps. And for this, they are convinced, you need to start before the age of three. There are two possible strategies:

(1) Starting kibbutz-like day-care centers in which trained teachers would give children an excellent education from earliest infancy. In a reply to Jensen, Benjamin Bloom has just suggested that we learn from Israel's experience with the children of poor and mainly illiterate immigrants from North Africa and Yemen. These Oriental children have extremely low IQs when reared at home—an average of 85, compared with the 105 scored by Jewish children of European origin. When both kinds of children are raised in the same communal nurseries from birth on, however, both have an average IQ of 115—a jump of thirty points

for the Oriental children. Bloom points out that these children had spent twenty-two hours a day in the kibbutz nursery for at least four years.

(2) Producing major improvements in the way parents raise their children—the solution which Bloom, Kagan and many others in the growth sciences prefer, and for which White is actively preparing. This, too, is a form of prevention, apparently more palatable than widespread day-care centers, but not necessarily easier to carry out.

After spending $2 million on projects in which social workers, clinical psychologists and psychiatrists tried to change the child-rearing practices of lower-class parents by means of counseling, for instance, the National Institute of Mental Health's Committee on Social Problems learned from its chairman, J. McV. Hunt, that "nothing, absolutely nothing, so far as I can ascertain, has come of it." Hunt's book, "Intelligence and Experience" (1961), played a major role in sparking the current interest in the first three years of life. He now believes that when poor mothers are given something useful to do with their children they sometimes become just as effective as professional teachers.

One "serendipitous finding," according to Hunt, was that infants in a Durban, N.C., ghetto actually benefited from a research program aimed only at studying their psychological development, not interfering in it. After two years of tests at a Duke University laboratory, once a month, these toddlers scored close to 110 on the Binet IQ test, while other two-and-one-half-year-olds from their neighborhoods scored only 70 to 80. Hunt thinks that the babies' mothers—who were present throughout the tests—must have noticed which items they did well on and which they failed, and then given them practice where they needed it. "They appear to have been exceedingly effective as teachers," he says. "This suggests that poor children's decline can be prevented."

When Merle B. Karnes of the University of Illinois trained the mothers of fifteen disadvantaged three-year-olds to make inexpensive educational materials—sock puppets, lotto and matching games, etc.—to use at home, she made a similar discovery. These mothers also served as assistants in Karnes' experimental nursery school, being paid three dollars for each two-hour training session. Within less than three months after they began, their own children, who had stayed home, suddenly gained 7.5 points of IQ. Later on these children did as well as those in Karnes' professionally run nursery school. Karnes concluded that teachers should take on a new role: Training parents, rather than just teaching children, and involving the entire family in the education of preschoolers.

The burden of the new research, then, is to put ever more burden on parents—which generally means mothers, since fathers have been strangely ignored by the growth sciences. Interestingly, when the mothers in Karnes' group realized how much time and effort are required to do a good job of raising preschool youngsters, they headed en masse for the local chapter of the Planned Parenthood Association —they felt they could never teach their children enough if they had babies every year, as before.

This does not solve the problem for the 1.5-million youngsters under the age of three whose mothers work away from home, however. Few of these women can either afford or find a first-rate nurse who is interested in stimulating their babies' intellectual and social growth. Even fewer have access to a day-care center with a strong educational component. The government has utterly failed to take their needs into account, but now private industry is beginning to enter this field and an upsurge in specialized day-care centers may be expected in the near future.

Both approaches—the educational day-care centers and the training of parents—have already come under attack. "What do you mean, have a white professor come here and tell us how to raise our kids?" sputtered a black militant when he heard about a new program for parents. Others object to the idea of "taking children away from their mothers and putting them in day-care centers from birth on—it's totalitarian!" Sociologists argue that one shouldn't impose middle-class values on the poor, who have their own culture. Community leaders declare that if any day-care centers are opened in their area *they,* not outsiders, should decide what will be taught.

The people in the growth sciences know it's going to be an uphill fight, but they are fascinated by the possibility of giving each child a chance to "realize his full potential." According to Hunt, "Most of the skills we are talking about—cognitive skills, language skills, pride in achievement, and so on—are not a matter that is black or white or green or yellow. In order to survive in a technological culture, one *must* have these skills." The best time to acquire them is in early childhood. He also points out that if one wishes to maximize a child's development, "you need to maximize it all along. Competence—like deprivation—is cumulative."

As these ideas spread, the nation's educational efforts are likely to include ever younger children, and soon the years from birth to three may become a target of first priority.

14 How Different Are They?

Stanley F. Yolles

In the following article a distinguished psychiatrist examines both biological and social sex differences and their implications for educational policies. He suggests that classes segregated by sex will produce the most well-adjusted children.

Experts on behavior hesitate when Henry Higgins asks, "Why can't a woman be more like a man?" Parents who wonder why little girls don't act like boys are assured by one authority that the differences are of "no consequence." A Stanford University professor of psychology now documents what little boys and girls are made of. The details, distilled from some 900 studies, show that boys and girls are indeed quite different. This notion is hardly a news bulletin for parents, but science has documented the obvious generalizations with facts and has also uncovered some fresh answers to the eternal question of Henry Higgins. Here they are as outlined in the book, *The Development of Sex Differences,* written in part with National Institute of Mental Health support and edited by Dr. Eleanor E. Maccoby:

Little boys start more fights, make more noise, take more risks, think more independently, are harder to educate and are the more fragile of the sexes. While many more males are conceived, more miscarried fetuses are male. More males than females die in the first year of life and in each decade after that. They are much more likely to stutter, to have reading problems and to suffer emotional quirks of every sort. They lag a year or more behind girls in physical development. By the time they start school, even their hand muscles are markedly less mature.

In contrast, little girls are more robust and mature, yet much more dependent, passive, submissive, conforming, unadventurous. They are more interested in people than in things, show more concern for others and are more sensitive to their reactions and are more likely, by far, to remember names and places.

Science has found no difference in IQ between boys and girls in childhood, yet their styles of thinking and learning are different. Girls excel in verbal abilities—even before they know they are girls. They talk first, and later on they spell better and write more. Boys outclass them in abstract thinking including math and science. Boys are also more likely to be creative.

The New York Times Magazine, February 5, 1967. © 1967 by The New York Times Company. Reprinted by permission. When this article appeared, Dr. Yolles was director of the National Institute of Mental Health.

How do we explain these basic and early differences? Some experts believe most of these differences are taught to the child. Other experts, such as Dr. David Hamburg, chairman of the department of psychiatry at Stanford, think there may be hormonal and genetic causes. Dr. Hamburg writes that hormones may act on the brain even before birth, or right after, to organize certain circuits into male or female patterns. The evidence for this comes from experiments with the hormonal systems of newborn rats. When male rats are castrated within the first twenty-four hours after birth, they retain a basic female-type system for regulating hormonal secretions later in life. If castration is delayed until the second twenty-four hours, only a few males retain the female patterns. By the third day, all male rats have developed a male-type pattern.

In addition, Dr. Hamburg points out that their genetic make-up is different. The female has a chromosomal composition that seems to lend her protection against disease and infection. It protects her against blood-clotting disorders, color-vision defects and one type of rickets.

Scientists at the National Institute of Mental Health who have observed infants right after birth and in the weeks that follow have seen sharp differenccs too early in life to have been caused by the environment. These differences have been uncovered through ingenious tests. Drs. George Weller and Richard Q. Bell hooked up recording devices to forty newborns by placing sensors on their skins. By this method they were able to detect the faint electrical activity of the skin called "conductance," a property which turned out to be greater in the female. Since this increases as the baby gets older, it is taken as a sign of maturity. The female infant, therefore, is more mature than the male of the same age. The females also show more sensitivity to contact and to temperature changes on the skin, more proof of their greater maturity in this very early period of life.

Dr. Howard Moss, an institute psychologist who has watched three-week-old and three-month-old infants for seven and eight hours at a time is impressed with the "striking differences" between boys and girls. Boys sleep less, cry more, demand more attention. "Much more is happening with the male infants," he reports. Some boys, he found, also seem to be much more "inconsolable" than the girls, a sign of lesser maturity.

When children go to school, their differences become magnified. From first grade until well into high school, the girls usually make better grades. One ingenious researcher found that as early as the second grade, little boys think of school as a female institution and, therefore, one which is hostile to them. Our psychologists at the N.I.M.H. asked teachers in Arlington County, Va., to write their impressions of 153 seventh-graders.

According to the teachers, girls are 20 percent better than boys at sticking to a task. They are more conscientious, compliant, methodical. They are also friendlier to the teacher, and more attentive. And boys are 35 percent more hostile, domineering, aggressive, also more irritable, boastful, argumentative, quarrelsome. Paradoxically, boys are more introverted—depressed, sad, withdrawn.

Several years ago, educators in Fairfax County, Va., near Washington, D.C., decided to experiment with separate elementary classes for boys and girls.

One teacher said: "I learned things about boys and girls that I had never understood before. I had spent years trying to keep boys from disturbing everyone. This was just wasted effort. I found that boys can still concentrate even when they are noisy. You can learn to work in a boiler factory, if you have to, and that is just what I have done."

Another said: "I always liked girls best until I got a whole classful of them. In the beginning of the experiment, it dawned on me that the girls were not doing their own thinking. Parrot-like, they repeated everything that the teacher had ever said. What are we doing to these girls, I began to wonder, to make them so conforming?"

The results of the experiment were impressive. Both sexes did significantly better in their studies. The boys became much more interested in school. The girls grew more independent and original in their thinking.

Since it is scarcely practical to separate the boys and girls in most of our school systems today, educators might consider what they can do to achieve some of the same results. Principals and teachers can keep the differences in school performance between boys and girls in mind when they deal with problems in the classroom—either of discipline or of underachievement. Devices such as all-boy or all-girl contests, debates, or dramatic and musical clubs might give students the sense of confidence and enthusiasm found in the separate classes.

If schools can capitalize on the differences between boys and girls, parents can do so, too. Parents of a boy can now see that he may be at a disadvantage in early years at school, under the twin burden of the girls' better performances and the teachers' disapproval. If parents don't expect their sons' reading or handwriting to be of the best, it may take some unnecessary pressure off the boys.

The girls' problem is even more complex. Many families feel that education is not so important for a girl as a boy. Today, only one in ten Ph.D.'s is a woman, a drop from the one in seven of the 1930's. Teenage marriages are on the rise, with an accompanying rise in the divorce rate. The question is, are we properly fitting girls for a woman's life as it really is?

After raising a girl to conform and to be subordinate we expect her to face problems that require education, originality, dominance and drive. A new study of young married people points out that conformity and submissiveness often lead only to boredom in marriage.

Science has found that the brightest girls are those whose interests extend into the masculine range. They like math, motors and abstract problems. The brighter boys also show a sensitivity and responsiveness we call "feminine" although these children are by no means effeminate. The most creative boys, for example, are dominant and aggressive, yet show much more sensitivity to their surroundings than other boys.

In my experience, the most successful personalities are those who have the widest range of interests and abilities. I would like to see our boys and girls brought up with as broad and varied an experience as possible, with attention to the many facets of the human mind. This includes insight into the thinking of the opposite sex.

What can parents do to offer this kind of insight to the young child? One psychologist brought his three-year-old girl a truck when she asked for it, to the consternation of her grandmother. Another brought home an abandoned engine his pretty twelve-year-old daughter had longed to tinker with. One father makes a point of answering his girls' questions about science and about his business world, although he has to fight an ingrained tendency against it. He tries to pique them into forming interesting solutions to problems, and to build self-confidence in their mental abilities.

As for the boys, one mother encourages hers to experiment with cooking. She enjoys giving them the benefit of her feminine insight into human behavior and motivation. This insight into the female skills will stand them in good stead professionally as well as in their marriages. It augments rather than reduces their manliness, she argues.

It might be in order to revise our ideas about what the proper sex role is for our boys and girls, and how best to train them for it. Society needs men who are not limited to the so-called tougher masculine characteristics of aggressiveness and dominance. It needs men who are capable of showing the more "feminine" traits of warmth and sensitivity toward the feelings of others. And we need women who are less conforming, more original and daring, women who can think hard and straight.

Henry Higgins, who yearned for more "logic" in women, and Eliza Doolittle, for "a little kindness" in men, surely would agree.

15 Sexuality and Sexual Learning in Childhood

James Elias and Paul Gebhard

The data presented below were collected by the late Alfred Kinsey, and are based on interviews with children ranging in age from four to fourteen. Elias and Gebhard have noted the differences in socioeconomic classes in knowledge of human sexuality in order to help educators prepare teaching programs most appropriate to their different students.

The turn of the century saw an awakening interest in sexuality and sexual learning among children. The most significant work of this period was Freud's theory of infantile sexuality, which directed the attention of the world to sexuality in early childhood and its importance for the future adult role. A somewhat neglected work, by Moll (1909), was overshadowed by the Freudian wave; but Moll's observations on the sexual life of the child were the first comprehensive writings done in this field. In an earlier study, Bell (1902) examined childhood sexuality through the study of the activities of children.

Research Since 1917

Numerous studies resulted from this increased interest in childhood sexuality. Among them were Blanton (1917), looking at the behavior of the human infant during the first thirty days of life; Hattendorf (1932), dealing with the questions most frequently asked by preschool children; Isaacs (1933), studying the social development of young children; Dudycha (1933), examining recall of preschool experiences; and Campbell (1939), writing on the social-sexual development of children. Conn (1940a, 1940b, 1947, 1948) has done a series of studies dealing with various phases of sexual awareness and sexual curiosity in children. Other important studies were made by Halverson (1940), on penile erection in male infants; Conn and Kanner (1947), on children's awareness of physical sex differences; Katcher (1955), on the discrimination of sex differences by young children; and Ramsey (1950), on preadolescent and adolescent boys. Sears, Maccoby, and Levin (1957) present a discussion of labeling and parental sanctioning of sex behavior,

Phi Delta Kappan, March, 1969. Reprinted by permission. Mr. Gebhard is director of the Institute for Sex Research at Indiana University. Mr. Elias is an associate sociologist at the institute.

and Bandura and Walters (1959) examine parental response of sex information questions.[1]

Current research has tended to move away from direct studies of infant and childhood sexual behavior. Sexuality has its roots in man's biological makeup, and the development of gender role or sex differences has become one of the main focuses of present research.[2] Since the molding forces, or socializing agents, are the family and the peer group (among others), sexuality is being pursued as a form of social development. Receiving special emphasis are the development of the male and female role—for example, the part aggression plays in developing an aggressive adult male sexual role and the concomitant emphasis on nonaggressiveness in the development of an adequate female role. Other areas of current research are found in the work of John Money and Joan and John Hampson on the ontogeny of human sexual behavior.[3]

The Kinsey Data

This discussion utilizes previously unpublished data from the Institute for Sex Research, taken from case histories of pre-pubescents interviewed by Alfred Kinsey and his co-workers. These histories are somewhat outdated (before 1955), but the information contained in them provides one of the few sources of actual interview information on prepubescent children. Questions were asked regarding sources of sexual knowledge, extent of knowledge, homosexual and heterosexual prepubertal play, and masturbatory activity, all of crucial importance for any educator, counselor, doctor, or other professional who deals with children. Some of the critical problems encountered in preschool counseling find their source in the sexual area. Educators recognize that [an understanding of the] differences between males and females, ethnic groups, and socioeconomic status groups is essential for an understanding of the attitudinal and behavioral patterns that children exhibit. Adequate sexual adjustment in early childhood is a prime factor in later adult sexual adjustment, as healthy attitudes toward self and sexuality are the foundations of adult adjustment.

Partly through necessity, many school systems are presently moving into education programs with a maximum of speed and often a minimum of preparation regarding the specific needs of the population the particular program is to serve. Sex research can offer some aid to the educational community by providing information about critical factors in the lives of children and how these factors affect later adjustment.

The Sample

The sample consists of 432 pre-pubescent white boys and girls ranging in age from four to fourteen.[4] There are 305 boys and 127 girls in the study, and they are grouped by occupational class (social class) and age.[5] The occupational classifications originally used in the work at the Institute for Sex Research have been combined in order to increase the number of cases and to provide social-class categories. The occupational classifications consist of: 1) unskilled workers who are labeled as lower blue-collar, 2) semi-skilled and skilled workers who comprise the upper blue-collar, 3) lower white-collar workers, and 4) business and professional men, here termed upper white-collar. A mean age is given for the children in each social class to make explicit the unequal age distribution.

The sexual behavior of younger children often lacks the erotic intent attributed to similar adult activities, raising the question, in some cases, of the validity of labeling some childhood activities as sexual. This research does not label childhood behavior as sexual unless it includes one of the following: the self-manipulation of genitalia, the exhibition of genitalia, or the manual or oral exploration of the genitalia of or by other children. Of course, many of these activities could be motivated by mere curiosity concerning a playmate's anatomy.

The term "sex play" as used here includes those heterosexual and homosexual activities involving more than one person which occur before the onset of puberty. Among the males, 52 percent report homosexual prepubertal activity and 34 percent report heterosexual prepuberty activity. These percentages seem accurate when we compare them with the self-reports of adults in the earlier Kinsey volumes. Adult males recalled homosexual experience in their pre-adolescent period in 48 percent of the cases, just four percent less than is reported by these children in their preadolescence.[6] The adult males also indicated that heterosexual preadolescent activity occurred in approximately 40 percent of the cases, but the reports of the children indicate only about 34 percent of pre-pubescent males engage in heterosexual experiences.[7] However, many of the children in this study have not reached the average age at which these experiences first occur. The average age among males for homosexual play is 9.2 years and for heterosexual play, 8.8 years.

Among female children, 35 percent report homosexual pre-pubertal sexual activity and 37 percent report heterosexual pre-pubertal experiences. The incidence of homosexual activity in the females is much less than that reported by males, but is very close to the percentage recalled by adult females in the 1953 Kinsey volume (33 percent). The adult females recalled heterosexual preadolescent activities in 30 percent of the cases, and the reports of the children show 37 percent with such experience.

One of the noteworthy findings coming from this analysis of the case histories of preadolescents is the surprising agreement between prepubertal report and adult recall. Another important finding is the lack of any consistent correlation between sociosexual activity and parental occupational class. The percentages do vary, but in no meaningful way.

Masturbation

Masturbation is most often described as self-stimulation leading to sexual arousal and usually to climax or orgasm, accompanied (after puberty) by ejaculation on the part of the male. Some writers prefer to believe that pre-pubertal children do not masturbate but simply fondle their genitals. These present data concerning pre-pubertal masturbation are not derived from reported "fondling of the genitals" but rather from deliberate activity done for pleasure and often accompanied by pelvic thrusts against an object (e.g., a bed) or manual manipulation. Sometimes a state of relaxation or satisfaction comparable to the post-orgasmic state is achieved; in other instances indisputable orgasm occurs.

More males than females masturbate in childhood, as is the case later in adolescence and adulthood. Among pre-pubescent males, 56 percent report masturbatory activity, while only 30 percent of the females do so. In comparison, information received from adults in self-reports indicates preadolescent masturbation in 57 percent of the cases. These actual childhood reports are within one percentage point of the recall data from adults as reported in the earlier works.

Looking at age groupings and social class, one finds that the blue-collar classes contain the highest percentages of boys who have masturbated—60–70 percent. The majority of those in the blue-collar and lower white-collar classes who masturbate are in the eight- to ten-year age group. The upper white-collar class has the lowest percentage of those who have masturbated (38 percent), with more beginning in the three- to seven-year age group than at any subsequent time. The mean age for first masturbation is as follows: lower blue-collar, 8.6; upper blue-collar, 8.8; lower white-collar, 7.8; and upper white-collar, 6.0. The probable explanation for the lower mean age, lower percentage of those who have masturbated, and lower average age at first masturbation for upper white-collar boys is the fact that their average age at interview is 7.2 years, while the average ages for the boys of other social classes are two to four years older.

Fewer girls tend to masturbate than boys, and only 30 percent of the girls report that they have masturbated. The highest percentage is among the lower blue-collar females (48 percent); the other three classes have lower and quite similar figures (between 25 and 29 percent). The average age of masturbation for girls is lower than that of the boys. By class, it is: lower blue-collar, 7.5; upper blue-collar, 7:4; lower white-collar, 5.7; and upper white-collar, 6.7.

Masturbation has been designated in the past as the prime cause of mental illness, low morals, and stunted growth, among other things.

These stigmas are for the most part behind us, but tradition dies slowly and many children are still being told "old wives' tales" concerning the alleged effects of masturbation. This is unfortunate for in early childhood masturbation might influence the child to accept his body as pleasureful rather than reject it as a source of anxiety. Society has progressed to a point where few parents punish their offspring for masturbating, but it is noteworthy that fewer still encourage it.

Sexual Knowledge

In this study, additional measures are taken of current knowledge while controlling for child's age and occupation of father. The occupational level is dichotomized into lower (blue-collar) and upper (white-collar) classes for purposes of analysis. Presence or absence of knowledge about the following topics is examined: intercourse, pregnancy, fertilization, menstruation, venereal disease, abortion, condoms, and female prostitution. In general, the white-collar class surpasses the blue-collar class in all sex knowledge categories. Of special interest to the educator are some of the differences in learning which occur on the part of the children in these two groups. For example, while 96 percent of the blue-collar boys have an understanding of sexual intercourse by ages thirteen to fourteen, only four percent have any knowledge concerning the "coming together of the sperm and the egg"—fertilization. Twenty-seven percent of the upper white-collar group in the same age range understand the concept of fertilization, and this nearly seven-fold difference is indicative of the language level and sources (hence quality) of information for the two groups. Blue-collar boys learn about intercourse, abortion, condoms, and prostitution earlier than do other males, especially by age eight to ten. These words and activities become a part of the sex education of lower-class boys much earlier than of boys whose fathers are employed in higher-status occupations, as a result of most sex information being provided by peers on the street.

This earlier and more extensive knowledge of coitus is reflected in pre-pubescent heterosexual activity, wherein nearly three times as many blue-collar boys have, or attempt, coitus than do white-collar boys. Interestingly enough, more blue-collar males know of intercourse than know of pregnancy (except in the four- to seven-year-old group) and just the reverse is true for the white-collar males. The white-collar male surpasses the blue-collar male in sexual knowledge in later age groupings, perhaps indicating that many of the more formal aspects of his sex education come from his mother, with peers "filling in the gaps" concerning some of the more sensitive areas, such as methods of birth-control and prostitution.

The pattern for girls stands in marked contrast to that for boys. Pre-pubescent girls, unlike boys, are not inclined to discuss or joke about sexual matters. Also, the girl eavesdropping on conversation by adult females is less apt to hear of such matters than is the boy listening to adult males. Lastly, there is reason to believe that the lower-class mother is more inhibited about, and less capable of, imparting sex education to her daughter. Consequently, the lower-class girl generally lags behind her upper-class counterpart in sexual information. Thus, for example, in age group eight to ten, not quite half of the lower-class girls know of coitus, whereas close to three-quarters of the upper-class females have this knowledge. This gap is found even with regard to menstruation, a thing sufficiently removed from overt sexual behavior that one would expect it to escape from taboo. On the contrary, at lower social levels, menstruation is often regarded as dirty and somehow shameful. The result is that among eight- to ten-year-olds roughly a quarter of the lower-class and nearly three-quarters of the upper-class girls possess this inevitable knowledge.

On more technical matters the lower-class girls are equally or even more disadvantaged. For example, none of them grasp the concept of fertilization: the idea that pregnancy is the result of the fusion of an egg and a sperm.

Among upper-class girls from age group eight to ten on, the knowledge of pregnancy is universal, whereas many of their lower-class counterparts are unaware of where babies come from. Indeed, in age groups eight to ten and eleven to twelve, more lower-class girls know of coitus than of pregnancy. This situation, so incongruous to an upper-class reader, is explicable. Thanks to their contact, both physical and verbal, with lower-class boys (a substantial number of whom have attempted coitus), more lower-class girls hear of or experience coitus than hear of pregnancy. Note that while a boy may attempt to persuade a girl to have coitus, it is most improbable that he will defeat his aim by informing her of the consequence.

Lastly, the differences in knowledge between upper- and lower-class girls hinge to some considerable extent on literacy and on communication with parents. The upper-class girl, more prone to reading, and in a milieu where books and magazines with sexual content are available in the home, will educate herself or ask her parents to explain what she had read. The upper-class parent, having been told by innumerable magazine articles and books on child-rearing of the desirability of sex education, is far more likely to impart information than is the less knowledgeable and more inhibited lower-class parent. This statement will be substantiated in the following section on sources of sexual knowledge.

Sources of Sexual Knowledge

By looking at the sources of sexual learning for children, one can see the origin of sexual "slang" terms and sexual misinformation frequently unacceptable to the middle-class teacher. Though a large portion of this mislabeled and often incorrect information is the product of children's "pooled ignorance," the problem is only confounded by adult non-communication.

The main source of sex education for most boys is the peer group—friends and classmates. Nevertheless there are important differences, depending on the child's social class (measured here as father's occupation). The peer group is overwhelmingly important as a source of information for all the boys from blue-collar homes: from 75 percent to 88 percent of them report other boys as their major source. The boys of lower white-collar homes seem a transitional group, with 70 percent so reporting, while the boys whose fathers are lower white-collar men find their mothers as important as their peers with respect to information. The boys from upper white-collar homes derive little from their peers, most from their mothers, and a relatively large amount from combined educational efforts by both parents. These figures are in striking contrast to those of the blue-collar boys: only eight percent cite peers as the main source, 48 percent report the mother, and 24 percent both parents. This inverse relationship between parental occupation and the importance of peers as an informational source is one of the major, though anticipated, findings of this study. As the occupational level of the home increases, the child's mother plays a growing role in the sex education of her son, rising to nearly half of the cases for males whose fathers are upper white-collar men. For all occupational levels, the father seems to play a marginal role as a source of sex information for boys, and when he does play a role in his boy's sex education, it is mainly when both parents act as a team. While we can only speculate on the basis of our data, the mother is probably the "prime mover" of the parental educating team. Other sources as major channels of information (e.g., siblings, other relatives, simple observation, etc.) are statistically unimportant, never exceeding four percent.

Some children report that their sources of information are so evenly balanced that they cannot name one as the major source. Boys reporting this situation are more common (20 percent) in homes of lower blue-collar fathers. The percentages tend to decrease progressively as parental occupational status increases, but this trend is unexpectedly reversed by the boys from upper white-collar homes. This reversal is probably not the result of small sample vagary, since the same phenomenon is to be seen among girls. No explanation is presently known.

Teacher Unimportant as Source

It is interesting to note that the teacher is not mentioned by any of the children as the main source of sex education. In fact, throughout the study the contribution of the teacher and the school system to the child's information about sex is too low to be statistically significant. However, with the current proliferation of formal sex education programs in some of our nation's school systems, the role of the teacher and the school has no doubt increased in importance since the time these interviews were conducted, before 1955.

When looking at the main source of sex knowledge for girls, we see similar trends. Peers provide the main source of sex information for 35 percent of the girls whose fathers are lower blue-collar men and for 25 percent of the girls whose fathers are upper blue-collar workers. By contrast, only nine percent and four percent, respectively, of the girls whose fathers are white-collar men report the peer group as their main source of sex education. The mother's importance as a source of sex education increases with increased occupational status, being the major source for 10 percent of the daughters of lower blue-collar workers up to 75 percent of those whose fathers are upper white-collar men.

For girls, fathers provide very litle sex education, and then only as a member of a father-mother combination. It is interesting to observe that significantly more girls than boys report no main source of sex education, especially those girls from homes in which the father has a lower-status occupation. For example, 45 percent of the daughters of lower blue-collar workers report no main source of sex education, as compared to 20 percent of the boys whose fathers are at this occupational level. Other possible informational sources, such as siblings and printed material, are inconsequential.

Nudity

The general level of permissiveness regarding nudity in the home, a sex-related phenomenon, also varies in relation to the occupational level of the family. As a rule, boys are allowed more nudity than girls, except in homes where nudity is a common practice—in which case the girls report a higher incidence of nudity. Differences between occupational groups are great, with 87 percent of the lower blue-collar workers never allowing nudity among their sons, as compared to only 28 percent of upper white-collar men. Again for boys, 40 percent who come from upper white-collar families report nudity as very common, compared to only three percent whose fathers are lower blue-collar workers. Among girls, we find the same patterns emerging, with 44 percent of the girls from upper white-collar families reporting nudity as very common, and none of the girls from lower blue-collar families reporting nudity as usual in the home. Thus nudity in the lower-class home is more the exception than the rule for both girls and boys; in the upper-class home almost the reverse is true. This upper-class permissiveness regarding a sex-related behavior, nudity, fits nicely with our finding that upper-class parents communicate more freely on sexual matters with their offspring.

Implications for Education

The main implication of the reported data for those in the field of education is the need for educators to be aware of the differences in information and experience which exist between boys and girls, between different occupational and socioeconomic groups (and though not treated in this article) the differences which may occur between ethnic groups. An apparent problem regarding these differences, still evident in much of our educational system today, is an often inflexible adherence to the "middle-class yardstick."

The sexual experiences and the sexual vocabulary of the heterogeneous student population, especially the pupil who has not come from the same socioeconomic, occupational, or ethnic background as his teacher, create definite problems in expectations, understanding and communication between teacher and pupil. An adequate knowledge of the sources of sex education, types of experiences, and the vocabulary and attitudes of these students will enable the teacher to gain a wider understanding of some of the problems of pupils regarding sexual matters and to modify his or her teaching accordingly.

Counseling the child in the school system raises some of the same problems encountered by the classroom teacher in an even more intense, personal situation. The counselor should have some idea of differences in preadolescent sexual activities and knowledge, enabling him to aid the child and his parents more intelligently as they deal with questions and problems of sexuality. If the average age for preadolescent homosexual experiences, for instance, is around nine years, this activity should be recognized as possibly a part of normal sexual development rather than as a sexual aberration. There is great danger of confusing activities accompanying normal sexual development with pathological behavior.

It is also apparent from the data presented here that many lower-class children will probably experience problems in learning and adjustment because of the lack of accurate information from informed sources. Neither the teacher nor the parent will completely replace peer-group influence in the process of providing sexual information, especially in the lower class, but the educator has the opportunity to provide programs to meet the needs of children otherwise inadequately prepared to cope with sexuality because of restraints imposed by social-class position. Therefore education should continue to initiate programs which will help fill this void created either by peer misinformation or by similar misunderstanding and reluctance on the part of parents.

References

1. Sigmund Freud, "Three Essays on Sexuality," *Standard Edition of the Complete Psychological Works* (London: Hogarth, 1953), pp. 135–245; Albert Moll, *The Sexual Life of the Child* (New York: Macmillan, 1923) (originally published in German in 1909); S. Bell, "A Preliminary Study of the Emotion of Love Between the Sexes," *American Journal of Psychology*, (1902), pp. 325–354; M. G. Blanton, "The Behavior of the Human Infant During the First Thirty Days of Life," *Psychological Review*, (1917), pp. 956–983; K. W. Hattendorf, "A Study of the Questions of Young Children Concerning Sex: A

Phase of an Experimental Approach to Parent Education," *Journal of Social Psychology* (1932), pp. 37–65; S. Isaacs, *Social Development of Young Children: A Study of Beginnings* (London: George Routledge and Sons, 1933); G. J. and M. M. Dudycha, "Adolescent Memories of Preschool Experiences," *Pedagogical Seminar and Journal of Genetic Psychology*, (1933), pp. 468–480; E. H. Campbell, "The Social-Sex Development of Children," *Genetic Psychology Monograph* (1939), p. 4; J. H. Conn, "Children's Awareness of the Origin of Babies," *Journal of Child Psychiatry* (1948), pp. 140–176; "Children's Reactions to the Discovery of Genital Differences," *American Journal of Orthopsychiatry* (1940a), pp. 747–754; "Sexual Curiosity of Children," *American Journal of Diseases of Children* (1940b), pp. 1110–1119; J. H. Conn and Leo Kanner, "Children's Awareness of Sex Differences," *Journal of Child Psychiatry* (1947), pp. 3–57; H. M. Halverson, "Genital and Sphincter Behavior of the Male Infant," *Journal of Genetic Psychology* (1940), pp. 95–136; A Katcher, "The Discrimination of Sex Differences by Young Children," *Journal of Genetic Psychology* (1955), pp. 131–143; C. V. Ramsey, *Factors in the Sex Life of 291 Boys* (Madison, N.J.: published by the author, 1950); R. Sears, E. Maccoby, and H. Levin, *Patterns of Child Rearing* (Evanston, Ill.: Row, Peterson, 1957); A. Bandura and R. Walters, *Adolescent Aggression* (New York: Ronald Press, 1959).

2. R. Sears, "Development of Gender Role," in Beach (ed.), *Sex and Behavior* (New York: John Wiley and Sons, 1965); E. Maccoby (ed.), *The Development of Sex Differences* (Stanford, Calif.: Stanford University Press, 1966).

3. J. Money, J. Hampson, and J. L. Hampson, "Hermaphroditism: Recommendations Concerning Assignment of Sex, Change of Sex, and Psychologic Management," *Bulletin of Johns Hopkins Hospital* (1955a), pp. 284–300; "An Examination of Some Basic Sexual Concepts: The Evidence of Human Hermaphroditism," *Bulletin of Johns Hopkins Hospital* (1955b), pp. 301–319.

4. The following table presents the number of boys or girls in each category (N) and the mean age of that category:

		Males		Females	
			Mean		Mean
		N	Age	N	Age
Blue-Collar	Lower	59	11.2	21	9.5
	Upper	79	11.5	17	10.1
White-Collar	Lower	115	9.9	53	6.9
	Upper	37	7.2	35	6.6

5. The blue-collar—white-collar distinction provides an excellent indication of social level *vis á vis* the occupational level. The association between occupation and education (used in the original Kinsey publications) is very close. See p. 328, *Sexual Behavior in the Human Male* (Philadelphia, Pa.: Sanders, 1948).

6. A. Kinsey, W. Pomeroy, and C. Martin, *Sexual Behavior in the Human Male* (Philadelphia, Pa.: Sanders, 1948).

16 The Social Perception of Nursery-School Children

Frank J. Estvan

That children develop social perceptions in different ways and at different rates, and that the variations are greater with respect to affective as opposed to cognitive attributes are among the insights provided by the following study.

"That says beep, beep, tractor!" a boy in nursery school exclaimed.

Another child pondered and then said slowly, "I, um . . . this is . . . this is Pammy and Mickey and Daddy breakin' up the playground . . . Daddy an' the playground, look!"

Both boys were looking at the same picture, a view of a farm projected on a screen. Yet the two children had different reports on what they saw. What children "see" in a series of life-situations—that is, their social perception—is the subject of this report.[1]

The study examines three major questions:

Do the various components of social perception develop at the same rate?

Is there a relationship between level of social perception and type of life situation observed?

Do nursery-school groups differ in social perception?

The sample in the study was made up of seventy-eight children. Forty-two pupils took part in the first year and thirty-six in the second year. All the children were attending the Nursery School of the College of Education at Wayne State University.

About half the children lived in the housing project where the nursery school was located. The other children came from various parts of the metropolitan area and were chosen to get a balanced representation of racial and socioeconomic groups.

Included in the study were fifteen Caucasian boys, eleven Caucasian girls, twenty-one Negro boys, twenty-five Negro girls, and three boys and three girls of mixed parentage. In socioeconomic background these children ranged from the professional and managerial to families on welfare. The children's chronological age ranged from 31 months to 64 months. The mean age was 48.6 months.

Reprinted with permission from *The Elementary School Journal*, Volume 66, Number 7, April 1966. Published by the University of Chicago Press with the Department of Education of the University of Chicago, copyright 1966 by the University of Chicago. Dr. Estvan is Professor of Education, Wayne State University.

Data were collected through individual, projective-type interviews, based on a series of fourteen pictures of life situations. The pictures depicted community situations in rural and urban areas, social-status situations that contrasted upper- and lower-class living, and child-adult situations that showed differences in experiences commonly associated with age. The series depicted ten basic social functions such as conservation of human and natural resources; production, distribution, and consumption of goods and services; transportation; and government.

The interview consisted of three parts designed to bring about a gradual increase in personal involvement. In Part 1, black-and-white slides two inches square were projected on a screen thirty inches by forty inches. The child was asked, "What story does this picture tell?" In Part 2, the same pictures were presented as photographs eight and a half inches by eleven inches. This time the child was given eight cardboard figures of happy, sad, angry, and neutral boys and girls. From these figures, the child selected the one that "belongs in the picture" and gave his reasons for his selection. In Part 3, the child chose the two pictures he liked best and the two he liked least and again gave his reasons for his choices.

All responses were tape recorded and then typed verbatim. Two persons scored the protocols independently; differences in scoring were discussed until consensus was reached. The analysis yielded the following dimensions of social perception: recognition, spatial setting, temporal setting, attitude, picture preference, and figure selection. The classification scheme used to categorize responses follows:

Recognition Scale

Recognition:
> Synthesis (both structure and function)
>> Structure (external, objective features)
>>> Immediate (limited to scene)
>>> Extended (generalized)
>> Function (internal, dynamic processes)
>>> Immediate (limited to scene)
>>> Extended (generalized)
> Partial (description of part of scene)
>> Human elements
>> Natural environment
>> Cultural inventions and things
> Identification of significant elements

Non-recognition:
> General (description of non-related items)
>> Human elements
>> Natural environment
>> Cultural inventions and things

Inappropriate (inaccurate or erroneous)
Miscellaneous (listing non-related items)
Indefinite (garbled, vague, mixed)
No response (for example, "I don't know")

Spatial Setting Scale
Associational:
    Nature (for example, "in the country")
    Home (for example, "in the livingroom")
    Other institutions (for example, "in church")

Systematic:
    Community (for example, "in Detroit")
    State (for example, "in Michigan")
    Region (for example, "in the Midwest")
    Nation (for example, "in the United States")
    World (for example, "in Europe")

Indefinite:
    Mixed (placed in two incompatible areas)
    Unspecified (no mention of place)
    No response (for example, "I don't know")

Temporal Setting Scale
Associational:
    Diurnal (for example, "morning," "noon")
    Annual (for example, "springtime," "winter")
    Personal (for example, "time to eat")
    Social (for example, "wartime," "depression")

Systematic:
    Clock (for example, "nine o'clock")
    Calendar (for example, "July")
    Past (for example, "Abraham Lincoln's time")
    Present (for example, "a modern farm")
    Future (for example, "when I grow up")

Indefinite:
    Mixed (placed in two incompatible periods)
    Unspecified (no mention of time)
    No response (for example, "I don't know")

Attitude Scale
    Positive (attraction, happy figure)
    Neutral (no feeling tone expressed)
    Negative (aversion, sad or angry figure)
    Mixed (incompatible feelings)
    No response (for example, "I don't know")

A more detailed description of the instrument, the interview method, and the scoring technique appears elsewhere.[2,3]

Recognition

About two-fifths of the responses of these nursery-school children indicated some recognition of the pictures in the series. Of these, by far the largest proportion (24.5 percent) were partial descriptions, such as "a man on a tractor" in the farm scene. One reaction in ten reflected an integration of clues or wholeness in awareness. Of these responses most were centered on structure or objective characteristics (6.7 percent), as in the recognition that a scene was a farm. A few responses were centered on function or processes (1.6 percent), such as food production in connection with the farm. A synthesis of structure and function was achieved in 2.2 percent of the responses. One reaction in twenty (5.5 percent) represented the lowest level of recognition—enumeration. In these responses the child simply listed relevant clues. For the farm scene he might respond "a barn, cows, and horses."

The largest number of reactions classified as non-recognition were also descriptive, but so general (26.1 percent) that they gave no indication of the significance of the life situation. In the farm scene, these responses took such form as "a man sitting outside" and "a boy walking in the grass." About one response in ten (11.5 percent), was clearly inappropriate, such as "daddy digging up the playground" for the farm scene. An equal proportion (11.7 percent) represented a simple listing of miscellaneous items. Almost the same number were uncertain because the response was indefinite or garbled (7.4 percent) or because no response (2.7 percent) was elicited for a particular life situation.

In short, out of ten responses, five were devoted to parts of the life situations. Whether classified as *partial description* (recognition) or *general description* (non-recognition), three-fourths of these partial responses centered on people; the remainder were divided between cultural and physical elements.

For each of the life situations there were great variations in recognition. Appropriate recognition ranged from a high of 92.5 percent for the picture of the Bedroom to a low of 3.6 percent for poverty as depicted in the picture of the Poor House. Scenes that ranked in the top half in appropriateness and in non-recognition follow:

Recognition		Non-Recognition	
Scene	Per Cent	Scene	Per Cent
Bedroom	92.5	Poor House	96.4
Schoolroom	71.8	Capitol	95.1
City	71.4	Factory	93.3
Farm	70.6	Dam	91.7
Dock	59.3	Rich House	76.2
Church	50.0	Village	76.2
Old Beach	46.3	Resort	58.5

The situations that were more easily recognized show the influence of the primary institutions and childhood experiences available in a metropolitan environment. There are farms in this region. Many children identified their toy tractors and toy boats in the pictures. Lack of experience could explain the lack of perception in connection with such situations as the Capitol, the Factory, the Dam, and the Village. The scenes showing the Poor House, the Rich House, and the Resort, however, suggest another factor: a lack of sensitivity to qualitative or socioeconomic differentials in ways of living.

The scores of the two classes showed considerable divergence. All statistically significant differences occurred in the non-recognition categories. The children in the first class were more aware of human beings in their general descriptions; the next year's class had significantly more responses that were classified under *miscellaneous listing, indefinite, inappropriate,* and *no response.* For no single picture in the series, however, was the difference of such magnitude as to raise the question of skewness caused by undue weighting by one or more life situations.

Spatial setting

These children's perception of the locale for life situations was less developed than their powers of recognition. Seven out of ten responses (71.2 percent) were classified as *indefinite* in spatial setting in comparison with six out of ten scores (59.4 percent) which fell in the non-recognition categories. The great majority of responses (26.3 percent) that indicated some spatial orientation were at the associational level, as "in church," "at home," and "out in the country." Only 2.4 percent of the responses took a geopolitical form such as "It's in Detroit" or "That's Washington." Responses of this kind were classified as *systematic.*

By far the greatest number of indefinite responses were found in the category labeled *unspecified* (61.2 percent). The child may have noted "a man on a tractor" or even recognized the scene as a farm, but these recognitions were free floating as far as location was concerned. One response in fourteen (7.2 percent) revealed much vacillation or the use of incompatible referents at different points during the interview ("in the country . . . in the city"). These responses were classified as *mixed.*

Of the spatial referents used, almost half were institutional (13.8 percent. These were followed by *home* (9.5 percent), *nature* (3.0 percent), *community* (2.1 percent), and *nation* (0.4 percent). Of a total of 1,106 responses to pictures, not one placed a picture in a state, a region, or a world setting.

The distributions of *spatial setting* responses for the two classes were significantly different. The variance was confined to two categories at the indefinite level: the first class had a higher total in the *no response* classification; the second class had a higher total in the *mixed responses* classification. In the use of systematic and associational settings, however, both classes were alike.

Temporal setting

These children showed little sense of time. Most of their reactions (96.1 percent) were classified as *indefinite*. About one response in thirty (3.4 percent) was associational in character, and one in two hundred (0.5 percent) was based on a systematic or metric scale for recording time. This pattern was similar to that for spatial orientation although at a far lower level of awareness.

Hence, there were more unspecified responses in which no mention was made of time (92.8 percent) than unspecified responses in which no mention was made of spatial setting (61.2 percent). Among the associational referents, these nursery-school children used diurnal occurrences such as "morning" and "night" more frequently than certain routinized personal activities such as "time to go to sleep." One child showed an awareness of seasons in connection with swimming, but no child placed a life situation in the context of a social era such as "war," as older children or adults do. The occasional use of systematic referents included the calendar as in days of the week (0.4 percent) as well as the present and the future (0.1 percent). No child used clock time or placed any scene in the past.

This distribution of responses held true for both classes of children. The greater number who failed to respond in the first year provided the only significant difference between the two groups.

Attitude

Of a total of 1,092 summary scores for the picture series, five in eight gave evidence of a feeling tone, three in eight being negative (37.9 percent) and two positive (25.6 percent). Neutral responses accounted for 21.5 percent; 12.6 percent of the children's responses vacillated throughout the interview. These responses were classified as *mixed*. Only 2.3 percent of the responses were classified as *indefinite* because they were garbled or because the child failed to respond.

The great majority of children began the interview with responses that were neutral (86.6 percent) in tone. More feelings emerged in Part 2 of the interview, which called for the selection of attitudinal figures and for reasons to support choices. As might be anticipated, these reasons, as well as the reasons given to support the choices of preferred and disliked pictures (Part 3), tended to be less neutral. Both sets of reasons were also relatively high in indefinite responses (20.2 percent for selection of attitudinal figures and 21.3 percent for selection of pictures). Apparently the question "Why?" is not an easy one for young children to answer. The much larger proportion of positive reasons (49.8 percent) given for preferred pictures as compared to negative (28.9 percent) reasons for disliked pictures also suggests that the children were more certain why they liked a situation than why they did not like it.

Of the various components of social perception discussed thus far, the greatest differences between the two classes lay in attitudes. The first class was far more neutral; the next year's class was decidedly more positive in outlook. This difference in set or tone was evident in each phase of the interview. Both groups, however, displayed a preponderance of negative feelings and the same relative proportions of mixed and indefinite reactions.

Picture preference

Given two opportunities to select the "picture you like best" as well as the "picture you do not like," these nursery-school children identified a significantly greater number of the former (135 preferred pictures as against 89 disliked pictures).

Of the preferred pictures, two were distinct favorites: the Farm and the Schoolroom (twenty-two children each). These were followed by a group of three that shared about the same degree of popularity: the Rich House, the City, and the Bedroom (fifteen, fifteen, and thirteen respectively). Among the disliked pictures, none was singled out for extreme rejection. The Schoolroom and the Bedroom were highest (ten children and eight children respectively). These two were followed by a cluster of five pictures that were equally disliked (seven children each): Poor House, Dam, Old Beach, Capitol, and Resort.

TABLE 1. *Rank in Recognition of Life-Situation Pictures and in Preference and Rejection*

| | Preferred | | | Disliked | |
| | *Rank* | | | | |
Picture	*Preference*	*Recognition*	*Picture*	*Rejection*	*Recognition*
Farm	1.5	2.5	Schoolroom	1	4
Schoolroom	1.5	4	Bedroom	2	1
Rich House	3.5	9.5	Poor House	5	14
City	3.5	2.5	Dam	5	11
Bedroom	5	1	Old Beach	5	7
			Capitol	5	13
			Resort	5	8

Table 1 indicates a relationship between degree of recognition and picture preference. Four of the five most popular life situations ranked among the top five in recognition, while only two of the seven least popular scenes ranked this high. Familiarity and acceptance do not appear to be directly related, however, for two of the best-liked situations also ranked highest in rejection (Schoolroom and Bedroom).

Both classes focused more on likes than on dislikes. Each identified about the same ratio of most preferred to least preferred situations (1.5 to 1.0). The classes showed greater agreement on the pictures they liked than on pictures they disliked. Three of the four most-preferred pictures were common to both classes (Farm, Schoolroom, and Bedroom), but only the Schoolroom appeared high on both lists of rejections. The evidence suggests that children are quick to learn what they like and crystallize their preferences early. Their dislikes are more diffused.

Figure selection

In four out of five choices (79.3 percent) either a boy or a girl was designated as "belonging in this picture." The remaining selection was much more likely to be in terms of both boys and girls (13.2 per cent) rather than left indefinite (7.5 percent).

For the series as a whole, the proportion of boys and girls selected was about the same (boys—38.3 percent; girls—41.0 percent). However, there was a tendency to perceive certain life situations as more suitable for one of the sexes. The five that ranked highest for each sex follow:

Boys		Girls	
Dam	1.5	Poor House	1
Farm	1.5	Rich House	2.5
Bedroom	3	Schoolroom	2.5
City	4	Church	4
Village	5	Resort	5

Certain patterns are apparent in each of these lists. The situations that were regarded as suitable life space for boys, except for the Bedroom, are outdoor scenes. With the possible exception of the Resort, situations associated more closely with girls deal with the home, the school, and the church. The fact that the Poor House and the Rich House were highest on the girls' list would also indicate that nursery-school children do not associate sex role with socioeconomic status.

The two classes of nursery-school children differed widely in their perception of life space as revealed in their selections of figures. The first year's class gave decidedly more boy and girl responses as well as indefinite responses, while the next year's class designated a significantly greater number of boys only or girls only. For specific scenes, there was high agreement on situations designated as girls' life space. There was only one difference between the groups regarding girls' life space (Church), but only one agreement between the groups on boys' (Farm). This difference in perception of life space was not due to a disproportionate representation of boys and girls in the respective groups. Boys and girls were equally represented the first year (twenty-one each), and the difference in numbers was slight the following years (seventeen boys and nineteen girls). It appears that very young children, boys as well as girls, learn what the feminine role is in our culture before they learn the male role.

Some of the generalizations that emerge from this analysis of a heterogeneous group of nursery-school children may have broader application. These generalizations follow:

1. Development of young children's social perception is differential. In general, five-eighths of the perceptions of these children reflected attitudes toward life situations. Two out of five gave evidence of some degree of recognition based primarily on parts of the situation rather than on the whole. About one-fourth exhibited an awareness of space usually in association with institutions or the home. The occasional mention of time was associated largely with diurnal changes or daily personal routines. As Table 2 shows, this pattern is in keeping with trends noted for first- and sixth-graders reported elsewhere.[3, 4]

TABLE 2. *Social Perception of Children in Nursery School, in First Grade, and in Sixth Grade**

	Percent of Responses		
Component	Nursery School	First Grade	Sixth Grade
Recognition (total appropriate responses)	40.6	66.5	90.2
Spatial setting (total systematic and associational responses)	28.7	38.0	79.6
Temporal setting (total systematic and associational responses)	3.9	9.6	23.2
Attitudes			
Positive responses	25.6	44.3	58.8
Neutral responses	21.5	11.9	14.3
Negative responses	37.9	29.4	15.3
Mixed responses	12.6	14.3	11.7
Indefinite responses	2.3	0.3	0.0

* Reported in Frank J. and Elizabeth W. Estvan, *The Child's World: His Social Perception* (New York: G. P. Putnam's Sons, 1959).

Three- and four-year-old children tended to fixate earlier on their likes than on their aversions. An awareness of the feminine role in our culture appeared before that of the male. For the most part, there was little sensitivity to social status.

2. There is great variability in nursery-school children's perception of life situations. For the fourteen life-situation pictures, recognition ranged from more than 90 percent to less than 10 percent. Furthermore, there were very real distinctions in the children's valuation of situations, no one of which commanded complete approval or complete rejection. Different children perceived sharply contrasting values in the same life situation. This finding was supported by responses to two scenes that

were among the highest on the "best liked" and the "least liked" lists. No two children were alike in their social perceptions.

Scenes depicting primary institutions and urban environment were more readily perceived than scenes removed from urban regions or representing adult activities. Allusions to space and time also reflected the children's experiences rather than the more sophisticated geopolitical or other systems of measurement. Scenes most highly prized were those with which nursery-school children have much acquaintance. Unfamiliar situations tended to be rejected. Situations that were the target of extreme aversion, however, were also well known to children.

3. There is considerable variation in the social perceptions of different nursery-school groups. Although the main outlines of the pattern of social perception were the same for the two classes, statistically significant differences were discovered in each of the components.

Variations were greater in the affective, or feeling, attributes than in the cognitive. In each phase of the interview, this difference in "set" or tone was manifested by differences in the way children approached the various tasks. The well-established fact that no two groups are alike may be attributable to differences in perception as well as to differences in age, intelligence, and other factors.

References

1. This series of studies was made possible by research funds from the College of Education; and the co-operation of Norma R. Law, director of the Nursery School, and her teaching staff, Hui C. Wu and Jean M. Green; and Elizabeth Estvan, who conducted all the interviews.

2. Frank J. Estvan, "Studies in Social Perception: Methodology," *Journal of Genetic Psychology*, XCII (June, 1958), pp. 215–246.

3. Frank J. Estvan and Elizabeth W. Estvan, *The Child's World: His Social Perception* (New York: G. P. Putnam's Sons. 1959).

4. Frank J. Estvan, "Children's Social Perception," *Social Studies in Elementary Schools*, Thirty-second Yearbook, pp. 25–32 (Washington, D.C.: National Council for the Social Studies, 1962).

17   Early Childhood Education and Race

Frances J. Perkins

Racial awareness is present in some children as young as three. Here Frances Perkins discusses ways in which preschool teachers can foster positive racial attitudes in young children. The need for developing an appreciation for the many kinds of people who live in our world and for building positive attitudes toward human understanding is emphasized.

Some people think that awareness of race does not exist in early childhood. What could a three-, four-, or five-year-old know about such an adult concept? The fact that children of different races play together and are friends suggests that children are unaware of racial attitudes. This idea is naïve.

In the past twenty years, social scientists have studied the area of race and young children. Their studies show no evidence that racial prejudices are inborn, a belief held by some. It is equally untrue to assume that a young child is free from racial considerations. Surprisingly as it may seem, there is evidence that racial awareness is present in some children as young as three. However, not all three-year-olds have developed a conscious awareness of racial characteristics. Certainly, most four-year-olds have.

Consider Morris, who is three. His teacher is a Negro in a community where there are no Negro residents. One day, Muriel brought her beloved Negro doll to school and placed it on a table while she removed her coat. Morris looked at the doll and said, "I don't like that doll. She's dirty." The teacher didn't want to pass up a good opportunity to develop positive racial attitudes and said, "You know, Morris, that doll really isn't dirty. She has been loved a lot and is somewhat worn out. But even when she was brand new, she was that same color. If you look around this room, you will see someone else that color."

Morris carefully scanned the face of each child, then looked directly at his teacher and said, "No, there isn't." "Look again, Morris. There really is," said his teacher. Morris slowly repeated his investigation of children's faces, turned to his teacher, and said emphatically, "No, there isn't." His teacher said to him gently, "Morris, I'm the same color as Muriel's doll." Morris' eyes widened as he realized for the first time that his teacher had dark skin.

"Early Childhood Education and Race" by Frances J. Perkins. From *Colloquy*, April, 1969. Copyright, United Church Press. Used by permission. Dr. Perkins is Lecturer in Psychology and Director of the Brandeis Nursery School, Brandeis University.

The next time he saw a person with similar skin-coloring, he was in a supermarket with his mother. He pointed to the Negro woman and said, "Look, Mommy, there's another schoolteacher over there." At first, his mother could not understand his remark. Morris hastened to explain, "She looks like my teacher."

Morris was guilty of a three-year-old's hasty generalization. When he first came to school, he oriented himself by his feelings. Thoughts about his teacher's competency prevented his seeing her different skin coloring. In time, he would have noticed even without help. He felt positively about her so that his new awareness of a difference did not alter his feelings about her ability to care for him.

Three-year-old Adam was playing with a humming top he had brought from home. Kern, a Negro child of approximately the same age, wanted a turn and tried to snatch the top away. The teacher said, "It belongs to Adam. Ask him and perhaps he will let you have a turn when he finishes." Adams quickly said, "I don't want him to play with it 'cause he has a dirty face." Once again, the teacher was on the spot. She chose to clarify this misconception immediately. "You know, Adam, Kern's face is not dirty. As a matter of fact, it is almost the same color as mine. That's the color of our skin. Our skin has melanin in it that makes it dark, just like our mommy and daddy's skin."

Adam's glance remained on his top, but he paused in his activity long enough to let the impact of the explanation register. Slowly, he looked at the teacher, then to Kern, and then to his own hands. He spun his top vigorously. Then turning to Kern, he said, "Now it's your turn."

As children develop, they begin to acquire a sense of themselves and a sense of others. They begin to see more details. In time, they learn from the people around them that these details may have meaning. And they begin to assimilate these meanings according to the same values given them by others around them.

Unfortunately, too many children grow up thinking that black and white people are quite different kinds of people and that blacks are inferior to whites. Television shows black angry people who burn and steal and yell and fight. But who tells a child, in language he can understand, why people burn, steal, yell, and fight? Where is there in a child's experience an opportunity to understand that not all black people act like this and that those who sometimes do, also do other things? Ideally, foundations for real understanding can be effectively introduced during the all-important early years when a child's thinking is malleable and his mind responds to the excitement of learning. These years should be used to lay the foundation for thinking about people in ways consistent with our democratic philosophy.

If nursery-school classrooms could include black, white, and Oriental children, the task would be somewhat easier, providing the teacher has come to grips with her own feelings and is able to project good will toward all the children. Her goodwill can guide the children toward an understanding of feelings, actions, and reactions which have much in common with their own.

When Andrew, a Negro, continues to hit, push or shove children to get what he wants, the children say, "I don't like him. I don't want to play with him." To prevent the children from associating their legitimate dislike for Andrew's behavior with his dark skin, the teacher encourages the children to explore why they don't like Andrew. To Jimmy, she says, "I just saw Andrew push you away from the tricycle. Just as you were about to ride, he got on it and you didn't get your turn. You didn't like that, did you? Let's talk to Andrew about it." Together, they go to Andrew. The teacher asks him to slow down so she can speak to him. "Jimmy didn't like it when you grabbed the bike when it was his turn. He had been waiting a long time and he wants to ride now. You didn't even ask for a turn. It is Jimmy's turn now. You may have the next turn. I won't let anyone take your turn and I can't let you take Jimmy's turn either." By talking specifically about Andrew's behavior, the teacher takes steps to prevent his unacceptable actions from being related in some way to his dark color.

In similar circumstances, children angered by this kind of aggression have said, "I don't like you, you old black thing!" Once again, the teacher must step in and protect the dark child from racial epithets. He must learn to suffer the consequences of his aggressive acts but not negative racial attitudes.

Racial name-calling must be stopped as soon as it begins. Children need to understand that name-calling can hurt and that the classroom is a place where the teacher expects children not to hurt each other. Contact with a variety of children helps them understand that, despite certain obvious differences (skin coloring, texture of hair, type of features), children still are alike in more ways than they are different. While playing hiding games, they learn that almond-shaped, blue, green, hazel, and dark-brown eyes can all locate a hidden object. Washing at the bathroom sink helps them to discover that their playmates' dark skin does not wash off, even if the dirt from the sandbox does. Toilet routines help them to discover that one's skin is the same color all over. All this information is gradually assimilated in such a way that children feel comfortable with differences, especially when their teacher demonstrates that she is comfortable with a wide range of differences. The process is infinitely easier when human variety is a natural part of the classroom.

The absence of variety in a classroom in no way lessens the need for developing an appreciation for the many kinds of people who live in our towns, cities, country, and world. Realistic photographs may initiate children's awareness of those different from themselves. Facts about these children, given in a comfortable, relaxed manner, will develop understanding of and appreciation for them. Visitors from another school and visits to schools can extend the repertoire of real situations, which broaden children's horizons.

On one visit, two white girls had been missing from the playroom for a long period of time. The teacher found them in the bathroom and overheard one saying to the other. "Let's not play with those children today." The other replied. "Yes, let's don't." The teacher had no way of knowing if "those children" meant the dark-skinned children or the children who were strange because they had been seen only a week ago. She did not create guilt feelings in the girls with social platitudes like, "It's not polite to stay away from visitors too long," or "When friends come to visit, they have a better time when you play with them." In her wisdom, she said simply, "We missed having you in the room with us and hope you will come back soon."

Meanwhile, the rest of the children were having a great time frosting graham crackers for a special snack. Before long, the two girls realized they were having no fun staying away from the group. They returned to the room and were soon working with pink and green frosting. Their right not to participate until they felt ready had been respected. By making their own decisions, for reasons important to them, they became involved voluntarily instead of being coerced against their will. Their teacher demonstrated the kind of understanding that goes with the grain instead of against it. For the remaining six visits, the two girls joined their school activities. They realized they could be comfortable with and enjoy new and different children.

Today's nursery school children will be adults in a world of many different kinds of people. They will need to feel comfortable with human diversity. They will need to understand human variety. Hopefully, they will learn to respect people different from themselves. The cornerstone for such relationships can be laid during the early childhood years. Not enough people are committed to preparing children for racial democracy. Too much time has already been lost in pursuing these goals. Parents, schools, churches, and social institutions must provide young children with meaningful experiences, which can serve as a solid foundation on which to build positive attitudes toward human understanding.

Language Development and Communication

18 Suggestions from Studies of Early Language Acquisition

Courtney B. Cazden

What have psychologists discovered about ways children learn language before or out of school? This is an up-to-the-minute overview of significant research.

When we say that a child has learned his native language by the time he enters first grade, what do we mean he has learned? A set of sentences from which he chooses the right one when he wants to say something? The *meaning* of a set of sentences from which he chooses the right interpretation for the sentences he hears? Even if the sets of sentences and interpretations were enormous, the result would still be inadequate. Outside of a small and unimportant list of greetings like *Good Morning* and clichés like *My, it's hot today,* few sentences are spoken or heard more than once. Any speaker, child or adult, is continuously saying and comprehending sentences he has never heard before and will never hear or comprehend again in the same way. Creativity in expressing and understanding particular meanings in particular settings to and from particular listeners is the heart of human language ability.

The only adequate explanation for what we call "knowing a language" is that the child learns a limited set of rules. On the basis of these rules he can produce and comprehend an infinite set of sentences. Such a set of rules is called a grammar, and the study of how a child learns the structure of his native language is called the study of the child's acquisition of grammar.

When we say that a child knows a set of rules, of course we don't

Reprinted by permission of Courtney B. Cazden and the Association for Childhood Education International, 3615 Wisconsin Avenue, N. W., Washington, D.C. Copyright © 1969 by the Association.
Dr. Cazden is Associate Professor of Education, Harvard University.

mean that he knows them in any conscious way. The rules are known nonconsciously, out of awareness, as a kind of tacit knowledge. This way of knowing is true for adults too. Few of us can state the rules for adding /s/ or /z/ or /iz/ sounds to form plural nouns. Yet if asked to supply the plurals for nonsense syllables such as *bik* or *wug* or *gutch*,[1] all who are native speakers of English could do so with ease. Most six-year-old children can too. We infer knowledge of the rules from what adults or children can say and understand.

Children learn the grammar of their native language gradually. Might one assume, therefore, that the stages they pass through on their way to mature knowledge could be characterized as partial versions of adult knowledge? Not so! One of the most dramatic findings of studies of child language acquisition is that these stages show striking similarities across children but equally striking deviations from the adult grammar.

For example, while children are learning to form noun and verb endings, at a certain period in their development they will say *foots* instead of *feet, goed* instead of *went, mines* instead of *mine.*[2] Children do not hear *foots* or *goed* or *mines.* These words are overgeneralizations of rules that each child is somehow extracting from the language he does hear. He hears *his, hers, ours, yours* and *theirs;* and he hypothesizes that the first person singular should be *mines.* Human beings are pattern- or rule-discovering animals, and these overgeneralizations of tacitly discovered rules are actively constructed in each child's mind as economical representations of the structure of the language he hears.

Rules for formation of sentences show the same kinds of deviations. In learning how to ask a question, children will say, *Why I can't go?,* neglecting temporarily to reverse the auxiliary and pronoun.[3] And their answer to the often-asked question, *What are you doing?,* will temporarily be, *I am doing dancing.*[4] If the answer to *What are you eating?* takes the form, *I am eating X,* the child hypothesizes that the answer to *What are you doing?* is, *I am doing X-ing.* Only later does he learn that answers with *doing* require the exceptional form *I am X-ing.*

The commonsense view of how children learn to speak is that they imitate the language they hear around them. In a general way, this must be true. A child in an English-speaking home grows up to speak English, not French or Hindu or some language of his own. But in the fine details of the language-learning process, imitation cannot be the whole answer, as the above examples show.

Sometimes we get even more dramatic evidence of how impervious to external alteration the child's rule system can be. Jean Berko Gleason's conversation with a four-year-old is an example:

> She said, *My teacher holded the baby rabbits and we patted them.*
> I asked, *Did you say your teacher held the baby rabbits?*
> She answered, *Yes.*
> I then asked, *What did you say she did?*
> She answered, again, *She holded the baby rabbits and we patted them.*

Did you say she held them tightly? I asked.
No, she answered, *she holded them loosely.*[5]

Impressed by the confidence with which the child continued to use her own constructions despite hearing and comprehending the adult form, Gleason conducted a variation of her older test[6] with first-, second- and third-grade children. She asked the children to give irregular plural nouns or past tense verbs after she had supplied the correct form as she asked the question. "In the case of verbs, they were shown a bell that could ring and told that yesterday it rang; then they were asked what the bell did yesterday."[7] Even under these conditions, only 50 percent of the first-graders (7 out of 14) said *rang;* 6 said *ringed* and one said *rung.* Gleason concludes:

> In listening to us, the children attended to the sense of what we said, and not the form. And the plurals and past tenses they offered were products of their own linguistic systems, and not imitations of us.[8]

When sophisticated parents try deliberately to teach a child a form that does not fit his present rule system, the same filtering process occurs. The following conversation took place when a psychologist tried to correct an immaturity in her daughter's speech:

C. *Nobody don't like me.*
M. *No, say "Nobody likes me."*
C. *Nobody don't like me.*
   (eight repetitions of this dialogue)
M. *No. Now listen carefully: say "Nobody likes me."*
C. *Oh! Nobody don't likes me!*[9]

It happens that irregular verbs such as *went* and *came* are among the most common verbs in English. Children usually learn the irregular forms first, evidently as isolated vocabulary words, and later start constructing their own overgeneralizations *goed* and *comed* when they reach the stage of tacitly discovering that particular rule. Finally, they achieve the mature pattern of rule plus exceptions. Stages on the way to the child's acquisition of mature behavior may look for the moment like regressions, like new errors in terms of adult standards, and yet be significant evidence of intellectual work and linguistic progress.

With a very few pathological exceptions, all children learn to speak the language of their parents and home community. They do so with such speed and ease, at an age when other seemingly simpler learnings such as identification of colors are absent, that one wonders how the environment helps the process along. Just as the commonsense view holds that the child's process is basically imitation, so it implies that the adult's contribution is to shape the child's speech by correcting him when he is "wrong" and reinforcing him when he is "correct." Here too the commonsense view seems invalid. So far no evidence exists to show that either correction or reinforcement of the learning of grammar occurs with sufficient frequency to be a potent force. Analysis of conversations between only a few parents and children are available, but that generalization holds for them without exception.

Brown and his colleagues have found corrections of mis-statements of fact but not correction of immature grammatical forms in hundreds of hours of recordings of three children—Adam, Eve and Sarah—and their parents.[10, 11] Horner[12] found only correction of "bad language" (*pee-pee*) in her study of conversation between parents and two three-year-old lower-class children. Finally, students recording the acquisition of language in such farflung areas of the world as India, California and Samoa report the same lack of correction.[13]

Reinforcement of immature constructions could be expressed in many ways. Brown *et al.* have looked for two kinds of reinforcement: verbal signs of approval and disapproval and differential communication effectiveness. In either case, the critical requirement for the operation of reinforcement is that the parent's utterance must be supplied contingently—supplied when the child speaks maturely and denied when he speaks in an immature fashion. Without that contingent relationship, the adult behavior cannot reinforce the child's mature utterance and make it more likely to occur again. Brown *et al.* examined parental response to specific constructions—such as questions—at times when the children were oscillating between mature and immature forms (as with *went* and *goed* above). They found no evidence of differential approval or of differential communication effectiveness.[14, 15] Analyzing these same parent-child conversations, Bellugi-Klima concludes:

> The mother and child are concerned with daily activities, not grammatical instruction. Adam breaks something, looks for a nail to repair it with, finally throws pencils and nails around the room. He pulls his favorite animals in a toy wagon; fiddles with the television set; and tries to put together a puzzle. His mother is concerned primarily with modifying his behavior. She gives him information about the world around him and corrects facts. Neither of the two seems overtly concerned with the problems that we shall pursue so avidly: the acquisition of syntax.[16]

In modifying behavior, supplying information about the world and correcting facts, mothers of young children do seem to use simpler language than they address to other adults. At least, this is indicated in the only study in which the mother's utterances to her child and to another adult have been compared. The utterances to her child were both shorter and simpler.[17] Presumably, as the child's utterances become longer and more complex, so do the mother's. Other than this simplification, there is no sequencing of what the child has to learn. He is offered a cafeteria, not a carefully prescribed diet. And, seemingly impelled from within, he participates in the give-and-take of conversation as best he can from the very beginning, in the process takes what he needs to build his own language system and practices new forms to himself, often at bedtime.[18]

As far as we can tell now, all that the child needs is exposure to well-formed sentences in the context of conversation that is meaningful and sufficiently personally important to command attention. Whether the child could learn as well from an exclusive diet of monologues or dialogues in which he did not participate—as he could get from television—we don't know and, for ethical reasons, may never be able to find out.

The foregoing picture of how children learn their native language *before* school is fairly certain, though still incomplete. Implications for how to help children continue their learning *in* school are far less certain—indeed, are controversial in the extreme—and evidence on which the controversy might be resolved is insufficient. The most obvious implication is that teachers should act the way parents have acted: talk with children about topics of mutual interest in the context of the child's on-going work and play. This recommendation is made by many people in early childhood education in this country and in infant schools in England.[19, 20] And see Hawkins'[21] sensitive account of "the language of action and its logic" in six four-year-old children who are deaf. Controversy arises because so far experimental comparison of various preschool programs that focus on language development have failed to demonstrate the effectiveness of those programs based on the above philosophy.[22]

Two different explanations of this apparent anomaly can be very tentatively suggested. First, our diagnosis of children's communication problems may be inadequate. Children who need help with language may need very specific kinds of help: help in specific language knowledge such as word meanings, in specific communication skills such as communicating information accurately through words alone, in specific school language games such as answering questions posed by an adult who obviously knows the answers; or help in very general cognitive strategies like focusing attention in school and on tests. In short, maybe the kind of linguistic knowledge that has developed so well in the conversational setting of the home is not a problem in school at all, even for children from disadvantaged environments, and the problems that do exist respond better to more structured educational programs. Second, the test results in the more structured programs may look deceptively good. What the child has learned well enough to express on a test may not have been assimilated into his total linguistic and cognitive system.[23]

Hopefully, this controversy will be resolved in the near future. It is an issue of both practical and theoretical importance.

References

1. J. Berko, "The Child's Learning of English Morphology," *Word* 14 (1958), pp. 150–77. Also in S. Saporta (ed.), *Psycholinguistics* (New York: Holt, 1961), pp. 359–375.

2. C. B. Cazden, "The Acquisition of

Noun and Verb Inflections," *Child Development* 39 (1968), pp. 433–438.

3. U. Bellugi-Klima, *The Acquisition of the System of Negation in Children's Speech* (Cambridge, Mass.: MIT Press, Quoted material reprinted by permission of MIT Press).

4. Cazden, "Acquisition of Noun and Verb Inflections."

5. J. Berko Gleason, "Do Children Imitate?" *Proceedings of the International Conference on Oral Education of the Deaf,* June 17-24, 1967, vol. II, pp. 1441–48, copyright 1967 by the Alexander Graham Bell Association for the Deaf, Washington, D.C. Quoted material reprinted by permission of Alexander Graham Bell Association for the Deaf.

6. Berko, "Child's Learning."

7. Berko Gleason, "Do Children Imitate?"

8. *Ibid.*

9. D. McNeill, "Developmental Psycholinguistics," pp. 15–81, in F. Smith and A. Miller (eds.), *The Genesis of Language: A Psycholinguistic Approach* (Cambridge: MIT Press, 1966. Quoted material reprinted by permission of MIT Press).

10. R. Brown, C. B. Cazden, and U. Bellugi, "The Child's Grammar from I to III," in J. P. Hill (ed.), *1967 Minnesota Symposium on Child Psychology* (Minneapolis: University of Minnesota Press, 1969).

11. R. Brown and C. Hanlon, "Derivational Complexity and Order of Acquisition in Child Speech," in J. Hayes (ed.), *Carnegie-Mellon Symposium on Cognitive Psychology,* in press.

12. V. M. Horner, "The Verbal World of the Lower-class Three-year-old: A Pilot Study in Linguistic Ecology," unpublished doctoral dissertation (University of Rochester, 1968).

13. D. I. Slobin, "Questions of Language Development in Cross-Cultural Perspective," paper prepared for symposium on *Language Learning in Cross-cultural Perspective* (Michigan State University, September 1968).

14. Brown, Cazden, and Bellugi, "Child's Grammar."

15. Brown and Hanlon, "Derivational Complexity."

16. Bellugi-Klima, "Acquisition of the System of Negation."

17. Slobin, "Questions of Language Development."

18. R. H. Weir, *Language in the Crib* (The Hague: Mouton, 1962).

19. C. B. Cazden, "Evaluating Language Learning in Early Childhood Education," in B. S. Bloom (ed.), *Formative and Summative Evaluation of Student Learning* (New York: McGraw-Hill, in press).

20. ____, "Language Programs for Young Children: Notes from England," in C. B. Lavatelli (ed.), *Preschool Language Training* (Urbana, Ill.: University of Illinois Press, in press).

21. F. P. Hawkins, *The Logic of Action: From a Teacher's Notebook,* (Boulder, Col.: University of Colorado Elementary Science Advisory Center, 1969).

22. M. Blank and F. Solomon, "How Shall the Disadvantaged Be Taught," *Child Development,* 40 (1969), pp. 47–61.

23. J. Glick, "Some Problems in the Evaluation of Preschool Intervention Programs," in R. D. Hess and R. M. Bear (eds.), *Early Education* (Chicago: Aldine, 1968), pp. 215–221.

19 Listening Behavior:
Some Cultural Differences

Edward T. Hall

Teachers can never fully understand the inner world of childhood. Here a distinguished linguistic anthropoligist and author writes of listening behavior among disparate culture groups. His comments bear directly on the improvement of teacher-learner relationships, particularly in schools with culturally different children.

A United States ambassador I once knew was forced to return home from his assignment in a small tropical country. The reason—ulcers. Instead of warm relations with friendly neighbors, his experience had been so frustrating that it broke his health. Relations with the local people had soured—not because of diplomatic or personality differences, but due to a misreading of man's basic nonverbal communications systems: the meanings attached to time, space, material objects, and friendships.[1]

In the United States we value promptness and demand scheduling, and we evaluate each other's behavior in these terms. To arrive late for a business appointment has different meanings, depending upon how late one is, where one lives and works, and how well the people involved know each other.

Physical arrangement of buildings and rooms often tells us something of the relative value of the activities which they house. The seating of people at a banquet, formal discussion, etc., many times discloses something of their significance in that situation. Teachers occasionally ask students to come to the front of the room or to stand not only so that they can be better seen and heard, but to emphasize their statements. What is most interesting and crucial in the conduct of interpersonal relations is that these things that we do automatically and take so much for granted are actually part of a complex of learned behavior that varies from culture to culture. (It should be noted here that I am not referring to gestures, but to the deeper context in which all communications take place, all of which has been developed in more detail elsewhere.)[2]

Culture as a system of communication deeply influences the entire educational process. We are not talking now about beliefs and customs

This is a revision and expansion of the article which appeared in the March, 1969 *Phi Delta Kappan*. Reprinted by permission. The editors are deeply grateful to Dr. Hall, who is Professor of Anthropology at Northwestern University, for providing additional material and examples.

and the things that people normally think of when they refer to culture, but about the hidden structure that underlies everything else. When the implications of this are finally recognized, they will be as profound as the effects of modern linguistics on the teaching of language. In the meantime let's take a look at one aspect of hidden culture.

What does it mean to listen, and what is meant by "being a good listener"? More than you might think! Most of us take listening for granted, yet the way people show they are listening (that is, paying attention and playing the role of interlocutor properly) is as varied as the languages they speak. In fact it's part of language—not explicit but implicit, not spoken but silent.

I first became interested in the implications of listening behavior some fifteen years ago while developing orientation materials for Americans going overseas for the State Department. Fortunately, I had people around me who represented many of the major languages and cultures of the world. A number of them used to stop in my office and then stay to visit. As is often the case when interacting with people of other cultures, I would find myself impelled (as though pulled by hidden strings) to hold myself, sit, respond, and play out the listening part in quite different ways. I noted that when I was with Germans I would—without thinking—hold myself stiffly, while with Latin Americans I would be caught up and involved.

My foreign friends soon began to talk about how hard it was to know whether Americans were "tuned in" or not. When sufficiently at ease to talk freely, they said that Americans were rude. I slowly learned that the way one indicates that he is paying attention is different for each culture. The entire process of being an interlocutor in a conversation is highly stereotyped, culturally patterned, and regulated by rules that are seldom, if ever, spelled out. Nevertheless, like language, this complex process—the language of "Yes, I'm listening"—is learned. It is experienced so naturally that few people know it is like a language, and like language, can be either understood or misunderstood.

Western culture has a habit of artificially separating events that really belong together. Talking and listening, two intricately intertwined processes, are an example. Even when alone and "talking to one's self" there is a part of the mind that speaks while another part listens and monitors. What is important is that the listener has a profound effect on the speaker. That is, in Skinnerian terms, the listener is either positively or negatively reinforcing the speaker at all times. Without knowing it, he may even guide the conversation by a process of positive and negative cues, showing interest in some things or disinterest in or disagreement with others. Furthermore, status, the relationship of the conversers, their feelings about each other and the topic, as well as their self-images, are all communicated in the listener context. Children are carefully coached, not only how to speak in a manner appropriate to the topic, tone, etc., but how to listen properly in widely varied contexts.

Little or none of this teaching and learning is technical. It is more characteristically informal, which means the rules are seldom spelled out, but instead are learned through observing others. *To recapitulate briefly:*

1. The two interlocutors in a conversation are intimately intertwined.
2. Almost as much is communicated by how one listens as in what one says. To listen properly is important, as when status differences are involved in parent-child, teacher-student, or employer-employee interactions.
3. The interlocutor in a conversation provides the reinforcement schedule that guides the conversation.
4. Manners are also involved, as indicated earlier, because by the way one listens he communicates either respect or rudeness, attentiveness or boredom.
5. Last but not least, most of what I am describing is experienced very personally and is seldom viewed in the context of widely shared culture patterns.

This brings us to the crux of the matter: One of the most remarkable and paradoxical aspects of culture is that the most personally experienced features are the most widely shared. What is more, most aspects of culture that fall within the personally experienced cultural category are also included in those cultural events that are learned informally and which function almost totally out of awareness.[3] Most responses to out-of-awareness communications are nonspecific; that is, they are not focused. The subject has difficulty pinpointing what it is he likes or dislikes or what has caught his attention, so that difficulties in communication are likely to be attributed to deficiencies in *attitude* on the part of the other person. That is, the whole gestalt is mentally clustered by the observer and treated as an undifferentiated mass.

In the early thirties when I was working with the Navaho Indians, I was fortunate to have friends who were good models for interacting with the Navahos. A small point, but one which I learned was crucial to the entire tone of a transaction with a Navaho, is the way he uses his eyes. Unlike middle-class whites, Navahos avoided the direct open-faced look in the eyes; more likely, they froze when looked at. Even when shaking hands they held the other person in the peripheral field of the eyes, letting the message of warmth and pleasure at seeing a friend seep through a long-clasped, but delicately held hand.

I ultimately learned that to gaze directly at a Navaho was to display hostility. As an illustration of this, a colleague of mine told of seeing an adult Indian in a pickup truck pull up, stick his head out of the window, and with nothing but a look, chastise two misbehaving Navaho boys playing at the roadside.

Another Navaho taboo that I soon learned was the use of the name as a form of direct address. Nor were voices ever raised except in extreme anger.

By now some of my readers are undoubtedly thinking what it must have been like to be a small Navaho child in schools—where white teachers, frustrated by behavior they couldn't understand, would unconsciously raise their voices, fix the child with a beady eye and say, "What's the matter? Can't you talk? Don't you even know your own name?" Finally, after much embarrassment on everyone's part, some other child would intervene, saying in a barely audible voice, "His name Hosteen Nez Begay." Some teachers were more gentle than others; others were made so anxious by behavior they couldn't fathom that they allowed their own frustration and rage to break through. "Stupid Indians won't look at you and can't even tell you their own names!"

This experience was thirty-five years ago, and I am sorry to report that things have not changed significantly. The Navahos have changed, though, and now they look at us whites, which we find reassuring. Yet I've observed they still use the old forms when they're with one another.

However, it is not just the Navahos that have developed their own particular system for using the eyes while listening. Humphry Osmond, the psychiatrist, once wrote to me about his childhood experiences in England. His description not only tells us how these things are learned, but some of what is conveyed in the use of the eyes:

> When I was a small boy I was always encouraged to look at people "straight between the eyes." It took me some time to learn this art, because, particularly where adults are concerned, one's neck got tired looking up, and anyway you couldn't look at anything else. My father who was usually kindly and sensible, was easily distressed by this, for he was of the opinion that not to look at people "straight between the eyes" implied shiftiness or untrustworthiness.

What has all this to do with modern education? The practical educator might ask what percentage of today's school population is Indian. Actually, a small, though important, percentage; but there are other groups, much more numerous than the Indians, who are just as misunderstood and just as inappropriately handled. I refer to the rural as well as central-city blacks, and to the Puerto Ricans, Mexican-Americans, Spanish-Americans, and other culturally distinct groups.

For the moment I will describe only a small segment of lower income, poorly educated black behavior; for there are basic cultural differences which are out of our awareness, but result in what Erving Goffman calls "alienation in encounters,"[4] as well as H. S. Sullivan's parataxic relationships.[5]

Though there are those who would deny it, the existence of black culture is implicit in my discussion. This subject is much too complex and emotion-laden to develop here. However, according to my own definition of culture as set forth in *The Silent Language* and *The Hidden Dimension*, the French, the English, the Greeks, and the Navahos —to name only a few groups—have their own nonverbal culture, part of which is in the way they use their eyes and set distances. They also have definite patterns for the handling of time, space, and materials. Just as there are many languages not yet reduced to writing, there are many informal cultures that have not yet been technically described or given recognition.

I should make it clear at this point that when I started studying black-white encounters in America in detail, I wasn't sure that black culture was significantly different from the dominant white culture on this point of listening behavior. My research ultimately revealed that there does exist in lower-class black culture a series of responses governing the use of the eyes, the hands, orientation of the body, position of the body, and tone of voice. Any and all of these behavioral cues are frequently misread by whites and vice versa. I should point out, however, that (a) there is nothing genetic in what I am talking about—the entire process is learned; (b) middle-class blacks until now have been imprinted by white culture and have consciously or unconsciously used whites as models of what it is to be middle-class, just as one would use a Frenchman for a model in learning how to pronounce French, and thus middle-class blacks obviously do not exhibit the central-city core black culture behavior; and (c) when one is discussing cultural differences of the type here described, ranking is not only not implied, but is explicitly *excluded*. I am only saying that there are two systems—the two systems are different and cannot be read in terms of each other; they can only be understood in their own terms. With these points in mind and with the view that the context analysis is incomplete or perhaps even faulty, there are a few generalizations about black listening behavior that have caused difficulty when central-city or rural, under-educated blacks interact with middle-class whites.

Basically, the informal rule for lower-class black culture goes somewhat as follows: If you are in the room with another person or in a context where he has ready access to you, there are times when there is no need to go through the motions to show him you are listening, because that is automatically implied. When blacks interact with whites, the differences in how one communicates that he is paying attention can lead to difficulty. One of my black assistants, working as a draftsman, had trouble with his engineer boss who wanted to tell him something. Following his own culture, my assistant continued working at his drafting table without looking up, thus giving the engineer no visible or audible sign that he was listening. The man finally said, "John! Are you paying attention to me?" At which point John looked up and said, "Of course."

How often has a polite black school child cast his eyes downward as a sign of respect and failed to meet a teacher's eye when questioned? How many teachers have thought students were "tuned out" because they gave no visible sign they were listening? How many have said, in angry tones, "Johnny! When I talk, you listen! Is that clear?" What is the child to do? How is he to know that what the teacher is really saying is "Stop acting in black ways and start acting white." The situation gets complex when prejudice and ranking are present, but even when they are not, there is a monumental communication gap which is usually not seen for what it is by either side. Furthermore, for the members of *any* culture to assume the communication styles of another seems unnatural and awkward at first. Unfortunately whites as well as many middle-class blacks have assumed that the communication styles of their students were simply substandard versions of their own style.

When I discussed eye behavior with a black colleague, he observed, "When I punish my boy *I look at him,* and when I look at him I'm *mad.* I look at his eyes and they grow big and he *knows* I'm *mad.*" (Note the direct communication back and forth on both sides.) The reader may have the impression that eye behavior in the Navaho and the central-city blacks are the same or that American Indians all practice eye avoidance. Neither point is true. None of the different ethnic groups in the Southwest use their eyes in precisely the same way (Navahos, Hopi, Rio Grande Pueblo, Taos, Spanish-Americans, etc.). The difference between the central-city black and the Navaho are numerous; anyone who has worked with both would never confuse them. Not only are there postural differences, including position of the head, but the way they use their eyes is different. While the two patterns only resemble each other in the most superficial way, imagine for a moment what it would be like to be a black or Navaho child confronted with an adult white who gives cues with his eyes, hands, and tone of voice, all indicating in your own dialectology that he is angry with you.

Teachers often get angry when students don't "pay attention." This compounds the difficulty for students in situations where the ethnic background of the teacher is different from the students. The teacher's anger at what she thinks is "not paying attention" causes the student to become anxious, thus inhibiting his ability to learn, in turn making the teacher more angry. This cycle of miscuing can be avoided if people only realize and adjust to cultural differences in nonverbal communications.

In the past, attempts to remedy parataxic communications of this sort have been singularly unsuccessful, due in part to high ego involvement on both sides as well as to the nonconscious nature of the processes themselves. Another crucial factor is that most people consider culture as limited to a system of beliefs and customs—both of which can be manipulated consciously. Seen in this light, a child's failure to conform is often viewed as lack of intelligence or motivation. Both interpretations should raise flags in the educator's mind that there is a good chance that he is reading his students incorrectly.

This paper was prepared because it illustrates two common and serious errors in the educational process: (a) *The artificial separation of events that are really part of the same process* (in this case, talking and listening); (b) *the commonly held belief that cultural differences are superficial* and are not personally cathected (linked) to the ego, and are therefore only superficially involved in interpersonal processes.

It is the conviction of the author that until man learns not only to accept, but to capitalize on cultural differences, everything from minor classroom tragedies to world wars will continue to plague us.

References

1. Edward T. Hall, *The Silent Language* (Garden City, N.Y.: Doubleday, 1959); Edward T. Hall, *The Hidden Dimension* Garden City, N.Y.: Doubleday, 1966); Edward T. Hall and William Foote Whyte, "Intercultural Communication," *Human Organization,* 19 (Spring 1960).

2. Hall, *The Silent Language;* idem, *Hidden Dimension;* Erving Goffman, *The Presentation of Self in Everyday Life* (Garden City, N.Y.: Doubleday, 1959); Goffman, *Encounters* (Indianapolis: Bobbs-Merrill, 1961).

3. For further information on informal systems and how they are learned, see Hall, *Silent Language,* Ch. 4.

4. Goffman, *The Presentation of Self.*

5. H. S. Sullivan, *Conceptions of Modern Psychiatry* (Washington, D.C.: William Alanson White Foundation, 1947).

SECTION D

New Frontiers

20 Psychoneurobiochemeducation

David Krech

One of the most respected and stimulating contemporary experimental psychologists here discusses the promise and danger in recent advances in our understanding of the brain and its control. He foresees biochemists, neurologists, psychologists, and educators combining forces to add to the intellectual stature of man.

His hypothesis regarding "species-specific enrichment experiences" and his interpretation of the importance of language development make this article a provocative contribution to speculations on early childhood education.

I am a rat-brain psychologist with a weakness for speculation. Now time was when rat research was a fairly harmless activity, pursued by underpaid, dedicated, well-meaning characters. The world took little note and cared even less about our researches on how rats learned to thread their way through mazes. Oh, occasionally a misguided educator would take us seriously and try to fashion an educational psychology out of our rats-in-a-maze studies. But the classroom teachers—once removed from the school of education—would quickly see through such nonsense, and, forsaking all rats, would turn to the serious and difficult task of teaching children—unencumbered and unaided by our research and theory.

But time no longer is. Our psychology—especially when combined with educational practice and theory—must now be listed among the Powerful and, even perhaps, the Dangerous sciences. I refer specifically to the recent research developments in brain biochemistry and behavior —to some of which research I now turn.

The research I will discuss really concerns itself with the venerable mind-body problem beloved of philosophers and theologians. For brain biochemistry and behavior research seeks to find the *physical* basis for memory. In essence it asks the following question: In what corporal forms do we retain the remembrance of things past? What are the chem-

Phi Delta Kappan, March, 1969. Reprinted by permission. Mr. Krech is Professor of Psychology in the University of California, Berkeley.

ical or neurological or anatomical substrates of the evocative ghosts we call "memories"? Over the centuries of thought and decades of scientific research we have gained but very little on this question. Today, however, there is a feeling abroad that we are on the verge of great discoveries. Indeed, some researchers believe that we already know, in the rough, the form the final answer will take to the question I have raised. And it is this: The physical basis of any memory, whatever else it may be, involves either the production of new proteins, the release of differentiated molecules of ribonucleic acids (RNA's) or the induction of higher enzymatic activity levels in the brain. In a word, for every separate memory in the mind we will eventually find a differentiated chemical in the brain—"chemical memory pellets," as it were.

What warrant do we have for such a prophecy? To begin with, we have reason to believe that the storage of memory in the brain is a many-splendored, multi-phased, actively changing affair. That is, any single memory is not merely "deposited" in a completed form in the brain. Rather, it goes through a complex developmental history in the brain in which it changes from a short-term into a long-term memory. And each stage in this consolidation process seems to be dependent upon different although interrelated chemical mechanisms. Let me indicate to you one set (of quite a number which are now available) of speculative hypotheses concerning this developmental transformation of memories.

First we can assume that immediately after every experience, a relatively short-lived reverberatory process is set up within the brain. This process continues for a time after the stimulus disappears and permits us to remember events which occurred moments or minutes ago. But this reverberatory process fairly quickly decays and disappears—and as it does, so does the related memory. However, under certain conditions, the short-term reverberatory process, before it disappears completely from the scene, triggers off a second and quite different series of events in the brain. This second series of events involves the release of new RNA's or the production of new proteins and other macromolecules. And these chemical changes are relatively long-lasting and serve as the physical bases of our long-term memories.

Now it can be supposed that if we increased the robustness or the survival time of the initial reverberatory process we might increase the probability of converting the short-term memory into a long-term memory. There are several ways one could do that. Through the repetition of the same stimulus one could presumably prolong or continually reinstate the reverberatory process and thus, perhaps, make it more effective in inducing permanent chemical changes in the brain. The old-fashioned term for this procedure is "drill" or "practice" and drill and practice are indeed effective techniques for helping the conversion of short-term memoies into long-term ones.

But James McGaugh, at the University of California at Irvine, got the bright idea that he could achieve much the same results chemically. His argument—very much simplified—went something like this: A drug which would increase neural and chemical activity within the brain might either increase the vigor of the reverberatory process, or the ease with which the long-term chemical processes would "take off," and thus facilitate the conversion of short-term memories into long-term ones. Apparently his idea was a sound one, for with the use of chemical compounds like strychnine and metrazol, which are central nervous system stimulants, McGaugh has been eminently successful in raising the intellectual level of hundreds of southern California mice.

In one of his experiments which is most pregnant with social implications and promises and forebodings for the future, McGaugh tested the maze-learning ability of two quite different strains of mice. One of the strains was, by heredity, particularly adept at maze learning; the other, particularly stupid at that task. Some animals from each strain were injected with different doses of metrazol after each daily learning trial to see whether there would be an improvement in their ability to retain what they had learned on that trial—and some were not. The findings pleased everyone—presumably even the mice. With the optimal dosage of metrazol, the chemically treated mice were 40 percent better in remembering their daily lessons than were their untreated brothers. Indeed, under metrazol treatment the hereditarily stupid mice were able to turn in better performances than their hereditarily superior but untreated colleagues. Here we have a "chemical memory pill" which not only improves memory and learning but can serve to make all mice equal whom God—or genetics—hath created unequal. May I suggest that some place in the back of your mind, you might begin to speculate on what it can mean—socially, educationally, politically—if and when we find drugs which will be similarly effective for human beings.

But let me continue with my story. What chemistry can give, it can also take away—as Agranoff and his now notorious goldfish at the University of Michigan have shown. Agranoff argued that if we could prevent the brain from manufacturing the chemicals involved in the long-term memory process, then we would create an animal which might have normal short-term memories, but would be incapable of establishing enduring memories. Agranoff trained his fish to swim from one side of an aquarium to another, whenever a signal light was turned on, in order to avoid an electric shock. Goldfish can learn this task within a forty-minute period, and once it is learned, they remember it over many days. Now Agranoff varied his experiments. Immediately before, and in some experiments immediately after, training, Agranoff injected puromycin or actinomycin-D (two antibiotics which prevent the formation of new proteins or nuclear RNA) into the brains of a new group of goldfish. His findings were most encouraging (to Agranoff that is, not necessarily to the goldfish). The injected goldfish were not impaired in their *learning* of the shock-avoidance task since, presumably, the short-term reverberatory process which enables a fish to remember its lesson from one trial to another—a matter of a few seconds—does not involve the synthesis of new proteins or nuclear RNA. But when tested a day or two later the fish showed almost no retention for the task they had known so well the day before—indicating that the long-term process *is* dependent upon the synthesis of these compounds in the brain. Here, then, we find not only support for our general theory but we have a suggestion that there exist in antimetabolites whole families of chemical memory preventatives which seem not to interfere with the individual's immediate capacity to obey immediate orders, but which do prevent him from building up a permanent body of experiences, expectations, and skills. Conjure up, if you are of that mind, what evils such weapons can wreak in the hands of the Orwellian authorities of 1984—but I must hurry on to our next set of experiments.

A number of years ago, James McConnell at the University of Michigan threw all the brain researchers into a tizzy by reporting that he had succeeded in teaching planaria—a fairly primitive type of flatworm— to make a simple response to a light signal, that he then ground up his educated flatworms, fed the pieces to untrained fellow worms—and lo and behold, the uneducated flatworms wound up with the *memories* of the worms which they had just eaten, and, without any training, could perform the response of the late-lamented and digested "donor" worms!

But then all hell broke loose when other workers in other laboratories and in other countries reported that they could train a *rat,* make an extract from its brain, inject this extract into an untrained rat, and by so doing cause the recipient rat to acquire the memories of the now-dead donor rat. It is one thing to claim this for the primitive planaria, which, after all, do not have very much in the way of a structurally differentiated and organized brain. It is a very different thing to claim it for the rat, which *is* a serious mammal, with a highly developed brain, not too different in complexity, in differentiation, and in organization from our own.

The dust raised by these reports has not yet settled. Indeed, most scientists are definitely on the side of the nonbelievers—but the work goes on, and we cannot predict the final outcome of these experiments, many of which have given negative results. However, as a result of this work, a number of brain researchers have been moved, over the last two or three years, from the position of stiff-necked disbelief to the position of "well, maybe—I don't believe it, but well, maybe." And this is where *I* stand at the moment—fearless and foursquare proclaiming "well, maybe . . ." Now, if it should come to pass that McConnell and his fellow believers are right, then we will indeed have made a huge jump forward. For we would then have a most effective behavioral assay method which should enable us to zero in on this marvelous brain-goulash which can transfer information from one brain to another, and isolate and identify in detail all the "memory" proteins, enzymes, RNA's, or other macromolecules.

After that—the world of the mind is ours! But that day is not here yet. Let me leave these brave new world experimenters and go on with another question and another set of experiments.

Does the research I have reviewed mean that if and when we will have developed get-smart pills (à la McGaugh), or chemical erasures of wrong mental habits à la Agranoff), or specific knowledge pills (à la Mc-Connell), we will be able to do without Head Start programs, educational enrichment programs, school supervisors, educational research, and, indeed, without most of our educational paraphernalia? The answer to this question, gentlemen, is a most reassuring "NO." I might even say, "Au contraire." Precisely because of the advances in brain biochemistry, the significance of the educator will be greatly increased— and just as greatly changed. Let me tell you why I think so by describing to you the results of some of our own work in the Berkeley laboratories.

Some time ago we set ourselves the following problem: If the laying down of memories involves the synthesis of chemical products in the brain, then one should find that an animal which has lived a life replete with opportunities for learning and memorizing would end with a brain chemically and morphologically different from an animal which has lived out an intellectually impoverished life. For almost two decades now, E. L. Bennett, Marion Diamond, M. R. Rosenzweig, and I, together with technical assistants, graduate students, and thousands of rats, have labored—and some of us have even sacrificed our lives—to find such evidence. Let me tell you some of what we found.

At weaning time we divide our experimental rats into two groups, half of the rats being placed in an "intellectually enriched" environment, the other half—their brothers—in the deprived environment. While both groups receive identical food and water, their psychological environments differ greatly. The animals in the first group live together in one large cage, are provided with many rat toys (tunnels to explore, ladders to climb, levers to press), and they are assigned to graduate students who are admonished to give these rats loving care and kindness, teach them to run mazes, and in general to provide them with the best and most expensive supervised higher education available to any young rat at the University of California. While these rats are thus being encouraged to store up many and varied memories, their brother rats, in the deprived goup, live in isolated, barren cages, devoid of stimulation by either their environmental appurtenances, fellow rats, or graduate students. After about eighty days of this differential treatment, all the animals are sacrificed, their brains dissected out and various chemical and histological analyses performed. The results are convincing. The brain from a rat from the enriched environment—and presumably, therefore, with many more stored memories—has a heavier and thicker cortex, a better blood supply, larger brain cells, more glia cells, and increased activity of two brain enzymes, acetylcholinesterase and cholinesterase, than does the brain from an animal whose life has been less memorable.

We can draw several morals from these experiments. First, the growing animal's psychological environment is of crucial importance for the development of its brain. By manipulating the environment of the young, one can truly create a "lame brain"—with lighter cortex, shrunken brain cells, fewer glia cells, smaller blood vessels, and lower enzymatic activity levels—or one can create a more robust, a healthier, a more metabolically active brain. If it should turn out that what is true for the rat brain is also true for the human brain, and that by careful manipulation of this or that group's early environment we can develop among them bigger and better brains or smaller and meaner ones, the wondrous promises of a glorious future or the monstrous horrors of a Huxlian brave new world are fairly self-evident.

The second conclusion I draw from our experiments is this: Since the effect of any chemical upon an organ is, in part, a function of the beginning chemical status of that organ, and since—as we have just seen —the chemical and anatomical status of the individual's brain is determined by his educational experience, then the effectiveness of the biochemist's "get smart pill" will depend upon how the educator has prepared the brain in the first instance. Indeed, a review of all the data indicates that manipulating the educational and psychological environment is a more effective way of inducing long-lasting brain changes than direct administration of drugs. Educators probably change brain structure and chemistry to a greater degree than any biochemist in the business. Another way of saying this is: The educator *can potentiate or undo the work of the brain biochemist.*

But there is still more to report, and more lessons to draw. Consider the experimental problem we faced when we tried to create a psychologically enriched environment for our Berkeley rats. We did not really know how, so we threw everything into the environment, including, almost the kitchen sink, and called it "a psychologically enriched environment." The cages were kept in brightly lighted, sound-filled rooms; the rats were given playmates to relate to, games to manipulate, maze problems to solve, new areas to explore. They were fondled and tamed and chucked under the chin at the drop of a site-visitor. In other words, we provided our happy rats with almost every kind of stimulation we could think of—or afford. And it seems to have worked. But of course it is quite possible that in our "kitchen-sink design," many of the things we did were not at all necessary—indeed, some may have had an adverse effect. And so we undertook a series of experiments to discover which elements of our environment were effective and which were not. I shall not bore you with the details of the many experiments already run and the many more which are now being run in the Berkeley laboratory. Let me list, however, some of the tentative conclusions which one can already make:

First: Sheer exercise or physical activity alone is not at all effective in developing the brain. A physical training director seems not to be an adequate substitute for a teacher.

Second: Varied visual stimulation, or indeed any kind of visual stimulation, is neither necessary nor sufficient to develop the brain, as we were able to demonstrate by using rats blinded at weaning age.

Third: Handling, or taming, or petting is also without effect in developing the growing rat's brain. Love is Not Enough.

Fourth: The presence of a brother rat in our intellectually deprived rat's cage helps him not a whit. *Bruderschaft* is not enough.

Fifth: Teaching the rat to press levers for food—that and only that seems to help somewhat, but only minimally. Not every problem-set will do, either.

The only experience we have thus far found really effective is freedom to roam around in a large object-filled space. From a recent experiment in Diamond's laboratory there are some suggestions that if the young rat is given continuous and varied maze-problems to solve—that and little else—the rat will develop a number of the same brain changes (at least the morphological ones) which we had observed in our randomly "enriched" environment.

It is clear, then, that not *every* experience or variation in stimulation contributes equally to the development of the brain. But of even greater interest is the suggestion in the above data that the most effective way to develop the brain is through what I will call *species-specific enrichment experiences.* Here is what I mean: The ability of a rat to learn its way through tunnels and dark passages, to localize points in a three-dimensional space full of objects to be climbed upon, burrowed under, and crawled through is, we can assume, of particular survival value for the rat as he is now constituted. Presumably, through the selective evolutionary process, the rat has developed a brain which is peculiarly fitted to support and enhance these skills. The "effective rat brain," therefore, is one which is a good "space-brain"—not a lever-pressing brain or an arithmetic-reasoning brain. The effective stimulating environment, correspondingly, would be one which makes *spatial learning* demands on that brain—which "pushes" that particular kind of brain in that particular way. To generalize this hypothesis, I would suggest that *for each species there exists a set of species-specific experiences which are maximally enriching and which are maximally efficient in developing its brain.*

If there be any validity to my hypothesis, then the challenge to the human educator is clear. For the educator, too, you may have noticed, has been using the kitchen-sink approach when he seeks to design a psychologically or educationally enriched environment for the child. Some educators would bombard the child—practically from infancy on —with every kind of stimulus change imaginable. His crib is festooned with jumping beads and dangling colored bits and pieces of wood (all sold very expensively to his affluent parents); he is given squishy, squeaking, squawking toys to play with, to fondle, to be frightened by, to choke on. He is jounced and bounced and picked up and put down. And when he goes to school—he finds the same blooming, buzzing confusion. He is stimulated with play activities, with opportunities for social interaction, with rhythmic movements, with music, with visual displays, with contact sports, with tactual experiences, and with anything and everything which the school system can think of—or afford. But it may be that a "stimulating environment" and an "enriched environment" are not one and the same thing. It is not true that a brain is a brain is a brain. The rat is a rat and he hath a rat's brain; the child is a child and he hath a child's brain—and each, according to my hypothesis, requires its own educational nutrient. What, then, are the species-specific enrichments for the human child?

Of course I do not know the answer to this question, but let me share with you my present enthusiastic guess that in the language arts you will find part of the answer.

I can start with no better text than a quotation from my teacher, Edward Chace Tolman, who was a completely devoted rat psychologist. "Speech," he wrote, "... is in any really developed and characteristic sense, the sole prerogative of the human being. . . . It is speech which first and foremost distinguishes man from the great ape" (1932).[1] In my opinion, it is in the study of language, above anything else, that the psychologist will discover the psychology of man, and that the educator will discover how to educate man.

In the first place, and we must be clear about this, human language, with its complex and *abstract structure,* has *nothing* in common with animal communication. Language is probably the clearest instance of a pure species-specific behavior. This is true whether you study language as a neurologist, or as a psychologist. Let us look at some brain research first.

Recently Robinson, at the National Institute of Mental Health (1967), attempted to discover which areas of the monkey's brain controlled its vocalizations.[2] Now the monkey most certainly uses vocalization for communication, but principally for communications with emotional tone such as threat, fear, pain, and pleasure. In Robinson's study fifteen unanesthetized animals, with brains exposed by surgery, were used. Some 5,880 different loci or spots in the brain were stimulated by electrodes to see whether such stimulation could bring forth vocalization. The loci explored included neocortical areas as well as areas in the limbic system, that older part of the mammalian brain which is most intimately involved with motivational and emotional responses.

Robinson's results were clear-cut: First, despite his exploration of several hundred different neocortical sites he was unable to raise a single sound from his animals by stimulating their *neocortex.* Second, stimulation of the limbic system brought forth regular, consistent, and identifiable vocalizations.

These results differ sharply from those found with the human brain. While there is some evidence that human cries and exclamations— uttered in moments of excitement—are also controlled by the limbic system, *speech and language clearly depend upon neocortical areas*— areas for which there simply are no analogues in the brain of any other animal. These areas are, of course, the well-known Broca and Wer- nicke areas in the left hemisphere of the human brain. It seems clear, as Robinson puts it, that "human speech did not develop 'out of' pri- mate vocalization, but arose from *new tissue* [italics my own] which permitted it the necessary detachment from immediate, emotional situ- ations." Man's brain, *and man's brain alone,* is a language-supporting brain.

Corresponding to the neurological picture is the psycholinguist's view of language. Almost every psycholinguist is impressed not only with the unique nature of language itself but with its unique mode of achievement by the child. Whatever value so-called reinforcement or stimulus-response theories of learning may have for describing acquisi- tion of motor skills by people, maze-learning by rats, and bar-pressing by pigeons—these theories are assessed as completely trivial and utterly irrelevant when it comes to understanding that "stunning intellectual achievement" (McNeill, 1966),[3] the acquisition of language by the child. Indeed, in reading the psycholinguist's work one is left with the im- pression that we will have to develop a species-specific learning theory for this species-specific behavior of language. I must confess that I agree with them. And if we ever achieve an understanding of language de- velopment, and if we learn how to push the *human* brain with this *human* experience, then will we indeed be on our way.

I know that other people have proposed other ways with which to enrich the child's education. Some plug for what are referred to as "cog- nitive" experience or "productive thinking" experiences, etc. Let me hasten to record that I quite agree with them. As a matter of fact, I am not at all certain that I am saying anything other than what my cog- nitive friends propose. For I hold with McNeill's judgment that ". . . the study of how language is acquired may provide insight into the very basis of mental life." And, I would go on, being human *means* having an effective mental, cognitive life.

It is for these and many, many other reasons that I would urge the educator to turn to the psycholinguist—as well as to Piaget and Crutch- field and Bruner—for his major guides in designing a rational educa- tional enrichment program.

Whether my guess merits this enthusiasm or not will perhaps even- tually be determined by research. But here is the challenge and here is the promise for the educator. Drop your kitchen-sink approach, and specify and define for us the species-specific psychologically enriching experiences for the child—and we will be off and running!

Where will we run? Let me speculate out loud. It is perfectly reasonable to suppose that we will be able to find specific biochemical boosters and biochemical inhibitors for different kinds of memories and imagery, or for different kinds of abilities, or for different kinds of personality or temperament traits. With such chemical agents in hand, and with appropriate educational and training procedures, we may use them as supplementary therapy for those failing in this or that trait and thus will we be able to rectify and heal some of the mentally retarded and the senile. Of course we may use these agents for evil—to create docile, intellectually limited, but efficient human beasts of burden without memories beyond the order of the day (remember Agranoff's fish?).

But above all, there will be great changes made in the first and foremost and continuing business of society: the education and training of the young. The development of the mind of the child will come to rest in the knowledge and skills of the biochemist, and pharmacologist, and neurologist, and psychologist, and educator. And there will be a new expert abroad in the land—the psychoneurobiochemeducator. This multi-hybrid expert will have recourse—as I have suggested elsewhere —to protein memory consolidators, antimetabolite memory inhibitors, enzymatic learning stimulants, and many other potions and elixirs of the mind from our new psychoneurobiochemopharmacopia.

There is a grievous problem here, however. Experts, whatever else they may be, are notorious order-takers. *Who* will direct our psychoneurobiochemeducator where to work his expertise, and *what* shall we tell him to do? Here we are talking about goals, values, and aims. Shall our expert raise or lower docility, aggressiveness, musical ability, engineering ability, artistic sensivity, effective intellectual functioning? Shall different ethnic or racial or national or social groups receive different treatments? In past centuries, and even today, this differential group treatment is precisely what our relatively primitive but quite effective medical and educational experts have been ordered by us to carry out. And lo, they have done so! On one side of the town they have created enclaves of the sickly, the weak, the ignorant, the unskilled —in a word, the brutalized social vanquished. On the other side of the town they have created the social victors—the healthy, the strong, the knowledgeable, the skilled. Will we continue to do this in the future with our much more sophisticated and effective psychoneurobiochemeducators? Who, in other words, will control the brain controllers—and to what ends?

I have thought and worried about these questions, and I must confess to you that I cannot avoid a dread feeling of unease about the future.

At the same time I keep whistling the following tune in an attempt to cheer myself up: If there be any validity at all to my speculations this afternoon, they add up to this: The biochemist, neurologist, psychologist, and educator will eventually add to the intellectual stature of man. With this in mind, and clinging to a lifelong faith in the virtues of knowledge and the intellect (for certainly, at this stage I can do no less), I find myself believing that man who by taking thought will have added cubits to his intellectual stature, will also acquire the added bit of wisdom and humaneness that will save us all. Let me stop on this note— before I scrutinize this faith and this hope too carefully.

References

1. Edward Chace Tolman, *Purposive Behavior in Animals and Men* (New York: The Century Company, 1932).
2. B. W. Robinson, "Vocalization Evoked from Forebrain in *Macaca Mulatta*," *Psychology and Behavior* (1967), pp. 346–354.
3. D. McNeil, "The Creation of Language," *Discovery* (1966), pp. 34–38.

Part Three
Education of the Young Child

Curriculum: Theory, Practice and Evaluation

21 Day Care: The Problem Nobody Wants to Face

Maya Pines

*In this aptly-titled commentary on the serious problems and needs
that arise in connection with the day care of children, Mrs. Pines
outlines the challenges that we as a society must confront.*

"I know a lot of people say that mothers shouldn't work," Vice
President Humphrey declared recently, "but I have been brought up
to believe that what is, is." He called the lack of adequate day-care facilities for children of working mothers one of the greatest problems of
tomorrow's America.

Though nobody wants to face it, this lack is also the single most urgent problem of preschool children today. One out of every four
mothers of children under the age of six is in the labor force. The number of such mothers has doubled since 1950. Four million American
preschoolers now have mothers who work. Yet only 225,000 children
of all ages can be squeezed into the nation's licensed day-care facilities.

What happens to the others? According to Katherin Oettinger, chief
of the U.S. Children's Bureau, 38,000 children under six have no care
at all while their mothers work. Presumably they are just locked up
in their homes. Twice as many infants and toddlers are looked after by
a youngster under the age of sixteen.

Another 600,000 preschoolers spend the day in what is euphemistically
called "family day care." In theory this sounds fine: The mother leaves
her child with a friendly neighbor, who takes in several other children
at the same time, for a small fee. In New York City, where public day-
care programs have waiting lists as long as their actual enrollment,
and where the more centers are opened the longer the waiting lists

become, a study has just been made to find out what family day care is really like. Since the Board of Health actually licensed only twenty-five homes for family day care in the entire city, this study looked into the unlicensed homes which take in some 25,000 New York children, more than half of them under the age of six.

One of the interviewers for the Medical and Health Research Association of New York City, which did this study, still has nightmares about some of the places she visited. She recalls a day-care "mother" in Central Harlem who took as many as four children at a time into her cluttered apartment, getting $15 a week for each child. The hall was used by drug addicts and "winos." In the apartment itself "you had to fight your way past torn mattresses, broken springs, all kinds of stuff which she collected—but there was not a single toy in sight," says Anna Graziano, who spent months doing this research. A four-month-old baby lay in a dark, dank bedroom on a big double bed without any barriers to prevent him from falling. "While I was there, his bottle fell to the floor several times," Miss Graziano reports, "and the woman just picked it up and gave it back to him without washing it or making a single comment. Otherwise, she paid no attention to him. There was another little boy of about eighteen months who kept making noises, so she told me to wait a minute, took him to another room, and came back saying, 'Now we can chat.' But he howled so much that after half an hour I insisted on going in to look at him, though she didn't want me to. I opened the door and saw this child shrieking—she had tied him to his crib with diapers around both his hands and feet."

The woman knew nothing about the background of the children in her charge, points out Miss Graziano. She knew neither their age nor even their correct last names. "I asked if she had the mothers' addresses or telephone numbers so she could reach them during the day in case of emergency, but she said, 'Oh, no, I forgot to get it.' As to taking the children outdoors, her reply was, 'I took this youngster out to the street once, but it was too much bother.' "

Some of the women who take in children are drunkards. Many more, according to Miss Graziano, are physically ill—and their illness is the very reason for their doing this kind of work. She recalls a harassed twenty-year-old girl who had previously worked as a salesgirl but had lost her job because of a severe anemia which left her always tired. The girl lived in a three-bedroom house with her parents, her own out-of-wedlock daughter (aged two), her uncle, her aunt, and their two children. In this home she also took three other children for day care, being paid $32 a week for all three. She hated what she was doing. She had lost control over the six children to the extent that she did not even bother to find out what part of the house they were in. One youngster, aged four, did nothing but cry all day long, sitting alone on the top step of the porch. The girl said he was "spoiled."

The children's routine in most family day-care homes is limited to breakfast, TV cartoons, lunch, nap, and TV. The study showed that 34 percent of the homes lacked play materials of any kind. In 25 percent of the homes the children were never taken out-of-doors. As many as 84 percent of the homes were rated inadequate because they violated the Health Code, or because the children were severely neglected.

There were a few glowing exceptions, such as the day-care "mother" in Central Harlem who ran what amounted to a first-rate nursery school in her house despite incredible difficulties. She had three children of her own under the age of six. To supplement her husband's meager income, she took care of four more, going about it in a highly professional way. She had cleared her living room of nearly everything except a long table along one wall, where some children were busy with crayons. "I need the space for the children to run about," she explained. Her walls were covered with paintings—her own and those of the children. There were blackboards, easels, and a variety of educational toys freely available. She had printed instructions for the children's mothers. At various times of day she managed to drop some children off at school and pick up others, taking the whole brood along with her on each trip. Despite these interruptions, she preserved large blocks of time for the children to play with clay, paints, or whatever she had scheduled for the day. She was also keenly aware of each child's difficulties and feelings.

On Miss Graziano's treks in and out of many slums in some of the city's most dangerous neighborhoods, she was sometimes struck by such extraordinary victories of the human spirit. But for the most part, the children were given no more than the bare necessities for physical survival.

Throughout their study, the interviewers were assailed by desperate women who begged them to help find good day-care services for their children. They would try any trick to attract the interviewers' attention, hoping it might somehow lead them to space in a day-care center. The study's associate director, Milton Willner, a social worker with long experience in day care, concluded that two kinds of programs were urgently needed: a training program for women who would run licensed family day care for up to five children in their homes, bolstered by periodic inspections to make sure they provided enough play materials, nap facilities, and fresh air; and many, many more day-care centers, including some for children under the age of three.

Before such programs can be expanded, or even begun, the attitude of the public must change, Willner believes. It is not only a matter of money, although the cost of good day care runs high. It is the reluctance to interfere in what is generally regarded as a family responsibility, the desire to prevent mothers from working, and "a sense of guilt which weighs heavily on the field of day care when it is confronted with a request to accept a child."

Even when the child is between the ages of three and six—the standard age for full day care—and even when space exists, the social workers who rule these centers must first establish that there is a social need—that it isn't just a case of the mother wanting to get rid of her children and go to work, as one welfare worker put it.

"Suppose you have to go to work for financial reasons," says Willner, "and you want to find a good day-care center for your four-year-old. You go to one of the family agencies that run such centers and ask them for help. First they'll do a study. If they find you're a healthy kind of person, you get along with your husband and your children, and you simply want to work, you're sure to be turned down flat. But if you have marital difficulties and problems with your children—ah! then they'll lick their lips, take your child, and give you counseling."

This typifies the arrogance of many social workers in this field, who believe that no woman is fit to make decisions about her own life without their help. Their attitude tends to squelch efforts at providing decent facilities on a large scale, or making sure that every young child has access to certain services and care.

Those who have seen the actual conditions into which thousands of American preschoolers are being pushed by the lack of day care cannot be blamed if they feel that nobody listens to them. During World War II, when it became not only acceptable but positively patriotic for mothers to work, enough nurseries and day-care centers suddenly blossomed, with government aid, to accommodate about 1,600,000 children. Today, when the number of working women exceeds the wartime total by 6 million, day-care centers have shrunk to one-sixth their wartime capacity.

While the nation gave Head Start $150 million for its first summer program, it appropriated only $7 million for day care—and that went mostly for better licensing procedures. The licensing that existed until then generally applied only to such things as toilet and fire regulations; few states had any requirements concerning the day-care center staffs. Better licensing was indeed essential; but it would not relieve the desperate need for services.

The most desperate mothers of all are those with children under the age of three. A startling total of 1,600,000 American youngsters under the age of three have mothers who work. When these women look for day care, "they come up against a stern wall of disapproval behind which is a vacuum of services," declares Mrs. Oettinger. "We did try to hold back the ocean. We always said the only place for the child under three was at home. Yet at this very moment children as young as two to four weeks are in inadequate arrangements made of necessity. We don't condone it, but babies are suffering—and we should see that they are in appropriate settings."

To find out what an appropriate setting would be like for such young babies, the Children's Bureau is now supporting several experimental programs, including one run by Head Start's Dr. Julius Richmond and

Dr. Bettye Caldwell, who had written the ill-fated *Head Start Daily Activities* booklet number two.

This extraordinary Children's Center, in Syracuse, New York, violates every convention about day care as normally practiced in the United States: It takes babies as young as six months of age (all its clientele is under three), and it deliberately stimulates their intellectual development. "At the beginning," recalls Dr. Caldwell, "I almost had to apologize for setting up this program." Several of the experts whom she called on to help plan the center rebuked her for even attempting it.

As Dr. Richmond explains it, "There's a tremendous bias against day care in the field of child welfare, due to overinterpretation of data. Since group care under certain circumstances is bad, people assume all group care is bad. But after having seen the real circumstances, we felt no great qualms of conscience. We felt it was ethically appropriate for us to provide better care than what these children were receiving."

The "real" circumstances he mentions came to light when he and Dr. Caldwell did a study of one hundred babies from very-low-income families whose mothers brought them to the Upstate Medical Center in Syracuse for check-ups. This showed something that many people suspected all along, but that his study documented. "About one-third of the babies were *not* cared for by their mothers during their first year of life," he says. "Now this would not have come out if we had not gone into the homes and studied the families; since the mothers brought the babies into the clinic, one would normally assume that they cared for their babies themselves.

"Actually, the babies had multiple mothers; they were parked with baby sitters or others, often under circumstances that would make our hair stand on end."

The Children's Center opened in 1964 as a five-year demonstration of how "culturally determined mental retardation" could be prevented among high-risk infants and toddlers. The idea was to promote *both* emotional-social development and cognitive growth with equal vigor. These are symbiotic—one does not develop at the expense of the other, emphasizes Dr. Caldwell, a psychologist who is the mother of twins. It is important to develop these children's sense of trust in adults and in events, she believes. The center arranges situations that lead the children to certain cognitive operations—classification, conceptualization, learning sets. At all times, it tries to provide an atmosphere in which infants and children can thrive, not merely grow.

Physically, the center consists of a narrow old building formerly used by medical students, and a large, reconverted trailer specifically adapted for the babies. It stands next to a spacious yard with swings, sandpiles, and climbing equipment. Behind each classroom there is a closetlike area in which researchers can observe the children through a one-way mirror without disturbing them.

As I walked up to the second floor, I met a half dozen toddlers, about eighteen months to two years old, on their way out with their teacher. They were going to a farm to see the animals and, hopefully, ride some ponies while held by a teen-ager. "We've already taken the older group out. They had a wonderful time," said Dr. Caldwell.

From a researchers' nook I watched the two- to three-year-olds having juice and cookies as a story was read to them. There were two teachers for eight tots—a ratio of one teacher for four children, which Dr. Caldwell calls an absolute minimum. This ratio was often improved by the addition of student teachers. Each child, I was told, had one staff person primarily responsible for him, who cared for him when he awoke from his nap. Each one received the concentrated, individual attention of a teacher once in the morning and once in the afternoon, for at least half an hour at a time.

Although the center supposedly provides group care, to which many experts object for this age group, in practice it offers a highly individualized type of care. Its unhurried atmosphere hides the fact that the curriculum is carefully programmed to try and match each child's particular level of intellectual development.

Even the babies under one year of age do finger painting on plastic trays and take part in special learning games. They may listen to various sounds—bells, whispering, and stones in a box—or smell many odors, including vinegar. A one-year-old may learn object permanence: The teacher puts a toy behind a barrier to see whether the baby can find it; later on, she may use two detours, placing two different covers over the same toy. A slightly older child may work on the toy-string problem: He learns to pull a string to reach a toy, a lesson in cause and effect. Once a month they are given very informal tests to see whether they have grasped certain concepts such as "bigger" or "smaller."

The trailer in which all this takes place was originally used by the crew of a construction company. Airy and neat, it holds seven cribs for the babies to nap in, a large bathroom, a large indoor play area, and a kitchen area. It cost $3,400, plus another $1,000 for installation. Since the children's mothers have varied schedules, the bulk of planned activities takes place between 9 A.M. and 4 P.M.

While I was there the babies returned from their outdoor play in the yard, all aglow. Some had runny noses, which a teacher wiped. Most of the children were Negro. An attractive Danish teacher changed the smallest baby's diaper. Seated on a high chair, a seventeen-month-old was about to start his concept learning session.

"Do you want to play a game?" asked his teacher, a pleasant, matronly woman who frequently cuddled her charges. She placed two metal cups before the boy—one small and shallow, the other big and deep. Then she hid a Fruit Loop (a small, colored cereal loop) under the small cup.

"Let's look under the little one," she said. Perhaps accidentally, the baby picked up the right cup, while the teacher exclaimed, "Good boy!" and clapped. The baby ate the cereal. On other trials, he occasionally chucked everything to the floor.

Dr. Caldwell considers the babies' training the most important step in the center's program. She had expected it to be the most difficult to arrange, but it turned out to be the easiest. She ran into real problems only when she tried to systematize the older children's program, probably for cultural reasons: While our culture takes it for granted that babies must be treated individually, any situation that looks like a nursery school makes teachers want to teach the whole group. She tried to get around this by setting up a platoon system, under which the children were split up into small subgroups. She also insisted that each child be read to or played with individually for at least an hour a day. This met with great resistance from the teacher at first, she reports. Working with such small groups is accepted in theory, but it just was not happening. The complaint was, "I won't ever have time to read to them again"—meaning as a group—or, "They all enjoy pasting!" Some teachers objected because they wanted nothing but free play. For others, structuring activities meant a rigid schedule. "The word 'structure' has nothing to do with discipline or schedule—it means basically *planning*," says Dr. Caldwell. "You *stage* things a bit. You give form and shape to them. A well-placed question is a good example of structure." Now, she says, they have arrived at a more comfortable balance between free and planned activities, though the group still exerts a tremendous pull and the older children's activities are still not as individualized as she would like.

To fit the schedules of working mothers, the center is open from 7:30 A.M. to 6 P.M. five days a week. All the children spend nights and weekends at home. The first twenty-three children who entered the center did so for a variety of reasons. One came because his mother had had a nervous breakdown and was sent to a mental hospital. Another, the youngest of four children in a stable and apparently happy family, where both parents worked, came because his mother wanted to prevent the difficulties his older brothers and sisters had had in school. At his age—two and a half—they had all seemed bright and talked well, she said, but later they failed in school; she didn't want it to happen again.

The father of three other youngsters—aged three, two, and ten months—had died just before the baby's birth, leaving a total of ten children and a greatly overburdened mother. Some of the older children had already dropped out of school. Rather than break up the family by sending the children to separate foster homes—the mother simply could not cope with the situation any more—the Welfare Department decided to try the center, and it worked. Even though the mother required an operation and had to be hospitalized for a while, she managed to keep the family together, since the three youngest ones were taken care of during the day.

"Not all the children's mothers are working," points out Dr. Richmond. "Some are teen-agers who can't function as mothers because they haven't yet fulfilled their own narcissistic needs. One thing we learned very quickly: to have continuity in the child population, you've got to have transportation for the child. Parents will generally get their child to a car, even if they wouldn't bring the child by themselves. This means fighting the bias of middle-class people who often say, 'If they don't have the motivation, to hell with them!' We've done too much writing off of people of this kind—those who need it the most."

Because the center's program is so revolutionary, the first thing that had to be established was that it would do the children no harm. So far, the children seem to develop well on all counts: They have formed attachments to the staff, they get along well with each other, and their IQ's have shown a tendency to rise as they grow older, rather than decline with time, as happens with most high-risk babies.

By now this is no longer a test of group care for very young infants, states Bettye Caldwell. Rather, it is a test of whether any other kind of care can provide the necessary supplements for the child. These supplements cost nearly $200,000 per year, including research, for twenty-five children. The program could be run, without the research, for about $3,000 per year per child. The only alternative to the center is foster day care through the Department of Welfare, but finding foster homes for all the children who need help is just not realistic.

Day care *must* be expensive, if only because its first requirement is a high ratio of teachers to children. In Israel, where the communal settlements called kibbutzim have a long history of group care for infants and toddlers, great sacrifices have been made to provide this ratio— usually one *metapelet* or nurse, for every four children under the age of two—despite war and shortages of all kinds.

If people really care, a variety of child-rearing patterns are possible without producing pathology, declares Dr. Leon Eisenberg, professor of child psychiatry at Johns Hopkins, who has visited several kibbutzim. Though the mother is absent most of the day, she remains the central psychological figure of her child. This is multiple mothering, not deprivation. Describing the warmth of the metapelet and the general atmosphere of love and concern for all the children in the kibbutz, Dr. Eisenberg remarked that "if the children suffer from anything there, it's mother-poisoning, not mother-deprivation! There are mothers all over the place—and all making chicken-noodle soup!" Such an atmosphere leads children to expect good from all adults, he continued. But he warned that it doesn't usually happen in other types of institutions.

By cutting corners, reducing personnel, or packing in too many children, any institution can easily be turned into a snake pit. At best, an institution is a very unstable organism. It becomes particularly dangerous when dealing with human beings at their most vulnerable age.

Despite this danger, however, something must be done for children in this age group, and it is easier to provide proper safeguards in day-care centers than in "black-market" family day care. According to Dr. Caldwell, the climate of opinion on this subject is changing rapidly. Suddenly a large number of organizations want to start their own centers for very young children.

This change in climate is partly due to the work of a small but influential organization called Early Child Care Reexamined (ECCR), which became interested in the problem a few years ago. Its first conference was sparked by Dr. Caroline Chandler, chief of the National Institute of Mental Health's center for studies of mental health of children and youth, after a questionnaire she had sent out to every state in the Union revealed "the incredible, woefully inadequate services almost everywhere." The psychiatrists, pediatricians, and child-welfare experts who attended this first conference decided to take a fresh look at the whole infant field and clear up many common misconceptions—particularly the notion that group care for children under three was always bad. Although they clashed on many points, they agreed that in certain cases group care was not only desirable, but essential if one wished to avoid damage to the child's personality or cognition.

"I don't care under what label you start developing relationships with children," replied one ECCR psychiatrist when I asked him what he thought of Dr. Caldwell's center. "In order to work with cognitive development, you have to get involved with the children—and only good can come of that! That is, if you have warm people who don't treat babies like experimental animals, but like human beings."

The department of psychiatry of Washington's Children's Hospital, a cosponsor of the ECCR conferences, is planning to open a day care center of its own for high-risk babies, taking them as soon after birth as possible. It will also try to develop a new career for American women: trained nursery mothers who can work in day-care centers. The training program, which will last about one year, will be modeled after that of the famed Metera Babies' Center in Athens, Greece.

All over the world, people who deal with the formative years of the most important possession a country has—its children—are important professionals, points out Dr. Allen Marans, director of this training project. "The kibbutz metapelet has prestige and professional security," he says. "The Soviet Union gives its day-care people high prestige. In France, the director of the crèche is a very important person in the community."

The staffs of American day-care centers, on the other hand, clearly lack both status and decent salaries. Although the number of centers has not grown much recently, their personnel shortages are worse than ever since fashionable new programs such as Head Start can offer much more in the way of money and pleasant working conditions. The day-care centers are particularly short of teachers. Education, in fact, has never been their forte. If there are qualified teachers, it's a nursery school; if it's custodial, it's day care, is the working definition of the difference between the two.

The problem greatly surpasses anything that has been attempted so far to solve it. Nor can it be solved, says Mrs. Oettinger, until the nation assumes the responsibility and obligation to see that children are given good care during their developmental stage. People are still ambivalent about this, she notes. She looks forward to the day when legislators and taxpayers agree that we *must* do it—like making sure that every child in the country is vaccinated against polio.

Dr. Marans puts it more bluntly: "The United States is really not a child-centered culture," he declares. "People are startled when I say that, but it's true."

22 On Designing Supplementary Environments for Early Child Development

Bettye M. Caldwell

Drawing upon a rich and varied research base, the author documents what is known about supplementary environments that stimulate growth in the early years.

For some years now a scientific consensus has been emerging as to the importance of infancy and early childhood for the intake of experience capable of optimizing a child's developmental potential. The recommended experiences are usually fairly simple and should be easily planned and carried out by most care-taking persons (assuming minimal levels of understanding and motivation for child-rearing). Any time there is planning of experiences, no matter how casual the planning might be, environmental design is occurring. The mother who chooses a woolly lamb as a toy for her baby in preference to a celluloid duck, who decides in favor of a high chair rather than a baby tenda, who places a crib under a window rather than in some other spot in the room, and who decides to buy a savings bond rather than a bassinet is designing an environment for her infant. When done within the family setting, such deliberate acts seem fully within the province of natural child-rearing behavior. However, when translated into extra-family settings, similarly mundane designs acquire an aura of automation and dehumanization. And they worry us. They bring visions of 1984 (which is getting too close to be metaphorically effective) and a degree of regimentation which most of us find offensive. Yet such designing is crucial to any large scale attempt to foster optimal development by the establishment of small group settings or home tutoring programs intended to supplement the home environment.

In a recent paper[1] this author attempted to explore the generality of the currently prevailing concept of an optimal learning environment for the development of a child under three. Although in Israel and in several eastern European countries various models of group up-bringing

When this article was published Dr. Caldwell was Professor of Child Development and Education, Syracuse University. She is now Director of the Center for Early Development and Education, University of Arkansas College of Education, Little Rock, Arkansas.
Reprinted with permission from *BAEYC Reports:* Boston Association for the Education of Young Children, Vol. X, No. 1, October 1968.

have been encouraged, in America there has been no serious challenge to the philosophy that the optimal environment for the infant consists of the cumulative experiences associated with remaining within his own home with his parents (particularly his mother). To quote from the earlier paper: "As judged from our scientific and lay literature and from practices in health and welfare agencies, one might infer that the optimal learning environment for the young child is that which exists when (a) a young child is cared for in his own home, (b) in the context of a warm and nurturant emotional relationship, (c) with his mother (or a reasonable facsimile thereof) under conditions of (d) varied sensory and cognitive input. Undoubtedly until a better hypothesis comes along, this is the best one available. This paper has attempted to generate constructive thinking about whether we are justified in overly vigorous support of (a) when (b), (c) or (d), or any combination thereof, might not obtain."[2]

There is now a considerable amount of evidence available[3] that a warm mother-child relationship and varied sensory input are by no means consistent ingredients in the home environments of many infants. This fact alone mandates professional concern for the task of designing environmental supplements. But even in homes where material and personal resources needed for creating optimizing environments exist in abundance there is increased interest in the professionalization of child care during the infancy period. To some extent this has probably resulted from the desire of mothers to obtain quality child care which will permit relaxed maternal employment. But this author, at least, is convinced that it also represents evidence that parents have been drawn into the excitement which exists among specialists in the field of human development and that they accept the tenability of the hypothesis that learning experiences during infancy are critical for subsequent development. It is, of course, unfortunate that they are endorsing hypotheses rather than facts.

For some three years now this author and her chief colleague, Dr. Julius R. Richmond, and a constantly enlarging staff of dedicated people have been engaged in the task of trying to design and *create* a supplementary environment which will foster optimal child development, with particular emphasis on development of the child under three. The word *create* deserves italics because it is so much easier to design environments than to build them. Many components of the environment which has emerged are probably more accidental than deliberate, for we, like the mother who gets fast-talked into buying an encyclopedia when the family needs a new refrigerator, have undoubtedly made mistakes and have had to go on living with them. Similarly we do not claim any original theoretical architecture which provided the blueprints for our program structure. For, as indicated earlier,[4] our infant intervention program represents the test of a big hypothesis rather than the construction of a small theory.

The most conscientious efforts have been made to utilize only empirically tested ideas in effecting an enriching environmental supplement. And yet this is not an easy task. With human children younger than three, there have been only a precious few attempts to enrich their experience (outstanding exceptions are such efforts as the work of Rheingold, 1956;[5] Ourth and Brown, 1961;[6] White and Held, 1963;[7] Dennis and Sayegh, 1965;[8] Casler, 1965[9]), and most of the enrichments have been short-term and to some extent "artificial." Also such studies have been limited to children in institutions or hospitals where the amount and type of environmental input could be expected to deviate sharply from that of home-reared infants.

This shortage of empirical data on the effects of enrichment means that, by and large most of our guidelines about conditions necessary for fostering development have been derived from descriptive studies of *deficit* environments (e.g., children in institutions) or from differential studies contrasting groups presumably differing in certain input characteristics (e.g., lower-class and middle-class children). Thus to a large extent the existing literature on environmental factors associated with different patterns of child development can only yield inferences about environmental conditions to be avoided. As yet we have little evidence about environmental conditions proven capable of enhancing development. Finally, where empirical data are lacking about either enhancing or detrimental conditions, and yet where policy (as a basis for practice) is needed, ideas which have a high degree of professional consensus have been utilized. One might use as a criterion for the acceptance of such unbuttressed principles the requirement that there be no data which would refute it.

It is a major premise of this paper that, using such empirical and theoretical sources, one can generate a small number of growth-fostering environmental characteristics which can serve as guidelines for the planning of supplementary enrichment programs. Furthermore, it is the author's conviction that an articulation of such principles serves a most useful purpose in the training and orientation of the staff who have the task of making the optimizing environment live. That is, they can function as a bridge between policy and practice.

Characteristics of Growth-Fostering Environments

The following assumptions represent the author's synthesis of the scientific and professional literature about environmental conditions which foster development. The list is not regarded as exhaustive by any means; in fact, it represents just the opposite—something of a least common denominator. The principles have been generated with reference to a home supplement environmental model (one in which the child would have as much or more contact with his own family as with enrichment personnel); however, it is felt that they also represent environmental characteristics which will foster development in any setting. The purpose of this brief paper is to stimulate thought about these characteristics by articulating them and making brief reference to empirical support which can be supported in their behalf.

1. *The optimal development of a young child requires an environment ensuring gratification of all basic physical needs and careful provisions for health and safety.* This includes such essentials as adequate nutrition, maintenance of sanitary conditions, and provisions for minimization of and proper treatment for illness. These represent conditions which are necessary but not sufficient for optimal development and need no empirical or theoretical buttressing.

2. *The development of a young child is fostered by a relatively high frequency of adult contact involving a relatively small number of adults.* This assumption is derived most obviously from the literature on maternal deprivation[10, 11] and on child characteristics associated with multiple mothering.[12] It is consistent with data on language development as a function of ordinal position, with first and only children generally showing the most advanced language development.[13] It is also consistent with the theoretical position developed by Bowlby on factors which influence attachment[14] to the primary caretaker, the mother. However, at this stage one might well question the basic validity of the phrase "involving a relatively small number of adults" for the supplementary enrichment environment. It was part of the originally articulated Children's Center policy. ("Insofar as is possible, their care . . . will be provided by the same staff person.")[15] In practice, it has never worked, and the Center staff has many times considered the pros and cons of the position. Not only because of the inevitability of staff turnover which would disrupt this planned interpersonal continuity is it perhaps ill-advised, but also one could make a strong case for the inadvisability of having young children become too strongly attached to any *one* person outside the family setting. However, generalizing again from the family model, it would appear to be a desired characteristic of a growth-fostering environment.

3. *The development of a young child is fostered by a positive emotional climate in which the child learns to trust others and himself.* This is undoubtedly one of the most widely accepted working principles of persons who have the responsibility of protecting the welfare of young children whenever any type of substitute care must be obtained (foster and adoptive homes, caretakers in institutions, etc.). Yet in many respects this is one of the most difficult principles to buttress with empirical data. One could certainly cite here the finding of Spitz[16] that the IQ's of separated infants dropped after separation from their mothers. Of course, many have argued that, in the first place, the drop was spurious[17] and that, in the second place, any true decrement was due to the net loss in stimulation rather than to the emotional circumstances.[18] In a recent study with three-year-old children, Blank[19] presented some suggestive

data that might be interpreted as negative evidence regarding this assumption. From a group of twelve children enrolled in a traditional nursery school, she selected a group of four (presumably at random) who received some special individualized tutoring, another group of two who received individualized "tender love and care" for the same amount of time, leaving the remaining six children to serve as classroom controls. She found large gains in ten of the individually tutored children with no significant changes in either the classroom or the tender loving care controls. The implication was that it was the teaching and not the atmosphere that produced change. However, one would assume that the emotional atmosphere of the four tutored children was not negative and that they were being tutored in an atmosphere of emotional support.

One could certainly interpret some of the data on children who show "failure to thrive"[20] as compatible with this assumption. However, it is generally impossible to separate the emotional components of the environment from the sensory components. Perhaps one would have to conclude that the support for this assumption is more visceral than cortical; however, there are certainly no data to challenge it as a common sense working hypothesis.

4. *The development of a young child is fostered by an optimal level of need gratification.* This is perhaps the fuzziest of the assumptions. As originally articulated it referred to the necessity of giving sufficiently prompt attention to a child's physical needs "so that the young organism is not overwhelmed but not such prompt or complete attention that budding attempts at self-gratification are extinguished."[21] This is perhaps but a less elegant way of calling for the proper level of tension or homeostatic disequilibrium. Harlow has made impressive cases for the validity of the principle in teaching new responses to all types of primates. In a theoretical paper in which he questions the universal validity of the drive-reduction theory of learning, he commented in his usually pungent style: "The hungry child is a most incurious child, but after he has eaten and become thoroughly sated, his curiosity and all the learned responses associated with his curiosity take place."[22] With preschool children, Gewirtz and Baer[23] showed that deprivation of social contact heightened the effectiveness of social reinforcement.

The author knows of no data relating to the over-gratification side of the coin, although the anecdotal literature of child development is full of stories of children who did not learn to talk because "they had everything they needed." This would appear to be an easily researchable assumption and one fully deserving of more research attention.

5. *The development of a young child is fostered by the provision of varied and patterned sensory input in an intensity range that does not overload the child's capacity to receive, classify and respond.* This is the assumption that has undoubtedly received the greatest amount of attention in the recent literature which has scanned experimental studies for

implications for educating disadvantaged children.[24] It has also probably received the most fervent scientific endorsement. Within the package of social-emotional-sensory deprivation (often renamed cultural deprivation), the part most easily defined and thus most readily accepted is the sensory part. And yet, ironically, in some ways it is the most difficult to make a case for the culturally deprived child as suffering any sort of true sensory deprivation. Sounds, shapes, colors, kinesthetic input, tastes, and odors abound in an urban slum (perhaps more than in some of the barren enclosures of certain varieties of high-fashion modern interior decor and architecture). But whether such stimuli have identifiable patterns, whether they have on-off cycles that give them salience, and whether they are perhaps often so intense or so blended as to create refractoriness is quite another matter. The nature and variety (though not always the intensity) of sensory stimuli available in an enrichment environment are fairly easy to control; therefore, as inexperienced groups begin to translate ideas into specific environmental features, this principle is an easy one to use as a bridge from policy to practice.

6. *The development of a young child is fostered by people who respond physically, verbally, and emotionally with sufficient consistency and clarity to provide cues as to appropriate and valued behaviors and to reinforce such behaviors when they occur.* This is obviously the response side of the above statement. It represents the emitting of behaviors by the adults in the enrichment environment in such a way as to permit modeling or identification (cue-producing responses) and also to serve as reinforcement of approved behaviors. The influence of such social responses upon behavior acquisition or elimination in very young children has been demonstrated effectively.[25]

In regard to the timing of the dispensing of the many variants of adult attention, partisanship rather than consensus is the rule. For example, there are those who feel that adult attention may be most needed when a child is behaving negatively, indicating that he is too emotionally overwhelmed to cope with the situation and thus revealing a need for adult support. Others regard such desired but unearned adult support as inimical to rather than facilitative of optimal development. Nonpartisan data relating to this controversy are very much needed.

7. *The development of a young child is fostered by an environment containing a minimum of social restrictions on exploratory and motor behavior.* Hunt[26] has postulated that one factor associated with the downward drift of developmental quotients in children from disadvantaged families which occurs at some time between the ages of one and two is the restriction on motility enforced by the parents because of the greater inconvenience caused by a mobile child in a crowded household. Hersher, *et al*[27] have data supporting the assumption that low income parents show an abrupt decrease in permissiveness and tolerance for their children's change-worthy behavior at some point around one

year. Following that time mothers who were formerly proud of the motor prowess of their children began to complain of all the trouble they caused and to express hostility toward them. Perhaps the most persuasive evidence relating to this point is that presented by Dennis[28] in reporting on the grossly retarded motor behavior of institution-reared children. In one institution in Iran in which infants were customarily placed on their backs in soft cribs and given a bare minimum of adult attention, psychomotor retardation was severe. For example, only 15 percent of infants between the ages of one and two years could sit alone and none could walk. In contrast, the development of infants being reared in a "model" institution set up to demonstrate that good child-rearing conditions would be associated with more normal development more closely approximated norms for that culture. Dennis interpreted the retardation found in the first group as due in part to the lack of opportunity for motor response.

Until fairly recently, the "motor" side of "sensory-motor" intelligence was somewhat neglected, in spite of the fact that Piaget's terminology for the earliest period of intellectual development is now widely employed. One still hears items on early intelligence tests criticized as being "just sensory-motor items." However, the probable importance of the motor side of the hyphen is beginning to receive support from several sources—from work with motor-restricted animals,[29] from retraining efforts directed toward children with brain damage,[30] or with mental retardation.[31] And certainly Bruner's formulation[32] of early cognitive development as requiring an *enactive* phase prior to progression to true symbolic cognitive activities supports this principle.

8. *The development of a young child is fostered by careful organization of the physical and temporal environment which permits expectancies of objects and events to be confirmed or revised.* This is based more upon descriptive studies of family life in homes characterized by the poverty syndrome than upon any known data. Such studies[33] have frequently stressed that the home environment is characterized by physical and temporal chaos—clutter and crowding cause figure and group to blend; people come and go with no predictability; daily events (such as meals) occur erratically and inconsistently. Even objects have less predictability than they should—e.g., turn on the television set and it may or may not produce a picture; a chair with a broken leg may support your weight or it may not. Thus even the ordinarily "responsive objects" which provide important information and feedback to the young child do not respond consistently or properly. Such conditions create the classical paradigm for intermittent reinforcement (although by accident rather than schedule), a condition which has consistently been shown to be associated with delayed response acquisition and greater resistance to extinction. Such behavior—slow learning and resistance to change— have been repeatedly ascribed to children from disadvantaged families. In supplementary environments control of these physical and temporal

contingencies should be much easier to achieve than is the case in any home with limited economic resources.

9. *The development of a young child is fostered by the provision of rich and varied cultural experiences rendered interpretable by consistent persons with whom the experiences are shared.* This assumption perhaps represents little more than a statement of belief in the implications of the term cultural deprivation. That is, it is conceivable that there is some sort of gestalt, some intangible quantum of total experience that is necessary for an enrichment to be effective. If so, merely by increasing sensory stimulation, social contacts, etc. one cannot hope to revise drastically a child's developmental potential. One often hears reference to this in descriptions of the generally greater "know-how" of middle-class children. As stated earlier in the few experiments in which enrichment has been provided, the extra stimulation has been carefully defined and compartmentalized (e.g., verbal stimulation of a particular variety, kinesthetic stimulation, exposure to a complex visual environment, etc.). The closest one might come to "total cultural enrichment" would be something like a traditional nursery (with its program of field trips, visits from representatives of different social roles, etc.), and the author knows of no study on the effects of nursery school attendance which has utilized children under three. Thus at this stage, one would have to disclaim any substantial scientific validity for this assumption.

There is a second part of this assumption which deserves mention, but which again can claim no empirical support.

That is the phrase "rendered interpetable by consistent persons with whom the experiences are shared." This is again an expression of the author's conviction of the need of little children for continuity of care from a relatively small number of persons; however, no pretense is offered that this is much more than a conviction probably shared by many persons having educational or clinical experience with young children.

10. *The development of a young child is fostered by the availability of play materials which facilitate the coordination of sensory-motor processes and a play environment permitting their utilization.* The author feels that this assumption should be stated, even though she has visions of its appearing quoted out of context on the cover of a toy distributor's catalogue! Some of the enrichment experiments[34] have basically used toys (mobiles or stabiles) as their vehicle of enrichment. Toys represent the original "responsive environments." A baby doll whose eyes close as it is placed in the horizontal position is "responding" to the child's movements as is a car that rolls when it is pushed or a ball that rolls when it is thrown—all are responding to certain movements and actions of the child in such a way as to coordinate sensory impressions with movements and to provide natural feedback as to the possible consequences of a particular act. But, of course, toys cannot help in this process unless the child has an opportunity to utilize them,

to carry out his own experiments. Thus the assumption about the developmental contributions which can be made by play materials has no relevance without the rider that the environment should permit extensive utilization of them by the child.

11. *The development of a young child is fostered by contact with adults who value achievement and who attempt to generate in the child secondary motivational systems related to achievement.* The importance of early development of achievement motivation has been stressed by Crandall,[35] who has also explored parental antecedents of achievement behavior in young children. In the literature on disadvantaged children, it has been repeatedly observed that lower-class parents do not value achievement as much as middle-class parents and that, furthermore, their behavior is often inimical to the development of such motivation in their children. The data of Hess and Shipman[36] on teaching styles of lower-class and middle-class mothers certainly supports the suspicion that middle-class mothers do a much better job of helping children to anticipate support and gratification in the formal learning situation and in the adults who will monitor it. In intervention studies with children over three, Gray and Klaus[37] have made the fostering of achievement motivation a cardinal principle of their enrichment program. The short-term and long-term gains obtained for children in their program certainly attest to the value of such an approach; however, this component of the enrichment program could not be singled out as representing the most effective ingredient of the enrichment experience. Only when we have true comparative educational research relating to very young children will it be possible to do this. A most interesting feature of the work of Gray and Miller[38] is their finding of an apparent diffusion effect of their total enrichment offered parents of the enriched children. Subsequent children show behavior that is significantly advanced beyond the level achieved by the older siblings when they were the age of the younger ones. Such a finding suggests that participation in an enrichment program can produce effects in parents who can then mediate future behavioral advances in their children.

12. *The development of a young child is fostered by the cumulative programming of experiences that provide an appropriate match for the child's current level of cognitive, social, and emotional organization.* This last assumption is a very broad and inclusive one, restating to some extent Hunt's principle of the "importance of the match."[39] One can generate this from Piaget's theory of the way in which the processes of assimilation and accommodation work. The new experience must be sufficiently similar to previous experiences if it is to be assimilated and not simply disregarded; on the other hand, it must be sufficiently different to require some degree of accommodation or internal restructuring of existing schemata. Bruner[40] has also stressed the need for having experiences meet the needs of the child's current level of cognitive organization. Within the Children's Center, the staff feels

that some of the negative consequences of a too-rich sequential environment for young children are being manifested. That is, in our four-year-group, we seem to be coping this year with a group of children who have already "seen everything and done everything" and who thus occasionally appear just a little bit bored. There has always been a careful attempt to plan the curriculum so that, for any particular age group, the experiences are tailored to its developmental characteristics. But ours is a day care program, and children function in different areas at different times of day and occasionally have to be shifted from one room to another due to staff shortages. Thus their incidental exposure does not always fit the planned sequence quite as closely as one might like and might interfere with optimal event-schema matching.

Summary

There is one inclusive principle which hovers implicitly around all the others here formulated: the development of a young child is fostered by exposure to an environment in which the planning adults can articulate their objectives for the children entrusted to their care. It has not been stated as a separate principle because it is embedded like a hidden figure in all the others. Often we are unduly wary about voicing our objectives for the early childhood period. And yet we cannot develop effective enrichment programs without careful attention to the question of what we are enriching children *toward*. This requires knowledge of the probable range of responses which young children of varying ages can make, and also awareness of the plasticity of the children—i.e., awareness of the possible. It is easy for interested persons to acquaint themselves with both the probable and possible range of infant behavior. It is equally easy to realize that all the growth-fostering characteristics outlined here can be achieved by all persons who would submit themselves to a degree of training and orientation; certainly there is nothing occult or "difficult to understand" in them. Their validity is, of course, quite another matter, as is the question of whether other components of the enrichment environment need to be covered. They are presented here to serve as springboards for thought out of the conviction that environmental supplements for infants and young children are not only desirable but necessary for large numbers of very young children and that the environmental engineering necessary to create such supplements is not as difficult as it might appear on first thought.

References

1. Bettye M. Caldwell, "What Is the Optimal Learning Environment for the Young Child?" *American Journal of Orthopsychiatry*, 37 (1967), pp. 8–20.

2. *Ibid.*, p. 19.

3. H. Wortis *et al.*, "Child-Rearing Practices in a Low Socioeconomic Group," *Pediatrics*, 32 (1963), pp. 298–307; C. A. Malone, "Safety First: Comments on the Influence of External Danger in the Lives of Children of Disorganized Families," *American Journal of Orthopsychiatry*, 36 (1966), pp. 3–12; Eleanor Pavenstedt, "A Comparison of the Child-rearing Environment of Upper-Lower and Very Low-Lower Class Families," *American Journal of Orthopsychiatry*, 35 (1965), pp. 89–98.

4. Bettye M. Caldwell, "The Fourth Dimension in Early Childhood Education," pp. 71–81 in R. D. Hess and Roberta M. Bear (eds.), *Early Education* (Chicago: Aldine Publishing Co., 1968).

5. Harriet L. Rheingold, "The Modification of Social Responsiveness in Institutional Babies," Monographs of the Society for Research in Child Development, Inc., 21 (1956), pp. 5–46.

6. Lynn Ourth and K. Brown, "Inadequate Mothering and Disturbance in the Neo-Natal Period," Child Development (1961), pp. 287–294.

7. B. L. White and R. Held, "Plasticity of Sensorimotor Development in the Human Infant," pp. 60–70 in Judy F. Rosenblith and W. Allinsmith (eds.), *The Causes of Behavior II—Readings in Child Development and Educational Psychology* (Boston: Allyn and Bacon, 1966).

8. Wayne Dennis and Yvonne Sayagh, "The Effect of Supplementary Experiences upon the Behavioral Development of Infants in Institutions," *Child Development*, 36 (1965), pp. 81–90.

9. Lawrence Casler, "The Effects of Extra Tactile Stimulation on a Group of Institutionalized Infants," *Genetic Psychology Monographs* 71(1) (1965), pp. 137–175.

10. Leon J. Yarrow, "Separation from Parents During Early Childhood," *Review of Child Development*, 1 (1964), pp. 89–130.

11. Mary Ainsworth, "Reversible and Irreversible Effects of Maternal Deprivation on Intellectual Development," *Child Welfare League of America*, (1962), pp. 42–62.

12. Bettye M. Caldwell *et al.*, "Mother-Infant Interaction in Monometric and Polymatric Families," *American Journal of Orthopsychiatry*, 33 (1963), pp. 653–664.

13. Dorothea McCarthy, "Language Development in Children," pp. 492-630 in L. Carmichael, *Manual of Child Psychology* (New York: John Wiley, 1954).

14. John Bowlby, *Attachment and Loss* (unpublished manuscript, 1967).

15. Bettye M. Caldwell and J. B. Richmond, "The Children's Center—A Microcosmic Health, Education, and Welfare Unit," Progress Report submitted to the Children's Bureau, 1967, p. 468.

16. R. A. Spitz, "Hospitalism: An Inquiry into the Genesis of Psychiatric Conditions in Early Childhood," *Psychoanalytic Study of the Child*, 1 (1945), pp. 53–74.

17. S. R. Pinneau, "The Infantile Disorders of Hospitalism and Anaclitic Depression, *Psychological Bulletin*, 52 (1955), pp. 429–452.

18. Lawrence Casler, "Maternal Deprivation: A Critical Review of the Literature," *Monographs of the Society for Research in Child Development*, 26(2) (1961).

19. M. Blank, "A Tutorial Language Program to Develop Abstract Thinking in Socially Disadvantaged Preschool Children," *Child Development*, 39 (1968), p. 380.

20. R. G. Patton and L. I. Gardner, "Influence of Family Environment on Growth—The Syndrome of 'Maternal Deprivation,'" *Pediatrics*, 30 (1962), pp. 957–962.

21. Caldwell and Richmond, "The Children's Center," p. 21.

22. H. Harlow, "Mice, Monkeys, Men and Motives," *Psychological Review*, 60 (1953), pp. 23–32.

23. Jacob L. Gewirtz and Donald M. Baer, "The Effect of Brief Social Deprivation on Behaviors for a Social Reinforcer," *Journal of Abnormal Social Psychology*, 56 (1958), pp. 49–56.

24. J. McV. Hunt, *Intelligence and Experience* (New York: Ronald Press, 1961); idem, "The Psychological Basis for Using Preschool Enrichment as an Antidote for Cultural Deprivation," *Merrill-Palmer Quarterly*, 10 (1964), pp. 209–248; Casler, "Maternal Deprivation"; Martin Deutsch, "The Role of Social Class in Language Development and Cognition," *American Journal of Orthopsychiatry*, 35 (1965), pp. 78–88.

25. Yvonne Brackbill, "Extinction of the Smiling Response in Infants as a Function," *Child Development*, 29 (1958), pp. 115–125; Harriet L. Rheingold, Jacob L. Gewirtz, and Helen W. Ross, "Social Conditioning of Vocalizations in the Infant," *Journal of Comparative and Physiological Psychology*, 52 (1959), pp. 68–73; Paul Weisberg, "Social and Non-Social Conditioning of Infant Vocalizations," *Child Development*, 34 (1963), pp. 377–388.

26. Hunt, "The Psychological Basis for Using Preschool Enrichment . . ."

27. Leonard Hersher *et al.*, "Consistency in Maternal Behavior During the First Year of Life" (unpublished manuscript, 1968).

28. Wayne Dennis, "Causes of Retardation Among Institutional Children: Iran," *Journal of Genetic Psychology*, 96 (1960), pp. 47–59.

29. R. Held and A. Hein, "Movement-Produced Stimulation in the Development of Visually Guided Behavior," *Journal of Comparative and Physiological Psychology*, 56 (1963), pp. 872–876.

30. Marianne Frostig, "A Developmental Test of Visual Perception for Evaluating Normal and Neurologically Handicapped Children," *Perceptual Motor Skills*, 12 (1961), pp. 383–394.

31. N. C. Kephart, *The Slow Learner in the Classroom* (Columbus, Ohio: Charles E. Merrill, 1960).

32. J. S. Bruner, *Toward a Theory of Instruction* (Cambridge, Mass.: Harvard University Press, 1966).

33. Wortis, "Child-Rearing Practices."

34. White and Held, "Plasticity of Sensorimotor Development."

35. Virginia Crandall, "Achievement in Young Children," PP. 165–185, in W. W. Hartup and Nancy L. Smothergill (eds.), *The Young Child* (Washington, D.C.): National Association for the Education of Young Children, 1967).

36. R. D. Hess and Virginia C. Shipman, "Early Experience and the Socialization of Cognitive Modes in Children," *Child Development*, 36 (1965), pp. 869–886.

37. Susan W. Gray and R. A. Klaus, "An Experimental Preschool Program for Culturally Deprived Children," *Child Development*, 36 (1965), pp. 887–898.

38. Susan W. Gray and J. O. Miller, "The Vertical Diffusion Effect in Preschool Enrichment Programs" (unpublished manuscript, 1967).

39. Hunt, "The Psychological Basis for Using Preschool Enrichment . . ."

40. Bruner, *Toward a Theory of Instruction*.

23 A Proper Curriculum for Young Children

James B. Macdonald

A leading curriculum theorist presents a foundation on which to build a suitable man-made environment for the youngest clients in our schools.

With the findings and reports of recent research in the education of young children, a growing awareness of the importance of and increased need for formal programs for children of preschool age has made it imperative that some guiding conceptualization of proper curricula for young children be developed.

The term *proper* is a rather old-fashioned one; yet it carries a double meaning which focuses upon appropriateness and rightness at the same time. Thus, a *proper* curriculum for young children would be one which both suits the child's developmental processes and individual capacities and one which is right for him as a social being. As John W. Gardner once expressed, "The release of human potential, the enhancement of individual dignity, the liberation of the human spirit—those are the deepest and truest goals to be conceived by the hearts and minds of the American people."[1] A proper curriculum would provide the crucial beginning for the achievement of these goals.

There are several considerations in the development and assessment of a curriculum for young children: 1) the relevance of curriculum to the individual, 2) the relevance of curriculum to the society, and 3) the relevance of curriculum to the ethics of relationships.

Environment

One basic curriculum problem relates to changes in the environment of the average child. As man creates more and more of his environment through urbanization, mass media, and the like, the whole society begins to take on an educational aura. Whereas schools once constituted much of the man-made part of the child's world, today much more of his environment falls into this category. Thus it is possible for McLuhan and Fiore to talk about "Education As War" and "War As Education." "In the information age it is obviously possible to decimate populations

This is a revision and expansion of the article which appeared in the March, 1969 *Phi Delta Kappan.* Reprinted by permission. The editors are indebted to Mr. Macdonald, who is Professor of Education at the University of Wisconsin-Milwaukee, for the additional material.

by the dissemination of information and gimmickry. There is no question here of values. It is simple information technology being used by one community to reshape another one. It is this type of aggression that we exert on our own youngsters in what we call *education.*"[2]

Society must face the implications of this fact. If the child's environment is to be mainly man-made, it is better to plan it carefully and place our young in it for maximum exposure.

An illustration may reinforce this point. What if we could choose between letting a three-year-old watch commercial television five hours a day or placing him in a carefully planned environment for that time? Obviously, we would do better to bring our rational understanding to bear through a developmentally oriented school environment. Commercial television generally provides a series of unrelated, value conflicting, chaotic experiences.

Much of the rest of a child's "normal" life holds similarly competing possibilities. Playing with mother's pots and pans will fascinate the very young and is of great interest and value; but if the child were placed in a school setting with blocks and other carefully selected objects for developing perception and dexterity, would this not be a potentially better environment?

For years many of us have assumed that putting the child in school at an early age takes him out of his natural environment and puts him in a contrived setting. Only recently has our understanding of the ecology of human living and the nature of man's relationship to his technology clearly forced us to realize that the choice for educating young children is not between a contrived and a natural environment, but between a planned and a haphazard man-made one. This new understanding suggests that as a society we should deliberately intervene, as early and as often and for as long a time as possible, to provide the optimum man-made environment for our children.

If we accept this situation, then a rationally constructed environment becomes a crucial factor in education. Assuming that we agree with John Gardner, our environment must provide maximum opportunity for the development of individual potential. Individual potential can be developed when educators carefully consider and provide for the nature of the young, the kind of society in which we live, and the way we relate to each other.

Any given environment encourages the appearance of certain behavior in terms of the general structure of interpersonal relationships, facilities, resources, etc. Thus, some environments call forth artistic or aesthetic responses while others are more prone to stimulate technical ability. The environment thus points persons in certain directions; it elicits certain kinds of behavior and discourages others.

Furthermore, environments are filled with customary ways or rules of behavior. Thus, we encourage (elicit) youngsters to talk, *and* we shape the way they utter sounds by imposing rules concerning the sounds and patterns that are elicited.

Finally, the environment tells us, through our perceptions of how significant other people see us, what it means to be human. For example, when relationships are formal and impersonal we learn to see ourselves differently than when relationships are more relaxed and friendly.

The environment must, therefore, be constructed on the basis of criteria such as those mentioned. It must have qualities which elicit and shape human potential in an ethically acceptable way. Three basic questions arise: 1) what will be elicited? 2) how will it be shaped? 3) how will the child encounter the elicitation and shaping process?

Eliciting

Program planners must first decide what kinds of responses they hope to elicit. The difference between what is called for (elicited) and how elicited behavior is shaped is a crucial distinction. What is elicited teaches us what the range of our potential is, whereas shaping will determine the depth and competency of that development. If we value the development of all human potential, rather than a particular potential, the kind of environment in which the young are placed must be extremely complex and varied in its structure and dynamics. The full range of human potential would certainly extend beyond the concept of social or intellectual development dominating our school programs today.

Our present social needs for consciousness expansion through drugs, eastern religions, etc., are probably a result of being severed from our own potential at very early ages. A proper curriculum for young children, for example, would elicit responses which are now classified for study in the area of parapsychology, such as prerecognition and clairvoyance. It would further focus upon sensation, perception, and feeling to a much greater degree. An optimum environment for young children would stimulate and elicit human resources in the development of these potentials as well as others.

It is indeed odd that those who have raised the issue and documented the importance of early intellectual experiences, who have described the potential for changing intelligence through early experience, have not noted the failure of almost all men to actualize their potential. What may be needed for intellectual development are radically different consciousness-expanding elicitations rather than focus upon the early shaping of common, mainly verbal responses.

The proper curriculum would elicit a whole range of perceptions of shapes, colors, sizes, events, persons, and so forth. It would provide for maximum motor potential in the use of muscles and the development of skill. It would provide social experiences which would lead to greater sensitivity toward others and a better sense of identity for oneself. And of course it would continuously elicit verbal and nonverbal intellectual responses.

In many ways the breaking down of responses into the categories above is entirely artificial and segmented. How would a child live in an environment without some perceptual, motor, social, and intellectual processes going on? It is the danger of losing sight of the *whole* child that forces us to face the shaping and relating problem.

Shaping

The shaping process has primarily a social significance. Although we can say that we shape responses into acceptable social categories in order that childern may live in society, there is really no logical reason why society could not provide for, and even encourage, much more variation than it does in each generation. We *shape* for the sake of the society. We *elicit* for the sake of the individual.

The major shaping activities of the curriculum are related to assuming rule-based behavior in relation to objects, persons, and the symbolic universe. Thus, for example, we ask youngsters to learn our language patterns, our social formalities, our ways of perceiving, our modes of inquiry. Awareness and use of language and numbers are obvious instances of this. The important thing to remember is that a child's behavior is shaped by the "rules" of the game of using words and other symbols. Although this socially relevant task has been the main emphasis in curriculum over the years, it is not enough; in the long run it will have less importance than curriculum provisions for eliciting responses.

An analogy to broader social circumstances may be helpful here. The shaping activities are analogous to the structure of the system and establishment. Solution of long-range problems, however, will result from newly elicited structures rather than well-shaped activities within the old system.

We have most recently made our greatest strides in understanding the shaping aspects of programs for young children. Recognition of the importance of early shaping in language development is one illustration of this.

The revolutionary breakthrough in the analysis of the nature of intelligence and the development of cognitive abilities has freed curriculum planners from the idea of passive waiting for the predestined flowering of abilities. They now see themselves as active shapers and eliciters, encouraging the appearance of ability and creating environmental conditions which make this readiness possible.

A major problem today in the shaping of young childen's behavior is finding what Hunt[3] calls "the problem of the match," i.e., the junction between the environmental press of stimuli and the inner integrative patterns of the individual. The danger which arises is forced closure for shaping when internal patterns are not "matched" for this.

Lawrence Kubie[4] refers to a similar phenomenon when he talks about forcing the pre-conscious sampling of youngsters. Kubie feels that forced sampling in the early verbal shaping of children's cognitive growth may actually produce a situation where "erudition and creativity are often at war with each other," by cutting persons off from their creative sources for the sake of early academic success.

This suggests that ideas of flexible multi-dimensional programming with continuous possibility for child choice are principles for constructing the shaping characteristics of the environment. In other words, given the best rational packaging of potentially rewarding developmental environment, in order to protect the child and maximize the possibility of "making a match" the shaping movement in this environment must be free, with broad avenues of movement and choice. What is often called "play" will be a major avenue of growth and what is "played with" will undoubtedly be improved as our understanding of the nature and process of conceptualization grows.

Relating

To some extent the curriculum determines how people live together and encounter the world. To establish and control the dynamics of this encounter in an ethical manner is basic to the development of a proper curriculum for young children. The way that we do things is the living contextual meaning of what is elicited and shaped.

Once we have accepted this fact, the question becomes what criteria to apply to "relating." There are two major areas suggested here: 1) relationships would reflect ethical concern for the inherent worth, dignity, and integrity of all persons present; and 2) relationships should reflect the necessity of choice and freedom for all.

In many ways the principles upon which an "autotelic environment"[5] is built, or which reflect what K. U. Smith calls cybernetic principles of learning,[6] are the ethical ones. The environment must be so structured that the child can control the stimuli which are to be presented to him. Since no child can escape being in an environment, it can be argued that a rational, well-planned, man-made one is better than an irrational man-made one. However, the manner in which the child encounters the school environment is the crucial ethical and functional problem for learning.

The stimuli are packed into the environment by the larger society and they may be ordered in certain ways, but control over these stimuli must lie with those being educated—through their free choosing—in order to maximize learner control of stimuli.

Moral responsibility in relations with other human beings is important here. Since the young child is at a crucial stage in the formation of his self-concept, our responsibility to him is very great. The way we adults or significant others relate to the child will form the his perception of himself.

The central question here is, "What kind of persons should children become?" This is in contrast to the "What kind of persons can they become?" the question posed in both the eliciting and shaping areas. If we wish persons to be self-directed; self-actualizing; creative; sensitive to others; able to identify, face, and solve problems; and able to possess positive values, then young children must see themselves reflected back as those kinds of persons, capable of these behaviors. This is done by the way in which we create environmental possibilities for them through their relationships.

Summary

In summary, then, a proper curriculum for young children is a curriculum that is encountered by the young at the earliest appropriate time and for the longest possible involvement. It is a curriculum based upon criteria which reflect our concern for individual potential, social relevance, and ethical relationships. This curriculum, as man-made environment, can be seen in terms of its eliciting, shaping, and relating possibilities. The eliciting of behavior must go far beyond the narrow social and intellectual responses encouraged in most young children's programs. It must extend to areas of sensitivity, aesthetic response, mental potential, and human activity which provide for wholeness. In shaping activity we must take our key from the exciting work being done with responsive environments, always remembering, however, the crucial role of learner control of stimuli. And in relationships our knowledge of the impact of the learning context on the development of self and our concern for what children ought to become demand children's freedom, choice, and control within ethical relationships.

References

1. John W. Gardner, in preface to Arthur E. Blanstein and Roger R. Woock (eds.), *Man Against Poverty: World War III.* (New York: Vintage Books, Random House, 1968).

2. Marshall McLuhan and Quentin Fiore, *War and Peace in the Global Village* (New York: Bantam, 1968), p. 149.

3. J. McV. Hunt, *Intelligence and Experience* (New York: Ronald Press, 1961), pp. 267–288.

4. Lawrence S. Kubie, "Research in Protecting Preconscious Functions in Education," pp. 72–88, in Richard M. Jones (ed.), *Contemporary Educational Psychology* (New York: Harper Torchbacks, 1967).

5. O. K. Moore, "Autotelic Responsive Environments for Learning," pp. 187–219, in Ronald Gross and Judith Murphy (eds.), *Schools* (New York: Harcourt, 1964).

6. Karl U. Smith and M. F. Smith, *Cybernetic Principles of Learning and Educational Design* (New York: Holt, 1966).

24 On Reformulating the Concept of Early Childhood Education — Some Whys Needing Wherefores

Bettye M. Caldwell

To be effective, teachers must be able to define the issues and objectives of their programs; yet, early childhood educators often are confused by labels, vague about goals and objectives and critical of innovation. In the following article, the author asks pertinent questions in an effort to stimulate constructive rethinking of the role of early childhood educators.

While a great deal of attention is currently being given to fostering concept formation in young children, there appears to be relatively little concern with concept formation *about* the field most intimately concerned with child development. A teaching technique often relied upon as an aid to concept refinement is the asking of questions—"What do you notice about these two sides of the rectangle?" There is no reason to think that this technique would not be equally effective with ourselves as teachers and as trainers of teachers. In this paper a few questions will be raised which will hopefully stimulate constructive thinking about the identity of the person who performs for society the extremely valuable function of the teacher of its young children and that of the field which she represents.

This is a very exhilarating time to be functioning in the field of early childhood education, for it is enjoying more status than ever in its history. The field is being looked to as offering the most hopeful solution to many of our social problems associated with poverty and family disorganization and as representing a potential laboratory for exploring the limits of an environmental technology concerned with helping everyone achieve at an optimal level. This is all very heady, especially to a professional group that has always suffered from feelings of inferiority. As the progeny of two parents—education and child psychology—neither of which thought the offspring respectable enough to carry the family name, we seemed doomed to be relegated to a low-status

When this article was published, Dr. Caldwell was Professor of Child Development and Education, Syracuse University. She is now Director of the Center for Early Development and Education, University of Arkansas College of Education, Little Rock, Arkansas.
Reprinted with permission from YOUNG CHILDREN, Vol. XXII, No. 6, Sept. 1967. Copyright © 1967, National Association for the Education of Young Children, 1834 Connecticut Avenue, N.W., Washington, D.C. 20009.

role. For the one parent we seemed not sufficiently educational, and for the other not sufficiently scientific. With such a conflicting background, perhaps an adolescent identity crisis was inevitable. For, to be sure, we often do not seem to know exactly who we are and what we do. Yet in spite of this, our literature is filled with prescriptions as to what we should and should not do. The purpose of this unfortunately one-sided dialogue is to stimulate constructive thinking about issues that should be given serious consideration by all representatives of the field before we settle too comfortably into a self-concept that sells us short of our true birthright.

Why can we not be more explicit about our goals and objectives? Sometimes it is difficult to find out exactly how the field of early childhood education defines itself. The wide use of many different terms to describe programs that presumably represent the same field of endeavor is a good indication of this confusion. Are we involved in preschools? Or nursery schools? Or day-care centers? Or preprimary education? Or prekindergarten programs? The official change of name for the national organization from "National Association for Nursery Education" to "National Association for the Education of Young Children" is a good sign that leaders in the field are aware of some of this semantic confusion and are eager to help resolve it.

But organizational labels and organizational substance are not always isomorphic. Many specialists in the field appear to have difficulty in communicating its identity to outsiders. Consider the following statement from Todd and Heffernan:

> Preparation of a book in a rapidly expanding field such as that of preschool or preprimary education is complicated by the lack of clear-cut definitions. It becomes necessary to set up definitions that are mutually exclusive and in conformity with most, but not all, of the current practices.[1]

After this quite legitimate recognition of the existing ambiguities, the authors go on to attempt a definition of a nursery school as "group experience for three- or four-year-old children." Not exactly explicit or definitive. Similarly, in a widely used source book, Leavitt says:

> A nursery school may be conducted as a private venture (private tuition school), as a community social service supported by the Community Chest or similar organizations, as a cooperative operated and supported by the parents themselves, or by a local church. By virtue of the fact that they have completely different sponsors, each school differs a great deal in organization, management, and financing. . . . As a result, programs and activities are likely to differ from school to school.[2]

Some authors of texts in this area do not even attempt to cope with the question of who we are and what we do. Perhaps they make the assumption that everybody knows—at least everybody who is interested enough to consider taking training in the field. A not atypical organization of textbooks for courses designed to train students as teachers of the young is to devote more space to the physical environment and the necessary equipment that must be purchased before a school is launched[3,4] than to the objectives of the educational program. This diffidence about stating goals appears to be largely a modern phenomenon, with modern referring to the past one or two decades. In an influential earlier text, Updegraff and her colleagues[5] openly express their conviction that any institution concerned with the training of individuals must be cognizant of its influence upon those individuals and always keep clearly in mind the objectives of the training. Describing the task of the teachers as, in one sense of the word, "adjusting stimulation intelligently," they indicate that this adjustment of stimulation must be based upon an awareness of the ultimate objectives of the school program —developing the peculiar or particular capacities of each individual. They further indicate, in a prophetically modern vein, that schools have left more to chance than they might realize. The chief alternative to such a *laissez-faire* approach is to formulate clear objectives for the preschool experience within a framework of a meaningful theory of child development. Updegraff *et al.* summarize their formulation as follows:

> In the following pages an attempt is made not only to describe nursery-school practice but to relate it to a background of theory concerning the objectives of preschool education. The philosophy and procedures are those of this particular school at the present time. . . . They are presented as being descriptive of one attempt to further education at the younger age levels.
>
> If this educational philosophy can be condensed into a few words, it may be summarized under three points:
>
> 1. Consideration of individual differences is paramount. While ultimate educational objectives are stated in general terms which are applicable to all children, each child is thought of as an individual in relation to his particular needs and in regard to all phases of his growth.
>
> 2. Clearly defined educational objectives are essential. It does not follow that these are iron-clad and unchangeable or that the program is inflexible, but that there is a sincere attempt to think clearly concerning the purposes and practices of preschool education.
>
> 3. The school is considered as a supplement to the home, not a substitute for it. It is believed that because of social groupings, suitable equipment, and expert study and guidance during the school experience, the preschool may contribute to the child's development in ways which are not possible in most homes.[6]

This is indeed a clear formulation and one which is as appropriate now as at the time it was written.

Why, in the formulation of our current objectives and in the development of training programs, are we so a-historical? In your training, how much attention was given to acquainting you with the history of preschool education? Froebel, one of the leading figures in the formalization of education for young children, once wrote, "The duty of each generation is to gather up the inheritance from the past, and thus to serve the present and prepare better things for the future."[7] I am reasonably confident that every student of social work knows about the struggles and achievements of Jane Addams, but how much do we teach our students about the struggles and achievements of Pestalozzi,[8] of Montessori,[9] of McMillan?[10] As Montessori is once again in fashion, with most everyone familiar with her work in the slums of Rome, the comments here will serve to call attention to the much less publicized work of Margaret and Rachel McMillan in the slums of London.

In her writings, McMillan frequently used a very meaningful phrase —she eschewed the word "nursery school" and often referred to the "Nurture School." And she was eminently clear as to their reason for being: "Why, we are asked, do we want Nursery Schools? . . . Nurseries and Nursery Schools are wanted simply because little children want nurses. They, being children, need that very important kind of early education called nurture. Can this be given, and given entirely by, let us say, the average mother? The well-to-do mother never attempts to do it alone."[11] Thus she clearly envisaged the nursery school as a nurturing force and one which served as a supplement to, not a substitute for, the home. It was also thought of as primarily needed for the children of the poor, as was true of the common school which had emerged only a century or so before.

McMillan clearly expected the nurture school to exert a profound effect on the children attending and on the educational practices used with older children. She stated, "I assume in the start that the Nursery School will, if successful, change and modify every other order of school, influencing it powerfully from below."[12] And, still later, in commenting on the valuable aid to observation of young children which will be found in the nurseries, she prophesied, "It is here—the new observation centre, the place where the new world will not only be created but understood at last."[13] There was certainly nothing shy or timid in those declarations, and only optimism and big-think permeate her declaration that: ". . . the elementary teacher's work will be changed by this sudden inrush of new life from below. A new order of child will have presented himself for education, and the 'newness' will not leave intact or unchanged all the formula and methods of yesterday."[14] McMillan was thinking of "newness" in terms of intellectual, social and moral behavior that would release the child from the prison of the slums.

It is of great interest that the two early heroines of the nursery school movement—Montessori and McMillan—began their work with children of the slums. As the movement emigrated to America, it quickly lost its social welfare and health image, instead quickly acquiring a patina of middle-class status. And, it is just possible, that when it acquired status it lost stature. At least it suffered a turn in objectives.

It is the contention of the writer that the field once again needs to be fired with some of this missionary zeal, to feel that we are potential savers of children, to be convinced that we should influence formal education rather than always accommodate to it.

Why do we have so much trouble with labels? Why do we refer to ourselves as *pre*school teachers and our schools as *pre*schools? Reflect for a moment on the paradox implied in the term "preschool education." Would we be as willing to accept the label of "pre-educational schools?" I think not, and I hope not. But we seem unwilling simply to call ourselves teachers and our schools schools. This may in part relate to a fear of the bureaucratization that supposedly comes with the formal educational process. But surely we are sufficiently bureaucratized within our own structure that such concern is fatuous.

What is the essence of such a school? Must it be desks screwed to the floor and regular report cards? And what is the essence of a teacher? Must she lecture to her students or "tell them" something. Much of the literature on nursery education is a bit phobic about the dangers of having teachers rob children of the incomparable joy of self-discovery. This is not meant to make light of an extremely important point about learning; rather it is to ask whether there should be any more concern about this hazard during the early years than during any subsequent school years. In essence, all years are "school" years, and all constructive adult-child encounters are "teaching." Teaching and self-discovery are not incompatible.

Why do we resist innovations in educational programs and teaching techniques? Just below the surface in many teachers there appears to lurk a basic conservatism that is activated whenever anyone advocates a change in educational programs. In many ways teachers of the young seem to represent the far right in education and to be the champions of the status quo. Whereas for more than a decade the field of education has been in a ferment of new ideas and has actively sought new approaches to old problems and ways of implementing change when new ideas come forth, within the field of preschool education there appears to have been active resistance to innovation.

In support of this statement one can raise the question of how many schools are engaged in trying out some of the newer approaches designed to teach young children to read. The typical attitude is "We'd better leave the teaching of reading up to the schools—the three- and four-year-old is not 'ready' to learn to read." "Besides," we add as a quick rebuttal, "what is he going to do in first grade if we teach him to read in nursery school?" And that, of course, is the most conservative cut of all, for it reflects our unverbalized conviction that we are without power to affect the later education of the children who pass through our doors.

This conservatism appears to be largely centered around the area of intellectual development—the very area that our historical leaders expected to influence most and that current research suggests may well be the most critical experience of the first three or four years of life. Here the conservatism is entirely commendable, though probably misguided. For our resistance to heavy emphasis upon intellectual endeavors in the early years is primarily related to the working principle that to encourage a child to move forward intellectually will somehow stunt his social and emotional development. Thus, even though we might be chided for our conservatism, we cannot be criticized for one reason; it is based entirely upon our feeling that we have a responsibility to protect the welfare of the young and somewhat defenseless organisms entrusted to our care.

Why do we think that intellectual development and personal-social development are somehow opposed to one another? If, as just hypothesized, one reason for our seeming resistance to innovation in education is that we fear the consequences of an emphasis upon intellectual achievement, we should perhaps explore the validity of this anxiety. If development can best be described by a closed-system model and conceptualized as having finite limits, then the fear is indeed valid, as development in one area would reduce the extent to which development can occur in another area. But development is probably better conceptualized by an open-system model, which would mean that development within one sphere (i.e., intellectual) facilitates development within another sphere (i.e., socio-emotional), and vice versa.

Binet and Simon[15] and Piaget[16] have stressed the *adaptive* aspect of human intelligence, and adaptivity involves all artificially compartmentalized aspects of development. Recently White[17] has emphasized the importance of competence as a major stabilizing force in human personality functioning. The child who exultantly cries out, "I can do it myself," is undergoing a profoundly reinforcing social and emotional experience. Some of the previously suspected harmful consequences of attempts to accelerate intellectual achievements may have stemmed more from faulty teaching procedures rather than from the acceleration attempts per se. This is important to keep in mind when we find ourselves tempted to shy away from attempts to explore the limits to which early achievements may be guided.

Why are we not more concerned with pedagogy and curriculum development? Why have we, by and large, been content to let the big educational ideas come to us, when we are in the prime position to develop, to test, to reformulate, to modify and to disseminate the most important ideas about how young children learn? Why have we produced no major educational theorist? I think the answers to these questions all come under the category of good answers—for basically, as discussed above, any inadequacies on our part have been determined primarily by our strong and entirely valid needs to protect the children who are our charges.

But one can be both protective and concerned with curriculum development, and with the old-fashioned word, pedagogy. A counterforce to our own conservatism has come from an interesting source. We have educated too many young mothers about the importance of the early years for child development for them to sit idly by and let this period pass without maximal support from the institution designed as appropriate to help the child during that period—the "preschool." Thus a new left threatens our complacence. Within the last decade, mothers have not been happy with the studied avoidance of these issues on the part of the group that they regard as the experts. As a consequence we have had the so-called "grass roots" schools—mostly Montessori-oriented —springing up all over the country. In her helpful and provocative book, *Learning How to Learn*, Nancy Rambusch comments on this as follows:

> Young mothers are concerned with education at the "optimal" level (that is, below the age of six) as well as at the formal level. They see their young children attempting to learn but, paralyzed into non-intervention, they let their children flounder until the first grade. The source of many a parental trauma is to be found within the ranks of nursery and kindergarten teachers, within a group which expresses resistance, and frequently hostility, to certain kinds of learning experiences among young children (principally experiences leading to academic learning). Many a child eager to begin reading at three or four is being rerouted into bead stringing and block play by teachers completely convinced that the child is not "ready" to learn, when frequently it is the teacher who is not "ready" to teach him.[18]

This avoidance of concern with pedagogy has meant failure on our part to influence the school curriculum from below. Yet McMillan stressed that the nursery school *should* influence the schools from below. For the situation to be otherwise is an insult to our efforts. And to this writer it is ridiculous to assert, as some authors have done, that there should be no forward-moving continuity between nursery school–kindergarten–first grade. To quote Todd and Heffernan again:

> The tendency has existed to bring the curriculum down from higher schools without regard to whether the instructional methods and materials of the higher school were appropriate for younger children. Since a child goes from kindergarten into elementary school, for instance, there is a real temptation to overemphasize reading readiness in the kindergarten instead of leaving it primarily to the first grade. Furthermore, there is the temptation to make the nursery school child ready for kindergarten by having him learn, among other things, to sit quietly while waiting for the teacher to lead some large-group activity. The absurdity of such expectations is readily apparent to those who work with preschool children.
>
> The curriculum is determined, not by anticipation of later curricula, but by the nature of the children at a particular age level.[19]

Such a position is in one sense tantamount to saying that a premedical curriculum should be based on what college students are like, not on what the student will need to have been exposed to when he reaches medical school. We are always talking about the search for a culture-free intelligence test, realizing all the time that there is no such thing as culture-free intelligence. Any suggestion that the preschool curriculum can afford to disregard the kindergarten curriculum is essentially an advocacy of a culture-free education. We should not only plan our curriculum with the kindergarten in mind, but we should expect reciprocity. That is, we should influence the educational program for older children as well as accommodate to it.

To return to the point about the identity confusion implied by "preschool" versus "school" labels, to abolish that entirely artificial distinction makes it less awkward to think about education *both* in terms of what a child is like at three and in terms of what we want him to be like at four or seven or twenty.

Why have we not built into our programs a procedure for self-evaluation? In the area of evaluation, early childhood education has again been set apart from the mainstream of formal education. Whereas achievement tests are routine for all children past kindergarten, no such attempt to carry out formal evaluations of the effects of participation in preschool programs has ever been carried out on a large scale. Again it is interesting to speculate on reasons for this wariness about evaluation. Are we embarrassed to ask for help? Are we afraid of what we might find? Or do we just not care? I cannot believe that it is the latter; again I think that the culprit is a misplaced kindness and protectiveness.

Knowing what we do about the relative unreliability of most forms of mental measurements during the early years, we have tended to shrug our shoulders and act as though there was nothing that could be done. But descriptive, concurrent evaluation that makes no claims to life-span reliability or validity is in no way damaging to the child. Quite the contrary, it is extremely helpful in enabling us to know what we are accomplishing, and what we have failed to accomplish.

Here a brief personal historical note might be of interest. Following participation in some planning discussions about Project Head Start, the author agreed to compile quickly a simple assessment procedure which would not require trained psychologists for its administration and interpretation and which would provide a summarization of some of the major educational achievements of the child during his early years of development.[20] The evaluation procedure so assembled was originally labeled the Preschool Achievement Test; however, before its introduction to the people who were to use it, a suggestion was made that the name of the procedure should be changed to the Preschool Inventory, as the notion of an achievement test for preschoolers was not acceptable. Yet to this author such measures of tangible accomplishment as a consequence of exposure to an educational regimen are not only acceptable but essential.

It should be a source of considerable dismay that spokesmen for the field of early childhood education could not say to the planners of Project Head Start in the Office of Economic Opportunity in the spring of 1965, "Of course we can tell you what you can expect from an eight-week preschool program for disadvantaged children. After all, we have been running day-care centers for disadvantaged children in this country for 30 years; of course we know what to expect. . . ." But could anyone honestly say that? No. At the termination of the Iowa-California polemics about whether nursery school could increase the IQ some 20-odd years ago,[21] it became very unpopular to be concerned with effects. This would not be so alarming if it were not for the fact that, suddenly, so much is being expected of us. We have all been willing to be swept along with the publicity, with the promises of increased intellectual productivity of improved school readiness; only a few brave souls have dared to speak up and suggest, "Perhaps you are expecting too much of us." But we really do not know—and that is nothing short of a professional disgrace.

Epilogue

Although we have recently redefined our field as early childhood education, we do not on the whole seem to view ourselves as child educators. Rather we seem to view ourselves more as part of the milieu in which the education occurs—a piece of movable equipment, as it were—than as a catalyst or reagent as appears to be the case with teachers in the area of later childhood or adult education. This paper represents an attempt to generate constructive thinking about the goals and objectives of education of the young child and of the implications of these goals for defining the role of the chief practitioners of the field. Inherent in the questions raised is the exhortation that we be not timid, apologetic or conservative in our own self-concept. The teacher of the young occupies a position of crucial significance in the lives of the children with whom she interacts. Whether she formulates her objectives clearly and anchors them safely within the framework of a meaningful philosophy of education, or whether she avoids such a formulation as being inappropriate for a program of "group experience for the young," the children whose lives she influences will indeed infer her objectives from the type of program she permits to develop. Thus she will either formulate a curriculum by choice or by chance.

It is hoped that a rethinking of the questions raised in this paper will reorient the teacher of the young to a concern with pedagogy and will encourage closer affiliation with historic and contemporary activities within the broad fields of child development and education. This reorientation cannot but help to get our identity into sharper focus on the broad screen of social living.

References

1. Vivan E. Todd and Helen Hefferman, *The Years Before School.* (New York: Macmillan, 1964), p. v.

2. J. E. Leavitt (ed.), *Nursery-Kindergarten Education* (New York: McGraw-Hill, 1958), p. 2.

3. Sallie Beth Moore and Phyllis Richards, *Teaching in the Nursery School* (New York: Harper, 1959).

4. Catherine Landreth, *Education of the Young Child* (New York: John Wiley and Sons, 1942).

5. Ruth Updegraff *et al., Practice in Preschool Education* (New York: McGraw-Hill, 1938).

6. *Ibid.,* p. 4.

7. Cited in J. MacVannell. *The Educational Theories of Herbart and Froebel* (New York: Teachers College, Columbia University, 1905).

8. Kate Silber, *Pestalozzi: The Man and His work* (London: Routledge and Kegan Paul, 1960).

9. Maria Montessori, *The Montessori Method* (New York: Frederick A. Stokes, 1912).

10. Margaret McMillan, *The Nursery School* (London: J. M. Dent and Sons, 1919; rev. ed., 1930).

11. *Ibid.,* p. 6.

12. *Ibid.,* p. 7.

13. *Ibid.*

14. *Ibid.,* 86.

15. A. Binet and T. Simon. *The Development of Intelligence in Children* (Baltimore: Williams and Wilkins, 1916).

16. J. Piaget, *The Origins of Intelligence in Children* (New York: International Universities Press, 1952).

17. R. W. White, "Motivation Reconsidered: The Concept of Competence," *Psychological Review,* 66 (1959), pp. 297–333.

18. Nancy McCormick, *Learning How to Learn* (Baltimore: Helicon Press, 1962), p. 3.

19. Todd and Heffermann, p. 154.

20. Bettye M. Caldwell, and D. Soule, "The Preschool Inventory," unpublished manuscript (Upstate Medical Center, Syracuse, 1966).

21. Beth L. Wellman, "Iowa Studies on the Effects of Schooling," *Yearbook, National Social Studies Education,* 39 (1940), pp. 377–399.

25 Early Learning for What?

Bernard Spodek

A specialist in early childhood education examines various traditional instructional models and goals for early learning. He suggests that a "transactional curriculum," in which the child and teacher establish goals and procedures uniquely fitting the individual, may be the most appropriate model for our time.

"Reading—The letters, which I originally had made for the trays, were kept in big wooden boxes, each with 26 letter places. These we still use and I think they form the best means of teaching reading and spelling, their use making appeal as it does to three distinct senses, the muscular, the tactual, and the visual. Falling back on these, particularly on the earlier senses, many of our pedagogical difficulties fall away."[1]

"No mention has been made of instruction in the Nursery School, because in any formal sense it has no place. No reading, no writing, no number lessons should on any account be allowed, for the time for these things has not yet come."[2]

Should we or should we not teach reading to young children in nursery schools and kindergartens? Observers of the field of early childhood education are aware that there is currently no agreement on this issue. The quotations cited above give evidence of the fact that the controversy is not new, that even the pioneers of nursery education could not agree on any answer fifty years ago. This lack of resolution is largely a function of the way in which the issue is framed and the kinds of evidence needed to respond to such a question.

Questions about the content of early childhood education are usually raised on the basis of what's good for all children, or at least for all children belonging to an identifiable group. "Should we teach reading in the kindergarten?" "Should two-year-olds be taught to read?" "Should we postpone reading instruction for all until they have a mental age of six and one-half years?" "Should we provide all disadvantaged children with language training?" It is the inclusivity of the questions, reflecting a need to find a single answer for educational problems, that plagues us.

Too often the question is asked as if its resolution required technical information alone. "What does research show?" "Has anyone successfully tried it?" Actually, the solutions to problems of content inclusion need to be based on more than technical data. There are moral issues relating to the aims of education that are not subject to empirical test. Furthermore, there is the issue of the relationship of curriculum content to edu-

---

Phi Delta Kappan, March, 1969. Reprinted by permission.

Mr. Spodek is Professor of Early Childhood Education, University of Illinois, Urbana.

cational goals. How consistent are the plans for schooling and their implementation to the stated aims? While such issues can be tested empirically, we often lack the technology needed for testing, or find that the process of evaluation requiring long-range follow-up would be so costly and so time consuming that we avoid it. Instead, we look at face validity, judging the apparent compatibility between what we do to children in school (or what we say we do to them) and what we conceive as the goals of education.

Arguments are again raging over the content of early childhood education. We are witnessing an unparalleled growth in early childhood education. Programs are being established for young children in communities where no public programs have existed, where there is no strong tradition of early childhood education. Many states are beginning to require that all school systems provide kindergarten education. Pre-kindergarten education is being offered to large numbers of disadvantaged children through federally funded programs and, in some areas, serious thought is being given to providing such educational opportunity for all children.

The question of what to teach in the nursery school or kindergarten can only be resolved when one has identified the purposes of education at this level. Nursery schools and kindergartens have been conceived differently at different times. Sometimes the concern has been for the nurturance of children, the need for broad support of the development of the young organism. At times early childhood education has been conceived as a socializing experience, giving children opportunities to learn to function with others within some code for group living. At other times these groups have been conceived of as primarily custodial agencies, "caring" for children, or as recreational settings, designed to support free, undirected play.

Today many educators view the kindergarten and the nursery school as a downward extension of the school. The goals for the nursery school and kindergarten are exactly those goals set for all schooling. The differences in activities found at these younger levels stem from developmental differences in the clientele rather than philosophic differences or differences of purpose. Presently the content of the early childhood curriculum must be related to how we define the goals of the school and how we conceive of schooling.

Models for Schooling

While many models for schooling exist, the following seem to be the most prevalently supported today. Often the goals of the models are not made explicit by those who advocate them, but they are identifiable. In some cases an existing school will not reflect any one model, but may combine elements of several.

The School as an Acculturator. This model was reflected in the Mission Kindergarten Movement of the turn of the century, in the 1922 compulsory public education law of Oregon, and in many current programs of compensatory education. Within this model the school's role is to teach a single acceptable pattern of behavior and values, often identified as the "American Way," to all children. In the Mission Kindergarten Movement, children of recent immigrants were taught the English language as well as American values and patterns of life. The school became the means of including these children and their families in the "melting pot" of American society. The Oregon law of 1922 in effect outlawed all private schools. The public schools were viewed as a means of teaching "Americanism" as a single set of beliefs and values to all children regardless of background. For many supporters of the law this was a way of lessening the influence of minority religious, cultural, and political groups.[3] In many programs of compensatory education the admonition to teach children "standard" English and to eradicate the children's native dialect, as well as the emphasis on teaching middle-class values and behavior systems, are a more contemporary example of this same model.

At the early childhood level, such a model would require that all children, but especially children from deviant and minority groups, be brought into the school early to be taught what could be characterized as a WASP* curriculum. Early childhood education becomes singularly important because of the possibilities of language learning at this level of development and the fact that teachers have a greater impact on children's values and behavior patterns in the early grades. Early schooling would mean that children could be acculturated early in the behavior patterns and value systems that would continue to be the central focus of the school. Teachers in schools reflecting these models would be careful not to allow any child's prior background or experience to enter into the classroom, since it might cause disruptions in the achievement of proper school learning.

The School as an Agency for Vocational Preparation. This model values the school for its utilitarianism rather than for its acculturating effects. The school is an avenue for teaching those skills needed by persons entering the world of work. Many current programs of compensatory education fit into this model of the school. These programs would concern themselves with teaching the disadvantaged student language skills and technical subjects because these are needed for the disadvantaged person to compete in the contemporary job market. Subjects that do not produce marketable skills are of secondary importance in these programs; thus such subjects as art or history may be downgraded or even eliminated in a program where many subjects are competing for available school time and resources.

At the early childhood level, vocationally oriented programs would

* White Anglo-Saxon Protestant.

emphasize those activities that provide a readiness to learn marketable, job-oriented skills.

The School as a Preparer for College Entrance. Schools fitting this model concern themselves with preparing students for more schooling. The prime goal of the elementary and secondary school is to ready the individual for entrance to college. (Since many colleges are vocationally oriented, this model may in some instances be an extension of the vocational model. The difference lies in the fact that schools prepare students for "careers" rather than "jobs"). The rationale for the inclusion of school subjects in secondary schools within this model is that these subjects are required for college admission. By downward extension, elementary school subjects and early childhood education are affected, being prerequisite for learning at the next higher level.

Sometimes the content of the class or the school is less important than the prestige of the school, especially when the concern is to get into the "right" college rather than merely "a" college. The competition of parents in large cities to get their children into selective nursery schools as their children's first step toward a proper college education is evidence of parental support for this model.

The School as a Miniature University. Within this model the school is conceived of as a transmitter of accumulated human knowledge. Significant human knowledge has been organized into disciplines which closely approximate the academic departments of a university. Only aspects of the human experience that are organized within the scholarly disciplines are worthy of attention in the school. While other content areas may be found in these schools, these areas are merely tolerated and do not represent the focal concern of the school. Emphasis on language and literature, science, social science, and mathematics characterizes this school, with less attention paid to the teaching of social skills, expressive skills, values, or aesthetics.

At the early childhood level, schools within this model might be organized around the Brunerian admonition that any subject can be taught to any child at any level of development, leading to a developmentally correct academic curriculum.[4]

The School as a "System." School bureaucracies, like other bureaucracies, develop a life and a rationale of their own, completely independent of any set of external goals. Some of the new critics of American education suggest that within American education one can identify many schools that fit this model of the school as a "system." The content of schooling is primarily designed to help children fit into the system with a minimum of conflict and allow for perpetuation of the system.

A recent article by Noyes and McAndrews reports several high-schoolers describing school:

> It's a system, you have to understand that. I guess it's because they have so many kids and they all have to be in school so many days a year, for so many hours. . . .[5]

> Schools are like roulette or something. You can't just ask, well, what's the point of it? . . . But you have to figure the system or you can't win.[6]

Jackson's *Life in Classrooms* describes elementary school activities that are inherent in this model, including learning appropriate classroom behavior.[7]

Alternative Models

Fortunately for children and for schools. the models identified above are not the only models available for early childhood education. Within the tradition of the early childhood education movement, other models have been developed and are being advocated. It is possible to conceive of a school that is not concerned primarily with having the child fit any particular mold or having all children achieve the same aims. It is possible to conceive of schooling as a partnership affair in which children, from the moment of their entrance into the school, are involved in determining purposes and goals as well as procedures. The early nursery schools, some of the kindergartens of the 1920s and 1930s, and the presently popular English Infant School reflect to some extent this model of schooling.

Within this model there can be no prior determination of curriculum. The questions "Ought we teach reading in the kindergarten?" and "Should all children learn to speak standard English?" are irrelevant, for each must be answered "yes" and "no," depending on the child, the teacher, and the circumstance. For the curriculum coordinator or the school superintendent, such a school might seem confusing, for goals and procedures cannot be carefully worked out in advance of schooling, nor can learning be evaluated by traditional tests. for all children will not be expected to go through the same programs, with individualization meaning individual pacing.

Such a model of schooling would develop what might be labeled the "transactional curriculum," a curriculum determined for each child through the transactions between the child, as client, and the teacher, as professional. At the early childhood level the teacher's role as professional would be to set the stage for learning, to provide legitimate alternatives for children's activities in school, and to serve a guidance function in the classroom. The teacher would provide alternative goals, help children clarify their needs and desires, help them anticipate the consequences of their acts, help them evaluate their activities, and help to see that school provides productive learning situations for all children.

As viewed within this model, the child is not a passive participant in the curriculum process. He will not simply be acted upon as the client in the situation. Nor will he dominate the decision-making process. The child, however, will have a role in instigating learning, in determining its direction, and in terminating any learning situation. In this transactional process, not only can the child achieve the traditional academic goals, but he can also learn to be self-determining. There can be outlets for creative thinking in the ongoing activities of the school. Divergent sets of values and patterns of behavior need not be squelched. Nor will anarchy reign in the classroom. For in the transactional process the goals and desires of the child can be modified and restructured. This provides at least a partial answer to the query, "Early learning for what?"

The involvement of the young child in curriculum decision-making suggested in the transactional model ought not to cease when the child leaves the nursery school and kindergarten class, but should continue as he moves through the many levels of schooling. The current student demand for a voice in educational policy making at the college level closely parallels a similar need at the early childhood level. This, too, is a part of education.

References

1. Margaret McMillan, *The Nursery School* (London: J. M. Dent and Sons, 1919), p. 111.

2. Grace Owen, *Nursery School Education* (London: Methuen and Co., 1920), p. 25.

3. David B. Tyack, "The Perils of Pluralism: The Background of the Pierce Case," *American Historical Review* (October 1938).

4. Helen F. Robison and Bernard Spo-
dek's *New Directions in the Kindergarten* (New York: Teacher's College Press, 1965) emphasizes this model.

5. Kathryn Johnston Noyes and Gordon L. McAndrews, "Is This What Schools Are For?" *Saturday Review* (December 21, 1968), p. 3.

6. *Ibid.*, p. 59.

7. Philip Jackson, *Life in Classrooms* (New York: Holt, Rhinehart, and Winston, 1968).

26 Teaching the Very Young:
Procedures for Developing Inquiry Skills
Frank J. Estvan

Children usually ask a lot of questions. But the adult's instant answer does less to enhance the child's learning ability than does an appropriate question in return. Such question asking causes the child to find the reasons and sources behind his problems. Mr. Estvan here discusses methods of helping the child learn, to think critically, and to solve problems.

Growing recognition of the importance of the first five years in shaping human development has renewed concern about the nature of the goals and procedures to be used in early childhood education. Some, for example, view these programs as an early start in the race to college. Others promote enrichment to make up for limitations in the background of culturally deprived children. The current interest in inquiry raises the question of the place of discovery methods in early childhood education.

Growing insights about human behavior shed some light on the purposes and methods appropriate for teaching the very young. One of these principles is that behavior is whole; it follows that educational goals for the early-age child, as for the teen-age child, must include a broad spectrum of ideas, feelings, and skills. Another principle is that development is continuous. Accordingly, any curriculum plan must begin at the beginning and provide for systematic development of behavior until a desired level of achievement is reached.

The decisions early childhood educators make, therefore, rarely are simple choices such as between social-emotional as opposed to intellectual goals or between "play" in contrast with highly structured methods and materials. Nowhere is this better demonstrated than in programs which attempt to help young children develop the power to think critically, to solve problems, to "learn how to learn."

Children and Inquiry

The child goes forth each day and, as Walt Whitman pointed out some years ago, becomes a part of the things he looks upon, and they become a part of him. Today's child goes forth into a much larger world, the product of family mobility, travel, television. To complicate

Phi Delta Kappan, March, 1969. Reprinted by permission.
Mr. Estvan is Professor of Education at Wayne State University, Detroit, Michigan.

matters, much more is going on in his world, and more of it impinges upon him at one time. As a result, a five-year-old last year may have known that Johnson was President, but when asked the President's first name replied "Howard!" He may wonder, too, in view of the antics on TV, whether a political party is the same as a birthday party.

Inquiry is a way of satisfying curiosities. The method is essentially one of raising questions and seeking answers.[1] These processes are not unknown to the young, for it is common observation that children are "full of questions" and that they are "always getting into everything." Unfortunately, the modern world makes little provision for being understood by young minds; neither do adults always have the time or skill to help children understand what they see and hear.

Teachers of the very young are in a unique position, for they can use the child's question as the organizing center for activities which help him learn the beginnings of inquiry skills. Such efforts will be effective to the degree that the teacher gives careful consideration to all the elements involved in instruction: goals, methods and materials, and evaluation.

Goals for Teaching Inquiry

All the various types of goals bearing on the various kinds of inquiry are suitable for nursery-kindergarten children, provided that they are appropriately defined. As is true for any age group, young children of the same age differ greatly; they are not at the same point in the development of any form of behavior. Studies of the social perceptions of three- and four-year-old children indicate that they are well beyond the zero point in the formation of many basic concepts. Three or more years of living in varied home environments, furthermore, have produced marked differences that are related to sex, race, social status, and age.[2] In view of this great variability and the rapid developments that occur between three and six years of age, inquiry goals should be designated in terms of levels to meet each child's requirements.

Cognitive objectives deal with knowledge and understanding. A basic step in learning to conduct inquiry is to acquire a meaningful grasp of the terms involved, for these are the concepts with which the child must deal. For a series of activities focusing on the question, "What makes flowers grow?," instructional objectives for a three-year-old, stated in behavioral terms, might be: The child *recognizes* basic vocabulary related to plants (seed, roots, bud, "to water a plant"). For a more mature child, the emphasis would be on a higher level of understanding: The child *uses* correctly basic terms related to plants.

Affective objectives, the feeling component of behavior, might center on the child's interest in discovering answers for himself and his persistence in the face of frustration. Behavior indicating an early step in the development of a commitment to inquiry would be: The child asks the teacher to read a book that will provide him with the needed information. (His own efforts to come close enough to birds in the play area in order to note their color and other characteristics proved unsuccessful.)

For a more mature child, the goal would be for him to take steps to find his own answers: The child leafs through old magazines or picture books looking for illustrations that give him the answer to his question. (Viz., different kinds of birds.) Hopefully, young children will ascend to higher levels of determination as they acquire more experience in facing obstacles and enjoying success. Instead of simply terminating inquiry, behavioral goals for a very young child might be: The child repeats his procedures when his first attempt fails. For a child who has had considerable experience in coping with difficulties and is beyond this point, an instructional goal could be: The child tries another approach when his first method proves unsuccessful.

Psychomotor objectives include all the skills involved in the inquiry process: formulating a question, collecting information, working with data, and confirming findings. An attainable goal for the very young child, who stands mute before the teacher with an object in his arms or tugs at her sleeve, would be: The child verbalizes a question that is understood after some clarification by the teacher. For the more verbal child, a higher goal can be set: The child asks a clear, direct question. Another objective might deal with the scope of the question. Stated behaviorally, a beginning level would be: The child asks one question about an object or event. Some children will be able to reach the following goal by the time they have finished kindergarten: The child asks a series of related questions about the phenomenon under observation.

Objectives for data-collecting skills can be expressed in terms of the number of senses involved and the child's ability to participate in experiments. For the child whose first exploratory move is to put an object in his mouth, a reasonable goal would be: The child uses a limited but increasing number of senses to obtain data. (He squeezes, pokes, pounds, shakes, lifts, drops.) With greater maturity the goal might be: The child uses all appropriate senses in finding out about the nature of an object. (A ghetto child might look at grass, chew it, stroke his hand over the turf to feel its texture, bend down close to the earth and smell it, and run on a lawn in his bare feet.)

Four levels in ability to participate in an investigation are listed below in ascending order of difficulty to indicate the range of data-collecting behaviors involved:

- The child *attends* to what the teacher is doing as she performs a demonstration.
- The child *reports* accurately the series of steps involved in an experiment performed by the teacher or classmates.

• The child *follows* the teacher's direction step by step as he performs an experiment.

• The child *plans* his own experiment for finding an answer to his question (e.g., he suggests that a dish of snow be placed in various locations, including the refrigerator, to test the hypothesis that "snow melts when it is brought inside").

Skill objectives for dealing with information include both the ability to differentiate and to synthesize data. Goals for analyzing skills can be based on the number of items involved: The child discriminates between two objects which differ in size or color or shape. A higher level goal is: The child detects the middle or median position among three objects which differ in some respect. For the synthesizing of data a low level behavioral goal is: The child classifies objects in terms of their functions. (A bed, pillows, and covers are for sleeping.) Given proper guidance and experience, the child should gradually be able to note relational generalizations as in the following goal: The child forms simple cause-and-effect associations. (Dark clouds often bring rain.)

Very young children take a significant step forward in their development of inquiry skills when they check results to confirm their findings instead of being satisfied with the manipulative aspects of their experience or of asking the teacher if they are "right." Two levels of behavioral goals which represent growth in this skill are:

• The child repeats his procedures to see if he gets the same results.

• The child compares his product with the real thing, a model, or picture.

Teaching Inquiry Behavior

The nature of inquiry processes dictates the tasks of the teacher: to help the child formulate questions that are important and meaningful to him and to aid him in his quest for answers.

Several conditions must be met if the child of five or below is to raise questions. The most important is to establish a classroom climate that is open to his queries. The child must be made to feel comfortable in voicing questions. He should have the assurance that his teacher and classmates will listen with respect to his wonderings, and that there is always the possibility that some of them will be acted upon. More than encouragement is required—the child should feel rewarded for initiating thoughtful questions.

The nursery-kindergarten teacher must also stimulate curiosities in areas that are not commonly available to the child. She must provide a wealth of wide-ranging experiences—indoors and outdoors, in school and in the community—that involve concrete, pictorial, printed media calling for manipulative, dramatic, creative, investigative activities. These should be introduced gradually so that there is always something fresh and new to capture the child's imagination, but never so much as to overwhelm him.

The way the teacher structures school experiences influences the kind of questions that are evoked. A child-structured situation, such as a "free" period, makes it possible for the child to pursue his own interests and get answers on his own. A teacher-structured experience, such as a story or a rhythms period, is more suitable for provoking new areas of interest. Between these two lies the semi-structured situation, such as show-and-tell and "juice" periods, in which the activity is designated by the teacher but the content and trend of the discussions are largely the children's.

The teacher will stimulate a broader range of questions if the child has opportunities for experiencing a variety of ways of working. There are times when he should work alone, seeking guidance from the teacher when he needs help. Because interests are contagious—one individual's enthusiasms may produce a snowballing effect on others—the child should also participate with his peers in small-group projects and total-class activities. Since attention time is a function of interest (a young child can concentrate for fifteen minutes or longer *if he is interested*), the scheduling of these various types of working arrangements should be flexible.

How the teacher deals with the child's questions will determine the kind of inquiry skills he develops. The great majority of his questions are direct, explicit requests for information: Why does it get dark at night? Who runs the train? How does the fireman know where the fire is? If the teacher readily supplies the information, the nursery child's customary reaction is to terminate his present explorations and turn to something else.[3] In such a transaction the child is learning to use human resources as a means of getting "instant" answers to his questions, but he is not learning how to discover answers by himself.

The basic canon, therefore, for helping children learn inquiry skills is: Don't tell—ask! *The teacher's questioning is the basic technique for guiding the very young child through the inquiry process.* Her questions perform two primary functions: that of focalizing the child's attention and directing his inquiry.

"Focalization" is the act of concentrating on an object or event so that it stands apart from the general stream of impressions which constantly bombard the individual. If the young child does not discriminate between the phenomenon to be studied and other stimuli, he cannot even begin to come to grips with it. Such discrimination is also necessary because of the way children perceive their world. The young child is highly selective in his perceptions; the teacher's questions can direct his attention to other important elements in the situation. Those elements which he does perceive are regarded globally and are differentiated only to the degree that is necessary for the circumstances; the teacher's questioning can lead him to note important details. The child also tends to perceive these elements in isolation; the teacher's questioning can lead him to see how these parts are related to constitute a whole.

The nature of the questioning employed by the teacher provides the child with clues as to the kind of thinking and procedures required to find answers. Replication of some of Piaget's work on the additive composition of classes suggests that children's ability to deal with the logical relationship between "some" and "all" (e.g., the sub-class "brown beads" to the total-class "beads") is related to the types of questions asked by the experimenter.[4] The order of questioning is important, too. Children find questions about the structure or external appearance of objects to be easier than those having to do with their function or how they work. Children also seem to deal more easily with differences than with likenesses, for in most cases the former are based on physical realities whereas the latter require them to engage in more abstract conceptualization. (A saw and a hammer are different because one is used to cut wood and the other to pound nails; they are similar in that both are tools.)

Lastly, the teacher's questioning can offer leads to the young child as to the kind of investigation that is needed. "Is it better to ——— or ———?" suggests that the child carry on an experiment. "Are big packages heavier than smaller packages?" identifies for the child the size-weight variables which he can put to test. "How can we fix this?" presents the child with a problem-solving situation. "I wonder how we can find out?" encourages the child to plan a method of procedure for discovering a solution.

There is no pattern of teacher questioning that can be used for all children for all questions. In a sequence of teacher-pupil interaction (consisting of a child-initiated question, the teacher's response, and the child's reaction to her response), the form, content, and function of both the nursery child's and the teacher's comments may be combined in innumerable ways.[5] Because children are different and thinking complex, the teaching of inquiry skills is a highly individual and personal matter which cannot be reduced to a simple formula.

Evaluating Inquiry Behavior

Decisions about every phase of instruction rest upon feedback gained from evaluation. The teacher's diagnosis of where the child is in his development will help her set up goals representing higher levels of achievement *for him.* If she has determined that the child can keep in mind one question that he is to ask on a field trip, she might decide that he is now ready to learn how to report the information back to the others. As learning experiences unfold, the teacher will evaluate the child's reactions to the various activities and related materials which were selected to bring about the desired learning. Does he appear to be sufficiently familiar with the situation to be able to cope with it, or is it so strange that he does not seem to know where to begin? Often it is simply a case of whether he understands the question or whether she should rephrase it. In terms of her evaluation, she may modify the goal, provide alternative learning experiences, or help him over a hurdle which is impeding his progress. On completion of a sequence of experiences, the teacher must evaluate to see whether or not the child has achieved the goals set up for the unit. Not only is she interested in knowing whether the child found an answer to his question, "Where does the store get the things it sells?," but if in the process of finding out he has grown in ability to carry on inquiry—to give a clear, concise report of his findings, for example.

Observation is the primary means of obtaining evidence of the progress being made by very young children toward the goals of instruction. By stating objectives in behavioral terms, as in the illustrations above, the teacher knows what to look for. Anecdotal recording of these observations over a period of time is probably the most common technique employed in early childhood education. Other techniques become more feasible as the presence of teacher aides, student teachers, high school future teacher club members, and cooperating parents grow and the use of instructional technology becomes widespread. An audio-tape recording can be made of several children discussing a large picture to find out "what is wrong"; a portable video-tape recorder can be used to record how a child of four or five goes about building an airport out of wooden blocks or tries to make a mechanical toy "work."

Regardless of which techniques are used to obtain evidence, the data must be summarized periodically. Rating scales and checklists are convenient forms for making such notations when the items reflect the specific goals of the program, and they are scaled according to degrees of proficiency so that growth can be noted. Explanatory or interpretive comments add to the usefulness of such ratings, and judgments about the adequacy of a child's progress will be more reliable if the results are viewed in terms of all the information contained in the child's cumulative folder.

Summary

The development of inquiry behavior is one of the most important functions of early childhood education. As in all instructional programs, the approach must be diagnostic and individualized. The child works best on questions which are important to him and geared to his level of development. He must have sufficient time to explore, create, and discover answers by himself, but this does not mean leaving him to his own devices. The teacher must intervene to direct the child's random (sometimes destructive) behavior into more inquiry-oriented channels, to assist him when frustration begins to mount. The primary means by which the teacher helps the child is by setting up a stimulating environment and by guiding his explorations through questioning procedures. Throughout, the teacher evaluates the child's behavior to determine the suitability of goals and teaching techniques as well as the progress he is making. The identification of specific goals, provision of appropriate learning experiences, and continuous evaluation are, of course, the prime requisites for effective teaching of any kind of behavior.

References

1. For a discussion of the nature of inquiry and types of skills involved see Frank J. Estvan, *Social Studies in a Changing World: Curriculum and Instruction* (New York: Harcourt, 1964).

2. Frank J. Estvan, "The Social Perception of Nursery School Children," *Elementary School Journal* (April 1966), pp. 377–385; idem, "The Relationship of Nursery School Children's Social Perception to Sex, Race, Social Status, and Age," *Journal of Genetic Psychology* (1965), pp. 295–308.

3. Dorothy Haupt, "Teacher-Child Interaction: A Study of the Relationships Between Child-Initiated Questions and Nursery School Teacher Behaviors," unpublished doctoral dissertation (Wayne State University, College of Education, 1966).

4. Eileen Thomas, "The Effect of Procedure on Piaget's Theory of Additive Composition of Classes," unpublished master's thesis (Wayne State University, College of Education, 1964).

5. Haupt, "Teacher-Child Interaction."

27 Kindergarten Is Too Late

Esther P. Edwards

Ferment about philosophy and methodology imbues the field of early childhood education. This author suggests some general directions for educators and urges an eclectic approach appropriate to the needs and interests of the individual child.

Education of the young child has come with a rush and a swirl out of the quiet backwater where it sat so long in its own reflection and has swept into the mainstream of American concern and controversy. At last we are hit hard with the fact that young children's experiences in their first years are of crucial creative importance for their total future lives. The heredity-environment dilemma having been laid to rest with the recognition that both are significant in continual interaction, we are ready to accept the thesis that intelligence is not fixed once and for all at birth but can be shaped by experience. We are just beginning to look seriously at the kinds of stimuli we provide for children. What should these be? When should they occur? How should they be presented? By whom? In what setting?

But what is the basis for this growing awareness that the early years are of incalculable significance? Any attempt to give a capsule explanation will be an oversimplification; yet the attempt must be made.

The word "cognition"—knowing—became respectable in American psychology in the Fifties. Piaget in Switzerland and Vygotsky in Russia had shown as long ago as the twenties and thirties that human intellectual functioning could not be sufficiently explained in any purely mechanical fashion. American psychology of the ruling behaviorist school came more reluctantly to recognize that thinking, learning, and behaving as we know them cannot be reduced wholly to a direct stimulus-response hookup.

What gives an intelligent adult the ability to focus his attention on *this* rather than on *that*? What allows him some degree of choice, of voluntary control? What gets him out from under the domination of his environment—not always, not entirely, but in part, and part of the time? Why can the absorbed reader fail even to hear the clock tick in the corner, the rain on the roof, the hiss of the fire, yet leap to instant attention when his child cries out softly in its sleep? Why, and how, have we human beings attained waking consciousness, that demanding burden and endless delight? What gives us alone of all life on this planet symbolic language—created, shared, used to build and sustain our cloud-palace cultures that float from generation to generation on the mind of man?

D.O. Hebb of McGill University has shown that there is a relation between the level of complexity of a species, the slowness and difficulty of early learning in its members, and the ease and speed with which they can deal at maturity with complex ideas. Whatever an ant learns— if it learns anything at all, functioning as it does chiefly through instinct—may be learned in the first moments of its life, learned once and for all. Thereafter it functions well as an ant, but with no possibility of varying its set pattern. "Go to the ant, thou sluggard"—but not for help with calculus. A rat reared in darkness, Hebb tells us, is capable of a selective visual discrimination, definitely learned, after a total visual experience of less than fifteen minutes; within an hour or so it has learned to function as well as its peers reared normally. A rat is an ingenious and canny beast, but calculus is not his meat either.

The young human creature spends months and years completing the intellectual structures which at his birth are present only as possibilities. Slowly he develops, with little visible change from hour to hour or day to day. His early learning is more laborious than that of neurologically simpler creatures. It is not only that the baby's period of development is longer than the ant's or the rat's, but that the human child is involved in a more difficult task. So difficult, indeed, that his first learning is less efficient, less fluent than any other creature's. It has been said: "The longest journey in the world is the journey from the back of the head to the front of the head." The infant is building the pathways that will make this journey at first possible, then easy, then lightning swift and marvelously effective. What pathways these, through what trackless jungle? Connected and interconnected systems of neurons, branching and coiling back, going off in new directions and returning, making patterned avenues through the forest of nine billion nerve cells that lies between the incoming sensory areas of the brain and the outgoing motor centers. Without this development, conceptual thought is forever impossible.

So at maturity the intelligent adult, whose potential has thus been translated into reality, perceives with understanding, speaks and thinks symbolically, solves problems, categorizes, appreciates, and does all this with an instantaneous flash of insight that is alone of its kind in nature. He deals conceptually with the universe—a universe he first had to construct for himself. How does he do this? As each of us must, he has built it during his earliest years out of the myriad perceptual cues coming into the nervous system from "out there"—cues impinging continually on nerve endings, but meaningless until his system has built the structures that allow a reading of the signals and a response to them.

This is what the infant in his cradle is doing. We adults, rushing about harassed and busy, look at the baby and think: "How restful—

to be fed, kept warm and clean, to have nothing to do but play with a toe, eat, cry a little, sleep. . . ." But the infant lying there is building his universe, and building himself. He must do both of these things, do them *then,* do them *at once* (for one is the converse of the other), or never do them at all. Never to do them is never to develop, to be cut off, to be a thing and not a man.

How construct a universe? The newborn baby possesses a nervous system which already receives and responds reflexively to signals from the outer world—to light, sound, temperature, pressure, and other stimuli. But though he responds through reflex action, the baby does not yet understand the signals: he cannot *read* them. He must learn to interconnect sets of cues—to see what he hears, for instance, and to learn that a light and a sound may describe one and the same object. So he begins to define reality. He must develop ability to deal with more and more signals at once. In time, perceptual cues gain meaning: the baby has begun to know what they signify. Memory, judgment, intention all stem from this moment in his intellectual life. First he acts as a purely physical being and learns how to solve problems by means of bodily acts. Then he learns to represent physical action by mental symbol, and thought has begun.

His first symbols are images, pictures which allow him to hang on to fleeting reality ("I remember my mother's face though she is out of the room"). Then the child learns a word, and another, and another, and begins to put words together. At eight months, or a year, he has begun to grasp the shorthand which allows him to hold in his head the whole of reality and to manipulate it, to solve the problems it sets him, through mental operations. Until he is five or six or older, the chief intellectual task of his life will be the creation of a symbolic vocabulary, or several of them (words, numbers, images, musical notes), which become the medium of his life as a human being.

How vital this is to human development is implied by the linguists' suggestion that the supremely difficult feat of building language recognition and response which takes place during the first years of life can occur because there is a built-in neurological mechanism for language learning present in every normal human organism. But like the image on the sensitized negative, this potential will not appear as reality unless the proper circumstances develop it. Experience—the right experience —is essential.

Heredity and environment interact. Hereditary possibilities are shaped by the influences that only human culture can provide; they are potentialities that must be developed while the young neurological organism is still rapidly growing, malleable, open to stimulus. If the "critical periods in learning" hypothesis applies to human beings (as we know it does to other creatures—dogs, for instance—and as evidence increasingly indicates it does to us), then the right experience must come at the right time, or the potential must remain forever unrealized.

Benjamin Bloom of the University of Chicago implies this when he says that the early environment, during the first five to seven years of life, is the significant one for intellectual development. This is why we are finally realizing that the young child's experience is of indelible importance, not only for his emotional life, but also in the formation of that aspect of man which is perhaps most crucially his own—his sapience.

If all this can be accepted as in some degree reflecting truth, where are we? We are at a point where we can see why education for the young child can matter enormously. It matters not as much as the family. The family is basic. But the good family is good precisely because it provides so much of the young child's education. Still, other appropriate experiences can add to what even the best family can do.

For the child born into a family which cannot give him what he needs in emotional security or intellectual stimulus, such experiences may act as a lifeline to essential development. What early education is offered to what children becomes, therefore, of first importance. Perhaps the right choices here can make a difference comparable to the release of nuclear energy—a release of human potential energizing our whole society.

This sense that the choices matter tremendously is why the present debate as to what constitutes good education for young children is more a battle than a scholarly discussion: Montessori—or not; "Teach your child to read at two"—or don't; imaginative play as the focus of the preschool experience vs. structured cognitive stimulation. Every aspect of the preschool is up for reconsideration, defended with zeal, attacked with fury. Partisanship is prevalent, the grounds for decision-making uncertain.

Part of this malaise stems from the attempt of psychologists and teachers to create activities appropriate for the thousands of urban—and rural—slum children who have come into preschool classes through such programs as Head Start. Once these children would never have seen the inside of a nursery school classroom. Now they are here. Teachers are responsible for them. And teachers have found that their tried and true techniques don't work with these childen. How do you make contact with a nonverbal, uncooperative, frightened, dirty, doleful, thumb-sucking four-year-old dragged to school by a slightly older sister who can't tell you anything about him except that his name is Buzzer?

So it is perfectly true that many Head Start programs are not making a significant difference in the intellectual capacities or the academic readiness of children thrust into them for a brief six to eight weeks the summer before they go to "real" school. Head Start has been oversold in an effort to enlist citizen support: "It will bring the slum child up to the level of his middle-class age mates in one quick and easy exposure." That was a line that salved the taxpayer's conscience with a minimum of damage to his bank account. But it was a lie. No one with the faintest understanding of the realities of mental, social, and emotional growth ever thought it could do any such thing. Head Start may be better than nothing (in some cases even this is questionable), but it is vastly less good—and *less* than is needed.

The solution, however, is not to damn previous educational goals and means across the board. New circumstances and children with new needs do not prove that the established ways of going at the education of young children are valueless—only that we now are dealing with a wider range of children and must supplement the older ways with different aims, content, and techniques. We need a more varied repertoire. We need to know when to do what, and why. That's all. But that's a tall order.

The situation, then, calls for a plea to the embattled camps in preschool education to beat a few swords into plowshares,. to leave their respective strongholds, to stop maintaining that each holds all the truth, and to begin to share questions and insights. A vast amount of hostility can be dissipated if we can accept two basic truths:

1) There is no one method of teaching young children which is ideal for all of them. Like the rest of us, they differ in temperament, in background, in needs, in readiness for this or that experience. As children vary, so must educational approaches.

2) Human beings are totalities: they have bodies, and they have minds; they exist in social context within which they act and feel. Small children are people and their life in school needs to be a whole life in which physical, emotional, intellectual, and social aspects of the self are all given adequate nourishment. It is wrong to leave out any major segment, though emphasis can and should vary with the particular set of circumstances.

Perhaps the first step is acceptance of the individual differences among children. Some of these are genetic in origin, others are caused by environmental accidents. Within groups of children from similar cultural and social strata are wide ranges in health, energy, temperment, aptitudes, and innate potential. Even among children in the same family this is so. Dozens of factors can affect the quality of early experience. One child's mother was sick when he was at a vulnerable stage; another child had an illness that required hospitalization; for a third, everything went along smoothly and success bred success. The gap between one socioeconomic group and another magnifies the differences. The early life histories of children living within a few blocks of each other in an American city may be as remote from one another as is the Arabia Desert from Manhattan. How foolish then to think that any one approach can be the best, much less the only one for such diverse bits of mortality, so variously shaped by their three or four years of life.

Proponents of cognitive preschool experience have recently leveled severe criticism at the less-structured types of nursery school curricula. "Only play," they say, "only messing around with finger paints . . ." The Montessori schools point to their abundance of graded materials which can be used by the individual child to move step by step from growing mastery of sensory-motor skills to a knowledge of letters, of numbers, of ordering and labeling. The child's attention span increases. He learns to work independently, systematically, following a coherent pattern established by materials and setting. For children from the often chaotic homes of poverty this may mean a significant gain.

O.K. Moore, of the University of Pittsburgh, uses his "talking type-writer" (actually a total language environment, rather than a typewriter in an ordinary sense) as a tool whereby children as young as three years have learned to read and write in the natural way in which they learn to talk—inductively—with personal choice of activity and pace. Carl Bereiter and Siegfried Engelmann, formerly of the University of Illinois and now of the Ontario Institute for Studies in Education, have created what is perhaps at the moment the most controversial program in pre-school education. It has been called a "pressure-cooker approach." In this setting, under direct academic force-feeding, groups of four- and five-year-olds from lower-class families are taught verbal and number patterns:

> This is a ball.
> This is a piece of clay.
> Is this a ball?
> Yes, this is a ball./No, this is not a ball.
> This is a what? This is a ball. . . .

The aim of this exercise is to develop the ability not merely to label "ball" and "clay," but to know the use and significance of such essential carriers of meaning as the simple word "not." Verbal skills, numbers, and reading are taught. Drill is the medium. The adults unashamedly pressure children to learn. Hopefully their own desire to achieve competence will be fired by the sense that they are doing something tough and important, but praise, exhortation, and tangible rewards and punishment are freely used. The atmosphere is intense. These children have no time to lose. They must move into the world created by adult society. The whole thrust of the program is to make this possible for them.

These and other preschool programs focused on cognitive development add a dimension that was underplayed if not lacking in the older nursery school, organized as these were around the child's social and emotional growth, his creative activity in the graphic arts and in music, and (with varying degrees of effectiveness) around introductory experiences in those areas recognized at a higher level as the basic disciplines (literature, mathematics, sciences, social sciences). Such a curriculum assumed that the young child entering preschool brought with him a fund of organized sensory and motor learnings. His language development was already well under way, chiefly through many months of interaction with an intelligent, loving, verbal, and attentive mother.

Often what he needed most was to be a child among children in an environment which allowed him to explore and to play. He had already been molded and stimulated by the adult world, represented by his vitally concerned parents, and every day he went home to continue this part of his education.

But the Head Start children come from homes which have failed to nourish them in health, in emotional stability, in intellect. They need desperately to develop language, to learn to think. For these children such a program as Bereiter and Engelmann's can perhaps give the all-essential forward thrust without which nothing else can have meaning. They come to school late in the day to establish basic learnings. Their tendency is *not* to listen, *not* to focus. They know in their bones that no one is paying attention to them. They have to undo false beginnings. From a mile behind the starting line they have to start the race their more fortunate peers are already running. Under such circumstances, if pressured instruction will get them ready for school, blessings on it, and let them have it.

But young children are being made ready for more than the first grade, and there is more to them than a brain, however vital that may be. William C. Rhodes of the National Institute of Mental Health writes in *Behavioral Science Frontiers in Education:*

> The imposition of culture upon the child, without relating the culture to his inner substance, is forcing a foreign body into his being . . . He will only mobilize defenses against the culture in an attempt to neutralize its harsh, abrasive denials of what he is.

This we must not make children do by being too demanding in our concern for cognitive growth. There are other values also of major importance.

Maya Pines, in her October 15, 1967, *New York Times Magazine* article "Slum Children Must Make Up for Lost Time," quotes disparagingly from the Head Start *Guide to a Daily Program,* which advocates that children:

> . . . learn to work and play independently, at ease about being away from home, and able to accept help and direction from adults . . . learn to live effectively with other children, and to value one's own rights and the rights of others . . . develop self-identity and a view of themselves as having competence and worth.

This is not mere cant. It is not necessarily accomplished, but these are worthy goals. Anyone who has worked with young children, whether they be culturally deprived or not, knows it to be the most sober of cold facts that such children do need to develop independence, social competence, and a sense of self. Until they do, their growth toward other sorts of learning is enfeebled. The child who lacks adequate ego development neither cares nor dares to learn.

Hopefully children can learn both to use their minds and to become

more fully human. Social and intellectual growth are not mutually exclusive. The valid criticism of the Bereiter and Engelmann program is
not made on the ground that it gives drill in cognitive patterns, but that
it gives little else except such drill, in a setting where teacher imposes and
child conforms. This is too narrow a segment of experience. It ignores
vital components of the totality that is a child. What the end result for
these children after some years will be, no one knows. But one must wonder whether so intense a focus on the growth of knowledge and the
means of its verification will not diminish other aspects of personality.

Preschool educators criticize the Bereiter and Engelmann program because of its frank admission of dependence on rewards (cookies, praise)
and its use of punishment (physical coercion, isolation in unpleasant
surroundings). These are gross inducements toward learning. If they
are used only to prime the pump, as is recommended, then one may consider them symptomatic not of the program so much as of the damage
already done to the child by his stultifying early experience, a damage
demanding heroic measures to overcome. But if they must remain in the
teacher's repertoire, if they are not left behind in favor of satisfaction
from the achievement itself, then they form an indictment of the mean-
ingfulness of this approach to children. A learning that takes place
only when the teacher doles out candy or brandishes a switch (hypothetical or not) is a learning without intrinsic satisfaction. Performance
can be evoked temporarily through pressure, but will not last. This is
one touchstone of valid education.

But why must we wait so long, and then resort to pressure? Already
there are several experimental programs which are attempting significant
intervention before the age of two in the lives of "high risk" children
(the younger brothers and sisters of academically retarded children from
deprived homes, or children from markedly nonverbal backgrounds). Appropriate education must be made available to every child as soon as
he can benefit from it. We know that as early as eighteen months disadvantaged children start trailing their middle-class age mates in tests
of general intelligence and language development. Already the subtle
undermining brought about by inadequate experience has begun. It is
simply not true that all lower-class children are lacking in potential
compared with their middle-class peers. Some, no doubt, are. But for
many, if not most, the deficit that so early becomes visible is more
likely caused after conception by various environmental lacks (poor
nutrition, the mother's ill health during the baby's intrauterine life, and
inadequate sensory-motor stimulation after birth). Such lacks can be
reversed, and they ought to be.

We are going to have to make educational stimulation available from
babyhood on for the children whose families cannot provide it for
them. Whether tutors should go into the homes, whether children should
be brought into carefully planned, well staffed *educational* (as distinct
from baby-sitting day-care) programs, we do not now know. Experiments

going on in several places in the country should help us decide. But however we do it, intervention by the age of eighteen months should be the rule for the children of deprived inner-city or poor rural families. As it is now, few children reach Head Start before the age of four. We are not making use of the golden period when we can most easily and effectively work with children without using pressure, without having to force on them a culture already so foreign that it cannot be learned unless, as William Rhodes says, we make the child "give up completely the content of the self." We are not coming to children when there is still time to help them build effective roadways through the neurological labyrinth, to help them create a universe rich, diverse, satisfying. We can, if we will. And we must.

We must build programs designed to amplify the child's world as the middle-class child's parents do, when he is still an infant in the crib. We must do this not to cut the lower-class child off from his home and his family, but to assist his overburdened mother, to help make the family milieu better for the child. We must create kinds of stimulation that become a constant part of his life, involving him daily in meaningful interactions, just as the child from a more fortunate home interacts with his mother every day for years, until the time that the thousands of exchanges, each modifying and adding to his understanding, give him mastery of thought and speech. We know that this is the most deeply meaningful education for the one-, two-, or three-year-old child. We must try to approach it for every child.

Such special interventions are not yet widely available. Large numbers of deprived children remain, in a sense, accident victims in need of first aid. Perhaps the Bereiter and Engelmann type of program is that first aid. Perhaps it is the best solution to an unfortunate situation. Perhaps it can build in children who have missed out on the normal growth toward competence some of the abilities they would have developed more gradually had their backgrounds been more intellectually stimulating. Perhaps it cannot. We do not know, but surely it is worth trying, with the sobering thought that force-feeding programs, though they rescue the starving, do not make up for deficits already incurred.

But because people who have been hurt need first aid is no reason to prescribe first aid as the all-important component of everyone's experience. Because deprived children may benefit from intensive work in the cognitive areas where they lack development does not mean that a broader, more inclusive type of program which meets the equally real needs of the intellectually advanced child deserves ridicule. What we really want is to bring into our repertoire a much wider range of experience from which we may select intelligently those aspects which are most useful and appropriate for each group of children—indeed for each child.

Here we take issue with Miss Pines's description of the "established" nursery school, quoted from her *New York Times Magazine* article but similar in tone to what she writes in her new book, *Revolution in Learning: The Years from Birth to Six*. Miss Pines states:

> Middle-class nursery schools operate on the theory that they can directly influence only the child's emotional and social development—not his mental growth. They assume that if they build up a shy child's confidence, or redirect any angry one's aggression, the child's intellectual development will take care of itself, following a sort of built-in timetable. Therefore they concentrate on teaching children to "get along with others" and "adjust to the group."

Undoubtedly this neglect of the cognitive dimension is true of many preschools, but it is not true of the good ones, and certainly it is false to the philosophy behind early education. It overlooks a range of experience which is very present when young children are well taught by intelligent teachers who are themselves cultivated and concerned people. Children do not get over being shy; they do not learn to redirect their anger or interact with others in a vacuum. They are able to develop as people, in the social and emotional sense, most effectively when their minds are occupied with challenging ideas. "Why does the ice cube melt? What is *melting*? Why does the wind blow, and what is air, and what are the words that let me talk about it? How can I draw a picture of what I felt like when I was in the hospital? What is a dream? Why am I afraid? How many nickels do we need to buy fresh food for our guppies if a box of fish food costs a quarter? What makes my baby brother cry at night and wake me up? How can a rocket go around the world so fast? When is tomorrow? How far is far?" These, and the millions of other questions small children ask every day, are *intellectual* challenges. The preschool exists to help children formulate them, examine them, and, in some degree, answer them. It can only do this by giving children some of the multiplicity of interlocking experiences through which they can move slowly toward mature answers. As nursery-school children they will not arrive, but they make progress.

Because in the past the intellectual component of the preschool has been implicit rather than explicit, this does not mean that it has been lacking. It means that the skilled preschool teacher has done a good job only when she has turned every experience to the benefit of intellectual growth as much as to social or emotional growth. It has given her the task of picking up the children's leads and building her program about these, on the presumption that children are readiest to learn in areas where they already show interest.

Let us not be so foolish as to say that the established nursery-school curriculum—if it is taught well—lacks intellectual content, or that it ignores children's growth toward cognitive ability, for it does not. It has been subtle in its approach to these. Perhaps it has been too subtle to allow the critics to recognize the presence of these strands of experience, but not too subtle for children to learn from them—provided the children were ready to do so.

But let us also admit that children who have lacked the requisite preparatory growth are *not* ready for such a program and need something else, something with a more explicit structure, something which is geared specifically to their level of attainment and their deficits. If these children are not always to be accident victims, they need educational intervention years sooner than we are giving it to most of them now. But in trying to do this, we must also bear in mind that to teach is not to bulldoze. Nonverbal, immature, dirty Buzzer is still a person, not a thing to be obtusely shoved into any mold we choose. This is why we need teachers to create programs that as yet do not exist, programs which can combine structured cognitive stimulation with full respect for the inalienable right of each human being to be himself.

Let us admit, also, that when we create these new approaches to cognitive growth, they may also be able to add something vital to the multiple stimuli offered by the middle-class nursery school. To object to an exclusive focus on structured intellectual learning for the middle-class child is not to say that he cannot gain from some of it. No one is talking in terms of taking the bloom off frail butterfly wings. Children who have learned how to learn are eager and resilient, and gobble up new information, skills, and insights in every conceivable way. If they are given some leeway to choose those aspects of a program on which they will spend most of their time, they can only benefit from encountering a wider range of possibilities. Teachers should know all the materials—the fullest spectrum of approaches—and should not be afraid to use them.

We are wasting time and energy, good humor and understanding, in opposing each other. No school of thought has all the light. There is no one ideal approach to learning for all young children. Instead, there are many possible variations of emphasis which can make the preschool experience maximally valuable for a wide range of children from differing family backgrounds, social strata, and levels of development. Let's stop this fruitless squabbling and instead fight ignorance (our own as well as that of others) and the limitations to children's potential growth, however these may occur. Let's be grateful for every addition to the armament of techniques and tools which we can use to help children. Let us try to find out how best to employ each approach: when, with whom, for what reasons, under what circumstances. And for heaven's sake, let's get going.

28 A Comparative Analysis of Preschool Curriculum Models

Rochelle Selbert Mayer

A number of innovative and experimental early education programs have been implemented in recent years. This author compares four early education approaches and examines how and why they differ. The issue of comparative effectiveness is explored.

In the nineteen sixties, educators became increasingly convinced of the importance of the early years in human development. Research pointed to the importance of early experiences for their effects not only on social and emotional development, but on intellectual development as well. Early childhood education that in the fifties had been almost exclusively the domain of the middle and upper classes, began to be viewed as a potential vehicle for solving the educational problems of the disadvantaged. While many social and political factors converged to bring about a national commitment to compensatory preschool education, the works of J. McVicker Hunt and Benjamin Bloom were particularly influential in developing the belief that such intervention could have a significant impact on intellectual development. In *Stability and Change in Human Characteristics,* Bloom's data pointed to the period before age four as the time of greatest intellectual growth, and therefore as the time when environmental factors exerted their greatest influence (for good or ill) on intellectual development. Hunt's *Intelligence and Experience*—drawing on Piaget—concluded that intervention at the preschool age level could provide the enrichment necessary to offset the educational deficits of disadvantaged children. Although the theoretical interpretation of these notions has not gone unchallenged,[1] it is widely agreed that educational experiences in the early years can promote learning and later school achievement. Such unanimity has not, however, produced uniform or definitive answers to the problem of methodology.

In recent years various experimental programs for the disadvantaged have been implemented with equally various premises and goals. Reports on individual programs, as well as comparative studies of their efficacy, are presently available; yet little has been written to explain the differences in instructional techniques and their respective theoreti-

This article was commissioned especially for this book of readings.
Rochelle S. Mayer is a doctoral candidate at Harvard Graduate School of Education.

cal rationales—to explain how and why the programs themselves differ from one another in their objectives, materials, and techniques. This paper will attempt to provide such an analysis by examining four early education curriculum models: the verbal-didactic; the verbal-cognitive; the child-development; and the sensory-cognitive.

The Child-Development Model

Let us begin by sketching briefly the major curriculum components of each preschool approach. We will first look at the child-development model which has served as a basis for most preschools serving middle-class populations and is also the model which, as in the beginning phase of Head Start, was most widely adopted for use with disadvantaged children. In its application to disadvantaged populations, the child development approach has been termed the "enrichment strategy."

The curriculum of the child-development model can be discussed in terms of "activity areas." There is a construction area with building blocks of different sizes and shapes, and accessories such as trucks and figures of animals and people. Many classrooms have a woodwork area with real tools and different sizes of soft wood to saw and hammer. There is an art area supplied with paints, clay, paper, crayons, scissors, and other art materials. There is a housekeeping area furnished with miniature stove, refrigerator, doll carriages, tables and chairs, tea set, dress up clothes, and so forth. There is a library corner stocked with picture books and story books, and a large area—often including a piano—for group activities such as music and movement, rest, and story time. There is a quiet area supplied with puzzles and games such as lotto and dominoes. The classroom also contains plants and animals and perhaps a science table with magnets, dry cell batteries, and similar materials. There is also an outdoor play area with swings, climbing apparatus, seesaws, and perhaps equipment for sand and water play.

In addition to classroom activities and outdoor play, another basic component of the curriculum consists of trips into the community. In some instances these trips become the focal point of themes, such as "transportation" or "community workers," providing a specific basis for the content of dramatic play, art work and other classroom activities.

A visitor to our four types of preschool classrooms would probably find this the "noisiest" one. At any moment some children will be building together or playing house while others listen to a story or paint; under the supervision of the teacher and her assistants, the children are free to choose and change activities according to their particular desires. One teacher might be stationed outside on the playground, another reading to or singing with a few children gathered around her, while a third might be helping others with individual projects, interceding in squabbles, and answering questions.

The Verbal-Cognitive Model

The classroom materials and "activity areas" of the verbal-cognitive model, here based on the Perry Preschool Project, are essentially like those of the child-development model. The difference is that, in the verbal-cognitive classroom, the teacher takes on a much more directive role, planning specific activities for the children which often require her to be the center of the children's attention. Throughout the day the teacher is continuously speaking to the children, questioning them and responding to them.

A typical day in such a classroom would begin with the children gathered in a circle for a "planning session." After general discussion and perhaps a group game, the teacher would present the activities for the first part of the day. She might show the group a paper plate and felt cutouts in the shape of eyes, nose, mouth, and ears along with a jar of paste. The children are asked what the materials are, where they could be found in the room, and what you can do with them. A child then demonstrates how you paste a face on the plate. Children are asked to point to their own eyes, noses, and so forth. Then a fire truck is taken out and the same procedure is followed. The third article might be a box of gelatin, and a discussion would follow about how you make gelatin and what happens to the contents in the box. Then each child selects an activity to begin the day and goes to the appropriate area. A teacher is stationed at each area to supervise or participate in the activity. In the block corner two children may be playing fireman and the teacher may take on the role of a victim of a fire. The children making gelatin are constantly being asked questions—what happened when we added hot water; what's going to happen when we put it in the refrigerator?

A child may finish an activity and remain in the same area doing other things, or he may change areas. Later, the group may be brought together for a story to be followed by small group activity such as sorting and classifying games, or discussion of the attributes of certain toys. Juice time also provides an opportunity for specific learnings: as the cups and napkins are passed out, they are counted and their colors are discussed. A child may also be asked to direct the distribution of cookies or juice as if he were the teacher. At the end of the day the children come back together for an "evaluation" session to discuss the events of the day.

The Sensory-Cognitive Model

The classroom of the sensory-cognitive model, based on the Montessori method, is arranged in an orderly and uncluttered manner. Low shelves with attractive materials line the walls. Each material has its own place and is visible and accessible. Although there are small chairs and low tables in the room, much of the floor space is free of furniture. Each child has his own small rug to roll out on the floor and many of the children's activities consist of working with various materials on their individual rugs.

The Montessori materials (which will be discussed in detail later in this essay) can be grouped into three broad categories: those designed to develop sensory skills; those designed to allow children to carry out practical life activities; and those designed for teaching writing and arithmetic. Children are free to select their own activities, although teacher suggestions are sometimes offered. The classroom atmosphere, as Dr. Montessori intended it, is one of "quiet activity." In general, children work individually with the materials, only occasionally joined by a teacher to demonstrate the use of a particular material. Opportunities for outdoor gardening, and care of plants and animals are also provided.

While the other models we discuss may or may not have children of different ages in the same classroom, the Montessori method is designed specifically to include children of different ages, and the materials are graded and sequenced in difficulty.

Children in the Montessori model take care of their own classroom: they wash the tables, sweep the floor, return materials to their proper place, and so forth.

The art activities and dramatic play found in both the child-development and verbal-cognitive models are not provided for in the sensory-cognitive model. An observer in a Montessori classroom might be struck by the extent to which the teacher remains in the background rather than directing children's activities, and by the children's sustained involvement with a particular material, working with that material over and over again.

The Verbal-Didactic Model

Our fourth classroom, based on Bereiter and Englemann's academically oriented preschool, will be termed the verbal-didactic model. Unlike the other curriculum models being considered, this program is designed to be used exclusively with disadvantaged children; it is intended to equip them with information and skills needed to succeed in first grade. The curriculum consists of direct instruction in language, arithmetic, and reading, while allowing time for periods of music and semi-structured play. During the latter, children have their choice of listening to a story, looking at a book, working on a puzzle, or drawing. For the music period the group meets as a whole and songs are chosen and words changed to reinforce the rules taught from the academic curriculum.

Each teacher in the program takes responsibility for one subject area. The children are grouped on the basis of ability into three smaller units that rotate from one subject area and teacher to the next.

The reading curriculum is based on a phonics approach and incorporates many of Fries' suggestions from *Linguistics and Reading*. The mode of instruction in language, as well as arithmetic, is intense oral drill. In the language curriculum, verbal formulas or sentence patterns are taught to the children. The basic sentence pattern is the identity statement. (This is a *cup*. This is not a *cup*.) When this pattern is mastered other more complex patterns are introduced. (This *cup* is *full*. This *cup* is not *full*.) Concepts are taught as rules which are to be learned by rote and then applied to analogous examples. In arithmetic, the sentence pattern is replaced by the number pattern. For example, children learn $1 + 0 = 1$, and the rule "when you add zero, you always end up with the number you started out with." The pattern is applied to other numbers plus 0. Children learn to recite in unison: "$1 + 0 = 1$; $2 + 0 = 2$; $3 + 0 = 3$; . . . $9 + 0 = 9$."

Topology of Curriculum Models

Schemes of classifying the differences among various educational approaches have been undertaken on the basis of objectives,[2] theoretical orientation,[3] and curriculum methods.[4] In addition to each scheme's internal problems, however, their scope makes any particular one insufficient for the present purpose—to conceptualize the differences in program approaches in a way that will shed light on *how* they are different (curriculum methods and structural characteristics) and *why* they are different (delineation of goals and theoretical orientation); and to provide a framework within which to interpret research results on comparative effectiveness of program approaches.

We will attempt such a scheme of classification on the basis of the structure or design of a program. The *American Heritage Dictionary of the English Language* defines structure as "the configuration of elements . . . in a complex entity; the interrelation of parts or the principle of organization in a complex entity." The basic components of a preschool classroom are teachers, children, and materials. Their interrelationships can be described in terms of interactions—between teacher and child, child and material, and child and child.

Weikart[5] and Karnes[6] have also used the term "structure" as a means of classifying program models by curriculum methods. However, their use of the term is considerably different. Weikart and Karnes conceptualize differences in curriculum methods by positing a spectrum of "structuredness." Programs are placed on this continuum according to the degree to which teachers plan or prescribe program activities and sequence presentations. Thus, the verbal-didactic, and to a lesser extent, the verbal-cognitive models occupy the high end of this continuum while the child-development model is relegated to the opposite pole. Even though the sensory-cognitive model is clearly low on teacher direction, it is not usually placed on the low end of the spectrum because the materials are highly "structured." As we can see from this last example, the criterion of structuredness is not truly unidimensional; we may be referring to the external organization of the child's experiences by the teacher, the sequencing of a child's activity inherent in the design of materials, or both. A unidimensional analysis of structure obscures differences present in types of instructional sequencing and their possible significance. Indeed, it is difficult to understand how such dissimilar instructional strategies can be used to rank programs along a single continuum of structure.

However, there is another and more important objection to classifying programs on the basis of "degree of structure." When we posit a spectrum of "structuredness" we lose sight of the very premise of "formal" education; namely, that it is not a set of random experiences in some instances and of planned experiences in others, but rather that *all* well executed educational programs represent "conscious designs." All curriculum models have been conceived so as to yield interactions among teachers, children, and materials in a way that is believed to facilitate the objectives of the design. In short, all well executed educational programs are highly "structured," though the type of interactions emphasized and the nature of sequencing children's experiences—as well as the emphasis of program objectives—differ. The task of conceptualizing operational and theoretical differences in program models is the task of understanding and schematizing their "conscious designs"—of analyzing and comparing how, and to what end, teachers and children interact with each other and with the learning resources made available in their environment. Such an analysis implies that the type of interaction(s) stressed by a program are logically related to the high priority objectives of that program and to theoretical notions about how children learn best what the program considers most important.

To eliminate differences across program models, we can begin by examining the emphasis various programs place on teacher-child, child-material, and child-child interactions. We can rank each program *relative to the other programs* on the basis of the frequency of each type of interaction.

For the purposes of this analysis we will rank teacher-child interaction proportionate to the amount of the child's time during which his learning is being mediated by a teacher. Child-material interaction will be defined as the amount of the child's time during which his learning is being mediated through individual manipulation of materials. The criterion for child-child interaction will be the amount of the child's time during which his learning is being mediated through cooperative play and conversation with other children.

Using these criteria, the interaction analysis can be depicted graphically as follows:

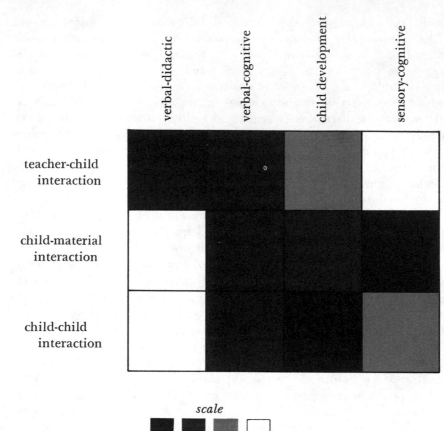

scale

most————————least

By depicting this pattern* of teacher-child, child-material, and child-child interactions we can see which instructional strategies are most important in each program. We will examine the ways in which these strategies are related to the objectives and theoretical orientations of each program. As we will see, the interaction most emphasized by a particular program also indicates the learning strategy where the most extensive instructional sequencing is present. Application of this point will become clearer if we first examine each of the *black* boxes individually before analyzing the diagram horizontally.

Teacher-Child Interaction: The Verbal-Didactic Model

The Bereiter/Engelmann program, which ranks highest on teacher-child interaction, aims to increase the child's learning of specific infor-

---

*This ranking has yet to be verified by research and has been attempted here on the basis of observations and what should hypothetically be true according to program descriptions from such sources as Bereiter and Engelmann (1966), Read (1966), Montessori (1914), Weikart *et al.* (1969), Weikart (1967), and Kamii and Radin (1967).

mation and rules in the areas of language, arithmetic and reading. Objectives [8] include: (a) ability to use affirmative and *not* statements in reply to the question "What is this?" (This is a ball. This is not a ball); (b) ability to handle polar sets (big-little; up-down); (c) ability to perform simple if-then deductions; (d) ability to name the basic colors; (e) ability to count objects correctly up to ten; (f) ability to recognize and name the vowels and at least fifteen consonants; and (g) a sight reading vocabulary of at least four words. The mode of teacher instruction is highly verbal and highly sequenced. "First order" statements (This is a cup) and yes-and-no questions (Is this a cup?) are to be mastered before "second order" statements (This cup is empty) and "what" questions (What can you tell me about this cup?) are introduced.

Teacher mediation is patterned on principles of learning theory.* This theoretical orientation holds that learning—which is defined as changes in behavior—can be most efficiently induced through "instruction involving repetition of associations between teacher's stimulations and the child's responses."[9] Rewards or reinforcements should follow correct responses so that the new behavior does not become "extinguished" or forgotten. Accordingly, Bereiter and Engelmann employ extrinsic reinforcers—both verbal (That's right, you're so smart today!) and nonverbal (handshakes, cookies)—in line with behaviorist learning theory. The motivation to learn is seen as contingent upon events in the environment rather than being viewed primarily as an intrinsic part of human nature.

The emphasis on teacher-child interaction and de-emphasis on child-child and child-material interaction follows from the reliance on direct instruction and the emphasis on language development. Bereiter and Englemann note that their objectives represent "kinds of learning that do not arise easily and naturally from casual conversations and experiences."[10] They are not the learnings which are likely to accrue from children playing together or with blocks and clay. Rather, teacher directed learning is necessary.

Kohlberg identifies the Bereiter/Engelmann approach with the "culture training" stream of educational thought. This approach assumes that "what is most important in the development of the child is his learning of the cognitive and moral knowledge and rules of the culture and that education's business is the teaching of such information and rules to the child through direct instruction."[11]

Child-Material Interaction: The Sensory-Cognitive Model

If we view the teacher-child dimension on our graph as indicating the emphasis placed on teacher-mediated, verbal learning, then we can

---

*Also termed "behaviorism," "socialization theory," "internalization theory," or "behavior modification."

interpret the child-material interaction as the degree to which learning is to occur through "doing" with emphasis on nonverbal, concrete experience. Here the sensory-cognitive model, which aims to develop the child's sensory discrimination and motor abilities, would rank highest. Objectives include: (a) ability to match and discriminate shades of color, sounds, textures, weights; (b) ability to order objects along a dimension of increasing size, pitch; (c) ability to differentiate an order of increasing weight from one of diameter; (d) care of plants and animals; (e) ability to care for oneself (washing, dressing); (f) counting; (g) development of motor skills for writing; (h) learning the sounds of letters; and (i) development of attention.

We have posited the notion that the more a program emphasizes a particular interaction, the more sequencing there is built into the nature of the interaction. While the child in a Montessori program is free to choose his activity and to move from task to task at his own pace, both the didactic materials and activities such as polishing and washing are carefully sequenced.

This is demonstrated by Montessori's three sets of solid inserts.[12] Each block of wood has ten cylinder inserts which can be easily removed from their holes. The child's job is to remove the cylinders—which vary on different dimensions—mix them up, and replace them in their respective slots. In the first set, which is the easiest for the child to master, the cylinders decrease in diameter only. In the second set they decrease in both diameter and height. In the third, the cylinders decrease only in height.[13]

While these exercises require the child to order the materials on the dimensions of size and shape, different materials will require ordering and classifying to proceed from other sensory dimensions such as color. Colored tablets, for example, are first presented to the child as a matching task of same and different; of pairing together the blue, red, and yellow tablets. Later, tablets of the same color but different shades are introduced, and the task is to order the tablets from dark to light.[14]

The activities for motor education are also presented in a carefully prescribed manner. Each activity is reduced to specific ordered components which the children must proceed through: children learn *how* to polish their shoes, *how* to set the table, *how* to wash their hands and tie their shoes. The teacher demonstrates these activities with "few or no words at all, but with very precise actions."[15] Montessori's de-emphasis on language instruction stemmed from her belief that the preschool years were not among the most sensitive periods for language development.

Montessori's view of intelligence as the ability to order and classify, her belief that development evolved through the child's interactions with the environment and proceeded through "stages," brings her very much in line with Piagetian thinking, as does her emphasis on intrinsic motivation, and the sensorimotor roots of intelligence.[16]

Child-Child Interaction: The Child Development Model

The child development nursery school emphasizes child-child interaction. Here we find objectives focusing primarily on social and emotional development. These include: (a) learning to interact and cooperate with other children; (b) developing inner controls in accordance with appropriate behaviors; (c) developing a sense of self-esteem and confidence; (d) extending abilities for self-expression and creativity in language, music, and art; (e) refining perceptual-motor coordination; and (f) learning about the wider environment.[17] The child development nursery school, as it evolved during the post–World War II period, saw its major contribution as providing an environment which would meet the young child's developmental needs for playing with other children, and for extending his experiences beyond the home.[18]

In examining the nature of planning and sequencing as it applies to child-child interactions, it is important to keep in mind the child development tradition's belief in sequences of development. Learning to interact and cooperate with other children is considered a developmental task for which the child must first be ready. Once ready, a supportive environment is required to enable the child to succeed in this task.

Prior to the 1960s the concept of maturational readiness was seen by proponents of the child development approach as a key factor in learning. The recent thinking about intellectual development which has underlined compensatory preschool efforts has altered this concept as it is applied to the "enrichment strategy."

> "Readiness is not conceived of solely as a maturational phenomenon but more as an interaction of maturation and experience. . . . Rather than suggesting that children be held out of school for a period in order to allow them to mature, children are given opportunities for school experience designed to create a readiness for school learning."[19]

The whole of the child development nursery school program is set up to encourage and facilitate child-child interactions. Rather than providing activities which require individual involvement or interaction with an adult, activities such as sociodramatic play, blockbuilding, and art all offer opportunities for joint child-child participation without a teacher's intervention.

The planning for facilitating social-emotional development, however, goes beyond providing activities toward this end. Indeed, regard for sequencing the child's experiences in a way that will enable him to adjust to an environment away from the home and ultimately to socialize in productive ways with other children is a prime concern. Read, for example, carefully outlines the steps to be taken in helping the child adjust to a group situation. The child's first visit to the classroom should take place when school is not in session, thus providing a "manageable" experience in which he can become familiar with the physical set up. This is to be followed with a short visit while school is in session. Later, the child—with his mother present—begins to attend school for part of each session. When the child is ready, he begins to attend without his mother and begins to stay for longer periods of time.[20]

In the child development nursery school the child's skill, development, and difficulties in getting along with others are noted carefully by the teacher. When possible, she makes provisions for facilitating the child's ability to form friendships. This might include sitting next to the timid child at a table where there is an empty seat for another child to join; or, if a child has trouble approaching others, the teacher might offer suggestions such as "If you'd like to play with them, you might knock first or ask Michael if he needs another block."[21] Sears and Dowley accurately describe and summarize the teaching strategy of the child development nursery school as "watching and waiting for the child's needs to emerge . . . (to) determine the timing of different activities."[22] A teacher may sequence a child's experiences in subtle ways. If the child is being introduced to a big dog, for example, he may feel more comfortable petting the dog if there is a fence between them. The sensitive teacher would allow for this, recognizing that the fence would be unnecessary in the case of a smaller dog, or after the child had become familiar with the larger one.[23]

The delineation of social-emotional objectives in the child development approach stems from the work of such men as Freud, Erikson, and Gesell. This theoretical orientation holds that experiences in the early years have lasting impact on later, adult personality. The process of personality development is described in terms of maturational stages —conflicts and abilities unfold as the child grows. Erikson's theory of psychosocial development identifies the preschool period as a stage of "vigorous unfolding." The child is "eager and able to make things cooperatively, to combine with other children for the purpose of constructing and planning, and he is willing to profit from teachers and to emulate ideal prototypes."[24]

The activities of the child development nursery school are designed to fit this developmental stage. Specific learnings and direct instruction are excluded because the preschool child is considered to lack the developmental readiness to profit from such instruction. Rather, young children learn best by doing; learning experiences are concrete, linked closely with the child's personal experiences in his immediate environment.

Trying to hasten development through training or direct instruction is considered inappropriate and possibly disruptive to the child's total growth pattern.[25]

The Verbal-Cognitive Model

The verbal-cognitive model presents an interesting pattern of interactions. Because the diagram ranks each interaction *relative to the interactions of other programs,* the verbal-cognitive model does not have a black box. Nevertheless, in terms of the relative emphasis placed on each type *within* each program, the verbal-cognitive model would yield a fairly even distribution—as the diagram suggests. Furthermore, each type of interaction has considerable sequencing built into it, reflecting the objectives and theoretical rationale of the verbal-cognitive approach.

The Perry Preschool Project, the basis for the verbal-cognitive model, not only incorporates social-emotional goals (with emphasis on their importance for cognitive development), but delineates cognitive objectives based on Piaget's theory of intellectual development. In addition to stressing language development through teacher verbalization, objectives for a Piagetian cognitive program include: (a) development of physical knowledge (glass breaks); (b) development of social knowledge (tables are to *sit at,* not to *sit on;* a doctor does certain things); (c) development of logical knowledge in classification, seriation, number, space, and time; and (d) development of representation at the symbol level.[26]

Perhaps the most fundamental principle to be extracted from Piaget's work on the development of sensorimotor skills and conceptual intelligence is that schemas, or mental structures, develop through the child's internalization of actions on objects. Consequently, "One of the most important functions of preschool . . . is to provide many opportunities for the child to use and manipulate a variety of real objects."[27]

The kinds of materials used in the verbal-cognitive model parallel those found in the child development classroom (unit blocks, clay, paints, dolls, trucks, puzzles, pictures). Unlike the child development model, however, child-material interactions in the verbal-cognitive model are geared toward specified cognitive goals and the child's experiences with materials are sequenced accordingly. To illustrate, subsumed under the goal of the development of representation is the development of the use of objects to represent other objects (make-believe). In order to facilitate this objective Sonquist and Kamii suggest a three step process whereby, for example, a game is played first using realistic toy cars, then blocks with wheels, and finally with the blocks alone.[28] Similarly, to develop pre-classification abilities, the child is initially asked to group "same" and "different" objects—unit blocks with unit blocks and trucks with trucks. Later tasks require classification by attributes—for example, separating long unit blocks from square ones—allowing the child to move eventually from work involving dichotomies to work with trichotomies.[29]

Child-child interactions are also seen as important vehicles for cognitive development. A detailed rationale for the nature of child-child interactions provided for in the verbal-cognitive approach is available in the work of Sara Smilansky.[30] In her book *The Effects of Sociodramatic Play on Disadvantaged Preschool Children,* Smilansky suggests that "sociodramatic play helps the child crystallize his experiences and facilitates both this emotional and intellectual adjustment to the environment."[31] Such role playing, she feels, leads the child to bring together divergent experiences which he can best integrate and absorb by an imaginative reaction of them through action and verbalization.[32] Smilansky's research points out qualitative differences in the sociodramatic play of advantaged and disadvantaged children, and suggests ways in which active teacher participation and group trips into the community can improve such play among disadvantaged children.

Smilansky lists six components essential for "good" or mature sociodramatic play: (a) imitative role-play; (b) make-believe in regard to objects; (c) make-believe in regard to actions and situations; (d) persistence (ten minutes of play); (e) interaction (at least two children); and (f) verbal communication related to the play episode.[33] She considers teacher direction of and participation in sociodramatic play to be viable teaching strategies. Thus, while the child development and verbal-cognitive models both provide opportunities for sociodramatic play, the verbal-cognitive model differs in that teacher mediation is incorporated into the design of the activity.

Teacher direction, or what Smilansky terms outside intervention, does not include teacher role playing, requiring instead teacher comments in line with the child's play. Such comments take the form of questions (How is your baby today?); suggestions (Let's take your baby to the clinic); clarification of behavior (I did the same when my baby was ill); establishing contact between players (Can you help her, please, nurse?) and straight-forward directions (Show the nurse where it hurts your baby. Tell her all about her).[34]

In teacher mediation through participation in play, the teacher takes on a role and governs her behavior so as to emphasize with each child the component he lacks in his play. "If, for example, he knows that Miryam, who is playing mother, does not use make-believe in regard to objects, the teacher acting as a nurse will suggest to her, 'Mrs. Ohajon, here is the medicine' (while pretending to hand her something) 'Give it to your baby twice a day.' "[35]

As the foregoing analysis indicates, the role of teacher mediation in child-material and child-child interaction takes several forms in the verbal-cognitive model, three of which are discussed and recommended by Sonquist and Kamii. These include (a) direct teaching—the teacher asks children to perform specified tasks (compare size of measuring spoons during a baking activity); (b) making discovery inevitable—the teacher arranges the environment or an activity so that the children must perform the task (make size discrimination inevitable by having measuring spoons replaced on a pegboard where their outlines have been drawn); and (c) discovery—the teacher arranges the environment so that learning can occur (give children measuring spoons in the hope that they will notice size differences).[36]

Another aspect of teacher mediation which deserves further clarification is the nature of teacher verbalization. The strategy for teacher verbalization in the verbal-cognitive model is termed verbal bombardment: "the teacher maintains a steady stream of questions and comments to draw the child's attention to aspects of his environment . . . the complexity of the language is increased as the child's verbal ability develops."[37] The child's manipulation of objects is accompanied by the teacher's speech in an attempt to strengthen symbolic processes—to help the child create a foundation for representation at the verbal level.[38]

The principles set down by Blank and Solomon to develop abstract thinking in socially disadvantaged preschool children are similar to those of verbal bombardment. They suggest that teacher verbalizations should be constructed to help children develop "skills involving the ability to organize thoughts, to reflect upon situations, to comprehend the meaning of events, and to structure behavior so as to be able to choose among alternatives."[39]

The following account of the verbal-cognitive program at Ypsilanti, Michigan provides an example of these intentions.*

(The children have entered the classroom and have gone to the bathroom. Most of the children are now sitting in a circle in front of the teacher, though stomping of feet and voices can still be heard coming from the direction of the bathroom.)
Teacher: Is there anybody still in the bathroom?
Child A: Yes.
Teacher: How do you know?
Child A: You can hear.
Teacher: Who could it be?
Child A: Don't know.
Teacher: Could it be Tommy?
Tommy: No, I'm *here*!
Teacher: Who could it be?
Child A: Harold?
Harold: (giggling) No, I'm here!
Teacher: Who could it be?

---

*Personal observation.

In this example the teacher's questions require the child to process and apply information gained from available clues, and to perform the abstract if—then deduction (*if* Tommy is HERE, *then* he can't be in the bathroom). It is particularly important to observe that the child's response can be verified—he can go into the bathroom to check his own answer.

Comparative Analysis of Teacher-Child Interaction

In order to justify our ranking of programs, and to further investigate differences among the various kinds of interactions, a horizontal reading of the interaction diagram will now be helpful. In regard to teacher-child interaction, the verbal-didactic model ranks highest, reflecting Bereiter and Engelmann's belief that disadvantaged children respond best to oral drill and direct teaching generally. Only during the brief semi-structured period during which children have their choice of listening to a story, looking at a book, drawing, or playing with a puzzle or game is it conceivable that for some children their activity will not be directed by a teacher.

The verbal-cognitive model also ranks high in teacher-child interaction. Such interaction occurs not only during the group planning session at the beginning of the day and the group evaluation session at the end, but also during the other activities where children interact primarily with materials and/or other children. Yet because the verbal-cognitive model does not consider teacher mediation the only viable learning strategy, it must be ranked lower than the verbal-didactic model in this area. The classroom itself is structured to encourage more than teacher-child interaction. Although the teacher stationed at each activity area is likely to become directly involved in at least one child's activity, other children will often be interacting with materials and/or each other without teacher mediation.

Teacher-child interactions are even more reduced in the child development and sensory-cognitive models. In the former—with the exception of such group experiences as story time—the teacher's time is spent setting up materials (preparing paints), facilitating the ongoing work and play (maintaining order and safety, working out squabbles), and observing the children. In the sensory-cognitive model, teacher intervention is even less pronounced and is essentially nonverbal. The Montessori teacher may, in some instances, suggest an appropriate activity for an idle child, or demonstrate the use of materials. She is also directly involved in teaching letters, numbers, and beginning reading with older children. Nevertheless, more so than in any other program, the Montessori teacher remains in the background observing, while the child spends long stretches of time with materials and activities requiring no teacher mediation.

Comparison of Teacher Verbalizations

It has already been observed that an important aspect of teacher-child interactions is the nature of teacher verbalization. As between the verbal-didactic and verbal-cognitive programs, the amount of teacher verbalization is not significantly different since both demand a fairly constant stream of speech.[40] However, there are obvious differences in the content, variety, complexity and sequencing of teacher verbalizations in each program. Compare, for example, the language sample from the Ypsilanti verbal-cognitive program (page 299) with the following excerpt from Bereiter and Engelmann.[41]

> *Teacher:* [Presents pictures of knife, cannon, pistol] This is a weapon. This is a weapon. This is a weapon. These are weapons. Say it with me. This is a weapon. This is a weapon. This is a weapon. These are weapons. Let's hear that last one again. Make it buzz. These are weaponzzz.
> [Refers to knife] This weapon is a_____. Who knows?
> *Child E:* A knife.
> *Teacher:* Yes, a knife. Let's say it. This weapon is a knife. Again. This weapon is a knife.
> [Refers to cannon] This weapon is a_____. Who knows?
> *Child C:* Battle.
> *Teacher:* That's pretty good. You use this thing in a battle, but it's called a cannon. This weapon is a *cannon.* Say it, everybody. This weapon is a cannon. . . .
> *Child A:* I got a cannon at . . . [stops talking as teacher holds outstretched hand only a few inches in front of child's face].
> *Teacher:* Here's the rule: [claps rhythmically] If you use it to hurt somebody, then it's a weapon. Again. If you use it to hurt somebody, then it's a weapon. Say it with me. If you use it to hurt somebody, then it's a weapon.
> And if it's a weapon, what do you do with it?

The verbal-didactic approach implicitly assumes that knowledge of vocabulary and verbal rules or formulas will advance thought processes.[42] A correct verbal response is considered sufficient evidence of learning and understanding. The verbal-cognitive approach, on the other hand, does not concentrate on verbal labeling and cautions that verbal responses which on the surface indicate the presence of cognitive structures may be deceptive—familiarity with the multiplication table does not prove knowledge of the multiplication operation.[43] Piaget explains that:

> The structures that characterize thought have their roots in action and in sensorimotor mechanisms deeper than linguistics. The more the structures of thought are refined, the more language is necessary for the achievement of this elaboration. Language is thus a necessary but not sufficient condition for the construction of logical operations.[44]

The verbal-cognitive program, then, emphasizes manipulative experiences, using teacher verbalization to facilitate cognitive stage development.

However, such development is not an aim of the verbal-didactic program. Kamii responds to Bereiter on this point stating:

> The most questionable sentence in Bereiter's article may be the following: "If . . . a teacher is interested in educating young children so that they will become better thinkers in the long run, the last thing he need be concerned about is getting them to attain Piaget's stage of concrete operations, since he can be asured they will all reach it anyway without his help!" The attainment of concrete operations indicates that the child's intelligence has become more mobile and better structured so that he can now reason logically. The ramifications of this achievement are enormous (e.g., the ability to measure, to add and subtract, to multiply and divide, etc.), and if the child is two years behind in this achievement, he will theoretically have 2000 hours of class time during which he will assume the role of a "slow learner" at least part of the time.[45]

Though the significance of the differences between the two approaches has yet to be fully investigated, Bissell, using John's process-product distinction, feels that the emphasis on developing a verbal *product* in the Bereiter and Engelmann program, as opposed to the emphasis on developing thought *processes* in the verbal-cognitive model is responsible for differences in effects. While children from both programs, at the end of the first grade, performed equally well on the reading vocabulary sub-test of the California Achievement Test, children in the verbal-cognitive program out-performed children in the verbal-didactic program on the reading *comprehension* sub-test.[46]

The kind of word drill found in the verbal-didactic model is purposely avoided in the child development model as it is believed to hinder the child from discovering the creative possibilities of speech.[47] Rather than simplifying and sequencing teacher utterances, Read recommends that they be expanded to convey more information:

> The nursery school teacher needs to talk with children and to give them opportunities to talk with her about their experiences. She may say, "Bring me the yellow cup on the top shelf" rather than "Bring that dish." In the first case the child's attention has been directed to a color, yellow, to a specific description, cup, rather than a loose one, dish, and to a position, top. He has a pattern for a more exact speech and way of thinking as well as a richer vocabulary.[48]

Differences between teacher verbalizations in the child development and verbal-cognitive approaches are brought into sharp focus by Blank and Solomon.[49] Perhaps the most striking difference is that in the child development approach teacher questions tend to be open-ended and not subject to the child's verification. The following sample illustrates this:

> There were boxes of small plants in the room. . . . As she entered, Julie immediately looked at these flowers. The teacher noticed this and said:

Teacher: Have you seen the flowers?
Julie: I saw a beautiful flower outside.
Teacher: A beautiful flower? What color was it?
Julie: I don't know. It's a beautiful flower.
Teacher: Did you put it in the ground?
Julie: I picked it up.
Teacher: You picked it up? What kind was it?
Julie: I don't know.
Teacher: Was it little and yellow? Maybe it was a dandelion? Did you
    plant the flower? Was it a seed and now it's a flower?
Julie: (nods.)[50]

In the verbal-cognitive approach questions tend to focus on cause-and-effect reasoning, and are "verifiable" as the following sample demonstrates:

(Julie has drawn lines on the blackboard with green chalk)
Teacher: If you put this sponge over your lines and wipe them, what will
    happen?
Julie: (moves sponge over drawing)
Teacher: What's happening to the lines, Julie?
Julie: (with surprise). They're not there anymore!
Teacher: (Holds sponge down to prevent child from lifting it) If I lift up
    the sponge, what color is going to be on the sponge?
Julie: White.
Teacher: Why white?
Julie: Green.
Teacher: Tell me why you said green? Why do you think it will be green?
Julie: Cause I wipe it off.
Teacher: What did you wipe off?
Julie: The green color.[51]

Teacher verbalization in the sensory-cognitive model is not emphasized, yet there is a specified strategy for verbal labeling. *After* the child has discriminated the large from the small, the smooth from the rough, etc., using the didactic materials, the teacher intervenes, and holding the appropriate objects says: "This is large"; "This is small." "Now, give me the large one"; "Give me the small one." Finally, the teacher pointing, asks "What is this?"[52]

Individualized versus Small Group Instruction

Another aspect of teacher-child interactions which produces major differences in the nature of the interaction is the distinction between individualized and small group (or whole class) teacher mediation. While the verbal-didactic model almost exclusively employs small group instruction techniques, teacher mediation in the sensory-cognitive model is almost wholly individualized. The verbal-cognitive and child development models employ both individualized and small group teacher mediation, the difference being one of emphasis: the verbal-cognitive model emphasizes interactions between the teacher and a small group of children, while the child development model emphasizes interactions between the teacher and the individual child.

Comparative Analysis of Child-Material Interaction

A horizontal reading of the child-material interaction indicates that the sensory-cognitive model, which views such interaction as the medium through which sensory discrimination can best be developed, ranks highest. The child development nursery school, though not as devoted to individual manipulation of structured materials, also emphasizes the importance of concrete, nonverbal learning—learning through doing. And although it may not be readily apparent, this model places greater stress on such learning than does the verbal-cognitive model. For while the activity areas of the two models are similar, and the time spent in these areas also seem comparable,* the teacher mediation accompanying child-material interactions in the verbal-cognitive model indicates its smaller reliance on *nonverbal* concrete learning. The verbal-didactic model excludes concrete manipulative experiences from its curriculum.

Let us now consider the differences in the nature of child-material interaction in the verbal-cognitive and sensory-cognitive models. While the materials used in both programs are obviously different—Montessori's structured materials versus unit blocks, art materials, and so forth—the sequencing of tasks is similar. Although we are dealing with instruction through the design of materials on the one hand, and instruction through teacher mediation on the other, both models provide for matching tasks of "same" and "different," and both then move on to ordering objects by attributes. In our discussion of the Montessori materials we noted Montessori's belief that cognitive abilities develop from sensory discrimination. The tasks, therefore, involve the introduction of increasingly finer discriminations, and the child is required to differentiate increasingly minute details.

The theoretical orientation of the verbal-cognitive model does not see sensory discrimination as the key to conceptual ordering. Piaget views the development of classification abilities as also dependent upon the child's ability to mentally select and retain a criteria for grouping. "In the cognitive orientation, therefore, the direction of programming is not toward more minute details, but toward enhancing the child's ability to select and 'hold' criteria for grouping."[53]

In the verbal-didactic model, objects or illustrations are used to clarify concepts, but are not manipulated by the child. There are work materials for reading, but these are not the kind of concrete materials presently under consideration. In fact, Bereiter and Engelmann inten-

---

*Not yet verified by research.

tionally exclude manipulative experiences on two counts. First, the curriculum of the verbal-didactic model has been specifically designed to compensate for the learning deficits of disadvantaged children, and there is little reason to believe that such children lack concrete manipulative experiences. Second—Bereiter and Engelmann cite as proof the academic success of blind children restricted in sensorimotor experiences—concrete manipulative experience is not thought to be the crucial factor in the development of academic aptitude as Hunt and others, following Piagetian theory, make it out to be.[54]

In summary, if we examine the curriculum of each model in terms of the relationship between language and concrete experience, we find the following: (a) the verbal-didactic uses objects to illustrate verbal labeling; (b) the verbal-cognitive unites teacher verbalizations with the manipulation of objects; (c) the child development has teachers and children communicating naturally in the context of ongoing work and play; and (d) the sensory-cognitive has the teacher provide a verbal label (thin, thick) *after* a concept is mastered on a sensory motor level.

Comparisons in Sequencing Content

Another interesting set of differences among the four models revealed most clearly on the child-material dimension is the way each model provides for or documents advances in learning. In the Montessori program a child's developing skills are evidenced by his mastery of new didactic materials. In the child development model, the child is using the same materials at the end of the year that he was using at the beginning. The environment is not simplified and the activities are not sequenced in terms of difficulty. Learning is not witnessed through the use of new materials, but rather through the more elaborate, refined, and imaginative use of the same materials (more elaborate block structures, more refined woodwork, more mature forms of dramatic play).[55]

Unlike the child development model, the verbal-cognitive model does start with a simplified environment to facilitate the development of pre-classification abilities. "During the first weeks of school, the block and truck areas should have shelves with only two sizes of blocks, cars, trucks, and figures of animals and people. As the year progresses, the environment can be enriched by adding more categories of items in more than two sizes."[56] Thus, the environment is made more complex as the children are able to handle increasingly difficult grouping tasks.

In the verbal-didactic model, the curriculum is sequenced in terms of difficulty and complexity of concepts. All of the children proceed through the same curriculum, but since the pace of particular groups may vary, some children cover more material than others. The child's level of achievement, then, is witnessed by the portion of the curriculum mastered.

The child-material dimension of the diagram also indicates the amount of student choice of activity. A ranking of this particular characteristic would parallel the ranking of child-material interaction.

In the Montessori method student choice is an essential ingredient. Hunt has observed that allowing the child to choose from an array of prepared materials sequenced in difficulty, allows him to solve "the problem of the match"—the problem of providing for each child that experience which "matches" his level of cognitive development.[57]

The verbal-cognitive model allows for a fair amount of student choice, but the choice is limited and defined by the teacher. During the planning session three or four fairly specific activities are outlined; while children are free to choose and change activities, they do so in a controlled fashion. Each child has a card with his name and picture on it which he hangs on a hook provided for that purpose in each activity area. If he changes activities, he is to bring his card with him and "sign in" at the new area. Finally, choice of activity is not present during the small group periods where teachers direct the activity.

Significant student choice is also present in the child development preschool. Although children are brought together for group singing, for stories, or to listen to a special visitor, they are more often allowed to move freely among the activity areas. In fact, only in the verbal-didactic program is a child's choice of activity greatly restricted—limited to the short semi-structured play period; the other models allow for flexible, (or nonexistent) scheduling so that a child involved in one activity may continue it without interruption.

Comparative Analysis of Child-Child Interaction

Turning to child-child interaction—the amount of the child's time during which his learning is being mediated through cooperative play and conversation with other children—we would expect the child development model to rank highest. As we discussed earlier, both the objectives and organization of the child development preschool aim to facilitate the social development of children. And while the child development classroom is arranged like the verbal-cognitive, the increased teacher mediation of the latter suggests that the child spends less time directly interacting with other children. Whether this is actually true would have to be verified by research. In fact, in classrooms with disadvantaged children we might find less child-child interaction if teacher mediation is absent—especially in light of Smilansky's findings that disadvantaged children engage in less sociodramatic play than advantaged children.[58]

The sensory-cognitive model does not discourage child-child interactions. Children may work together washing dishes or watering plants, or may engage in parallel play, working side by side on separate tasks. Montessori placed great emphasis on children's ability to learn from watching and imitating one another. Thus, the parallel play and mixed aged grouping (younger children learning from older children) are an important part of the nature of child-child interaction in this model. Nevertheless, since many of the Montessori activities can only be carried out individually we would expect to see less child-child interaction. Moreover, sociodramatic play, a major vehicle for child-child interaction, is omitted.

We can feel safe in describing child-child interaction as only incidental to the small group instruction sessions in the verbal-didactic classroom. Children do need to learn the appropriate behaviors for small group instruction, but learning to cooperate in this setting means attending to the teacher, not talking with your neighbor.

Sociodramatic and Symbolic Play

One of the subsets of the child-child dimension which deserves further elaboration is the position each model takes in regard to sociodramatic and symbolic play. Both the child development and verbal-cognitive models provide opportunities for sociodramatic play and view such play as an important component of the curriculum. As we noted earlier, the verbal-cognitive model includes teacher participation in the child's play while the child development model does not. There are also differences between the objectives and rationale each model provides for the inclusion of dramatic play. The child development model views dramatic play as an avenue for creativity and self expression, as a vehicle for social development, and as a medium through which children can work through emotional conflicts and traumatic experiences. The verbal-cognitive model, while incorporating the social-emotional objectives of the child development view, gives equal, if not more, emphasis to the cognitive components of such play:

> The major goals in using sociodramatic play as a teaching device are to develop the concentration and attention skills of the child: to help him integrate scattered experiences; and to enable him to consider possibilities in his mind as well as with his hands, that is, to engage in "make-believe" rather than depend wholly on toys . . . through sociodramatic play, the child develops his ability to use symbols and broadens his comprehension of the relationships among things and events in his environment.[59]

Unlike the verbal-cognitive and child development models, the Montessori method does not encourage sociodramatic play. Montessori's exclusion of symbolic and dramatic play followed from her observation that young children have difficulty in distinguishing between reality and fantasy. She believed that the preschool could facilitate this differentiation by adopting a "reality orientation": providing children with an environment in which "real" adult activities, such as cleaning and polishing, could be carried out.

An alternative view is expressed by Kohlberg who objects to Montessori's exclusion of dramatic play on the grounds that a child's ability to distinguish between reality and appearance develops naturally:

> The young child's involvement in symbolic play is neither an unhealthy preoccupation with fantasy, nor, in the adult sense, a manifestation of creativity. Its modulation and decline with age is not the stifling of the child by adult repression but the result of cognitive growth.[60]

The verbal-didactic model's exclusion of sociodramatic play stems more from practical than theoretical considerations. The disadvantaged child has a limited number of hours to spend in the preschool, and selectivity of content is therefore crucial. Bereiter and Engelmann, observing that children can engage in sociodramatic play out of school anyway, consider it less essential to future academic success.

Relationship Between Social-Emotional and Cognitive Development

Another interesting set of differences which are related to the design of child-child interactions is the position each model takes regarding the relationship between social-emotional and cognitive growth. The child development model views the child's ability to learn as dependent upon his emotional well-being. An underlying theme of this position is perhaps best expressed by Elkind's statement: "An emotionally distraught preschooler is cognitively disorganized as well."[61] The primary concern is to enhance the child's self concept and social competence in order to facilitate his intellectual growth.

The verbal-didactic model takes the opposite position. The child's academic achievement is viewed as a catalyst for the development of self-esteem, which is seen as a natural by-product of the program. Bereiter and Engelmann point out that a good teacher-child relationship can develop in a direct teaching situation as well as in a play-oriented classroom.

If we depict the child development position that social-emotional development feeds cognitive development as follows:

social-emotional ──────────────→ cognitive;

and reverse the direction of the arrow in the case of the verbal-didactic model:

social-emotional ←────────────── cognitive;

then we can represent the verbal-cognitive position with arrows going in both directions:

social-emotional ⇄──────────────⇄ cognitive.

Kohlberg writes: "According to Piaget, social development, play, and art all have large cognitive-structural components and contribute to, and are contributed by, cognitive development in the narrower sense."[62]

Unlike the other models, the Montessori program emphasizes individual cognitive activity. Kohlberg, discussing the implications of a Montessori program on social development—especially as it applies to disadvantaged children—stresses the reciprocity between cognitive and social-emotional development: "cognitive maturity appears to be the prime personality determinant of peer cooperation."[63] He goes on to point out that "some of the most striking and obvious cognitive defects of culturally disadvantaged children are defects in attention. . . . There is little doubt that either sustained teacher-pupil dyads or solitary or parallel task-activities much more easily sustain prolonged and stable attentional behavior than do group programs."[64] Kohlberg argues, then, that the "stimulation of cognitive development by the school may be both easier to accomplish and more important in serving the long-range social development of the child than either direct efforts to change the child's deeper emotional needs or the imposition of adult social authority upon him."[65]

Summary

As the foregoing comparative analysis indicates, the various educational approaches emphasize different kinds of learnings. Each has a different sense of what is most important to a child's education. The various foci on social-emotional growth, cognitive stimulation, sensory discrimination, and academic work, reflect their different theoretical positions in regard to growth and learning. We have tried to highlight some of the major theoretical differences of the preschool curriculum models and to explain how these differences relate to the delineation of teaching strategies and the design of curriculum materials. We have proposed a way of conceptualizing differences in preschool educational approaches as a function of the interactions emphasized by each program, and suggested that these interactions are also those most consciously sequenced. Finally, we have tried to investigate not only the comparative emphasis of "types" of interaction, but also differences in the nature and quality of each type of interaction in the several models.

Comparative Efficacy of Program Models

We have contrasted and accentuated the differences among various preschool education approaches. With evaluations from Head Start and other experimental intervention programs now available, what have we learned about the relative effectiveness of various curriculum models?

In a 1967 paper "Preschool Programs: Preliminary Findings," Weikart reviews the intervention evaluation literature to that date stating that "the debate between the so-called traditional (child development) and structured methods seems to be over. The traditional nursery school methods . . . are ineffective in accomplishing the basic goals of preschool intervention with the disadvantaged child."[66] Since 1968 Weikart has been directing a preschool curriculum demonstration project to test, in a controlled study, three of the models discussed in this paper for their impact on the cognitive, social-emotional, and academic growth of disadvantaged children. The three models studied were the verbal-didactic, the verbal-cognitive, and the child development. While the first two are truly representative of the models we have discussed, the child development or "unit-based" model included more deliberately planned activities and made greater use of themes to organize them than a traditional child development program. As of 1969 Weikart reports: "In analyzing the data from intelligence tests, teacher ratings, and classroom observations, *no statistically significant differences in results have been found between the programs. The gains in intelligence tests are unusually high in all three programs.*"[67]

In trying to understand the Ypsilanti findings, Weikart points to a number of characteristics common to all three programs which could be expected to affect the quality of the results. Two of the most striking characteristics were: (a) involvement of the mother—the classroom experience was supplemented with a home teaching component where children were tutored individually, and where the mother was actively involved in the education of her child* and (b) the staff model—team teaching with two teachers and aides for each class of less than twenty pupils; extensive planning; supervision. One almost needs to restate the findings as: given well trained enthusiastic teachers and aides, a 1-4or5 adult-pupil ratio, parent involvement and home teaching, a well-equipped classroom and well planned day, good supervision and close cooperation—curriculum, per se, does not produce differences!

The element of extensive planning in the Weikart project recalls our characterization of educational programs as "conscious designs." To quote from the project report:

> Essential to the demonstration aspect of the project is that all three programs have clearly defined week-by-week goals. The curriculum implementation follows a carefully planned daily program designed by the teachers themselves to achieve the goals of each curriculum. . . . Planning forces the teacher to devote particular attention to the use of time in the classroom and to the goals of her curriculum. It provides opportunity for an ongoing review of curriculum effectiveness.[68]

This planning was in evidence operationally. While all three programs *were* different, Courtney Cazden was able to make the following

---

*The home teaching component of the project is being eliminated this year to control for this effect.

observation: "All the programs get the children to focus and sustain attention and inhibit random, purposeless activity in favor of deliberate and planned action." [69] In other words, with extensive planning and supervision all of the teachers were effective in engaging children in productive goal-directed activity. This is a particularly important factor since the models we have discussed make different demands on teachers. The verbal-didactic model, for example, could be characterized as relatively "teacher-proof" in the sense that the curriculum and teaching strategies have been elaborated in detail. Others, particularly the child development model, are "teacher-dependent." While a philosophy is present and general guidelines as to appropriate activities are available, the job of operationalizing that philosophy and capitalizing on learning experiences on a day-to-day and moment-to-moment basis is left to the ingenuity, resourcefulness, skill and experience of the individual teacher. A common theme of the child development nursery school literature states that the teacher is the most significant factor in the effectiveness of the program. [70]

The seemingly disappointing results of Head Start—where programs were based largely on the child development model—may have reflected the teacher-dependent nature of the model. It is easy to understand how evaluation findings would favor those experimental programs where specific goals were consciously being made operational. *

Let us now examine the comparative evaluation studies which included Montessori programs. In both the Karnes (Urbana, Illinois) and DiLorenzo (New York State) studies, five program models were compared for effectiveness, four of which resemble those discussed in this essay. The fifth, labeled "community-integrated" is essentially a child development approach which includes children from different socio economic backgrounds. In both studies the children in the sensory-cognitive and community-integrated programs showed poor gains as compared with those in the verbal-didactic and verbal-cognitive programs. Children in the child development program placed in the middle. [71]

Yet, in Kohlberg's study of a Montessori program large gains were reported. [72] It is important to note, however, that though this was a Montessori program, it differed from the traditional sensory-cognitive model in that efforts were made to increase verbalization and representational play. Here, the effectiveness of the program seems to indicate

---

*Our distinction of "teacher-dependent" as opposed to "teacher-proof" models is perhaps the characteristic which Weikart (1967) was trying to clarify by categorizing programs along a continuum of "structuredness." His classification seems to present an attempt to rank programs by the degree to which they specify what the teacher is going to do during the day (how he will spend his time and what he will say) and the extent to which the children's experiences are predetermined and carried out in a prescribed manner. While such a distinction is important in that it seems to represent a characteristic of programs which may help to explain differences in effects when they arise, as demonstrated in the section on topology of curriculum models, it falls short as a viable scheme of classification.

that an added emphasis on language development may make a difference.†

While the Karnes and DiLorenzo studies are particularly interesting in that the *relative* efficacy of the different program models was the same in both studies, an even more pertinent finding—and one that supports the belief that planning is the crucial variable—was that "all of the programs in New York State were less effective than similar programs in Urbana."[73] The major difference between the two intervention efforts was that the New York State programs "were generally larger and less supervised, with personnel who were not as well trained and goals that were not as well formulated as their Urbana counterparts."[74] In other words, the differences among types of curriculum models at any one level of planning (high planned or low planned) were far smaller than differences between the two modes of planning.*

Our brief review of the evaluation literature indicates that other than the inclusion of an emphasis on language, curriculum components are less crucial to a program's effectiveness than the planning component. However, this conclusion must remain tentative owing not only to conflicting evaluation reports, but also to the weaknesses in assessment techniques and the state of the art of evaluation at the preschool level. Sophisticated instruments with which to measure such elusive quantities as self-esteem and social development are not available. Even in the cognitive realm, the IQ test and other instruments used to assess preschool gains were never intended for that purpose. Moreover, very little has been done to analyze differences in programs, such as those discussed in this paper, so as to be able to identify variables which affect program outcomes. Rather, the evaluations are based on program labels with little descriptive information or observational research documenting how children and teachers *actually* spend their time. Consequently, attempts to explain results as a function of differences in program models are still premature.

If the planning variable does prove to be salient, however, the implications for the role of curriculum development are clear. The development of additional materials can go far toward supporting teachers in their planning efforts. Especially in the case of teacher-dependent models, a more specific elaboration of teaching strategies is needed so that teachers can learn to be as effective as possible in helping children learn.

---

† This probably also reflects the fact that assessment instruments emphasize language abilities.

*For a full examination of the question of comparative effectiveness see Joan Bissell, *The Cognitive Effects of Pre-School Programs for Disadvantaged Children,* a thesis presented to Harvard University, 1970. One of Bissell's interesting findings is that the degree to which children are disadvantaged apparently affects which program they will benefit from most. The verbal-didactic and verbal-cognitive programs "tend to be most effective with the *most* disadvantaged of lower-class children or to be equally effective with all lower-class children, . . . (while the child development programs) tend to be most effective with the *least* disadvantaged of lower-class children."

References

1. See L. Kohlberg, "Early Education: A Cognitive-Developmental View," *Child Development*, 39 (1968), pp. 1044–1055.

2. C. Kamii, "Evaluating Pupil Learning in Preschool Education: Socio-Emotional, Perceptual-Motor, and Cognitive Objectives," in B. S. Bloom, T. Hastings, and G. Madaus (eds.), *Formative and Summative Evaluation of Student Learning* (New York: McGraw-Hill, in press).

3. L. Kohlberg, "Early Education: A Cognitive-Developmental View," *Child Development*, 339 (1968a), pp. 1013–1062.

4. D. P. Weikart, "Preschool Programs: Preliminary Findings," *Journal of Special Education*, 1 (1967), pp. 163–181.

5. *Ibid.*

6. M. B. Karnes, "Research and Development Program on Preschool Disadvantaged Children," Final Report, vol. 1, University of Illinois, Contract No. OE-6-10-235, U.S. Office of Education (1969).

7. C. Bereiter and S. Engelmann, *Teaching Disadvantaged Children in the Preschool* (Englewood Cliffs, N.J.: Prentice-Hall, 1966); Katherine Read, *The Nursery School: A Human Relations Laboratory*, 4th ed. (Philadelphia: W. B. Saunders, 1966); M. Montessori, *Dr. Montessori's Own Handbook* (1914) (New York: Schocken, 1965); D. P. Weikart, C. K. Kamii, and N. L. Radin, "Perry Preschool Project Report," in D. P. Weikart (ed.), *Preschool Intervention: A Preliminary Report of the Perry Preschool Project* (Ann Arbor, Mich.: Campus Publishers, 1967); c.f. Weikart, "Preschool Programs"; C. K. Kamii and N. L. Radin, "A Framework for a Preschool Curriculum Based on Some Piagetian Concepts," *The Journal of Creative Behavior*, 1 (1967 summer).

8. See Bereiter and Engelmann, *Teaching Disadvantaged Children*, pp. 48–49, for a complete list of objectives.

9. Kohlberg, "Early Education," p. 3.

10. Bereiter and Engelmann, *Teaching Disadvantaged Children*, p. 49.

11. Kohlberg, "Early Education," p. 105.

12. A detailed description of Montessori's didactic materials and activities can be found in *Dr. Montessori's Own Handbook*.

13. *Ibid.*, pp. 66.

14. *Ibid.*, pp. 83–85.

15. *Ibid.*, p. 57.

16. L. Kohlberg, "Montessori with the Culturally Disadvantaged: A Cognitive-Developmental Interpretation and Some Research Findings," pp. 105–118, in R. K. Hess and R. M. Bear (eds.), *Early Education* (Chicago: Aldine, 1968); also D. Elkind, "Piaget and Montessori," *Harvard Educational Review*, 37 (1967).

17. For a complete list of objectives, see Kamii, "Evaluating Pupil Learning."

18. Read, *The Nursery School*; Kamii, "Evaluating Pupil Learning."

19. A. Frazier (ed.), *Early Childhood Education Today* (U.S.A.: Association for Supervision and Curriculum Development, 1968).

20. Read, pp. 113–123.

21. *Ibid.*, p. 101.

22. P. S. Sears and E. M. Dowley, "Research on Teaching in the Nursery School," p. 864, in N. C. Gage (ed.), *Handbook of Research on Teaching* (Chicago: Rand McNally, 1963).

23. Read, illustrations, p. 130.

24. Erik H. Erikson, *Childhood and Society*, 2nd ed. (New York: Norton, 1963).

25. Kohlberg, "Early Education," p. 11.

26. For a complete listing of objectives, see Kamii, "Evaluating Pupil Learning"; Kamii and Radin, "Framework for Preschool Curriculum"; H. D. Sonquist and C. K. Kamii, "Applying Some Piagetian Concepts in the Classroom for the Disadvantaged," in D. P. Weikart (ed.), *Preschool Intervention: A Preliminary Report of the Perry Preschool Project* (Ann Arbor, Mich.: Campus Publishers, 1967); Weikart, Kamii, and Radin, "Perry Preschool Project Report."

27. Sonquist and Kamii, p. 92; cf. Peter H. Wolff, "The Developmental Psychologies of Jean Piaget and Psychoanalysis," *Psychological Issues*, 2 (1960), Monograph 5.

28. *Ibid.*, p. 94.

29. *Ibid.*, p. 98.

30. Sara Smilansky, *The Effects of Socio-dramatic Play on Disadvantaged Children* (New York: John Wiley, 1968).

31. *Ibid.*, p. 72.

32. *Ibid.*, p. 3.

33. *Ibid.*, p. 98.

34. *Ibid.*, p. 102.

35. *Ibid.*

36. Sonquist and Kamii, p. 101.

37. Weikart, Kamii, and Radin, p. 59.

38. Sonquist and Kamii, p. 96.

39. M. Blank and F. Solomon, "A Tutorial Language Program to Develop Abstract Thinking in Socially Disadvantaged Preschool Children," *Child Development*, 39 (1968), p. 380.

40. Kevin Seifert, "Comparison of Verbal Interaction in Two Preschool Programs," *Young Children* (September 1969), pp. 350–355.

41. Bereiter and Engelmann, pp. 107–109.

42. Kohlberg, "Early Education," pp. 1039–1044; Sarah Moskovitz, "Some Assumptions Underlying the Bereiter Approach," *Young Children*, 24 (October 1968), pp. 24–31.

43. L. Kohlberg, "Reply to Bereiter's Statement on 'The Educational Implication of Kohlberg's "Cognitive-Developmental" View,'" in *Interchange, A Journal of Educational Studies*, 1 (April 1970), pp. 40–49.

44. Kohlberg, "Early Education," p. 1042.

45. C. Kamii, "Piaget's Theory and Specific Instruction: A Response to Bereiter and Kohlberg," in *Interchange, A Journal of Educational Studies*, 1 (April 1970), pp. 33–40.

46. Joan Bissell, unpublished paper, 1970.

47. Read, p. 301.

48. *Ibid.*, p. 66.

49. M. Blank and F. Solomon, "How Shall the Disadvantaged Be Taught?" *Child Development*, 40 (1969), pp. 47–61.

50. *Ibid.*, pp. 56–57.

51. *Ibid.*, p. 55.

52. M. Montessori, *The Montessori Method*, (Frederick Stokes, 1912; reprinted

Cambridge, Mass.: Robert Bentley, 1965), pp. 124–125.

53. Kamii and Radin, p. 321.

54. Bereiter and Engelmann, p. 29.

55. M. Lay, "Comparisons of Preschool Programs on Selected Structural Dimensions," second presentation in symposium on *Analyzing Preschool Environments* at American Education Research Association Meeting (February 1969), p. 7.

56. Sonquist and Kamii, p. 99.

57. J. McV. Hunt, "Revisiting Montessori," introduction to M. Montessori, *The Montessori Method* (New York: Schocken Books, 1964). Reprinted in J. L. Frost (ed.), *Early Childhood Education Rediscovered* (New York: Holt, 1968), p. 120.

58. Smilansky, 1968.

59. C. Silverman (ed.), *Ypsilanti Preschool Curriculum Demonstration Project* (October 1969), pp. 14–15.

60. Kohlberg, "Montessori with the Culturally Disadvantaged," p. 108.

61. David Elkind, "The Case for the Academic Preschool: Fact or Fiction?" *Young Children*, xxv, #3 (1970).

62. Kohlberg, "Early Education," p. 1014.

63. _____, "Montessori," p. 111.

64. _____, "Early Education," p. 109

65. _____, "Montessori," p. 111.

66. Weikart, "Preschool Programs," p. 180.

67. Silverman, p. 27.

68. *Ibid.*, pp. 25–26.

69. C. B. Cazden, personal communication.

70. Read, *The Nursery School*.

71. Karnes, "Research and Development Program"; L. T. DiLorenzo and R. Salter, "An Evaluative Study of Prekindergarten Programs for Educationally Disadvantaged Children," *Exceptional Children*, 35 (1968), pp. 111–119.

72. Kohlberg, "Montessori."

73. Bissell, unpublished paper, 1970.

74. *Ibid.*

29 Some Problems in the Evaluation of Preschool Intervention Programs

Joseph Glick

In February, 1966 Dr. Glick participated in a Conference on Pre-School Education, *sponsored by The Committee on Learning and the Educational Process (Social Science Research Council) in Chicago. His article raises sobering issues of theoretical and practical importance about the problems of evaluating intervention programs at the preschool level. He demonstrates the need for a developmental framework in interpreting effects and conducting research.*

To express doubts about a conference such as this one makes me feel a little like Caliban plotting against a brave new world with such wondrous people in it. But I have doubts and feel a need for more critical and analytic thinking concerning the area of preschool intervention. By this I mean to indicate that maybe we have not clearly enough identified the problem or assessed the nature and implications of our interventions. My feeling is that we have not learned the lessons of our history well—we might be in danger of eclecticizing when we should be sharpening the issues.

In the following, I should like to formalize these feelings in terms of several dimensions of analysis: (1) a distinction between performance and capability; (2) a distinction between process and achievement; and (3) considerations about the nature of developmental change.

Performance and Capability

The distinction between the performance of a particular act and the capability to perform that act is a commonsense distinction which may have profound consequences for assessment and attempts at improvements of the "deficits" of the culturally disadvantaged.

If we do not pay serious attention in our thinking to the probable discrepancies between performance and the ability to perform, we are likely to make several interrelated assumptions which may be in error. First, we are likely to interpret performance measures such as intelligence test scores as reflecting some underlying cognitive structure which we call intelligence. Second, we are likely to interpret changes in test

Reprinted from Robert D. Hess and Roberta Meyer Bear, editors, *Early Education* (Chicago: Aldine Publishing Company, 1968); copyright © 1968 by Robert D. Hess and Roberta Meyer Bear. Joseph Glick, formerly of the University of Minnesota, is now with the Developmental Psychology Program, City University of New York.

score to reflect some change in underlying ability. Third, we are likely to relate this "change in ability" to the interventions that we have specifically planned.

In keeping with these assumptions, we have been regaled with reports of IQ changes of substantial degree which are presumed to reflect some change in intellectual capacity achieved by our intervention programs. To be sure, many of these programs have been so broad-scaled as not to allow for the particular assessment of the particular kinds of experiences provided and their particular effects on IQ. Nonetheless, we all react with a good deal of optimism when presented with such data.

Perhaps, however, this optimism may be a bit tempered by considerations as to what has been changed by our interventions. Is it an underlying ability? If so, of what type? Or is it rather the "nonunderlying ability" of being motivated to look good on IQ tests?

If we keep in mind the distinction between performance and capability, these questions arise. Some recent work by Zigler and his associates has suggested that Binet scores are not necessarily measures of cognitive abilities alone. They may, in fact, be looked at as being multiply determined by cognitive capabilities and other (possibly) motivational factors. In a recent and as yet unpublished study, Zigler and Butterfield (1967) have shown that Binet scores for underprivileged children vary by a mean of ten points depending upon whether the child is tested under standard testing conditions or under conditions designed to draw out the child and thus to obtain his optimal level of performance. In addition to assessing the difference between optimal and standard forms of testing IQ, Zigler and Butterfield compared both of these measures on children prior to their entering a preschool nursery program and after seven months in that program. The rather striking finding of this study was that tested IQ (under standard test conditions) showed a rise during the course of the year, while optimal IQ measures showed no corresponding increase. Data such as this suggest the importance of the distinction between performance on a test and capability to perform. If we take the optimal testing condition as a rough estimate of "underlying ability," the data show that there is no change in ability as a function of the preschool intervention. Where the changes have occurred, however, is in the area of the *relationship* between *ability* and *performance*. Here it was shown that the difference between standard tests and optimal tests decreased as a function of the preschool intervention. These data caution us against being overoptimistic in our assessments of changes in intellectual structure coincident with preschool intervention programs.

This observation in no way detracts from the presumably beneficial effects of preschool intervention. It does suggest, however, that our optimism may be misplaced. It appears that we are not producing "supermen" or restoring "normalcy" to "deficient" men by instilling cognitive factors which normally would not occur. We may, in fact, merely be producing children who are well motivated to "play the game." In the school situation, this is extremely important. However, I believe we should recognize that many false conflicts are introduced by interpretation of IQ changes due to preschool intervention as fundamental changes in cognitive structure. (Additionally, with the current changes of our concepts of cognition, it becomes more and more difficult to see either change or lack of changes in IQ scores as having relevance to statements about cognitive structures.)

Process versus Achievement

A second analytic dimension to keep in mind in evaluating preschool programs is a distinction that was made by Heinz Werner in 1937 between behavioral achievement and the process or structure underlying the achievement. This distinction is closely allied to the performance-capability distinction described above. It differs from it, though, in significant ways. While the "performance-capability" distinction refers to the possibility that different behavioral outcomes (for example, changes in IQ scores) might be subserved by the same cognitive structures, the process-achievement distinction refers to the possibility that the "same" behavioral outcome may be subserved by different structures.

The basic notion focused on in the process-achievement distinction is that a given outcome in behavior can be achieved by means of a variety of analogous processes. These processes may be ranked from developmentally *more primitive* to developmentally *more advanced,* although in restricted situations the behavioral outcomes may in fact be identical.

Two examples might be offered here. First, let us consider the behavioral "achievement" of locomoting between point A and point B. If we take as our criterion measure of this achievement the time taken in traversing the distance between these points, we might be able to show that there is little difference between a child of one year and a child of two years of age. Of course, what is obscured in this analysis is that one child traverses the distance by crawling and the other by walking. While this example is intentionally gross, the distinction between process and achievement can be applied more subtly, as is attested to in Collin's paper.

A second example might serve to drive this point home. There is a current controversy in the child development literature, centered around Piaget's work, about the age at which concrete transitivity of length is achieved. Originally, the achievement of the ability to integrate two propositions of the form $A > B: B > C$ into a transitive series ($A > B > C$) so that $A > C$, had been placed at about the age of seven years. Braine, utilizing arguments derived from a performance-competence distinction (Braine, 1959) ostensibly showed that when sources of verbal confusion are eliminated, children are able to make concrete transitive judgments by about the age of five years. Smedslund (1963), arguing from a process-

achievement distinction, attempted to show that the criterion performance which Braine interpreted as indicating transitivity could be subserved by a developmentally lower process which *in restricted situations*
yields results which look like transitive judgments. By introducing a
slightly different set of conditions, Smedslund was able to demonstrate
that a "transitive" judgment may in fact be achieved on the basis of a
"non-transitive" hypothesis. More recent work by Glick and Wapner
(1966) tends to substantiate this claim. Although the issues at stake have
not been resolved, this controversy has served to indicate the centrality
of both the performance-competence distinction, and the process-achievement distinction for developmental analysis (Smedslund, 1965).

These illustrations indicate potential sources of difficulty in evaluating
the effects of any preschool program. One may be able to show, for
example, that in achievement on certain criterion performances there
may be vast "beneficial" effects of either preschool intervention in a
remedial sense or in terms of making younger kids precocious. However,
until investigation is made which is oriented toward uncovering the
basic processes underlying the achievement, one must take this evidence
in a rather critical vein. It is not enough to simply demonstrate that
criterion performances (that is, achievements) increase with age or are
changed by intervention. What is necessary in order to make any argument which is basic to developmental questions is to show that the processes underlying the achievements have in fact been shifted up to a
higher developmental level. Evidence for such "process" changes may be
obtained by use of multisituational designs oriented toward the investigation of any shift in factors that determine behavior, or from close
analysis of the *patterns* of responses in any given situation.

The Nature of Developmental Change

The issues involved in the process-achievement distinction may be
extended in terms of their implications for our notions of developmental
change, and particularly for our notions of change induced by preschool
interventions.

From the previous analysis of the process-achievement distinction, the
possibility may be raised that intervention programs may lead to achievement gains, but without any real changes in process. Children may
improve "achievements" simply because developmentally primitive processes have been brought out. At any rate, there have been few, if any,
investigations oriented toward this question—few transfer designs have
been used, and few studies have gone into detailed analysis of the patterns of response.

This ambiguity in previous data must be resolved, since one of the
critical issues in the analysis of developmental change is involved. This
issue may be phrased in terms of a question—"To what extent does the
availability of primitive means of achieving criterial performance hinder

or help the development of developmentally more advanced means of achieving that performance?"

There is evidence on this issue from the field of perceptual pathologies. Goldstein (1939) and S. C. McLaughlin (1964) have indicated that in cases of amblyopia, adaptation to this condition is hindered by attempts to maintain function in the weaker eye. It is in this case the persistence of an earlier mode of adaptation that hinders attempts at achieving a new level of adaptation. Similar deficits in higher functioning due to the maintaining of developmentally more primitive means of adaptation have been reported by Luriia (1960) in the case of a subject with a well-developed memory based upon perceptual imagery, and by Luriia and Yudovitch (1959) in the case of language development in twins which was retarded by the availability of more primitive means of communication. What we have in these examples is an "einstellung" problem phrased in developmental terms.

These examples would suggest that achievements based on developmentally primitive means are something that must be overcome rather than encouraged by our intervention programs. It therefore becomes quite important to analyze changes in criterion performances in order to determine the processes being used. If we have made kids "look smarter" by encouraging the use of lower means, we may, in the end, have defeated our own purpose. For example, let us suppose we are able to teach children arithmetic at a very early age, by showing them the use of such primitive means as counting on fingers. Within a narrow range of problems, we might be quite impressed by their precocity, and, accordingly would congratulate ourselves on a stunning educational achievement. However, this optimism might be a bit tempered when we begin to wonder whether the too facile use of this means of calculation, at too early an age, might serve to impede the adoption of more sophisticated means of calculation, or the use of number systems that are not to the base 10.

An appropriate model of developmental change must take into account the "transformational characteristics" of change. Rather than development being the gradual acquisition of more and more "adult-like" behaviors, it seems to be governed by a set of different structural levels which fundamentally transform and subordinate previous levels. In addition to the remarkable observations of Piaget, a particularly striking example of this type of change may be seen in the ontogenesis of the use of strong and weak verb forms.

Observations suggest that children first learn the appropriate form of strong verb conjugations, for example "I have"—"I had," etc. Here their performance is like that of the adult. However, in subsequent development, this appropriate usage is "transformed" by the application of the weak verb rules, so that subsequently children conjugate, "I have" —"I haved," etc. Only later is this regularizing form superseded by correct usage again.

If the analysis of development in terms of a series of structural transformations is applicable, then one of our duties as researchers is to
investigate the fundamental problem of whether specific training of
performance at one level will retard or advance the transformation to
the next level of functioning. An ancillary question which applies specifically to the problem of the underprivileged concerns the question
of whether the "undertraining" of performance at a lower level hinders
subsequent transformations.

I believe that questions such as these should occupy a considerable
part of our research effort. The analysis of criterion performances alone
is insufficient to answer this question. We should shift away from being
satisfied solely with change in criterion performances. We should shift
toward the development of means of analysis of the processes underlying
performance and changes in performance.

At this stage of the game, we need a good deal of basic research. The
decisions being made now will be central to the course of the social
evolution of the underprivileged, and cannot help but have radical
implications for educational practices throughout society.

We are thus obligated to answer questions about what the nature of
our interventions are. What kind of education are we offering, and what
are our best estimates of its probable effects? Here is the area where
our responsibilities as social scientists constrain our role as social en-
gineers. Accordingly our statements must be based on research rather
than well-intentioned optimism.

30 Play Equipment for The Nursery School

Jessie Stanton and Alma Weisberg

The materials and activities employed in a school program are important in the education of the child, but they are often forgotten in the quarrels over curriculum content, financial budgeting, teacher vs. administrative control. The following article suggests some realistic and helpful materials and methods for the "preschool" program.

Introduction

This outline for nursery school equipment suggests a broad range of areas for a teacher to explore with her children rather than a prescription for material. It is hoped that the extent and variety of materials suggested will serve to stimulate the development and implementation of an educational program, challenging and satisfying the children's intellectual and emotional development.

The environment, indoors and out, often dictates greater concentration on certain materials (e.g. children living near rivers often use many varied boats). Each group of children will have individuals with special needs and interests (e.g. some children need more egg beaters for water play, finding it difficult to wait for turns) which will call for adaptation of materials or provision for extra items of equipment. Where the nursery school has more than one classroom, materials not in daily use can be shared between groups. The best guide for purchasing is the children's creative use of what the school provides during the course of a year.

It is neither expected nor desired that all schools be equipped as suggested here. Variations in the children's learning processes and experiences should and will affect the school program as much as the underlying philosophy and goals of the school influence the actual course of the curriculum. Where a school strives to enrich the cultural lives of the children, more books may be purchased, or more provision made for trips. On the other hand, schools with a sophisticated and verbal population may find some of its five-year-olds ready with preliminary experiences with writing, reading and written numbers. Any introduction of academic skills, however, should be given only to children with

Jessie Stanton, Alma Weisberg, and the faculty of the Bank Street School for Children, *Play Equipment for the Nursery School*. New York: Bank Street College of Education, 1962. Reprinted by permission.

a very fine background of experience and fund of information, and be a minor part of the total school program.

The role of the teacher cannot be overlooked in equipping a school. A teacher unfamiliar with the free use of varied art materials will probably not present more than basic materials until she gains skill and knowledge with these. A music teacher might use all of the instruments and perhaps help the children make simple instruments.

Each school's circumstances will limit its choice of materials. A one-room school will need more variety in the classroom than a school where special materials can be shared by the groups. A classroom used after school for other purposes may need extra storage facilities. A benevolent climate and a good outdoor area may make greater use of the natural environment and space, and need less indoor material. The school's budget may limit equipment purchase; here great ingenuity will be needed in finding and using free and inexpensive materials.

But while good materials support the children's independent explorations and help the teacher in carrying through her work, the value of the school program will be measured finally by the effectiveness of its practices, based on a clearly defined educational philosophy. A vital program is one which enlists the interest of each child in the group, working actively and comfortably under the guidance of a warm and skillful teacher.

For Block Play

Unit blocks have become a staple material in nursery schools and many primary grade classrooms because they are an unstructured material challenging the child to rebuild and recreate, in miniature, his conception of the world about him. His structures communicate his ideas and can therefore be shared and used by others. The mathematical relationships of block sizes and shapes offer him early experience with tangible arithmetic and geometric facts.

A new block shape, an interesting accessory, a well-timed question, or rare help with engineering problems confronting a child, encourage a child to implement and augment his ideas. Children gain greatest satisfaction, growing skill, and deepest learning when the teacher observes their work, limits her comments and questions to the most meaningful aspects which the children perceive in their work.

Where floor space permits, the experienced builder enjoys seeing his building kept up, often for a few days, as he adds to his scheme and uses it as a basis for dramatic play.

As children have more experience with blocks, greater varieties and quantities may be needed. Four-year-olds who have used blocks actively for a year or two, for example, will often use even more blocks than suggested for five-year-olds.

For Block Play

Set of blocks for a group of 15-20 children

	3 Years	4 Years	5 Years
Half units	48	48	60
Units	108	192	220
Double Units	96	140	190
Quadruple Units	48	48	72
Pillars	24	48	72
Large cylinders	20	24	32
Small cylinders	20	32	40
Circular curves	12	16	20
Elliptical curves	8	16	20
Pairs of triangles (large)	4	8	12
Pairs of triangles (small)	8	16	18
Floor boards (11″)	12	30	60
Roof boards (22″) (not illustrated)		12	20
Ramps	12	32	40
Half pillars (not illustrated)		12	16
Y switches	2	2	4
Right angle switches, and/or X switches (not illustrated)		4	8

Block Forms and Names

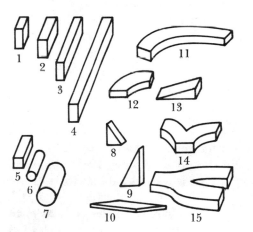

1 Half Unit
2 Unit
3 Double Unit
4 Quadruple Unit
5 Pillar
6 Small Cylinder
7 Large Cylinder
8 Small Triangle
9 Large Triangle
10 Floor Board
11 Elliptical Curve
12 Circular Curve
13 Small Ramp
14 Right Angle Switch
15 Y Switch

Block Accessories

The suggested materials below demonstrate the range of materials children use to augment not only the block buildings but their play with the structures. While the figures, animals and vehicles are sufficiently varied to fulfill children's most recurrent themes, often the child's keen observation and commitment to realistic detail requires other supplementary materials. There is often deeper satisfaction and a greater variety of imaginative themes when materials are suggestive of many uses rather than of a single function.

Rubber or wooden wedgie figures (adults about 5" high)

2 families: mother, father, boy, girl, baby, grandparents

12 community figures, farmers, workmen, milkmen, doctors, firemen, etc.

16 farm and domestic animals: cow, bull, calf, 2 horses, colt, sheep, ram, lamb, 2 pigs, piglets, cat, dog, etc.

1 set zoo animals

Vehicles (Plastic, rubber or wood recommended for younger children. Rounded-edge metal is safe for older children)

2 sets trains and tracks (for older children), 2 sets interlocking trains (sand-trains) (for younger children)

24 small cars, airplanes, busses, assorted trucks and tractor (according to environment). Axles should be enclosed to prevent loss of wheels.

4 jumbo trucks (if floor space permits)

6 small and large boats (tugboats, barges, liners, ferries, etc., according to environment)

Other accessories (May be stored in open window boxes or sturdy baskets)

1 box one-inch kindergarten cubes (often used for decoration)
Small pieces of fabric, rug, and linoleum samples
Set of sturdy wooden doll-house furniture
Large hollow building blocks
Pulleys, gears
Batteries, wire, bulbs
String, thumbtacks
Colored paper or cellophane

Block Storage

Block cabinets should be sturdy, on a 3" baseboard, using ¾" x 12" lumber, have a solid back, and should be divided into cubicles for orderly storage. The overall dimensions for a block cabinet for 15 three-year-olds might be 4'6" x 3' high.

Cubicles should be 11¾" high, with small cubicles (13" wide) for half units, cylinders, ramps, floor boards, pillars; medium cubicles (18" wide) for trains, cube boxes, triangles, switches, curves, arches, small cars and boats; large cubicles (24"-37" wide) for units, double units, quadruple units, roof boards, animals, people, other accessories.

Blocks should be presented in their shelves in such a way that their mathematical relationships can be perceived in terms of sizes and of categories of shapes. They should be arranged with the following considerations: large blocks and large vehicles should be near the bottom both for safety in removal and proper weighting of cabinet; each shape and type of accessory should have its own space for easier finding and orderly pick-up; the most popular shapes (units, double units, quadruple units) should be divided, where quantity is sufficient, to encourage building in front of different parts of the shelving (younger children and novices tend to build immediately in front of the shelves). Longer and lower cabinets (or two smaller cabinets) help in dispersing areas in which children build.

For Household and Dramatic Play

Five-year-olds with school experience often need equipment inviting dramatic play, but less suggestive of specific housekeeping functions: e.g. a low cabinet, rather than a stove, a sturdy small cot, which could be a seat or bed, a table with drawers for office desk or dressing table, etc.

> Rubber dolls
> Washable doll clothes with large snaps or buttons
> Large doll bed or cot (long and sturdy enough so a child can get into it) (for younger children)
> Smaller doll bed
> Blankets (several sizes, not wool)
> Mattresses for doll beds
> Fabric lengths for sheets, blankets and doll wrappers
> Small pillows and cases
> Clothesline and clothes pins (regular size)
> Fabric lengths (for dressing up)

> Ladies' and men's hats
> Assorted workmen's hats
> Ties
> Vests
> Ladies' medium-heeled shoes and men's shoes
> Costume jewelry
> Handbags, briefcases, small valises

> Mirror
> Wooden stove (large, sturdy)
> Wooden cupboard or shelves for dishes
> Kitchen sink (large basin with work space on side)
> Table and chairs
> Small unbreakable tea set (standard size cups and saucers for younger children)
> Telephones

> Brooms (short handled)
> Dustpan and brush   } hung on hooks
> Mops (short-handled)

> Cash register (for older children)

Dress-up clothing can be hung on hooks in a cabinet or on a peg board. A small dresser is often helpful for storage of small items. Other provisions for storage might include: shelves for fabric lengths, shoe-bags, boxes for hats and handbags, etc.

Note: As children's play develops more complex themes, many materials are used in more refined modes. The water tank is often a starting place for play at cooking; water and soapsuds are then used less as a material for their own sake but rather as a material in dramatic play.

For Water Play

Sink (See Household Play)
Large, deep water tank with ledges on side for work space. (This can be a washtub on a low table, or a deep box lined with galvanized metal, with a threaded spout on the bottom for easy emptying)

Many small materials can be placed on shelves or hooks. Waterproof aprons, sponges, and mops should be nearby.

3 12″-18″ wide open shelves for storage.
Small pitchers
Water cans
Washcloths
Towels
Soap and soap dish
Sponges
Corks
Lengths of hose
Measuring cups
Funnels
Egg beaters
Ladles
Plastic bottles
Bowls of various sizes (with broad bases)
Soap suds
Straws

Manipulative Toys for Table Play

2 shelves for storage, 30″ wide, 12″ deep
Color cones
Nested blocks or barrel sets
Hammering benches
Hammer and nail sets with celotex boards
Lock boards or boxes (A board or box with locks, hinges, bolts,

doorhooks and eyes, etc. screwed on to board, or ready-made equipment from educational supply companies)

Wooden beads for stringing

Pegs and pegboards (larger pegs for younger children)—assortment

Sets of small blocks: cubes, parquetry, plastic interlocking, snap-in, etc.

8 wooden inlay puzzles of varying degrees of difficulty

Games

For three-and-a-half to five-year-olds: Picture lottoes, large dominoes, picture dominoes, etc.

Sewing and Weaving

For four-and-a-half and five-year-olds.

Sewing needles (with large eyes)

Heavy thread or wool

Needle threader

Fabric remnants

Handlooms

For Creative Art Work

Painting

Water paints (Variety of strong, clear colors, always including red, yellow, blue, black and white)

Easels (14″ from floor to trough for threes; 18″ from floor to trough for fours, 22″ from floor to trough for fives)

Newsprint paper (18″ x 24″)

Variety of paper (brown paper 36″ and 48″ wide, butcher paper in rolls, etc.) for individual and mural painting

Easel paint brushes (with long handles, ½″ and ¾″ wide)

Easel clamps or right-angle hooks on easel to hold paper

Plastic jars with tops or juice cans (use kitchen wrap for tops)

Plastic aprons or smocks

For older children: 6 sets of glass furniture coasters for individual colors, and empty coasters for mixing, small water jar and sponge for cleaning brush, placed on 10″ x 13″ aluminum cookie sheet for individual painting and color-mixing.

Crayoning and Pasting

Crayons (large hexagonal kindergarten crayons, kept in box or basket; individual boxes for each child, or 5 boxes for 15 children)

Manila drawing paper (9″ x 12″ and 12″ x 18″)

Construction paper (assorted colors) (9" x 12" x 18")

8 pairs scissors (high quality blades, blunt ends)

Bits of bright paper, cloth, feathers, lace, fabric bits, wallpaper samples, etc.

Paste (library paste, liquid pastes) and paste brushes

Cardboard, varied papers

Clay Modelling

Clay (gray, non-firing, moist; can be bought in 50 lb. tins)

Scoop

2 Plastic covered pails—8 quart size (tightly covered—to soak dried clay for re-use)

Clay boards (12" x 12") or washable table surface

Tongue depressors

Other Plastic and Creative Art Materials

Play dough: made from 3 cups flour, 1 cup salt, vegetable coloring and water added. Alum (1 tablespoon) keeps dough smooth and retards spoilage.

Storage: Play dough may be kept for a week or so if wrapped in a damp towel and put in a plastic container.

Possible accessories: Powdered sugar shaker for flour; small rolling pins; cookie cutters, tongue depressors; clay boards or washable surface; wooden mallets; for decoration: spices, lentils, macaroni shapes, etc. (Dough soon becomes an adjunct to housekeeping play.)

Finger Paint: (wheat paste and water, mixed with water paint and soap flakes can be used with safety only by children who will not taste this inedible mixture)

For three-year-olds: Primary colors (introduce one at a time)

Plastic or metal dinner trays, or plastic-top table surface

For older children: Finger paint paper or white shelving paper

For cleanup: sponges, bucket or sink nearby, rubber squeegies (for scraping up excess paint)

Stable and Mobile Materials (for children three-and-a-half and up)

Select from:

Small pieces of wood (3" x 4" approx.) for stabile bases

String—colored and white

Armature wire: 2 thicknesses

Florist wire: thin and heavier weight

Colored wooden toothpicks

Wire clippers

Stapler, cellophane tape and dispenser, masking tape

Stringable materials: macaroni, bright beads, perforex, short pieces of colored drinking straws, strips and squares of colored corrugated paper, etc.

Stapler, cellophane tape and dispenser, masking tape

Other decorative accessories: colored pipe cleaners, colored cellophane, mesh fabric bits, colored tissue papers, etc.

Other materials for art work might include: paper and paste for papier maché; white wood glue for sculptural collages on wood scraps with shells, lentils, macaroni, mosaics, buttons, sand, pebbles, metal washers, etc., small sponge pieces for sponge painting; richly colored chalks for use on drawing and construction paper, damp or dry, etc.

For Woodwork (where supervision permits; three-year-olds should begin with simple hammering, later learn to saw)

Workbench with 2 vises (24"-30" high)
4 hammers
2 crosscut saws (14")
1 rip saw (for five-year-olds)
1 drill with assorted bits
Nails with large heads or thick finishing nails (assorted lengths and widths)
Sandpaper (heavy and medium grades)
Lumber: soft pine, assorted sizes and thicknesses
Large box for lumber storage
Paint brushes ($3/4$"-$1\frac{1}{2}$") and easel paints
Rasp, file
Other Accessories:
  1 large C-clamp
  Corrugated nails and staples
  Button-molds or wooden wheels (assorted sizes)
  Lengths of dowelling
  Buttons, washers, nuts, bottle caps, corks, wire
  Hooks and eyes, hinges, screws and nuts, etc. (for older children)
  Pencils, yardstick, rulers, glue
Woodwork supplies may be supplemented with materials from other areas, e.g. fabric bits, paper, etc.
All tools should be of good quality, well balanced, kept sharpened. Children become discouraged with inefficient tools.

For Science Work

Assortment of science books
2 goldfish or other hardy fish in large bowl with pebbles, greens and snail
1 or 2 turtles in bowl with dry rock or pebble pile
Other pets: hamster, male or female guinea pig(s), chickens, ducks, rabbit, cat or dog, etc.

Pulleys, rope, etc.

Bottles, lengths of tube, corks, etc. for simple experiments

Magnets, iron filings

Terrarium and supplies

Prisms

Magnifying glass

For planting: soil, pebbles, pots or coffee tins, watering can; avocado pits, onions, potatoes, carrot tops, lentils, grapefruit seeds, pumpkin seeds, etc. for quick growing; seeds and bulbs (quick-sprouting)

For advanced five-year-olds: large indoor-outdoor thermometer; large dry-cell batteries, electric wire, flashlight bulbs and sockets, telegraph key, buzzer, buzzer switch, small screwdriver.

For Cooking (Many accessories can be used from housekeeping and water-play areas)

2 large bowls and large pot; mixing spoons, rubber scraper

Tongue depressors or blunt knives (for spreading)

2 measuring cups with clear marking

2 measuring spoon sets

Hot plate or large electric frying pan or cooker (where supervision permits)

Plastic or metal spoons

Rolling pins

Vegetable scraper

Sifters (rotary)

Food mill, etc.

For Reading and Number Skills

Carefully selected assortment for various age levels, including story anthologies. Display in book rack.

For five-year-olds (where children show interest) for introduction of reading and writing skills: ¾″ lined paper, thick (primary) pencils, chart paper, pocket charts, blackboard and chalk. For introduction of number skills, such materials as a Cuisenaire set, Katherine Stern materials, Montessori materials or other tangible numerical materials.

For Music

Piano (if space permits, it is helpful to have a piano available in school)

Triangles

Tambourines

Drums and padded drum sticks

Cymbals
Sleigh bells
Jingle clogs, American castinets, or castinets mounted on handle
Maracas
Finger cymbals
Rhythm sticks
Chromatic bells (Xylophone-type)
Auto Harp
Phonograph—3 speed
Records (carefully selected)
Music books
Note: musical instruments should be of good quality.

For Rest Time

For brief mid-morning or mid-afternoon rests: washable bath
mats or plastic mats for each child.

For rest hour: sturdy cots (nesting aluminum frame or folding
wood-frame), canvas or plastic with sheets children can put on
cot, blankets provided by home or school.

Rest-time toys: either from shelves or in special large baskets:
small manipulative toys, small dolls with wardrobe, viewers
with slides, books, portfolios of pictures, puzzles, plasticene,
boxes of tiny objects, etc.

Classroom Arrangement

The way a room is set up and the way the materials are arranged in
it are of vital importance, for this will influence the children's play and
learning. The nursery school teacher must keep in mind that the *classroom is a young child's workshop*. With this idea foremost in her mind,
she will plan purposefully. A generous amount of floorspace away from
the main traffic stream will be allocated for active block play close to
the shelves that house the blocks and block accessories. The housekeeping corner might be set up near the water play and the room's sink or
bathroom. Tables and chairs should be near the materials children use
when they work at tables, and the easels should be near the light with
water and clean-up materials nearby. The workbench should be placed
away from the quieter table work. The bookrack or shelves can form a
cozy library area. Shelf space should be provided for drying clay, a
clothes rack, perhaps, for paintings, table space for painting woodwork,
while tops of shelves are kept free for displaying children's newest work
and for plants.

A well-arranged room should have fluidity for play which moves between working areas. It should be sufficiently flexible to permit minor
rearrangement as the year progresses and play patterns change: the sink

moved closer to or separated from the housekeeping area, more space allotted for block building or table space for enthusiastic painters. Materials not presently in use can be removed to nearby storage places, available with the teacher's help, but not becoming distracting clutter. The large storage closet should be sufficiently spacious to hold materials to be introduced at different times of the year.

The total atmosphere of the room should be considered in both aesthetic and functional terms. An attractive furniture arrangement, a proper balance of colors of furniture and walls, good lighting, in fact a basic interior arrangement which provides a background for the children's work and materials are an important aspect in making a room inviting and workmanlike for children. Windows should be left free for light and air to pour in omitting heavy dust-catching draperies. The pictures on the walls should be the children's; a bulletin board might be used for a changing display of pictures representing children's current interests.

All the furniture that goes into the room must be sturdy and well built. The creative material must be provided in plenty so the children can use it freely. All materials in daily use should be presented attractively and clearly, arranged so that children can use them independently with minimum help from the teacher.

Where space permits, some large-muscle play materials from the outdoor area might also be provided indoors: a small climber, or hollow blocks, steps, slide, jumping board, slower wheel toys, etc.

Suggested Outdoor Play Equipment and Materials

All outdoor material should have two coats of weatherproof house paint; hardwoods may have several treatments with linseed oil.

For Active, Big Muscle and Dramatic Play

> Jungle Gym (small climber for three-year-olds)
> 2 Swings (where space and supervision permit)
> Ladder box
> Horizontal ladder
> Push Trucks
> Wheelbarrows
> Four-wheeled "cars" or "horses" manipulated by child's feet
> Wagons
> 2 Steering wheels on stand or mounted on large blocks
> 2 Doll carriages, or large wooden box on wheels sturdy enough to accommodate child
> Tricycles (where sufficient paved paths available)—heavy-wheeled, well-balanced and sturdy (12″ pedal wheel for three-year olds
> 16″ pedal wheel for four-year-olds
> 20″ pedal wheel for five-year-olds)

Balls (assorted sizes and colors)

Large pieces of canvas or large washable blankets (for making houses, etc.)

Rubber dolls, small blankets

Clothesline (cut in 6' length for use in dramatic play)

For Building

2 Packing cases, 42" x 30" x 30"

2 Packing cases, 35" x 23" x 16"

2 Ladders, 44" x 14" (with end cleats, rungs 8" apart)

1 6' cleated board (for making slide, see-saw, walking board)

1 8' flexible jumping board

6 Saw Horses 2' x 12"
6 Saw Horses 2' x 16" } or 8 metal or wooden "fences" with 3 rungs

8 Kegs, 15" high x 12" diameter

48 Playboards, 4' x 5½" x ¾"

24 Hollow Blocks, 5½" x 11" x 11"

12 Hollow Blocks, 5½" x 11" x 22"

For Small Muscle Play

Sandbox with cover (if there is no natural sand or dirt in school environment)

Sand

Shovels, scoops, wooden spoons (no metal shovels for young children; long-handled children's snow shovels for older children)

Small dishes and cups (metal or plastic, assorted sizes and shapes)

Strainers, collanders, sieves

Brooms, dustpans

Pails (small size, rubber, galvanized iron or soft plastic)

Paint Brushes (flat, 1½" wide, for painting with water)

Plastic or rubber trucks: loading, dump, snowplow, etc.

Outdoor Arrangements

In setting up an outdoor play space, it is necessary to plan for the utmost safety. All fixed climbing equipment should be located on a soft surface such as grass, dirt or other impact-reducing material. There should be plenty of space between each piece.

On the other hand, the building materials are more easily and safely used by children on a smooth, flat surface such as cement or black top. It is worthwhile to stack blocks, boards, kegs, etc. separately in regular places at the end of the day, so that the children can start out the next day with fresh ideas, although again as in indoors, older children will sometimes want to keep working with an attractive structure for a few days.

A shed should be built to house the movable equipment and materials that rust outdoors if left unprotected. Such a shed serves a double purpose. After the material is taken out for use, it becomes a fine play house for the children.

It is most important to provide sufficient open areas for safe running, riding or pulling wheel toys without interfering with other play. Space might also be provided in warmer weather for tables and chairs for quieter play, tubs for planting, or tanks for refreshing water play.

The same principles of arrangement apply to outdoor space as to indoor space. Thoughtful planning which takes into account the kind of activities that will be going on there will help promote creative and meaningful play.

The Role of Educational Media

31 Media and Early Childhood Education

W. C. Meierhenry and Robert E. Stepp

What role may educational media play during the early years of child-hood? This is a review of recent research and development which indicates the growing importance of artfully designed equipment in the nursery school.

There are various notions of the place of media in the education of young children. At one extreme, some McLuhan enthusiasts might propose that all the world's people, including infants and young children, are really transistors being bombarded constantly by electrons, in which case all we need to do to turn on the young learner is develop the right circuitry. Others would argue that the young learner is such a fragile bit of humanity that the main prerequisite for learning is a personal and intimate relationship with other people, particularly his parents, his family, and his peer group; since media have nothing to contribute to positive personal feelings, they have no place in learning systems. We suggest that the best answer lies somewhere between these two extremes.

There are several bases for the proposals made later on as to what media can contribute to the education of younger children. First, there is a difference between mass media and media developed for learning purposes. This is not to argue that mass media messages fail to affect behavior. Obviously, advertising especially is effective in doing this. But commercial programs are seldom designed to produce the type of behavior educators are interested in. In this article the word *media* will be shorthand to signify stimuli designed to produce a certain type of educationally approved behavior.

Second, this article is built on the premise that all young children, including those who are disadvantaged, need experience which requires

Phi Delta Kappan, March 1969. Reprinted by permission.

Mr. Meierhenry (668, University of Nebraska Chapter) is Professor of Education and Chairman, Department of Adult and Continuing Education Teachers College University of Nebraska. Mr. Stepp (932 University of Nebraska Chapter) is Professor of Educational Administration and Director of the Midwest Media Center for the Deaf at the same institution.

some restructuring on the part of the individual child. Play and creative activities which assist the child to develop self-discipline are necessary, but such activities alone are insufficient. It is necessary to push beyond natural growth stages in order to prepare for genuinely demanding intellectual tasks. This is not an endorsement of the so-called "pressure-cooker" approach; but something more than a neutral position is required concerning the stimulation and direction of a child's intellectual development.

Third, there is the distinct possibility that all cultures place far too much emphasis on verbal symbols. In fact, some of the developing nations have become aware that literacy programs can lead to discrimination between those who possess the symbols and those who do not. The writers accept the stress on language which many early childhood education specialists emphasize, but do so with some hesitancy. Man's future developments may place much greater reliance on capacity to manipulate a wide range of symbols, especially mathematical symbols, rather than, as now is the case, mainly verbal ones.

The place of media in developing more fully the capacity for handling of all types of symbols is obvious. We turn to some of the research and theory which point to the need for the in-depth study of media as they relate to the education of the child from birth through age five.

Media and the Very Young

Birth to 15 months. A number of research studies have been performed on animals featuring an almost complete absence of perceptual stimulation. Such deprivation at early stages has a permanent deleterious impact on the development of the animal.

As attention has increasingly focused on the very young child in our society, many types of study have been made. For example, orphanage babies have been placed for some time in cribs covered with white sheets. When the cribs were uncovered, the infants were able to see only a white and figureless ceiling. Children reared in such an environment were found to be very much slower in developing the capacity to differentiate among various kinds of visual configurations so necessary for beginning to read.

Studies have been carried on with infants where bumping or striking an apparatus caused movement of colorful items in the crib or threw various kinds of flashing lights on the ceiling. Infants repeatedly triggered the mechanism which produced the visual stimuli. Subsequent studies indicated the superiority of the subjects in tasks requiring visual discrimination.

Various types of experience are necessary, therefore, even in the earliest days after birth. Infants should probably be propped before television sets even if only commercial programs are being telecast in order to give appropriate stimulation and training to visual perception.

Better yet, special telecasts could be prepared which would deal not only with colors, shapes, and forms but textures as well.

Furthermore, attention should be given to affixing apparatus to the crib which can be activated by the swing of an arm or the kick of a foot. These mechanisms might produce static or moving visual displays immediately above the crib or on the ceiling.

In the earliest months of life, then, it would appear that much more attention should be given to providing visual stimuli than is now the case. Although much of early human life is given to the refinement of physical skills, there is strong evidence that a base is already being developed immediately following birth for future intellectual activity.

The Pre-linguistic Stage. A child begins to respond to language long before he can speak, of course. In order for the child to speak his native tongue with facility at a later stage, he must have exposure to spoken language at all stages, but particularly from one to three years of age. The earlier a child is exposed to a great deal of talk and conversation, the more he intuitively masters linguistic patterns.

It has been known for some time that reading to an infant helps him to learn to read early. It is pretty well accepted by researchers that the disadvantaged child is often slow to read because he fails to separate the "talk" which surrounds him from the other noises. Some research indicates that as much talk goes on in the disadvantaged as in the advantaged home, but the infant's attention is not focused on the human communication.

Other research indicates that mechanical devices are valuable in exposing an infant to linguistic patterns. Again, television can be used at this stage. Radio, particularly FM with its greater clarity, could serve. Even more to the point is the use of records and transcriptions, and most of all of tapes. With the advent of low-cost cassette tape playback machines and their ease of recording, it is even possible for a family to record its conversations for replay to provide additional contact with familiar voices and consistent linguistic patterns.

Aural discrimination training begun at birth should be continued into year one, and the period from one to three should make generous provision for methodical linguistic input.

Two and One-Half to Five. From birth to three years was a period in the child's life when major activities were predominantly of an internal nature. Therefore, media which require a limited restructuring of stimuli by the child could be used. Beginning around three, the child requires an environment which is interactive in nature, feeding back in such a way that he must begin to manipulate abstractions in order to develop his own cognitive structure.

In addition to initiating a cognitive structure, the child at this stage also begins to recognize himself as an individual and begins to sense his status and role in regard to others with whom he associates. He begins to understand that others expect much or little of him, that they accept or reject him, that they believe in him or doubt his capabilities. There is a need, therefore, to begin to give attention to the affective area—the child's feelings—lest the child's self-image and ego wither through lack of positive attention.

Because developments in both the cognitive and affective areas require interaction, either human or through media, it can be argued that some type of more definitely structured schooling should be initiated around age three to complement what the home should do. In many instances the school may find it necessary to do the entire job. The type of material and equipment needed will be similar, whether education is carried on in the home or in the school.

The media chosen for cognitive development presumably will need to be of a programmed type, so that a response made by the child to visual or auditory stimuli will present alternatives to which the child will make further responses. Most of the equipment currently available for young children tends to be one-way presentation devices. Needed additions to such equipment will display colored visuals on a small screen and auditory stimuli by means of a record. Further, they will require the child to make certain responses; when a response is correct, further new material will be presented. At this stage of human learning it is evident that equipment, along with the required programs, becomes more complex and thus more expensive. It also becomes evident that breakthroughs in the improved use of equipment are necessary. For example, such pieces of equipment as the computer (with a cathode tube or some similar display mechanism) is excellent for model cognitive development. The potential of the computer for interaction and interplay may, for practical purposes, be virtually unlimited.

One of the manufacturers of children's toys has marketed a device which requires that the child assemble blocks in a certain order to produce a correct linguistic pattern in audio form. Greater attention needs to be given to the development of such toys, games, and instructional materials. They require the active participation of the child in developing various patterns related to cognitive structure.

One of the newer developments in school construction is the creation of an environment which is related to what is being learned. For example, if a teacher wishes to create the environment in which an Eskimo lives, she merely pushes a button. The appropriate setting is called up from the computer bank and visually "sprayed" on the walls of the classroom. It is also possible to provide the auditory stimuli to accompany the visual setting and, if required, the odors as well! There is no reason why children should not be able to call up from the data bank any setting which they desire. Thus the schoolroom of the future is likely to provide a total environment for young children enabling them and their teachers to create a psychedelic setting to expedite learning.

The child of this age should see himself and others in the best possible way. First of all, he needs to know how he appears and the features of his friends. The use of mirrors should probably be more widespread in schools for such small children. In addition, the teacher should make more frequent use of the 35mm and 8mm cameras and of tape recorders to help the young children to know themselves and to gain confidence in their own abilities. Further, the camera and the tape recorder might become the child's instruments for capturing the world, confirming and reinforcing his own ideas, and enabling him to communicate his ideas to others. Through such recorded materials teachers can begin to make preliminary identification of those individuals who may need attention of various kinds, including in some cases the possibility of psychiatric treatment.

Conclusion

Enough is known about the significance of the first several years of life for later intellectual, physical, and emotional development to warrant major research and the study of development needs during these years. Nothing completely takes the place of the warmth, concern, and activity of a good home. However, even in a good home, and later in a good nursery school, provision for the appropriate use of media must be made if the fullest cognitive and affective development of each child is to be achieved. This article attempts to suggest a few of many approaches which might be utilized. Much more special equipment will need to be developed for use with children from birth to five, because most of what we now have was developed for older children. Special equipment and material designs to evoke particular behaviors will certainly make possible greater leaps forward for this stage in the child's life, which only now is beginning to be recognized as his most critical and formative years.

Bibliography

Almy, Millie, Edward Chittenden, and Paula Miller. *Young Children's Thinking*. New York: Teachers College Press, 1966.

Bruner, Jerome. "Up From Helplessness." *Psychology Today* (January, 1969), pp. 31–33, 66–67.

Hechinger, F. M. *Pre-School Education Today*. Garden City, N.Y.; Doubleday, 1966.

Krown, Sylvia. "Pre-School Programs for Disadvantaged Children." *Children* (November-December, 1968), pp. 236–239.

Leitman, Allan. "The Workshop Classroom: Furnishings in the Learning Module," pp. 101–16 in *Symposium on Research and Utilization of Educational Media for Teaching the Deaf*. Lincoln, Nebraska: University of Nebraska, 1968.

Pines, Maya. *Revolution in Learning*. New York: Harper and Row, 1966.

Ray, Henry W. "Creating Environments for Learning," pp. 141–56 in *Symposium on Research and Utilization of Educational Media for Teaching the Deaf*. Lincoln, Nebraska; University of Nebraska, 1968.

Research Experimental Center, Las Vegas, Nevada. Brochure prepared by Clark County School District, Las Vegas, Nevada.

Saturday Review. "The Child." *Saturday Review* (December 7, 1968), pp. 71–82, 87–88.

Wann, K. D., M. S. Darn, and E. A. Liddle. *Fostering Intellectual Development in Young Children*. New York: Teachers College Press, Columbia University, 1962.

32 Designing a Program for Broadcast Television

Gerald S. Lesser

"Sesame Street" is by now a household word. In this article the principal consultant for CTW presents briefly the rationale behind the program's implementation and execution and then discusses the role of formative evaluation in the project.

On November 10, 1969, a series of 130, one-hour television programs for young children, an experimental series called "Sesame Street," began broadcasting over the 170 educational channels throughout the country.

With grants from both private and public agencies—Carnegie, Ford, the Office of Education, the Office of Economic Opportunity, and the National Institute of Child Health and Human Development—a group called the Children's Television Workshop currently is producing this five-day-a-week, twenty-six-week television series for three-to-five-year-old children, primarily but not exclusively from urban families, and then will assess the impact that viewing these programs has on the development of these children. This paper focuses on the role that child watching, or formative evaluation, has been playing in guiding the design and construction of the television programs.

"Sesame Street" is not intended as a substitute for other forms of early childhood education. Nor is it intended as a comprehensive program of early education. But there are some compelling facts about the television viewing of very young children which led us to consider national television programming as a complement and supplement, as one option to be added to other approaches to early education, an option that might achieve certain limited, selected goals quite well.

Television sets are in greater supply in American homes than bathtubs, telephones, toasters, vacuum cleaners, or newspaper subscriptions. Even for households with less than five-thousand-dollar incomes, over 90 percent own at least one television set. For example, in the "hollers" of Appalachia, where the median income is about three thousand dollars a year, and where homes are in such remote locations that preschool children cannot possibly reach an organized school, over 95 percent of the

Reprinted with minor deletions with permission of both the author and publisher from *Psychology and the Problems of Society* (Frances F. Korten, Stuart W. Cook, and John I. Lacey, editors). Washington, D.C.: American Psychological Association, Inc. Copyright © 1970 by the Association. Dr. Lesser is Charles Bigelow Professor of Education and Developmental Psychology, and Director of the Laboratory of Human Development in Harvard University.

families have at least one television set, and these sets are on for an average of over fifty hours a week. By the time a child born today reaches age eighteen, he will have devoted more of his life to watching television than to any other single activity except sleep.

Over four-fifths of the three- and four-year-old children in this country do not attend any organized form of school, but the television medium is used by these young children for enormous numbers of viewing hours. What can we do with its message to capitalize on the inherent fascination that television seems to hold?

A compelling fact about television is its capacity to show children events that they have never seen before and are unlikely to ever have the opportunity to see in person. These events, in sequence, can add up to stories, and these stories can contain and convey ideas. With these stories and ideas, conceivably (with luck) we can touch the child and catch his imagination. We all know the power of the television medium to succeed in that most difficult accomplishment—catching the child's imagination—sometimes accidently and perhaps sometimes in ways that seem trivial or unworthy. But if we only can begin to understand what really moves a child and what really excites him to want to know more about what he sees and hears, that would be an achievement worth any investment.

The film sequences I will discuss illustrate the role of formative evaluation in program design. Of course, they will be out of the context of the total show, which combines warm human beings (who treat each other and their viewers in a gentle, dignified way) with puppets, live-action films, and short, animated segments.

Anyone who has children knows—mostly to his anguish—how readily young children learn commercials, in which pace, style, repetition, and the use of jingles are key elements. We are experimenting with short commercials to teach letters and numbers, and one of our early efforts is a commercial to teach the letter J.

> The J commercial is a cartoon animation in which the letter J appears from the top of the screen to two boys resting on the ground and talking. The boys ask each other what it is, suggest that it looks like a fishhook, and the J replies that it is the letter J. Thereupon, the J recites a nonsense rhyme containing a number of words which start with the letter J. The narration is accompanied by illustrative animation. At the end of the story, the boys discuss the letter J, one saying, "So that's the letter J," while the other consolidates the little story with a nonsense rhyme of his own using words which start with J.

We have had considerable criticism of the J commercial from adult audiences, who do not like the slang, the Judge hitting someone on the head, and the "negative attitude toward jails." More important, of course, were the reactions of young children, who take it simply as a nonsense rhyme—which is the way it was intended. They watch it and enjoy it, but some child watching told us that, despite its ability to hold the child's attention, it was not a really effective teaching device. One of our premises is that entertainment and instruction can complement each other, but we now find from watching children that we sometimes create a competition between the two—that because the animated characters in the J commercial, for example, are so successful and appealing to the child, and draw his attention so strongly, he is distracted from the letter we are trying to present. So the next approximation tried to maintain the appeal of animation, but to make the letter more salient to the child. The animated sequence about Wanda the Witch is an effort to teach the sight and sound of the letter W.

> Like the J sequence, Wanda the Witch is an animated cartoon sequence with rhyming narration. Here, however, the letter W is significantly more mobile and plays a larger role in the animation than the letter J did in its first usage. Ws were used in the animation whenever possible to represent the wig Wanda wore, and such things as snowflakes and the portion she brewed. Many of the key words which are in the rhyme are illustrated.

An even more direct focusing of the child's attention on the material to be learned is achieved in this next segment. Here, the letter itself is an actor and the child has an opportunity to get a good, long look at it. You also meet Kermit, an important member of our repertory company.

> In this live, videotaped sequence Kermit the Frog, a Muppet puppet, delivers a lecture on the letter W, represented in the scene by the letter itself, made of foam rubber and therefore movable. As Kermit begins, unaware that the letter is capable of moving, he mentions words which start with W such as Wiggle and Wobble, and the letter reacts accordingly. Kermit is startled by the W's behavior, but passes it off as a figment of his imagination, then continues his lecture, mentioning words such as Walk and Wander. At this point the letter begins wandering toward Kermit, who is nonplussed. The letter moves in closer to Kermit and attacks him. Kermit explains to his audience that words like Wrestle and Wack start with W as well. The scene ends with the letter W victorious and Kermit saying, "Woe is me."

The Role of Formative Evaluation

Let us return now to the function of formative evaluation in the design of children's television. The ultimate success of "Sesame Street" will depend upon the appeal of the programs and the impact they have on children. But there already has been one highly successful result of this experiment. Children's Television Workshop has a research staff responsible for child watching to get a detailed, moment-to-moment view of what goes on in the child's mind—what he actually sees and hears—when he is watching "Sesame Street," and to convey this information to the producers of the show to guide their efforts in building progressively better shows. The remarkable achievement is this: The researchers and producers actually have learned a great deal about how to be useful to each other. The researchers not only have learned to make useful observations about what works or does not work with children, but to convey this information in a usable form to the producers. Equally remarkable is the producers' ability to absorb and use this information and to ask reasonable questions of the research staff.*

The general function then of formative evaluation is to serve production. As the shows have been developing, research is assessing both their appeal for children and what children learn from them. To accomplish this, Edward Palmer and his group have developed several techniques of child watching, one simple but very effective one being the "distractor." Here, a child can watch either the television set or a television-sized projection screen on which slides are changing constantly. Fluctuations in the child's attention are recorded and graphed, and then reviewed in detail with the producers.

These and other techniques of child watching are yielding much specific information about program elements and some general understanding of children's viewing behavior; the role of context, pace, and repetition, of familiarity and incongruity; the appeal of animation and pixilation (an old Buster Keaton, speeded-up action technique); the attentional drifts of the child; and the cues he uses in deciding very selectively whether he should watch or not. When television sets are turned on for an average of fifty-six hours a week in the homes of young children, they must become highly selective in monitoring what to watch, and they do. For example, very rarely will a young child watch for long if an adult is on the screen talking full-face to him. In contrast, contrary to the ancient folklore among television producers, children do enjoy other children in action and listening to their talk.

Another effort—in this instance, an effort to teach the concept of "round"—illustrates some of these general observations through its relative failure.

> Using live-action film this short essay depicts objects with round shapes, such as manhole covers, Frisbies, clocks, soap bubbles, car wheels, holes, marbles, telephone dials, etc. This film is fast paced with lively music.

Although this segment does hold the children's attention and creates many images that they can recall and describe, child watching indicates that it fails to teach the concept of round. Many round objects are depicted, but children apparently fail to abstract the concept of roundness from those objects.

Thus, in attempting to teach other concepts—around, through, and

---

*Those interested in how this successful collaboration between researchers and producers is coming about please contact Dr. Edward Palmer, Research Director, Children's Television Workshop, who is responsible for the formative evaluative phase of its operation.

over—the action and language of children were added, with considerable repetition and redundancy.

In another live-action film, a group of children demonstrates by playing "follow the leader" the concepts of *around, through* and *over.* The children first go *around* some sheets hung on a clothesline but the smallest child does not understand and runs into them, getting tangled up in the clothes. The older children return, untangle him, and then go around the clothesline again so that the little child can learn correctly. He does, and they go on to the next two tests which take them *through* a large pipe and *over* some boards on sawhorses. The little child, of course, fails to go through and over on his first attempts, but his playmates help him to do it again, and he succeeds. The film ends with the children playing leap frog, running through each other's legs, and romping in a grassy plot.

The production of "Sesame Street" represents the first time that child watching research is being applied systematically to the design of televised instruction for young children. This research is proving to be of great value, not only in improving the quality of a specific set of programs, but in generating some general understanding of how young children learn, what moves them, and what catches their imagination.

Administrative and Program Concerns

33 Schools for Young Children: Organizational and Administrative Considerations

Robert H. Anderson

School administrators alert to the new demands documented by Messrs. Shane and Krech elsewhere in this volume will find in this article a rationale and concrete suggestions for planning and executing a program in early childhood education.

In a new policy statement[1] by its Research and Policy Committee dated July, 1968, the influential Committee for Economic Development has issued a strong appeal for the fundamental improvement of American education. The document includes these passages:

> We . . . recommend extensive experimental activity in preschooling, not only in the substance and process of instruction but also in organization, administration, and finance.[2]
>
> We are convinced that reconstruction of instructional staffs, instructional patterns, and school organization must lie at the heart of any meaningful effort to improve the quality of schooling in this country.[3]

That advances in teaching techniques, materials, and technology depend ultimately on ways the staff is trained and organized is another theme in the report.

Accepting the committee's conclusions, at least to the extent that organization does matter, let us turn to a discussion of some ways programs for educating young children might be set up.

General Organization

There is no automatic supposition in this discussion concerning *where* the education of children ages two through five will be located

---

Phi Delta Kappan, March 1969. Reprinted by permission. Mr. Anderson, of Harvard University, is co-editor of this volume.

or in what manner it will be administered and financed. The Committee for Economic Development, it may be noted, favors a "mixed" system including both public and private preschools, with nonprofit schools serving as demonstration units. At present, virtually all programs for children below age five are under the sponsorship of private groups or public agencies other than the local public school district. Head Start, for example, is only rarely affiliated with a public school. There are only a few school districts that sponsor "junior kindergarten" (or equivalent) for four-year-olds, and even tax-supported kindergarten sevices for five-year-olds have, until very recently, been available to less than half of American children. Where such services have not been offered, private and church-related groups have provided them on a fee basis. Meanwhile, the public schools have faced an ever-growing problem of how to finance classroom construction and other operating costs when and if kindergarten services are added.

The few existing school programs for two-year-olds are usually intended to cope with special problems and to equalize developmental opportunities for the culturally deprived. Though most such programs are now independent of the public school, it can be argued that all so-called preschool programs ought to have ties with a public school district. This might provide a small measure of needed guidance; at least it would enable the school district to begin building a record of the child's developmental history. Various community agencies, especially those concerned with health, should also be closely involved.

Harold and June Shane[4] have envisioned what they call a "mini-school" for three-year-olds, emphasizing experiences designed to increase the sensory input which is so essential if children are to develop their full intellectual potential. These small units might exist in housing projects, store fronts, or even in regular schools. Next the Shanes envision a two-year preprimary continuum for the four- and five-year olds, to replace the present kindergartens. Following this flexible unit would be a "seamless" primary unit, succeeded in turn by the middle school and the secondary continuum. Implicit in the Shane predictions, as indeed in most current writing about school unit organization, is that the successive units of the school should overlap and "flow into" each other in ways that greatly reduce the painful historic problems of unit articulation.

The size of the preprimary school program, whether in separate units or all under one tent, will of course vary from place to place. Ideally, for reasons that are documented in other articles of this volume, each group of children should be a heterogeneous mixture within which occasional homogeneous subgroupings are possible. It should be in the care of a team of adults, including professionals and nonprofessional aides. The professional staff should include one or more teachers who coordinate and supervise the work of aides, tutors, resource persons, and other personnel, plus health workers, guidance specialists, and others who assist in the various functions of pupil diagnosis, program planning, instruction, and evaluation. Depending in part on the maturity of the children, the program itself should add, to the "regular" class experience of a group of young children, such other experiences as individual exploration, small group or individual interaction with an adult, small group activity with a considerable degree of independence, and larger group situations in which stories, TV, and other presentations are involved.

Much of what happens will be in the context of play situations, but, especially for some children at the upper age levels, there may be relatively structured lessons. Obviously, such a program requires the close co-involvement of several adults whose professional talents, personalities, interests, and styles are sufficiently diverse so that they are capable, collectively, of appropriate response to a wide range of pupil needs. It also requires that time, space, and resources be organized and utilized very flexibly.

The needs and characteristics of younger children call for a somewhat different and presumably less "open" pattern of staffing and organization than those appropriate for children in middle and later childhood. The young child is obviously less ready to cope with complicated instructional machinery, with a great many types of social situations, with an extensive and varied physical environment, and with a large number of adults each of whom presents different opportunities and challenges to him. Therefore various organizational and instructional trends now gaining in acceptance in upper-elementary and secondary levels, especially cooperative staffing patterns and mechanized instruction, will necessarily be used in preprimary schools with a degree of caution.

Of interest in passing is that nursery school teachers have in the past often worked within an informal, collegial pattern of staff organization. Over the past decade many elementary schools have been experimenting with a variety of new ways of utilizing teachers and aggregating pupils for instruction. It is not yet clear which of these emerging staffing and grouping patterns will work best in preprimary schools with different kinds of people, but it seems no longer in much doubt that the autonomous teacher working continuously with only one class of children will in the future be an exception rather than the rule in all levels of schooling.

Apart from the inherent advantages for teachers as they work, share, and study together, it is good for the children to live in the same family with a group of adults whose behavior offers a constructive model for their own. By being themselves, by fulfilling different roles, by exhibiting different interests and views, and especially by living and working together in reasonable harmony, the teachers help the children to understand and appreciate important truths about human interaction.

That the teachers are a heterogeneous lot stands to benefit children in yet another way. One of the chief aims of the school serving young children should be to collect, analyze, and act upon a vast array of data concerning each child's life history (short though it has been!), the out-of-school environmental situation in which he lives, the present state of his intellectual and social development, and other clues to his needs and potential. This implies that the school staff must therefore include a variety of persons whose training and personality equip them to examine and understand many different dimensions of the child's world, including his health and medical history, his views of himself and others, his verbal competency, and even the aesthetics of his life and environment. It also implies, by the way, that this broadly talented school staff must devote large blocs of time to the functions of interviewing, advising, and assisting parents and other significant adults in each child's life. Ideally, the home-school relationship should be nurtured in ways that insure complete two-way communication and also a maximum of mutual assistance.

The child will reveal his interests, predispositions, and needs through the way he responds to the various stimuli the school situation presents, including the personalities and offerings of the several different children and adults he encounters. By observing these responses and the conditions under which a particular child seems best to function and to learn, the staff can then deploy itself and groups of children in ways that exploit and capitalize the insights in hand.

School Linkages

When the early childhood program is included within or as a part of a regular elementary school building, the organization plan of the school should provide at least three lines of communication reaching out from the preprimary unit. One of these would be to other units and services within the school, and would seek links not only with adults but with the older children. Another would be to outside agencies and resources, important examples being the public library, social service departments, and church-sponsored or private preschools with which functional linkages might be arranged. A third would be the school's community, including especially the parents of enrolled pupils but also resource people from the neighborhood. Other linkages are possible, notably with television workers if plans for educational programs beamed at preprimary children and their families are successful.

Within the school, the most obvious ties of the preprimary people are with the primary unit itself. Hopefully, the relationship can be so close that barriers ordinarily separating kindergarten from "first grade" will cease to exist. More mature preprimary children might spend part of their day in primary classrooms, and some primary children might similarly spend part of *their* day in the more relaxed environment of the preprimary. Teachers could, likewise, move freely between the units; it would even be desirable, each September, for one or more of the preprimary teachers to "move up" with the six-year-olds into the primary, while a former primary teacher reclassifies herself as a preprimary teacher for a year or more. This practice would not only foster continuity in the teacher-pupil relationships that develop and ensure a smooth transition for each class, but it would greatly improve inter-staff relations and also stimulate professional growth. As Gorman[5] contends, the occasional reassignment of teachers is a stimulant to new learning experiences and also facilitates the development of new structures such as nongrading.

A new and promising trend is in linking older children, not only the "star pupils" but also those of average or below-average attainment, with those in the lower classes in a tutorial or other helping role. It will be remembered that in the little red schoolhouse, in historical plans using prefects or monitors, and in developing countries where "each-one-teach-one" has been practiced, more advanced students served in effect as teachers and often gained a great deal in the process. Evidence mounts to support this contention; and it seems highly desirable to provide even greater opportunities for older pupils to "teach" younger children, to play a big-brother role, or to have some other responsibility which will help themselves as well as the younger children to grow in various ways.

Parents and other community adults (and teenagers) can also play a significant role in the daily school life of the young children. Many small cooperative nursery schools operate regularly with unpaid parents doing not only housekeeping chores but also the work of "assistant teachers" under the director's supervision. The use of parents and others as resource people is also quite common, as is the use of college students (some of these being older women) who are in early stages of teacher training. These practices ought to be continued and expanded; and in addition there should be a closer tie-in between the school and the home, especially in cases where tutoring and other forms of compensatory assistance can be provided to children in underprivileged families. Recent studies at Catholic University, Syracuse University Medical School, and elsewhere have shown that it is possible to raise the intellectual effectiveness of infants quite dramatically through tutoring which consists of play activities, reading and talking to the children, the taking of walks and trips, and other experiences some children miss: the crucial element evidently being the one-to-one relationship in which the adult's attention is focused on the child. Continuation of special help of this sort will be necessary for some children even after they are in school; and there is reason to believe that older children as well as adults can assist in such programs.

Launching New Programs

It seems altogether likely that American education is making ready for some fairly radical changes, among them being the long overdue inclusion of the preprimary offerings in the regular school program.

Granted that the cost will be high and problems of launching and housing this new service will be enormous, it nevertheless seems that parents and politicians alike will soon be persuaded that this next step is necessary. . . .

In many ways such a development will cause headaches among schoolmen. For one thing, there is a flimsy foundation of experience on which to build. That the provision of high-quality preprimary education is a relatively new cause among educators, however, has certain advantages worth noting. In most communities, habit-ridden teachers and fossilized preprimary curricula are not yet on the early childhood scene, nor are inflexible classroom spaces and outdated educational equipment. Even where these already exist, the prospect of significant expansion means that new teachers, new spaces, new equipment, and (let us pray) new approaches and content in instruction will be entering the picture. As a result, and despite the many problems in tooling up for the "golden age" that hopefully lies ahead, there is a real opportunity to launch fresh, imaginative, and sound programs in physical settings that are truly appropriate. It is, of course, important to implement the expansion only as adequate resources become available. Headlong expansion without good planning could be disastrous.

But reckless expansion seems very unlikely. The catch-up cost of providing classrooms to meet the actual need for kindergarten space alone (much less the total preprimary requirement) will reach billions of dollars. A significant increase in operating costs, particularly salaries, will also be necessary and most communities will find it expedient to absorb these costs by stages. Furthermore, recruitment and training of sufficient professional personnel will prove a demanding task for the colleges.

Lest we be overwhelmed by these practical limitations, and as a way of gaining experience and momentum, why not move toward full-scale programs one step at a time? Our priorities can go, first, to the provision of kindergarten services where they have not existed. Next, heeding Esther Edward's advice that "kindergarten is too late," [6] we can move to extend the kindergarten program by adding the four-year-olds. Finally, the "mini-school" can be incorporated. The master timetable can extend over any given number of years, although obviously the fewer the better.

One potential hang-up is the extent of the service to be provided. Some may argue that the program should be five (full- or half-) days per week within the school environment, especially for the older children. Until housing and financing for a full program become available, however, it would seem reasonable to offer a *modified* program which brings each child into the school (or, whatever other space is being used) at least one or two half-days per week. A hard-pressed community could begin, for example, with a once-per-week arrangement while it is constructing new classrooms and building up its staff and program.

In a year or two, the offering could be increased to twice per week, and then to three days per week, and so on.

Especially during the growth period but perhaps as a permanent feature, the basic in-school program could be augmented by television offerings (to help parents as well as children), by parent-directed activities for groups of children in homes and churches, and by such additional activities as may be possible with the cooperation of local libraries, museums, and community centers.

Housing the Preprimary

With respect to facilities, the profession now has the benefit of over ten years' experience in developing architectural and engineering solutions to the space problems posed by current educational innovations. At the elementary level, experience with team teaching, nongrading, teacher aides, programmed learning, flexible scheduling, educational television, and a wide range of electronic and mechanical resources, with instructional materials centers, independent study, new curricula, clinical teacher education programs, and other "new" or newly important arrangements has helped educators to appreciate how the school plant can contribute to the growth and effectiveness of both children and teachers. It is no longer unusual for new buildings to be flexible and functional. Even the taxpayer now seems persuaded that beauty, comfort, and even excitement are legitimate considerations in school planning. This acceptance of the creative role of the physical environment must be brought into play for the youngest children as well.

Very timely are three excellent new publications which describe the kinds of facilities modern preprimary programs require. One of these is *Designing the Child Development Center*,[7] a U.S. Office of Education booklet outlining the physical properties of a Head Start center. Its comments on personnel, site, the outdoor playscape, a range of interior environments for the children, and space provisions for community people as well as school staff can prove useful not only to Head Start leaders but to educators in general. Also exciting and informative is a new Educational Facilities Laboratories report, *Educational Change and Architectural Consequences*.[8] Though it deals with all school levels, its discussions of current innovations and of "the instructional encounter" in varying sized groups are informed and perceptive and contain, in each instance, examples from early childhood education. A section on the preprimary school describes and illustrates a kindergarten facility. It includes a testing center which resembles a very small nursery school and which has an adjacent observation room and a nursery play yard. Near this center are the school's chief instructional spaces: one room and outdoor play area for the less mature children and another for more sophisticated activities, many of which center around learning to read. The outdoor play areas, similarly are designed for both less advanced and more advanced pupils. A small projection arena called a "theaterette," is shared by and linked with the two classroom areas.

A third booklet, *The Prepared Environment*,[9] examines and discusses school and equipment design implications of certain concepts, for each of which an educational rationale is presented, followed by architectural interpretations. There are five such discussions: dependence, independence-interdependence; early stimulation and learning, manageable complexity; the play of young children; and the role of the teacher.

(Editor's note: a fourth publication about preprimary facilities, which appeared subsequent to the printing of this article, is *The Early Learning Center,* Stanford, Connecticut, by Sherwood Kohn. Published by Educational Facilities Laboratories, Inc., in January 1970. 30 pages.)

Passing the Roadblocks

In the EFL booklet, as in most of the current literature in support of structural and educational reforms, it is acknowledged that the new approaches have yet to take hold of any significant scale. That they are consistent with, and supportive of, the goal of providing truly individualized instructional opportunities to many different types of children makes it all the more urgent that their full-scale adoption becomes widespread. Most of the theoretical roadblocks to organizational reform, particularly the mythology surrounding self-contained classrooms, have eroded in the face of recent evidence and experience. Roadblocks that remain, however, include the lack of flexible or even adequate facilities and the failure of school administrators to provide real leadership in helping teachers to understand and to implement the newer options in pupil grouping, scheduling, use of resources, and deployment of adult personnel.

These general observations obtain at all levels of schooling. From the viewpoint of early childhood education, the problem is exacerbated by the failure of most school administrators (including college deans and department heads) to comprehend and to sympathize with the functions and importance of nursery school and kindergarten offerings. The great majority of administrators are men, and unfortunately preprimary education and for that matter elementary education generally have tended to be a woman's world. In addition, most superintendents and deans were themselves secondary school teachers in their early careers and, except perhaps later as parents, they have had little exposure to preprimary teaching. We may hope that recently the necessity for redressing this situation is becoming apparent to school officers generally.

One fact that has often inhibited the educational administrator, and which must ultimately be accepted by taxpayers, is that appropriate school offerings for young children are necessarily more expensive than those for older children. Ratios of adults to pupils must be more favorable, and unsupervised individual work is more rare, in preprimary classrooms. However, evidence now exists to support the argument that in the long run there is a significant saving to the society when priceless human resources are recognized and developed before it is too late. It is, to put it more directly, even probable that appropriate and well-financed preprimary and elementary school programs can lead to radical changes and significant economies in the presently wasteful enterprises of secondary and higher education.

It would seem, then, that the successful implementation of down-ward school expansion depends to a significant extent upon the under-standing, the skill, and the *zeal* with which superintendents of schools, deans of education, and other key leaders accept this new challenge. Badgered as they are by political and financial problems, they will need all the support and encouragement that the other friends of early education can muster.

References

1. Committee for Economic Development, *Innovation in Education: New Directions for the American School* (A Statement on National Policy by the Research and Policy Committee, 477 Madison Avenue, New York 10022: CED July, 1968).

2. *Ibid.*, p. 15.

3. *Ibid.*, p. 14.

4. Harold G. Shane and June Grant Shane, "Forecast for the 70s," *Today's Education* (January 1969), pp. 29–32.

5. Charles J. Gorman, "Annual Reassignment of Teachers: An Important Ingredient of Nongrading," *Elementary School Journal* (January 1969), pp. 192–197.

6. Esther P. Edwards, "Kindergarten Is Too Late," *Saturday Review* (June 15, 1968), pp. 68–70, 76–79. See chapter 27 of this volume.

7. Ronald W. Haase and Dwayne Gardner, *Designing the Child Development Center* (Washington, D.C.: Office of Economic Opportunity, 1968).

8. Ronald Gross, Judith Murphy, *et al.*, *Educational Change and Architectural Consequences: A Report on Facilities for Individualized Instruction* (Educational Facilities Laboratories, 1968).

9. Margaret Howard Loeffler, *The Prepared Environment and Its Relationship to Learning* (Oklahoma City, Okla.: Casady School, 1967).

34 Seeking Continuity in Early and Middle School Education

Joann H. Strickland and William Alexander

The authors of this article feel that the present structure of segmented education should be replaced by a system which is more continuous, which draws more upon the constants of the child's life—the family and community.

Historically, the development of educational programs for young children has been stimulated primarily by wars, religious and political movements, and geographical and social expansion. The rise of the crèches, day nurseries, infant schools, and nursery schools of Europe— programs that gained impetus from those initially developed by Jean Oberlin of France and Robert Owen of Scotland—were influenced first by agricultural reforms and then by the Industrial Revolution, which transferred the family from agricultural to industrial areas and transformed the mother into an out-family worker.

The kindergarten, an idea originated by Friedrich Froebel of Germany, began and survived in this country mainly as a social regeneration movement with religious and philanthropic overtones, rather than as an integral part of the public educational system. Although a number of state and local educational systems are currently operating kindergartens, it cannot be assumed that even this level of early childhood education is yet a widespread, established part of public education in the United States. Over the past one hundred years, the percentage of preschool programs has increased and declined, depending on public enthusiasm for economic, political, and social reform. For example, a remarkable increase in nursery schools came as a result of the economic crash of 1929. Federally supported nursery education provided jobs for many unemployed teachers, doctors, nurses, dietitians, clerks, janitors, seamstresses, and others. The programs offered protection and development for children and opportunities for their parents to learn better methods of child-rearing. When nursery schools were no longer needed to provide job opportunities, the government discontinued financial support and the result was a marked decline in the number of programs established for young children. In the main, the responsibility

Phi Delta Kappa, March 1969. Reprinted by permission.
Miss Strickland is director of the Early Childhood Curriculum Laboratory, University of Florida, Gainesville. Mr. Alexander is director, Institute for Curriculum Improvement, also at the University of Florida.

for nursery education swung back to the churches, private businesses, and philanthropic organizations.

Impetus for Current Programs

During the past decade, political change and social conflict have opened new frontiers and the greater society we seek as a national goal has again brought attention to early childhood. The Economic Opportunity Act of 1964, which provided Project Head Start for preschool children of low income parents, and the Elementary and Secondary Education Act of 1965 were the major vehicles on which early childhood education was orbited back into the public spotlight. On the heels of these two continuing programs came additional federal support. Project Follow Through, and the Parent-Child Centers, which significantly encouraged primary schools to adopt proven Head Start practices and aided the development of educational programs for economically deprived infants and their parents.

Even today, when scientific evidence compels us to recognize that man's early years are the optimal time for increasing his capacity to know and become, the child's education remains primarily dependent on adult whims for national reform. Likewise, significant experimentation in early learning is facilitated and effectively implemented in public programs to the degree that financial support is made available. Through the programs of the 1960s—reforms which stress improvement of opportunities for the poor—knowledge and innovations in early childhood education are gaining momentum, emphasizing valid practices of the past and bringing new theories, questions, and changes to the public educational system. These innovations cause us to question once again the efficacy of traditional patterns of education past the early years.

Development of the Middle School

Another current innovation in the broad scope of childhood education, one which may have great impact on the other end of the ladder of public education, is the emerging middle school, designed for children "in-between" earlier childhood and adolescence.

Let us examine some of the relationships and policies educational leaders will need to keep in mind as they seek to develop continuity in childhood experience from nursery education through the middle school and into adolescence.

The middle school is defined as:

> . . . a program planned for a range of older children, preadolescents, and early adolescents that builds upon the elementary school program for earlier childhood and in turn is built upon by the high school's program for adolescence.[1]

This newer organization also reflects many previous efforts to find a better way to serve children, in this case the transescent stage of development. To understand how continuity can be created, we first will present a concept of the middle school with which the early childhood years may be linked in the future.

The upgraded primary school was replaced by the eight-grade grammar school, then the six-grade elementary school plus a three-year junior high school. Now a new middle school is beginning to provide greater stimulus to the developing interests of children, encouraging independent, self-motivated learning rather than the somewhat sterile patterns of the traditional intermediate and upper elementary or junior high school years. The new program is intended to reflect society's current emphasis on the teaching of the young to become lifelong learners rather than mere memorizers of soon-to-be-forgotten and oftentimes obsolescent facts.

Advocates of the middle school have, through investigation and concentrated effort, created a new organizational pattern within the educational establishment. It is a promising innovation for providing variations in instructional patterns to meet the varying learning styles and rates of children between the ages of ten and fourteen. The purposes of the educational program may be summarized as follows:

1. To serve the educational needs of the "in-between-agers" (older children, preadolescents, early adolescents) in a school coming between the school for earlier childhood and the high school for adolescence.

2. To provide optimum individuation of curriculum and instruction for a population characterized by great variability.

3. In relation to the foregoing aims, to plan, implement, evaluate, and modify, in a continuing curriculum development program, a curriculum which includes provision for: a) a planned sequence of concepts in the general education areas, b) major emphasis on the interests and skills for continued learning, c) a balanced program of exploratory experiences and other activities and services for personal development, and d) appropriate attention to the development of values.

4. To promote continuous progress through and smooth articulation between the several phases and levels of the total educational program.

5. To facilitate the optimum use of personnel and facilities available for continuing improvement of schooling.[2]

Perhaps the strongest case to be made for this emergent middle school is the possible freedom for innovation found in a new organization unshackled from the dominant traditional patterns of elementary school self-containment and secondary school departmentalization. The new middle school is viewed by its proponents and builders as an opportunity to put the best of what is known into operation at a newly defined level that promises to strengthen the earlier and later years that children spend in school. We now suggest some of the ways in which the middle school, by its nature, meshes effectively with the earlier years of childhood.

Early, Middle Schools Compared

There are many similarities between the spirit of the five aims for education and the "in-between" age child and certain inherent aspects of early childhood education programs and investigations. For example, because of the unpredictability of federal support and its changing goals, early childhood educators have been forced to maintain flexible, experimental plans for implementing, evaluating, and modifying the curriculum of the preschool.

Additional resemblance between the early and middle segments of childhood education can be detected in the results of studies of basic learning sets and cognitive styles, studies which have established a rationale for a sequence of concepts for the young child. The most recent experimental and operational early education programs appear to agree with Fowler's ideas that it is important to concentrate upon both single object structures and abstract classificatory structures in beginning concepual learning. He explains further:

> The first discrimination and generalizations acquired become foundation concepts upon which subsequent discriminations and generalizations must be erected. All ensuing concepts formed serve as cumulative con straints determining which higher order paths to abstraction and which set of representations of reality we come to comprehend.[3]

Apparent in the middle school's plan for continuing curriculum development with a continued focus on individuation and the above explanation is the acceptance of human variance in developmental sequences. Even if all children were presented with the same initial sets of stimulus objects, learning styles and choices of more complex representations of reality would differ among most individuals. With these basic agreements in philosophy and practice, cooperative curriculum planning between the middle and early schools should promote continuity in the educational ladder, another important aim associated with the middle school concept.

Similarities in teaching strategies can be identified in early childhood education and in the middle school. Proponents of the middle school encourage the teacher to help the child improve his methods of discovery and inquiry, while research in early childhood education emphasizes the value of the child developing those methods as learning-to-learn skills. In addition, team teaching arrangements are currently prevalent in both programs. A model of instructional organization assumes that each middle school student is a member of an instructional group taught by a team of four specialists representing language arts, social studies, mathematics, and science. Variations in teaching skills and roles, the use of special centers staffed by other specialists, and the coordination of professional and nonprofessional staff are an integral part of the team teaching concept at both levels.

Categories of rank for the middle school team may include master teacher, senior teacher, associate teacher, assistant teacher, intern teachers, and assorted teacher aides. Although Head Start programs have listed some of the same rank categories, they have developed extended staffs to provide more comprehensive services such as social and child welfare, medical and dental prevention and treatment, nutritional education, and parent involvement. The teams of these child development centers serve the child, his family, and the community.

To better meet the variations in developing interests and abilities of children, the emerging middle school as well as many early childhood programs maintain flexible grouping. For example, the Centerettes of Dade County, Florida, a program provided through Project Head Start and Titles I and II of the Elementary and Secondary Education Act, are trying a "family style" approach to grouping. Seventy-five children who range in ages from four through seven years are housed in a large room designed with all the comforts of a middle- or upper-middle-class home, including bathtub, shower, living room, dining room, and kitchen. Each room is staffed with a team of three teachers, an aide, and a National Teacher Corps intern. Although each "family" spends most of its time together, there is some cross-grouping between "families," on the basis of age, interests, lack of interest, academic abilities, and social characteristics[4] Current middle school patterns include special interest grouping of children of all ages included in the school.

Another family style approach was initiated by the Frank Porter Graham Child Development Center at Chapel Hill, North Carolina. In this program a "family unit" consists of only twenty children, ranging in age from early infancy through the kindergarten years. The infants and toddlers spend the major portion of each day in the family unit. The two-year-olds are away from the unit, engaged in special classes and recreation programs, for one or two hours in the morning and one hour in the afternoon. The three-, four-, and five-year-olds generally spend even more time away from "home," especially as they become increasingly involved in more advanced educational and recreational activities.[5]

This provision for special classes and special personnel is analogous to, though different from, the middle school's staffing of both curriculum area and learning process specialists. It does not seem realistic to maintain that the child, even at a very early age, cannot relate to more than one adult at a time.

One historical and important aspect of preschool education to which the developers of the middle school have so far given little mention is the recognition of family and community life as prime determinants in the child's total development. A decided disadvantage suffered by the early kindergartens as they were integrated into the public educational system was that they were forced, through lack of interest among school officials, to eliminate their parent education and social welfare programs. The public school should function as an educational center for the entire community. Parental interest in the education of their children through at least the period of preadolescence, can be much more fully utilized to bring about continuity in education.

Improving Continuity

The points of common focus in innovating programs in schools for early and middle childhood point to several possibilities for improving continuity of education at least through preadolescence. And the authors would fervently hope that similarly common foci of the middle school and the high school would lead to a much higher degree of coordination in planning and programming the entire period of public schooling.

These suggestions would, we believe, help in developing such continuity:

1. Interested groups should develop alternative models of schooling which utilize closely coordinated program and staffing patterns in school levels previously labeled at preschool, early childhood, elementary, intermediate, middle, and junior high.

2. School faculties serving young and older children, preadolescents, and adolescents should cooperatively and continuously construct curriculum sequences which allow for human variance in the development of communication skills, cognitive processes, concept formulation, creativity, values and attitudes, and individuality.

3. In any local educational system, plans for coordination between the early, middle, and higher school levels should include ways of jointly and efficiently using special programs and facilities such as the library; the reading, mathematics, science, music, and art laboratories; the materials center; the health clinic; and the psychological and social service center.

4. Programs of teacher education should provide early and extended experience in team work, with each neophyte team member having an opportunity to work in varied capacities with children of several age levels before beginning specialization in any function, area, and level.

5. Program planning for early childhood, later childhood, and preadolescent education—even adolescent education—should draw heavily upon family and community involvement. Continuing attention should be given to the common effort to be made by school and home and community in maintaining focus upon the developing learner and his successive learning experiences rather than on discrete levels and separate educational organizations.

References

1. William M. Alexander *et al., The Emergent Middle School* (New York: Rinehart and Winston, 1968, p. 5.

2. *Ibid.,* p. 19.

3. William Fowler, "Concept Learning in Early Childhood," *Young Children* (November 1965), p. 84.

4. "Dade's First Little School—Education Family Style," *Quest* (Miami, Fla.: Dade County Public Schools, February 1968), p. 6.

5. Halbert B. Robinson, *The Frank Porter Graham Child Development Center* (Chapel Hill, N.C.: University of North Carolina), pp. 3, 4. (Mimeographed).

35 Involving Parents in Programs of Educational Reform

Gordon Hoke

Where once parents were only involved in the schools through the PTAs and parent-teacher conferences, in many areas they are now assuming more responsibility and active interest. The following selection discusses some of the programs which have been attempted in several cities, and the effects of involving parents in the education of their children.

Background

In his latest work, Archibald MacLeish pays tribute to Jane Addams by stating: "Hull House was not a house: it was an action."[1] It is significant that MacLeish refers to a notable achievement in the field of social service, for public schools today are caught up in a demand for social action. Various forces in the United States, including the federal government, are insisting that educational institutions act as agents of social and economic reform. Nor is this demand a new phenomenon. Jane Addams herself questioned whether education is an adequate substitute for direct political action in the alleviation of poverty.[2]

Whether or not schools should be expected to fulfill the role cited above, however, has long been a hotly controversial issue. For example, the requirements of devising a theoretical base and the operational procedures essential to successful implementation of current programs of compensatory education represent a perplexing situation for school personnel. True, federal projects such as Head Start and Follow Through have provided additional funds for satisfying new demands. But many of the concomitant tasks—for example, involving parents in the education of their children—are fraught with numerous difficulties.

The Problem

For many years, the Parent and Teacher Association was the only organization through which parents were involved in school issues. Numerous accounts have described the limited impact of this organization. Critics point to the relatively narrow base of active membership as a major factor in negating the P.T.A. model as an effective agent

With permission from ERIC Clearinghouse on Early Childhood Education, 805 West Pennsylvania Avenue, Urbana, Illinois 61801.

of change. But there are other problems, too. Hence, simply extending the base of membership of the P.T.A. would only improve one organization and not necessarily solve the problem of involving parents in educational change.

Effective Communication—Theory

It is important to note that comprehensive programs of parent involvement in public education will cut across social-racial-economic lines in the community. Conflicts over school management in New York City, disputes in many communities concerning the administration of Head Start summer programs, the animosities displayed in proposals for school integration, all illustrate the problems created by the interrelationship between educational issues and social problems. One of the most basic of these problems is how to encourage effective communication among the people involved.

Although considerable research on the social psychology of communication has taken place in the past decade, the complexity of this field was spotlighted over a generation ago in the work of Kurt Lewin.[3] Several points of caution cited by Lewin are worthy of careful study by those engaged in school-community endeavors.

1. "Reality" for the individual is, to a high degree, determined by what his reference group accepts as reality. That is, the recipient of a mass-communicated message is seldom reached directly; instead, his understanding of the message is heavily influenced by the close, informal groupings to which he also belongs.

2. The significance of these informal ties also means that even first-hand experience does not automatically create correct knowledge. Moreover, intellectual understanding of an issue does not necessarily result in changes in attitudes. The resistance of highly-educated suburban dwellers to plans for open housing or school integration is one manifestation of this difference between intellectual understanding and actual changes in attitudes.

3. Programs designed to bring about a change in behavior must lead to the active involvement of individuals in the dialogue concerning the planning and execution of these programs.

4. This crucial element of personal involvement is reflected in such areas as voluntary attendance, informality of meetings, freedom of expression in voicing grievances, the presence of an atmosphere of emotional security, and avoidance of pressure.

Effective Communication—Operational Procedures

The consequences of poor communication are portrayed in the following remarks. They initially appeared in the text of a speech given by Dan W. Dodson, Director, Center for Human Relations and Community Studies, New York University, under the heading, "The Crisis in School-Community Relations."[4]

As the community comes into conflict over goals of education, the leadership of the schools becomes insecure and rigid. This exacerbates the problems. Hence in minority neighborhoods it is extremely difficult to create the climate between school and community which makes for a viable educational program. For instance, as the community becomes segregated and the whites withdraw their pupils, the minority community begins to suspect that if prejudice is so great that whites will not go to school with them, it is also so great that white teachers really do not like them either, and are there to teach only because it is a fat job. They become suspicious of the teachers, and frequently hostile toward them.

Unless school-community relations can be improved so teachers believe they have the support of the community in dealing with children, it is going to be impossible for them to do the job required of them. Unless the community believes the teachers are genuinely interested in their children and accepting of them they are not going to give that support. Most school leadership is unwilling to engage in the type of dialogue necessary to develop that understanding.

Current attempts to establish meaningful discussions between schools and the parents of *all* the children are described on the following pages. These accounts were extracted from sources prepared by personnel active in the field of school-community relations.[5] Common to all of the approaches cited is a reliance on techniques which reflect Lewin's principles in action.

New Orleans, Louisiana—The program described in *Project Kindergarten, 1965–66* by the Division of Instruction of the New Orleans Public Schools stresses the importance of beginning with problems of immediate concern to adults. Excerpts from the New Orleans publication follow.

Recognizing that optimal results could be achieved only if home and school reinforced each other's efforts, Project Pre-Kindergarten focused attention on actively involving parents. Their ideas, inspiration, service, and support were solicited.

Parents participated in a family-education program. They were invited to bi-monthly meetings in each center. Sometimes these were large group meetings to hear a lecture, view a film or witness a demonstration. More often, these were "kaffee klatches" with small groups, to talk informally of the work and aims of the classroom.

Study groups were planned around the problems of making a home and rearing children. Discussions and workshops were devoted to family needs, such as budget, homemaking tips, and information on existing legal and social service facilities; aspects of child growth and development, such as the early stages in child development, child rearing, and discipline; physical needs, such as nutrition, hygiene, and the identification, prevention, and treatment of childhood diseases; and various phases of the educational program, such as school goals, story-telling techniques, and games and finger plays for carry-over experiences in the home.

Resource persons and discussion leaders included project and school system personnel and volunteers from the community. Among these were physicians, nutritionists, and college professors. In all meetings, an effort was made to avoid professional pedaguese and to encourage an easy, informal interchange of ideas. Leaders were impressed with the participants' eager responses and receptiveness to ideas, which avid interest is contrary to the charges of indifference traditionally leveled against this class of parents.

Teachers held frequent conferences with parents. Some were scheduled meetings; others were informal conversations during the dinner hour or when the parents brought or called for their children. Parents were invited to participate in classroom activities, to assist with the preparaion of materials, and to accompany youngsters on field trips. Because most classes were conducted in the late afternoon, the majority of field trips were held on Saturday, thus permitting the attendance of working parents. Such participation enabled them to become familiar with and adopt the teacher's approaches and techniques.

In addition to home visits by the nurses and social worker, teachers visited the home of each pupil on at least two occasions. These interviews afforded opportunities for furthering mutual understanding of the child and for discussing appropriate home and school experiences.

Parents were asked to make suggestions and recommendations for improving the program. In future projects, they will be invited to serve on planning and advisory committees.

Oakland, California—A somewhat negative support for the New Orleans emphasis on individual involvement in issues of immediate concern comes from a report on the Ford Foundation Great Cities School Improvement Program in Oakland, California. Calling attention to one of the projects which experienced little success, the report concludes:

> On the whole this project was not successful because very few neighborhood organizations developed. Those organizations which were successful tended to direct their activities toward goals which they could realize in the immediate future. Projects in which neighborhood residents built a playground, undertook trash collections, or pressured the authorities to improve street lighting were successful. Projects designed to call mass meetings on problems of unemployment, race relations, and urban renewal rarely turned out more than a handful of people.[6]

Las Cruces, New Mexico—School District No. 2, Las Cruces, acts as the legal agent for a Title II, Public Law 89-10, project: "A Sustained Primary Program for Bilingual Students." In this program cooperation of the home is sought in a variety of ways. A school-home coordinator conversant in both English and Spanish is a vital component of the project. Teachers and administrators from the schools go to the homes to personally invite parents to visit their children's classrooms. Study of the Spanish culture and its influence in the United States is an integral part of the daily school program.

The Las Cruces approach is one more illustration of the close cooperation often found between parents and the schools when young children are involved. However, it is critically important to sustain this relationship as students move up into the secondary levels. The role of specialized personnel in welding teachers, administrators, and parents into a working team for continuous support of student effort is described below.

The parents of the incoming youngsters often had to be encouraged to become part of the new school and to see it as their own. They were sometimes coached in the kinds of social skills that they needed to be able to deal effectively with school personnel. School officials sometimes asked team members to attend and participate in meetings of parent groups concerned with future desegregation as well. Thus, the integration specialists assisted in establishing and maintaining communication and liaison between the school system and parents. The importance and success of this function was perhaps best illustrated at protest meetings where it often seemed clear that the integration specialists were respected and trusted by parents and other protesters as well as by school personnel being protested against.

One factor incidental to the integration program, its special *Administrative* demands, could have provided a major irritant to already overworked school personnel had not the team members been available to carry much of this load. For example, integration specialists often handled reassignment problems for youngsters who seemed unable to adjust in their new schools or who needed assignments to special classes, they arranged for the transmittal of necessary records between schools, they followed up cases of absence (from school or from the bus), forgotten lunches, and the like. Further, the specialists served as a link between the school and incoming youngsters who were lost and floundering in a new setting and needed help in coping with it. In this sense, the integration specialist may be seen as the advocate of the youngster who is unable, either directly or through his parents, to deal with his new school.

Despite wide personality differences, the three team members assigned to individual schools utilized similar strategies in developing, communicating, and implementing essentially similar roles. All had agreed in advance that their constituencies would be the schools in which they worked rather than the newly desegregated youngster alone. This reflected the conviction that the school as an institution, rather than individual students, was the primary client as well as the relatively small number of youngsters who were desegregated. Consultative work with faculty rather than direct service to students was emphasized whenever possible.[7]

Implications for the Future

Head Start and Follow Through programs underscore the idea that schools should be the coordinating agency through which various forms of social services are made available to children and their families. In order to discharge this responsibility a number of changes in financing as well as organizational and instructional practices will be required. Government funds provide a partial answer to the question of additional finances. But the Head Start guidelines which directed schools to develop programs for parents, i.e., classes in sewing, nutrition, literacy, job training—involved educators with factions the schools had not customarily dealt with in the past.

An outstanding illustration of the benefits accruing from a program whereby schools are committed to a joint endeavor with individuals and the community is found in Flint, Michigan. Excerpts taken from a recent address by Mr. Fred Totten, director of the Mott Foundation Program in Flint, pinpoint certain noteworthy features of the community school approach.

> Reading is basic to upward mobility and to successful life. A large percentage of people in poverty cannot read. They cannot read instructions given by an employer. They cannot look up a name or a number in a telephone directory nor can they read the want ads in a newspaper.
>
> The parents of the children in one school were given a series of lessons on how to help their children with reading and a set of rules and practices to follow for the reading program at home. Nothing was done with the parents of the children in the other school.
>
> Children in the first group gained 5.4 months in reading level in a 5 month period, while those who had no help from their parents gained only 2.7 months.
>
> In a recent year the number of crimes committed by juveniles in the United States increased by 17 percent. During the same year there was a 12 percent decrease in juvenile offenses in Flint.
>
> It was during the first two-year period that the counseling team approach was used as a pilot program in one of the Flint high schools that the number of juvenile offenses in the school district decreased by 32 percent.
>
> During a ten-year period the percent of registered voters who actually voted in the ten most socially and economically depressed areas of the city increased from 66.2 percent to 81.8 percent. One district changed the voting record from 17 percent to 72 percent in the ten-year period.
>
> During the last twenty years every school millage has been approved by a substantial majority. This is a rather rare circumstance.

Mr. Totten adds that a true community school of the future will resemble a human development laboratory. In his words, this laboratory will become a place where

> Expectant parents receive instruction in prenatal care and preparation for parenthood.
>
> Babies receive clinical examinations and medical care.
>
> Preschool children get ready for kindergarten experience.
>
> Children and youth use their free time for creative expression in such areas as science, reading, music, and crafts.
>
> School dropouts are reclaimed as a part of society.
>
> Mothers learn how to purchase, prepare, and conserve food and how to construct, launder, and maintain clothing.
>
> Persons displaced by automation retrain and learn new salable skills.
>
> Adults learn basic academic skills including reading and writing.

Older citizens become aware that they are still a useful part of society.

Summary

Greater participation by community elements in the actual operation of schools, as in P.S. 201 in New York City where neighborhood parents are hiring teachers and administrators and making policy decisions, may be frightening to large numbers of educators; but it can also represent the nucleus of a solution to the problem of inferior education. In this sense, the rural slums of Appalachia confront many of the same sources of difficulty that are present in metropolitan areas. Years of neglect and indifference to issues of public schooling have characterized the reactions of groups living in the ghettos and in the impoverished rural regions; likewise, formal education has done little to reach out and directly involve these same people.

To the extent that educators can work with, through, and for new combinations of federal and state government funds, foundation assistance, and local parent groups, they may be able to accomplish something of lasting benefit for modern society. Schools will have to assume the positive attitude of going to the community by getting parents involved in the educative process rather than the negative one of simply reacting to forces developing outside the educational system. This surely is one of the major lessons to be drawn from the Flint experience.

It is equally true that parent involvement requires a thorough appraisal of the dangers and pitfalls that lie ahead. However, to those who can conceive and develop quality programs embodying this principle, the future holds out the promise of operating a school system more attuned to the needs of this country.

References

1. Archibald MacLeish, *A Continuing Journey* (Boston: Houghton Mifflin Company, 1968), p. 23.

2. Actually, she criticized it as being "a fine Victorian example of rose water for the plague." Jane Addams, *My Friend, Julia Lathrop* (New York: The MacMillan Company, 1935), p. 57.

3. Kurt Lewin, "Conduct, Knowledge and Acceptance of New Values" *Resolving Social Conflicts* (New York: Harper Bros., 1948) (Reprint: Charles E. Merrill, Inc., 1965).

4. *Five Crises of Urban Education.* Paper delivered before the closed session hearing of the National Advisory Commission on Civil Disorders (Washington, D.C., November 2, 1967).

5. Readers may be confused by the apparent dissimilarity of such terms as "School-Community Agents," "Detached Workers," "Integration Specialists," etc. While certain phases of their job performances will differ, individuals in these positions will serve as specialists in the realm of fostering worthwhile school and community interaction.

6. *Social Intervention and Research in A Gray City Area: Oakland, California.* presented to AERA (February, 1966). (Mimeo).

7. *School Desegregation & Integration: Lessons From a Medium-Sized Northern City,* Jerome Bekert (Syracuse University Youth Development Center, Syracuse, New York). (Mimeo).

36 Supervision and the Involvement of Paraprofessionals in Early Childhood Education

Frances Litman

With the rapid growth of programs in early childhood education, there arise many problems of selecting, preparing, supervising, and helping the adults who will work with young children. In the material that follows, two aspects of this situation are examined. In section I, the author proposes that early childhood education requires supervisory models more closely related to the special conditions of the field than are those most commonly applied in elementary and secondary schools. In section II, she describes the emerging importance of paraprofessionals. At the conclusion, there is a discussion of inter-relationship of the ideas expressed in the two sections.

I. Supervision in Early Childhood Education

Although the field of early childhood education has produced its own literature with respect to history, philosophy, and pedagogy, it is interesting to observe that there is no comparable tradition in the area of supervision. The operational models used by supervisors in early childhood education are for the most part extracted from the general literature on supervision in secondary or elementary education. These models are not necessarily applicable for the supervision of students who will be teaching very young children. There is a need for supervisory models which can relate to the specialized values, goals, and philosophy of early childhood education.

The education of both young children and the teachers of young children has been influenced and guided to a large degree by philosophies and assumptions common to both. In the eighteenth and nineteenth centuries, both Rousseau and Froebel expressed a philosophy of naturalism and developmentalism which has had a lasting impact on early childhood education. Although much has been learned regarding child development and early childhood pedagogy since the nineteenth century, preschool programs (with the possible exception of intervention programs) are still largely based on free play. The preschool

---

Mrs. Litman is Assistant Professor at Wheelock College, Boston. This paper was commissioned especially for this book of readings.

environment is one which allows children to grow and develop naturally; the teacher's role is to guide the process.

The typical approach to supervision of student teachers in early childhood education has reflected this developmental philosophy. The supervisor's role is to create a climate in which the unique quality of the embryo teacher's personality will emerge, and she will then be able to use newly discovered knowledge and become an effective teacher.

This approach to student teaching supervision is not confined to early childhood education. The concept of the emergent "self as an instrument" has been well articulated in the teacher preparation literature. Arthur Combs suggests that the good teacher possesses something intensely and personally his own. "Artists sometimes call this 'the discovery of one's personal idiom.'[1]—an effective teacher is a unique human being who has learned to use himself effectively."[2] He goes on to say that the supervisor's task is to help the student find "his best ways of teaching."[3]

Although this view is widely accepted today, it was not always so. During the first quarter of the twentieth century, supervision was dominated by a classical view of man and institutions.[4] Teachers were closely supervised to ensure that they carried out the methods and procedures advocated by administrative superiors. In pre-service supervision, the concept of the supervisor as a "critic teacher" evolved from this view. Emphasis was on the teaching act and what the student did. The supervisor observed the student and then presented to the student immediate critical judgments relative to her performance. Although today we still see remnants of this approach, it is losing popularity as it is being replaced by a more humanistic attitude.

In the second quarter of the century, supervision was seen as the practice of human relations.[5] This view acknowledges the importance of the student's feeling and attitudes. The writings of Combs[6] and the eclectic view of the Association for Supervision and Curriculum Development stress the human dimensions of supervision.[7]

More recently, operational models for supervision are expanding the human relations approach to include an analytical and cognitive dimension. Robert Goldhammer calls this "clinical supervision."[8] Robert H. Anderson in the Foreword to Goldhammer's book[9] suggests that the clinical approach to supervision is best exemplified by the analogues of certain forms of teaching and ego counseling. He also suggests that there is a "relative dearth of a significant literature on which viable teacher-supervision models can be based."[10] This observation seems particularly applicable to supervision in early childhood education.

One model which might have implications for supervision in early childhood education is the Lucio-McNeil concept which stresses the importance of accountability and sees the supervisor as an agent of change.[11] They suggest that instead of extolling the importance of the teacher's growth, the supervisor should give priority to the objectives of instruction. Teachers have often become facile in discussing child growth and development without altering classroom practice in accordance with new knowledge.

The decade of the sixties has produced a renaissance of interest in early child development and preschool education. A spate of compensatory and research programs has resulted in new knowledge and often new educational goals, at least in regard to the disadvantaged population. The role of the supervisor as a supportive, helping person who assists the student teacher to "discover herself" may be comfortably compatible with traditional values and goals, but it is not enough. What is needed presently is a concept of teacher-supervision which also includes articulation of objectives and courses of action. This is not to suggest a recipe book. On the contrary, it suggests that the supervisor seeks to involve the student teacher in the analytical process of judgment regarding his own behavior. The supervisor asks "what are your objectives for this child and why? What kinds of strategies can you conceive of which will accomplish these objectives?" It removes the emphasis from the teacher's personal characteristics and focuses constructive thought on the child, the curriculum and the results to be achieved in the classroom. This approach offers options which are based on thoughtful analysis of goals and strategies rather than on intuition, experience, or possibly incorrect assumptions.

The goals of early childhood education are measurable, although we have preferred to say they are not. In the last five years, researchers have shown us that we can collect evidence showing the extent to which our procedures are successful. It should be the supervisor's role to help the teacher make use of new knowledge in child development and early education by making explicit what is required to achieve the desired objectives. It is also the supervisor's responsibility to help teachers learn to state behavioral objectives and to select appropriate strategies to achieve these objectives.

Another aspect of the Lucio-McNeil approach, which seems particularly applicable to early childhood education, is the expanded role of the supervisor. We recognize the need for the supervisor to be a teacher and counselor; however, in this day of changing social values, it is important that the supervisor also see himself as an agent of change. In the past the college supervisor in early childhood education has often been a transmitter of values and knowledge to the student as well as a liaison person between the college and the school. When confronted with school administrators or cooperating teachers who expressed divergent philosophies or methods, the supervisor usually puts on the diplomat's hat to maintain the relationship—and the status quo. We are learning that if educational institutions are to keep pace with the enormous inputs of knowledge and with changing social values, neither diplomacy nor defensive polarization will do. The supervisor must articulate the view of the educator-scholar to the community while still listening to the voice of the community. The supervisor must see himself as a learner as well as a teacher and be able to interpret the community to the college.

In summary, we are proposing an approach to supervision in early childhood education which can prepare teachers more appropriately than the derivative models. This approach is basic to a still-to-be-designed operational model which, though eclectic, would be responsive to the particular goals and values of early childhood education. Basically humanistic in approach, it would also include a reasoned objectivity which focuses on the consequences of the teacher's behavior. It would see the supervisor as a teacher, an ego counselor, and a catalyst for change.

II. Teacher Aides: Relationships Between Teachers and Paraprofessionals

The previously static and self-perpetuating structure of the early childhood education establishment has been profoundly changed by several convergent forces—social, economic, and educational. Innovative responses on the part of educators were necessary because of an increased awareness of the special learning needs of young, disadvantaged children and the polarized styles which separate home and school in low income communities. One of these responses, utilization of low-income, under-educated persons as auxiliary personnel in Head Start, offered an opportunity for society to respond to a serious economic and human problem while also serving the needs of young children.

It is estimated that, with the growth of antipoverty programs, roughly half of the 40,000 to 50,000 paraprofessionals employed by Community Action Agencies are in school services primarily as teacher-aides in Head Start programs.[12] The paraprofessional is also beginning to gain recognition and acceptance in public school systems. An NEA teacher opinion poll conducted in 1967 revealed that almost one in five public school teachers had aides. The survey indicated that nine out of ten teachers felt the aide service was helpful, and more than half said the service of aides was of "great" assistance. Aides, the survey revealed, were happy and found the experience interesting and rewarding.[13]

In day-care centers and community-organized schools, the paraprofessional is not only a teacher's aide or assistant teacher, but frequently a Head Teacher. The career development concept, which is now built into all Head Start guidelines, is putting pressure on agencies and school systems alike to recognize the need to establish behavioral criteria for teacher selection. The argument is that the college educated, middle-class teacher with a bachelor's or master's degree has not been able to meet all the demands of children in ghetto schools. The paraprofessional understands the social and economic characteristics of her community and, with training, can sometimes be more effective in the classroom than the middle-class teacher with "irrelevant" certification.

Although the data regarding the impact of the use of paraprofessionals in education are only suggestive, there is strong evidence that paraprofessionals can and do make a positive contribution. In a report dated June 1969, Alan Gartner, associate director of the New Careers Development Center, says that there is mounting evidence that "paraprofessionals working alone or in conjunction with professionals can improve an agency's service product—i.e. children's learning, patient care, etc."[14] He goes on to say that there is no hard evidence showing how paraprofessionals affect children's learning. He conjectures that potential benefits derive from such factors as the "closeness" of the paraprofessional in style, color, race, and language patterns to the children and parents when both are from the same community; the system "know-how" which the paraprofessional brings to her task; the role model which may be provided by the paraprofessional; and the "bridge" role the paraprofessional can play between home and school.[15]

There is growing empirical evidence showing the beneficial effect of the paraprofessional in the classroom not only on the child's learning but also on the educational process, the school, and the teacher. One has only to observe Head Start classrooms, day-care centers, parent-child centers, kindergartens, or Follow Through programs where paraprofessional aides and professional teachers are working together to discern the benefits which are derived from new staff patterns.

Value of the Paraprofessional

Teachers in low income communities are often strangers to the people living there. The teachers are seen as different in the eyes of the children and the parents. Their subculture gap can be detrimental to the child's emotional, social, and academic adjustment. Aides in the classroom can help provide a bridge between the two subcultures: the classroom becomes a place where teachers and aides can alter each other's perceptions, attitudes, and behavior.

A good aide-teacher relationship gives the middle-class teacher an opportunity to gain insights and to become more aware of the real problems facing poor people. She has the opportunity to become less judgmental and more appreciative of the unique strengths of the children and parents with whom she is working. A young Head Start teacher with a middle-class background said with great humility, "I have learned so much about my children from my aide."

Teachers and aides working together can provide more individualized attention for the children with emphasis on small group experiences. They can also offer more one-to-one relationships and independent activities. Conferences between aide and teacher about children and curriculum create a diagnostic atmosphere in which attitudes about a child's behavior are analyzed and better understood in the light of shared knowledge.

When the relationship is functioning optimally, the teacher encourages the aide to recognize her own strengths and be aware of the ways in which her special qualities help children to grow and learn. Aides gain a new feeling of confidence and aspiration and, consequently, their self-image is improved.

In Minneapolis, pupil learning in kindergarten classes with an aide was reported to be fifty percent greater than in classes with no aide.[16] The "Early Child Stimulation Through Parent Education" project at the University of Florida found that educationally disadvanged aides who were trained to work with preschool children and their mothers had produced a marked effect upon the children's development of skills.[17]

In summary, there seems to be consensus that low income, educationally disadvantaged people can be trained to contribute to the learning-teaching process. The extent of the aides' involvement in this learning-teaching process and the effectiveness of the working relationship are dependent on three essential elements: 1) the ability and potential of the individual aide; 2) the quality of the training program; and 3) the basic assumptions underlying the attitudes of the professional teacher and the paraprofessional aide toward each other.

Effective Working Relationships

The quality of the working relationship which develops between the professional and the paraprofessional is crucial to the achievement of the objectives of the educational program and to career development. A recent study by Claire Jacobsen among professionals and paraprofessionals in Head Start suggests that the paraprofessional has a great deal of difficulty in developing an autonomous identity and is often in conflict with the professional.[18]

The solution to the conflict between the professional and the paraprofessional and to the problem of role identity does not rest with the paraprofessional alone. Successful working relationships among professionals and paraprofessionals lie in the recognition and acceptance by both cooperative models of staffing and role differentiation.

There are probably as many possibilities for models of teacher-aide relationships as there are teachers and aides. We will examine three models of teacher-aide relationships which are commonly encountered, and discuss the underlying attitudes and assumptions which determine each relationship.

1. *Teacher-Dominated Model.* One type of teacher-aide relationship can be characterized as teacher-dominated. The teacher makes the decisions, she organizes and plans the programs and the curriculum. Sometimes she shares her plans with the aide, but usually she simply tells her what to do, often with minimal explanation. She sees the aide as a nice person, a good helper who can do the children no harm as long as she, the teacher, is in control of the classroom. The aide finds herself assigned to menial tasks such as cleaning up, serving juice,

and occasionally reading a story or comforting a child. She gets increasingly less satisfaction from her work but often stays with it because she doesn't know what else to do or for financial aid or various other reasons.

Such teacher-dominated relationships are based on the assumption that the teacher is the authority figure in relation to both the children and the people who work with her. This perception is currently shared by many paraprofessional aides and teachers, and is widely accepted in our society and perpetuated in our educational institutions. Implicit in this model is the notion that because the teacher has the knowledge, the title, and the credentials, she should also have the power.

An individual's attitude, skills, and knowledge are the products of previously experienced interactions. Thus, when the aide and the professional teacher, both of whom have learned through repeated experience to accept the teacher-dominated model, come together in a working relationship, they continue to accept and practice what they have already learned.

The underlying attitudes implicit in this model are also a reflection of learned societal attitudes and values. The paraprofessional probably is poor and less educated, and often has minimal training in child development or education. She probably fears that she has little to contribute to the learning-teaching process. The traditional teacher may see the aide as a subordinate and have little appreciation of her as a person with value or as a paraprofessional with high potential for learning and growing. The aide has learned throughout a lifetime of painful experience to accept this attitude on the part of her superiors. Indeed, she probably sees herself in the same way.

Although the civil rights movement and antipoverty programs have both had some impact on this situation, there is ample evidence that basic changes in attitudes and assumptions regarding the authoritarian role of the teacher have not taken place. Static and stultifying attitudes are all too evident in many classrooms.

2. *Teacher-Leader Model.* Another kind of working relationship can be called the teacher-leader model. In this situation, the teacher is the leader of the team, but she works smoothly and efficiently with the aide and both have an appreciation of each other's value. There is sensitive communication between them, with the aide responsive to the verbal and nonverbal cues of the teacher. The teacher recognizes the aide as a learner and is willing to communicate knowledge about young children and education. The aide feels confident about making her own contribution to the discussion because the teacher has encouraged her participation and respected her judgment. It is possible to identify the teacher as the leader despite the smoothly orchestrated rhythm of their working relationship; this teacher maintains her leadership role in subtle but observable ways. Although the teacher is per-

ceived as the leader of the team, each appreciates the other's unique contribution. The relationship is built on attitudes of mutual respect and trust, and each learns from and teaches the other.

3. *Cooperative Model.* Finally, there is a model which is just beginning to emerge as professionals and paraprofessionals work together. This model—the cooperative model—is a result of changing attitudes and assumptions concerning differentiated roles and the nature of the learning-teaching process. The hierarchical titles of teacher and aide, which can impose subtle restrictions on the ability of people to work together, are replaced by experience and training so that they learn to see each other as co-teachers.

Basic to such a relationship is the belief that the needs of young children are not met by one person working in isolation, but are more effectively served by a team of people working together. The team should bring together people whose knowledge, experience, and personalities complement each other. The underlying attitudes of the people who work together cooperatively are based on deep respect for each other's individuality; the co-teachers are guided by the assumption that the teacher is a facilitator of learning for the children, rather than custodian of knowledge or wisdom.

The cooperative model is built on shared responsibility and shared values and goals. This is not easy to achieve when, as is often the case, each is the sum total of widely differing life styles. But it can be achieved if the co-teachers see each other as co-learners. The working relationship becomes a mutual learning experience.

Training

Effective utilization of paraprofessionals, whether in the cooperative model or the teacher-leader model, is not easy. Some people who have a natural talent and skill in working with young children do not have the same skill in working with adults. The key element seems to be in the training component, as confirmed in a recent study.[19]

Most training programs focus on the paraprofessional only. Both on-the-job training and specially designed pre-service training courses are being tried. Out of the experience and challenge of educating paraprofessionals, much is being learned which will have an influence on all of education. One of the important lessons we have learned is that there should be two aspects of training if paraprofessionals and professionals are to work together as an integrated team. One must be the meeting of the academic and professional needs of the paraprofessionals; the other should be the bringing together of professional and paraprofessional for training in human relations and communications skills.

Old assumptions and attitudes and hierarchical working relationships die hard. Educators and leaders must be aware of the tired assumptions and attitudes which guide them. They must be taught to replace them with new interaction behaviors. Professionals and paraprofessionals alike must be taught how to listen to each other and how to talk to each other, how to plan and how to share. They must be taught to appreciate each other's strengths and abilities. They must be taught how to function as a cooperative entity.

The Supervisor and the Paraprofessional: Agents and Change

We have suggested that the traditional role of the supervisor in teacher education has been primarily that of teacher and counselor. In early childhood education the supervisor has also been a transmitter of prescribed knowledge and values. In a time of changing social values, the supervisor's role must be expanded to include two additional dimensions: he must promote an analytical study of teaching, and he must see himself as an agent of change. It is in the latter role that we see a parallel between the paraprofessional and the supervisor.

The supervisor is a liaison between the college faculty and the school. He can bring to the college the voice of the school and the community, and he can bring to the school new knowledge accrued through research and analysis. He can be instrumental in establishing a climate where students, college faculty, and the school work together as a cooperative entity.

The paraprofessional is similarly a liaison between the community and the school or agency. She can interpret the community of which she is a part to the professionals. She can be effective in bringing to them special insights which represent the community orientation. The corollary of this proposition is also valid, though too often ignored. The paraprofessional as a member of the educational team can share with the community her new knowledge and an appreciation of the educational process, and problems. Her intervening role can be of value in influencing program goals and educational objectives. The supervisor and the paraprofessional as agents of change can promote a new concept of teaching in which the paraprofessional and the professional see themselves as co-learners as well as co-teachers.

Early childhood education, like society, is in a process of revolution. One of the most important issues to be faced today is whether education as an institution shall perpetuate historical values and patterns, engage in practices which are consistent with traditional assumptions of "good" education or whether it shall be responsive to societal needs and produce results.

The supervisor and the paraprofessional as mediators between college and community and between community and school are in a unique position to implement needed change.

References

1. Arthur Combs, *The Professional Education of Teachers, A Perceptual View of Teacher Preparation* (Boston: Allyn and Bacon, 1965), p. 9.

2. *Ibid.*

3. *Ibid.*, 106.

4. William H. Lucio, and John D. McNeil, *Supervision, a Synthesis of Thought and Action* (New York: McGraw-Hill, 1962), p. 3.

5. *Ibid.*

6. Arthur Combs, *The Professional Education of Teachers.*

7. Robert R. Leeper (ed.), *Supervision: Emerging Profession* (Washington, D.C.: Association for Supervision and Curriculum Development, N.E.A., 1969).

8. Robert Goldhammer, *Clinical Supervision: Special Methods for the Supervision of Teachers* (New York: Holt, 1969).

9. *Ibid.*, Foreword; see also Robert H. Anderson, "Supervision as Teaching: An Analogue," *Supervision: Perspectives and Propositions* (Washington, D.C.: Association for Supervision Theory, National Education Association, 1967).

10. *Ibid.*

11. Lucio and McNeil, *Supervision*, pp. 193–194.

12. Edith F. Lynton, "The Non-Professional Scene," *Head Start Career Development*, 1 (December, 1969), p. 11.

13. N.E.A. Research Division, "How the Profession Feels About Teacher Aides," *NEA Journal*, 56 (November 1967), pp. 16–19.

14. Alan Gartner, "Do Paraprofessionals Improve Human Services: A First Critical Appraisal of the Data," *New Careers Development Center*, New York University (June, 1969), p. 5.

15. *Ibid*, p. 2.

16. *Ibid.*

17. *Ibid.*

18. E. Grotberg (co-ordinator of research), "Review of Research 1965-1969," *OEO Pamphlet 6108–31*, Project Head Start (June 1969).

19. Garda W. Bowman and Gordon Klopf, *New Careers and Roles in the American School* (New York: Bank Street College of Education, September 1967); see also Sylvia Sunderlin, *Aides to Teachers and Children* (Washington, D.C.: Association for Childhood Education International, Bulletin 24-A, 1968).

Appendix A

Sources of Further Information

I.   Research Centers for Child Study

Bank Street College of Education
69 Bank Street
New York, New York 10014

Center for Early Development and Education
University of Arkansas
College of Education
Little Rock, Arkansas 72202

Fels Research Institute for the Study of Human Development
Yellow Springs, Ohio 45387

Gesell Institute of Child Development, Inc.
Yale University
New Haven, Connecticut 06520

Institute of Child Development
University of Minnesota
Minneapolis, Minnesota 55455

Institute of Child Study
University of Maryland
College Park, Maryland 20742

Institute of Human Development
University of California
Berkeley, California 94720

Institute of Child Behavior and Development
University of Iowa
Iowa City, Iowa 52240

Merrill-Palmer Institute
71 East Ferry Avenue
Detroit, Michigan 48202

National Institute of Child Health and Human Development
U.S. Department of Health, Education & Welfare
9000 Rockville Pike
Bethesda, Maryland 20014

Philadelphia Center for Research in Child Growth
University of Pennsylvania
Philadelphia, Pennsylvania 19104

Society for Research in Child Development
Purdue University
Lafayette, Indiana 47907

Appendix A

Sources of Further Information

II. Agencies and Associations

Association for Childhood Education International
3615 Wisconsin Avenue, N.W.
Washington, D.C. 20016

Child Study Association of America
9 East 89th Street
New York, New York 10028

Children's Bureau
U.S. Department of Labor
Washington, D.C. 20210

Department of Elementary-Kindergarten-Nursery Education
National Education Association
1201 Sixteenth Street, N.W.
Washington, D.C. 20036

ERIC Clearinghouse in Early Childhood Education
University of Illinois
805 West Pennsylvania Avenue
Urbana, Illinois 61801

National Association for the Education of Young Children
1629 Twenty-first Street, N.W.
Washington, D.C. 20009

Office of Economic Opportunity
Washington, D.C. 20506

Office of Education
U.S. Department of Health, Education, and Welfare
Washington, D.C. 20202

Superintendent of Documents
U.S. Government Printing Office
Washington, D.C. 20202

Index